THE EUROPEAN MOSAIC
CONTEMPORARY POLITICS, ECONOMICS AND CULTURE

Pearson Education

We work with leading authors to develop the
strongest educational materials in politics and
history, bringing cutting-edge thinking and
best learning practice to a global market.

Under a range of well-known imprints, including
Longman, we craft high quality print and
electronic publications which help
readers to understand and apply their content,
whether studying or at work.

To find out about the complete range of our
publishing please visit us on the World Wide Web at:
www.pearsoneduc.com

The European Mosaic Contemporary Politics, Economics and Culture

SECOND EDITION

Edited by

D. GOWLAND
B. O'NEILL
R. DUNPHY

School of Contemporary European Studies,
University of Dundee

An imprint of **Pearson Education**

Harlow, England · London · New York · Reading, Massachusetts · San Francisco
Toronto · Don Mills, Ontario · Sydney · Tokyo · Singapore · Hong Kong · Seoul
Taipei · Cape Town · Madrid · Mexico City · Amsterdam · Munich · Paris · Milan

PEARSON EDUCATION LIMITED
Edinburgh Gate
Harlow
Essex CM20 2JE
England

and Associated Companies around the world

Visit us on the World Wide Web at:
www.pearsoneduc.com

First published 1995
Second edition published 2000

© Longman Group Limited 1995
This edition © Pearson Education Limited 2000

ISBN 0 582 32896 9

British Library Cataloguing-in-Publication Data
A catalogue record for this book is available from the British Library

Library of Congress Cataloging-in-Publication Data
A catalog record for this book is available from the Library of Congress

10 9 8 7 6 5 4 3 2 1
04 03 02 01 00

Typeset by 30.
Printed and bound by T.J. International, Padstow, Cornwall, UK.

Contents

Preface

This second edition of a book first published in 1995 has involved updating in the midst of a time of rapid change, but also to some extent reorganising our presentation of the mosaic of contemporary Europe. Some new contributors have been brought in, and the range of topics considered has been slightly expanded. As in the first edition, the editors have tried to bring some degree of unity to the book, so that responsibility for its content rests primarily with the editors, relying on the expertise of the contributors.

While the work for this second edition was under way, Alex Reid, one of the editors of the first edition, unexpectedly died, leaving Chapter 9 nearly complete but not finally edited. His death deprived the editorial team of the enormous energy and cheerfulness of a good friend, the vast knowledge of a fine scholar, and the determined hard editorial work which contributed so greatly to the first edition. We should like to dedicate this second edition to him.

We should also like to thank Dr Chris Harrison and Emma Mitchell of Pearson Education for their constantly helpful advice and assistance.

David Gowland, Basil O'Neill, Richard Dunphy, School of Contemporary European Studies, University of Dundee.

Acknowledgements

We are grateful to the following for permission to reproduce copyright material:

Figure 2.1 reprinted with permission from *The Guardian* (14 February 1994); Figure 3.1 from *Britain in Europe: An Introduction to Sociology*, Routledge (Spybey, T. (ed.), 1997); Figure 3.2 and Figure 3.5 extracted from *A Social and Economic History of Twentieth-century Europe*, Harvard University Press (Ambrosius, G. and Hubbard, W. H., 1989); Table 3.2 extracted from *Beyond the welfare state?*, Blackwell Publishers (Pierson, C., 1998); Figure 3.3 from *Revolutions of our time: capitalism*, Weidenfeld and Nicolson (Vaizey, J., 1971); Figure 5.1 reprinted with permission from *The Independent* (31 January 1998) (Dyclos-Merilon-Turpin/FSP); Table 7.1 and Table 7.3 from *Yearbook of Nordic Statistics*, OECD (1997); Table 9.1 from *Business Central Europe*, World Bank, IMF (1993); Figure 9.2 from *The Guardian* (3 June 1994); Table 10.1 from Commission Services, The Office for Official Publication for the European Community.

Whilst every effort has been made to trace the owners of copyright material, in a few cases this has proved impossible and we take this opportunity to offer our apologies to any copyright holders whose rights we may have unwittingly infringed.

List of abbreviations

AFD	Alliance of Free Democrats (Hungary)
APL	Albanian Party of Labour
ASP	Albanian Socialist Party
AWS	Solidarity Electoral Action (Poland)
BSP	Bulgarian Socialist Party
CAP	Common Agricultural Policy
CDE	Conference on Disarmanent in Europe
CDR	Romanian Democratic Convention
CDU	United Democratic Coalition (Portugal)
CDU	Christian Democratic Union (FRG/Germany; Hungary)
CEFTA	Central European Free Trade Agreement
CFE	Conventional Forces in Europe
CFP	Common Fisheries Policy
CIS	Commonwealth of Independent States
CJTF	Combined Joint Task Force
CMEA/Comecon	Council of Mutual Economic Assistance
COREPER	Committee of Permanent Representatives
CPSU	Communist Party of the Soviet Union
CSCE	Conference on Security and Cooperation in Europe
CSU	Christian Social Union (FRG)
CzSSD	Czech Social Democratic Party
DC	Christian Democracy (Italy)
DCR	Democratic convention of Romania
DNSF	(Democratic) National Salvation Front (Romania)
DP	Democratic Party (Albania)
DU	Democratic Union (Poland)
EAEC	European Atomic Energy Community
EAPC	European–Atlantic Partnership Council
EAR	Greek Left Party
EC	European Community
ECB	European Central Bank
ECOFIN	European Council of Finance Ministers
ECSC	European Coal and Steal Community
ECU	European Currency Unit

EDC	European Defence Community
EEA	European Economic Area
EEC	European Economic Community
EFTA	European Free Trade Association
EMS	European Monetary System
EMU	Economic and Monetary Union
EPC	European Political Cooperation
ERM	Exchange Rate Mechanism
ESCB	European System of Central Banks
ETA	Euskadi Ta Askatasuna
EU	European Union
FCMA	Treaty of Friendship, Cooperation and Mutual Assistance
FDP	Free Democratic Party (Germany)
FIDESZ	Alliance of Young Democrats (Hungary)
FN	National Front (France)
FRG	Federal Republic of Germany
FYROM	Former Yugoslav Republic of Macedonia
GATT	General Agreement on Tariffs and Trade
GDP	Gross Domestic Product
GDR	German Democratic Republic
HDF	Hungarian Democratic Forum
HDZ	Croatian Democratic Alliance
HSWP	Hungarian Socialist Workers' Party
HZDS	Movement for a Democratic Slovakia
IMF	International Monetary Fund
IMP	Integrated Mediterranean Programme
INF	Intermediate Nuclear Forces
IMRO	Internal Macedonian Revolutionary Organisation
IU	United Left (Spain)
KKE	Greek Communist Party
KLA	Kosova Liberation Army
KOR	Workers' Defence Committee (Poland)
KPD/DKP	Communist Party of Germany (FRG)
LCY	League of Communists of Yugoslavia
LDDP	Lithuanian Democratic Labour Party
MDF	Hungarian Democratic Forum
MDS	Movement for a Democratic Slovakia
MEP	Member of the European Parliament
MFA	Armed Forces Movement (Portugal)
MFN	Most Favoured Nation
MRF	Movement for Rights and Freedoms (Bulgaria)
MSI	Italian Social Movement
MSzP	Hungarian Socialist Party
NACC	North Atlantic Cooperation Council
NATO	North Atlantic Treaty Organisation
ND	New Democracy (Greece)

NSF	National Salvation Front (Romania)
ODS	Civic Democratic Party (Czech Republic)
OECD	Organisation for Economic Cooperation and Development
OEEC	Organisation for European Economic Cooperation
OPEC	Organisation of Petroleum Exporting Countries
OSCE	Organisation for Security and Cooperation in Europe
PASOK	Pan-Hellenic Socialist Movement (Greece)
PCE	Communist Party of Spain
PCF	French Communist Party
PCI	Italian Communist Party
PCP	Portuguese Communist Party
PDS	Democratic Party of the Left (Italy)
PDS	Party of Democratic Socialism (Germany)
PDSR	Part of Social Democracy of Romania
PHARE	Poland and Hungary Assistance for Economic Restructuring Programme
PP	Popular Party (Spain)
PPI	Italian Popular Party
PS	Socialist Party (Formerly SFIO, France)
PSD	Social Democratic Party (centre-right) (Portugal)
PSI	Italian Socialist Party
PSL	Polish Peasant Party
PSOE	Spanish Socialist Workers' Party
PSP	Portuguese Socialist Party
PUNR	Party of Romanian National Unity
PUWP	Polish United Workers' Party
QMV	Qualified Majority Voting
SARK	Serbian Autonomous Region of Krajina
SDLP	Social Democratic and Labour Party (Northern Ireland)
SDL	Party of the Democratic Left (Slovakia)
SEA	Single European Act
SED	Socialist Unity Party (GDR; now PDS – Party of Democratic Socialism in united Germany)
SFIO	Section Francaise de l'Internationale Ouvrière
SIS	Slovak Information Service
SLD	Union of the Democratic Left (Poland)
SPD	Social Democratic Party (FRG)
UCD	Democratic Centre Union (Spain)
UDF	Union for French Democracy
	Union of Democratic Forces (Bulgaria)
USSR	Union of Soviet Socialist Republics
UW	Freedom Union (Poland)
VAT	Value Added Tax
WEU	Western European Union
WTO	Warsaw Treaty Organisation
WTO	World Trade Organisation

1 The historical legacy

Introduction

In the last decade of the twentieth century, western and eastern Europe redis-covered each other after almost sixty years of separation. Each side was keen to explore the other, but it was far from being a comfortable experience for west-ern leaders. In particular, they felt obliged in a newly integrated Europe to intervene and solve their first 'European' crisis, the wars which erupted from the disintegration of Yugoslavia. That conflict, which dominated the European agenda for most of the 1990s, revealed the limits of what the West could achieve in a region which had been the 'forgotten half' of Europe for three generations. Indeed, the euphoria surrounding the fall of the Berlin Wall and the unification of Germany (1990) had lasted only a short time. It was soon clear that the ideal of closer European unity would be immensely difficult, not least because of the segregation of East and West for over half a century.

After the Second World War, the democratic capitalist countries of western Europe began to be more closely linked together in economic and security terms through the European Community (EC) and the North Atlantic Treaty Organisation (NATO). By the 1980s the EC had spread to the continental periphery to include Britain, Ireland and the newly democratic Greece, Portugal and Spain. The process of integration associated with the EC involved a volun-tary attempt by states in the region to overcome the legacy of war, nationalism and economic rivalries that had so disfigured Europe in the period 1914–45. The concept of Europe as a common marketplace rather than a war zone was rooted in the view that the domestic welfare interests of individual states were best safeguarded through close, institutional links with neighbouring states.

The eastern half of Europe, however, had been forced into a distinct course of its own. From the time that Adolf Hitler expanded eastwards in 1939, the east European states had become increasingly locked into the economic and security system of Nazi Germany. Six years later, when this system collapsed, the region was quickly penetrated and succumbed to its eastern neighbour, the Soviet Union. Stalin's economic and security system was as exploitative as Hitler's, but in contrast, Soviet control of Eastern Europe would remain for over fifty years. Even if the Nazi and then Soviet dominance was not felt to the same extent in all parts of eastern Europe – Yugoslavia, for instance, was one area which was never a satellite – the general impact was to sever the region's links with the rest of the continent. At the same time, the economic, cultural and state development of each east European country was severely restricted by its communist authorities. Many national traditions or problems from the inter-war period were either put 'on ice' or were dealt with according to a specific communist agenda.

As a result, when communism collapsed across most of eastern Europe in 1989, many characteristics of the region re-emerged after sixty years to face the new democratic regimes. The colour of each state's political system, the direction of each economy, the question of national minorities, the fears for national security – all these issues which had dogged eastern Europe in the 1920s and 1930s now resurfaced and begged for answers in societies which were released from the communist strait-jacket. If these were the fundamental problems for each east European country, they were also of prime concern to the West. Most eastern European states in the 1990s saw in the West the means to solve, and indeed secure, their future in political, economic and international terms. The West in turn responded to eastern Europe's desire for such security, so as to integrate the region into the rest of the continent and prevent any new domination by Russia. But at the same time the western leaders laid down specific criteria for such integration, which was to be on western terms: the east European states were expected to move towards the western democratic and economic model, as well as a range of accepted western 'values' (towards national minorities for example). The ideal of integration was speedily thwarted, however, by the realities of the Yugoslav crisis. When the horror of 'ethnic cleansing' in Bosnia and Croatia emerged in 1992, public opinion in the West was brought face to face with the historical legacy of eastern Europe. It was clear that the region in the 1990s was not only adjusting economically and politically in the aftermath of decades of communism. It was also exploring historic issues which had remained unsolved or dormant since the 1940s.

The east European experience

The eastern Europe of the 1920s had broad similarities to that of the 1990s. New or 'liberated' states had emerged in 1918 on the ruins of old empires and claimed the right to existence on the basis of self-determination for one predominant nationality (the Poles in Poland, the Romanians in Romania, the 'Czechoslovaks' in Czechoslovakia). The region as a whole was able to explore its own identity within this new state-structure since both of its giant neighbours, Russia and Germany, were temporarily distracted by their own domestic problems. And, again to be repeated in the 1990s, nationalism proved a virulent force which the countries of eastern Europe often relied on in their search for a secure identity in a new, insecure world.

Most of the east European governments from 1918 faced identical difficulties in the ensuing twenty years of their independent existence. We can summarise these under four headings which would also feature on any present-day agenda: political instability; economic backwardness; national minority rights; and international security. After the First World War, the western victors expected the new states to be democracies on the western model. But everywhere except Czechoslovakia, the fledgling democracies had collapsed by the early 1930s. They all had major problems in adjusting economically in their first decade of existence, but this was exacerbated by their overwhelming reliance on an agricultural base and by a mutual animosity in the region which prevented any notable economic cooperation during the economic Depression after 1929. Most of the supposedly 'national' states were also bedevilled by the presence of national minorities within their borders. These not only challenged the legitimacy of the ruling nationality, but helped to sour relations with neighbouring states who shared the nationality of the minority. In turn, this issue added to the general insecurity which all the east European countries felt with regard to their neighbours. Inter-war eastern Europe did not act as a unit in international relations: on the contrary, it was divided into two or more camps which usually looked outside the region for international support. From 1933 this enabled Nazi Germany to exploit existing tensions, slowly penetrating the region economically, dividing and then dismantling the security network of eastern Europe as a prelude to territorial expansion.

Political instability

The inter-war experiment in democracy in eastern Europe proved to be a failure in all cases except Czechoslovakia, where coalition government was remarkably effective. In 1926 even some German minority parties joined the government in Prague, suggesting to the outside world that this country was a bastion of stability in central Europe. Elsewhere, however, universal suffrage was either adopted only in name (Romania) or not at all (Hungary); or it resulted in a mass of parties who by their in-fighting and intolerance rapidly discredited the parliamentary system and produced a series of *coups d'état* by the end of the decade (Bulgaria, Poland, Yugoslavia).

In a number of these states, a key reason for the failure to adapt was that the old privileged elite from pre-1918 was still effectively in power. In Hungary, for example, democracy was never really an option after the chaos of 1919 when a Bolshevik regime had ruled for 133 days; after a right-wing backlash, the old pre-war political system was reintroduced by 1922. In Bulgaria events took a similar turn, since there too the old elite retained crucial positions in society. In the face of a democratic electoral system which brought the peasantry *en masse* into politics, the Bulgarian urban elite moved swiftly in 1923 to overthrow the peasant leader, Stamboliski, and impose a semi-authoritarian regime. In Romania the fate of democracy was slightly different, but here again the old elite acted to protect their interests when mass-politics threatened. They carefully 'controlled' the elections, ensuring that the peasantry had no real voice and that King Carol could quite easily assume greater powers from 1930. Even when the main peasant party gained power for a few years, its leaders did not pursue policies to satisfy their peasant constituency, with the result that a large proportion of the latter turned towards the semi-fascist Iron Guard movement in the 1930s.

In two other states, Yugoslavia and Poland, the breakdown in democracy stemmed directly from a lack of domestic consensus over the character of the new state. The example of Yugoslavia is particularly instructive in view of its collapse at the end of the twentieth century. Both Czechoslovakia and Yugoslavia were artificial creations, born from the pre-war myth (which was perpetrated at the Paris Peace Conference of 1919) that there was a 'Czechoslovak' and a 'Yugoslav' nationality. In the former case there was sufficient consensus among Czechs and moderate Slovaks to serve as a basis for political stability for many decades. Yugoslavia, however – or the Kingdom of Serbs, Croats and Slovenes as it was known for its first decade – was created on rocky foundations from the start. It was a multi-national entity where few identified themselves as 'Yugoslav' (in fact only 5.4 per cent gave that as their nationality in the 1981 census). But the crux of instability was the clashing Serb and Croat perspectives on the new state. The Serbian authorities tended to view the rest of Yugoslavia as an extension of Serbia, as regions which they had liberated from the old Habsburg Empire. The Croats, under their popular peasant leader Stjepan Radić, expected a federal state and substantial autonomy for Croatia in line with Croatia's own 'historic tradition'. It was also the case that while Serbia saw in the formation of Yugoslavia a positive expansion of its own territory, many Croats and Slovenes entered the new state for largely negative reasons: to escape continued German or Hungarian oppression in the Habsburg Empire. Hence the country of Yugoslavia was founded on a fundamental conflict of perceptions from the start.

In the inter-war Serb–Croat struggle it was the Serbs, numbering 39 per cent of the population, who were victorious. They managed to impose the Serbian constitution on the country in 1921, creating a centralised state which was run from Belgrade for the next two decades. Ironically (in view of what occurred in the 1990s), the constitution was only voted through with the help of the Bosnian Muslims; they, like the Slovenes in the north-west of the country, consistently supported Belgrade in return for special privileges. In contrast, the Croats (numbering 24 per cent of the population) were never reconciled to the 1921 constitution, and the 'democratic' system ensured that they could usually be outvoted by a combination of the other parties. The clash of Serbian centralisation against Croatian semi-independence caused the breakdown of the parliamentary system by 1929. King Alexander stepped in with his own dictatorship, and vainly tried to cultivate a 'Yugoslav nationalism' in place of ethnic politics. Although this was abhorrent to Serb as well as Croat politicians, the latter simply saw in it 'Serbian dominance' in a new guise. The inter-war Yugoslav state therefore left deep traumas on all sides. For Croats, there was the memory of Serbian domination which was not extinguished by Belgrade's brief granting of autonomy to Croatia in 1939–41 (the so-called *Sporazum* or Settlement). For Serbs, there was the memory of Croatian intransigence which had 'sabotaged' the Yugoslav dream. In the Second World War, this memory would be overshadowed by the horror of a Croatian fascist regime which murdered hundreds of thousands of Serbs.

Despite the model which the West had encouraged, by the 1930s almost all of eastern Europe was ruled by authoritarian regimes. Only Czechoslovakia preserved a parliamentary tradition with some influence of the 'left' in politics. In the future (and post-1989 as well) this 'bourgeois regime' would be remembered with nostalgia by many Czech citizens who found it difficult to view critically the policy of their own government towards 'disloyal' national minorities within their borders. Elsewhere in the region, however, the western democratic model had been fully abandoned in favour of increasingly authoritarian structures which borrowed heavily from the vigorous example of Nazi Germany and fascist Italy: these seemed to be the exciting models for the future, not the weak and vacillating French example. Most domestic politics in eastern Europe was consequently dominated in the 1930s by the 'right', increasingly susceptible to fascist or even Nazi ideologies. It was a fact which played heavily into the hands of the communist parties after Nazi Germany's defeat in the Second World War.

Economic backwardness

Eastern Europe's economic legacy from the inter-war period was also a traumatic one. The states spent their first decade adjusting to economic independence, which usually meant autarky or relying on their own resources. The new national frontiers cut straight across many old trade routes, forcing a re-evaluation of markets at all levels of the economy. Poland was now abruptly cut off from the Soviet market to the east while a vicious tariff war with Germany (1925–34) soured relations to the west. To the south, in the lands of the former Habsburg Empire which had functioned as an economic unity before 1914, all states engaged in economic nationalism as old markets were severed. Slovak farmers, for example, were no longer able to take their produce to the Hungarian market but were forced to turn to the Czech half of their new state. Inevitably, there was also a long period of post-war transition for states like Poland or Yugoslavia. These regions had not only witnessed substantial war damage, but the new state authorities had to coordinate a range of tax, legal and transport systems from each country's previous territorial components; initially, four currencies were circulating in the new Yugoslavia. Since a few countries – notably Hungary and Bulgaria – were also designated as 'defeated states' and had to pay reparations to the Allied victors of the war (until the early 1930s), the whole region faced a mountain of economic challenges in the 1920s.

All the states depended on an injection of foreign credit as a basis for stability, particularly to stabilise the new currencies. Since this was not immediately forthcoming, there was a strong tendency, as in Germany, to print money, which merely fed inflation and exacerbated political instability. It was Czechoslovakia which set an example with a stable currency (1923), relying on its advanced industrial base in order to take the kind of lead which would also be evident in the 1990s. The other states either needed loans from the new League of Nations to stabilise their currencies (Hungary and Bulgaria, 1924) or were slow to do so because of an inherent suspicion of foreign investment (Romania, 1929). Indeed, although historians agree that as a result of foreign borrowing the general economic picture was favourable by the end of the decade, a heavy price would soon be paid. Both Hungary and Poland had accumulated a foreign debt of over $800 million each by 1930 in order to stimulate their economies. When the Depression hit and these short-term loans were withdrawn, the result was devastating. Moreover, for a region so heavily dependent on agriculture, the fall in foreign demand and the closure of many foreign markets (notably Germany) as tariff barriers were raised, seriously damaged eastern Europe's trade balance and caused widespread unemployment at home.

What is most striking in this long economic crisis is the degree to which the east European states failed to coordinate a common regional approach (for example at the Warsaw conference of 1930). Political tensions among the states were the main stumbling block. As a result it was Nazi Germany which stepped into the vacuum, offering a series of preferential treaties which provided a crucial market for the region's agricultural exports, and effectively pulled the states out of the Depression by the late 1930s. Poland and Czechoslovakia deliberately avoided this Nazi snare and sought new markets elsewhere. But Hungary, Yugoslavia and Bulgaria were firmly tied into the Nazi economic orbit (the value of Hungary's exports to Germany tripled from 1933 to 1936), allowing an opening for ideological penetration in the years ahead.

For many in eastern Europe, the lesson from the 1930s was that 'western capitalism' – as well as the rest of the 'western model' – had been tried and had failed. After the Second World War the communist regimes could exploit this memory in arguing for a centrally run socialist economy. They could equally benefit from the fact that the inter-war 'bourgeois' regimes had paid inadequate attention to the agrarian question. Although, apart from in the Czech lands, agriculture was the principal basis of eastern Europe's economy, the inter-war governments provided little investment; for instance, only 3 per cent of the Romanian budget was devoted to agriculture. The result was a backwardness in farming which left the region far behind western Europe for the rest of the century. It was compounded by inadequate land reform which fuelled overcrowding in the countryside. The most radical measures were taken in Romania, Czechoslovakia and Yugoslavia (in the latter case abolishing a system of serfdom in Bosnia which Muslim landlords had wielded over Serb peasants). But there remained glaring discrepancies in land tenure as a whole, with Poland and Hungary doing very little in view of the landed interests which continued to predominate there. 'Land reform' would be another important card for the communists to play to win peasant votes after 1945.

National minority rights

An even more striking long-term legacy from the 1930s was the existence of substantial national minorities within supposedly 'national states'. Ethnic multiplicity would be considerably reduced by the horrors of the Second World War and the mass expulsion of Germans from the region in its aftermath. But even so, with the 'liberation' of eastern Europe in 1989, the issue of ethnic minorities resurfaced and drew the attention of western Europe in the 1990s. It led in 1992 to the Conference on Security and Cooperation in Europe (CSCE) appointing Max van der Stoel as High Commissioner on National Minorities, his role being to visit sensitive areas such as Romania and Slovakia and make recommendations on minority policy to the native regimes. Such a role was very reminiscent of the international system of minority protection which had existed in the inter-war period.

The peacemakers in Paris in 1919 had tried to ensure stability in the multi-ethnic states which came into being after the First World War by giving the national minorities in them special protection under international law. It was the only time in the twentieth century that such a comprehensive system was attempted. A 'Minorities Section' was set up at the League of Nations in Geneva and all the east European states were obliged to sign a Minorities Treaty which guaranteed certain basic rights for the minorities within their borders. Any minority grievances could be sent in by petition to Geneva, which then took the matter up with the native government.

Certainly it was a very bureaucratic system, to which the governments objected as an infringement of their sovereignty. The minorities in turn complained that it worked to their disadvantage, since Geneva (ever sensitive to the issue of national sovereignty) tended to give the governments the benefit of the doubt. Nevertheless, it was not a total failure. The Hungarians in Romania and the Sudeten Germans in Czechoslovakia were probably treated slightly better because of international pressure upon the Romanian and Czech governments. Where the system broke down was in not being applied to older states like Germany, which in the 1930s was able to treat its large Jewish population as it wished without international censure. Nor could the system deal at all effectively with the ethnic clash in Yugoslavia, for the Croats there were treated as members of the majority 'Yugoslav' nationality, and could never claim a minority status under the state's minority treaty. Furthermore, the presumption that minorities had collective rights had its own dangers. As states like Czechoslovakia would argue, it provided ample opportunity for disaffected elements in Germany or Hungary to interefere in neighbouring countries where they had national minorities. Indeed, this would enable Czechoslovakia to be dismembered by its neighbours in 1938–9.

Not surprisingly therefore, the system of minority protection was not recreated after the Second World War. From 1992, however, Max van der Stoel had to grapple again with Geneva's inter-war dilemma: how far to interfere in the business of sovereign states in order to ensure protection for ethnic minorities and enhance regional stability. On this subject much might still be learnt from the inter-war experience. The crucial difference is the degree to which the West may now have more leverage over east European countries like Romania and Slovakia who wish to to be accepted into NATO and the European Union. On the other hand, the West has not been at all consistent in its approach after the experience of 'ethnic cleansing' in the Bosnian wars. In 1999 when the West adopted military action to protect the Albanian minority in Kosovo, it broke fully with precedent and laid itself open to the charge of blatantly violating the sovereignty of another European country (Yugoslavia). However, such a radical innovation in Europe was a specific response, on the one hand to the violent minorities policy of Slobodan Milosevic's authoritarian regime, on the other to NATO's perception that the continuation of such a policy would further destabilise the region. It has not undermined the possibility of a common 'minorities policy' on the continent in the future; but it has shown (as in the 1930s) the real limits of any such policy if a native regime refuses to cooperate. Many might therefore argue that closer European integration – and the concomitant moral pressure 'from within' a European union – is the best method of safeguarding the interests of Europe's ethnic mosaic.

International security

Most east European states in 2000 do not regard their own national resources as adequate for their national security. They aim for inclusion in the wider security system of NATO, which was achieved by the Czech Republic, Hungary and Poland in March 1999 (on the eve of NATO's offensive against Serbia). This attitude is the historical legacy of forty years within the Soviet orbit. But it is also based on the damaging inter-war experience, when the national and regional security systems of the newly independent states collapsed as the area was taken over by Nazi Germany.

Eastern Europe for part of the inter-war period was temporarily relieved of German and Russian influence, and was theoretically bound by the 'collective security' network of the new League of Nations. But in practice the region was consistently divided into two main camps and increasingly anarchic in terms of any regional security system. On the one hand, there were Hungary and Bulgaria. As enemies of the western Allies during the First World War, they were treated in the 1920s as 'defeated states', truncated at the Peace Conference and forced to pay reparations to the victors. They were consistently 'revisionist' states, eager for any opportunity to overturn the Versailles peace settlement in eastern Europe. Hungary in particular, which in the 1930s easily drifted into the Nazi-Fascist camp, has perhaps never recovered from the 'butchery' inflicted at Trianon (1920) when it lost 70 per cent of its territory. Even in the 1990s the Hungarian foreign ministry was anxious about any reappearance of hostile encirclement by neighbouring states which had been such a nightmare in the inter-war period.

Other states – Czechoslovakia, Romania and Yugoslavia – sought to uphold the Versailles settlement. They based their national security upon the League, upon west European support, and above all upon a regional pact known as the Little Entente. The history of the Little Entente illustrates well the dangers of building up a regional security network based on exclusivity and on a largely negative agenda. The Little Entente was principally directed against Hungarian revisionism; it had few other justifications for existence, for it failed to function well economically and by 1930 was (apart from Czechoslovakia) hardly a 'democratic bloc' in the region. It further weakened its potential by excluding Poland, largely due to Czech–Polish rivalry, so that the Poles decided by 1930 to go it alone in international affairs.

The result of this total disunity in the region, exacerbated by the Depression which raised protectionist barriers everywhere, was that Hitler was slowly able to sever any threads of regional cooperation. While Hungary and Bulgaria were natural adherents to his revisionist outlook, Poland rashly decided to make a separate bargain with Nazi Germany (1934); and by 1938 Yugoslavia and Romania had followed the same course, judging that a deal with the dictators would give them more security than reliance on western Europe or on the Little Entente. Consequently, the stage was set for Nazi Germany to begin the dissection of Czechoslovakia, aided by the Poles and Hungarians, while the Czechs' former Little Entente partners waited in the wings. By October 1938, with western Europe's full compliance, Hitler had successfully exploited the grievances of Czechoslovakia's German minority and annexed the strategically vital German districts of the country to the Third Reich. Less than six months later, he invaded the rump state, announcing that the Czech regions would form a 'Protectorate' within Germany; meanwhile, the Slovak leadership under Josef Tiso was bullied into declaring independence for Slovakia for the first time in its history.

If these events spoke volumes about the broader anarchy in European security which Hitler had successfully encouraged in the 1930s, they were also a blunt reminder for the future of the perils of regional disunity. The small east European states could ill rely on their own resources in defence against a large predatory neighbour.

The radical experiments of the 1940s

The inter-war period therefore sowed mixed memories in eastern Europe. On the one hand there was the positive achievement of statehood for countries such as Czechoslovakia and Poland. For the Czechs a democratic tradition seemed to have secured some firm roots and would still be viewed with nostalgia in the 1990s; for the Poles, a new national unity had at least been successfully cultivated and would surface again in a new Poland after the horror of the Second World War. On the other hand, for many in eastern Europe this was a period with largely negative connotations. Alongside fluctuating economic insecurity, many had been victims of the nationalist mood which predominated within and between states, while many others – even if initially enthusiastic about their own native triumphant nationalism in the 1930s (for example in Hungary or Romania) – lived on to witness the negative consequences as the region was slowly sucked into Nazi Germany's orbit, first economically and then ideologically and territorially.

Yet it was the following decade which would leave the most traumatic memories, setting eastern Europe on a course where its identity was subsumed into that of its German and then Russian neighbours. With the Second World War, the first half of the 1940s witnessed a radicalisation of many trends which had prevailed in the previous ten years. The region was now tied in varying degrees of tightness to the German 'hub'. While the Poles lost all statehood as Hitler and Stalin divided up the country in September 1939, the Czechs retained a threadbare and nominal autonomy in the 'Protectorate' within the Third Reich, their lands acting chiefly as an area for Nazi economic exploitation. Elsewhere – further from the German hub – Hitler allowed native authoritarian regimes to survive in east European 'satellite states' on the understanding that they would remain loyal, serving the economic and military interests of the Reich while ensuring stability in the region. It was particularly notable that Hitler preferred to work with conservative-authoritarian regimes, such as Marshal Antonescu in Romania or Monsignor Tiso in Slovakia, rather than giving free rein to those competing far-right elements which were ideologically closer to Nazi Germany. This ensured that nationalist and conservative governments prevailed until 1944, retaining a strong measure of native nationalist support. As a result, figures such as Antonescu and Tiso retained a certain fond status in, respectively, the Romanian and the Slovak memory as men who had at least tried to serve the country's 'national interests' during the war; in the 1990s both leaders would be to some extent rehabilitated at home for their nationalist (if undemocratic) credentials. Yet if their conservative regimes served to temper the degree of extremism in certain parts of wartime eastern Europe, they also sealed the fate of 'conservatism'. When the Soviet armies invaded in 1944, 'conservatives' of all shades were doomed through their association with Nazism, making a communist takeover of these countries far easier.

The most significant radical trend of the decade, however, was a demographic one. As was so clear in Kosovo in 1999, the anarchy of war allowed extreme solutions to be implemented to deal with unresolved ethnic issues. The Nazis went about this systematically, murdering over five million Jews in the death-camps on Polish soil (and leaving in the process a lingering controversy about the degree of Polish involvement in the Holocaust). Usually it required Nazi involvement or prompting for regional ethnic tensions to produce such a violent and sustained solution, but this was not always the case. The Romanian regimes of the early 1940s carried out their own small Holocaust (still barely acknowledged in contemporary Romania) with little Nazi encouragement, while the horrors in wartime Yugoslavia shocked even Nazi German observers.

After Hitler's attack on Yugoslavia in 1941, the country was dismembered and remained for the rest of the war a theatre of anarchy where native Yugoslavs turned on each other as much as on the occupying forces. In an obscure part of Europe where history was easily blended with myth in an oral tradition, the events of this bloody civil war were sustained in family memories and would emerge to be exploited by nationalist extremists in the Bosnian wars of the 1990s. Yet it was reality, not a myth, that during the war of the 1940s the Independent State of Croatia, ruled by a small group of Croat fascists (the Ustashe) under German–Italian auspices, tried to carry out a genocide of Serbs.

They killed at least 500,000 in the process. For Serbian nationalists it would be easy in the future to tar any idea of an independent Croatia with this fascist brush even though only 6 per cent of Croats actually supported the Ustashe. With the same distortion of history, some Serb commentators in the 1990s would claim that Serbs had always been on the Western side in the Second World War. The truth was as usual far more complex. The Serb version belied the fact that their disorderly guerrilla movement (the Chetniks) had actively collaborated with Italian fascists and was aiming anyway at restoring a Serb-dominated Yugoslavia which could never bring peace to the region. The communist regime of Josip Broz Tito, which assumed power in 1945, recognised only too well that it was building upon years of ethnic horror. It resolved to forge a new Yugoslav identity in the region and eclipse the memory of national hatreds. This was to be a very difficult task, not least because the communists' own legitimacy rested on their claim to have saved the country from fascism: they still needed, in schools and in historical literature for the next forty years, to remind the populace about the wartime miseries from which communist Yugoslavia had saved them.

The ethnic cleansing of whole populations which took place during the Second World War, whether through their murder or deportation, did not end in 1945. The ethnic map was further simplified when in the wake of the retreating Nazi troops, the new centre-left regimes in eastern Europe expelled their German minorities. In the Polish case this policy went hand in hand with the shift of Poland's frontiers one hundred miles to the west (as Soviet Russia encroached into former Polish territory). For the Czechs it was more a case of learning from Nazi behaviour in order to take revenge and expel wholesale Czechoslovakia's three million German minority. (The same solution was not achieved with the Hungarian minority which would continue to irritate Hungarian–Slovak relations for the rest of the century.) While Czech colonists moved into the districts formerly inhabited by Germans, the subject of the expulsion became a taboo in communist Czechoslovakia. It would be another forty years before the Czechs would be forced to consider the legitimacy of their action. On becoming president in 1989, Václav Havel immediately apologised for the expulsion and in a subsequent treaty, Germany and the Czech Republic expressed their common penitence for the events of the 1940s. However, the Czech–German relationship, like that of the Serbs and Croats, is rarely short of mutual blind-spots. A Czech–German historical commission set up in the 1990s with the dubious task of producing a common viewpoint of the historic relationship has, not surprisingly, found it difficult to fulfil its remit in any objective fashion. It is one more example of pre-communist chickens coming home to roost and disturbing the stability of post-communist eastern Europe.

The second radical experiment to hit the region in the 1940s came with the communist takeovers in the wake of invasion by the Soviet armies. In the nominally left-wing coalition governments which assumed power in the east European states, the communist parties dwelt heavily upon the real popular demand for social and economic reforms – land reform, the nationalisation of industry, the expulsion of 'fascists' – and ensured that they gained the credit for these measures. Where they faced an uphill battle (Hungary, for instance, where the Smallholders Party easily won the elections of 1946) the communists relied on the Soviet armed presence to ensure that rivals were fast discredited and eliminated. By 1948, through a range of devious methods, the communists had secured full power throughout the region and proceeded to impose a Stalinist political and economic conformity in line with Moscow's wishes. While historians agree that by 1948 a certain post-war economic recovery was beginning in eastern Europe, the Stalinist revolution of the next few years, in the words of one Polish economist, 'upset the whole applecart'. Under a tightly managed 'command economy', each country's priorities were measured against those of the Soviet Union which, like Nazi Germany a few years earlier, treated the states as satellites to be dealt with individually and exploited.

Only Tito's Yugoslavia escaped this servitude, not because Tito was less Stalinist but because he refused to accept the satellite status which Stalin expected. For Yugoslavia, it meant an abrupt break with the east European communist bloc and (from 1950) the need for Tito to set his country on a 'separate road to socialism' which was less doctrinaire. At home Tito tried to preserve a delicate balance between the national groupings, while abroad he flirted with western Europe and tried to balance Yugoslavia between east and west. For the rest of eastern Europe, Yugoslavia's expulsion from the bloc was equally traumatic. It produced its own 'terror' as communist officials competed to seek out their own 'Titos' and prove their commitment to Stalinist conformity by organising sham show-trials of those who were found to be 'traitors' to the cause.

This terror was at its height in eastern Europe when Stalin died in March 1953. The way that the region, having been locked in a five-year Stalinist conformity, began again to diversify after 1953 is explored in Chapter 9. But the events of the next forty years unfolded against the backdrop of oppression which had so coloured the region in the 1940s. Eastern Europe by the mid-twentieth century had effectively become a laboratory for ideological, biological (ethnic) and economic experimentation. If the real drive in this direction had come first from Nazi Germany and then from Soviet Russia, we have seen that the region itself possessed a whole cocktail of ingredients which made such experiments possible on its soil. This had been clear when the states tried to foster their own identities in the inter-war period and, on the whole, had found it impossible to develop the western national model in the 'mosaic' conditions of eastern Europe. Only in the 1990s was this western model tried again in the region and again it was found wanting. The Czech or Hungarian examples might indeed be highlighted as reasonable successes in the transition to westernisation. But further east and in the Balkans the model has looked decidedly shaky – if not wholly inadequate. Indeed, western Europeans at the millennium have been consistently reminded that the historical legacy of others, even on the same continent, is far different from their own.

The west European experience

This section on western Europe since 1945 focuses on the process of European integration and the evolution of the European Community/European Union(EC/EU) as one of the distinctive features of the west European experience in this period. West European states have been the principal actors in the construction of the EC/EU. This section therefore pays particular attention to exploring the dynamics of European integration in the light of the interests and interactions of states in the region.

Projects of west European reconstruction 1945–50

At the end of the Second World War in Europe in May 1945 the major European states experienced greatly reduced power and influence. Britain confronted the immediate price of victory in the form of the largest external debts (£4.7 billion) in its modern history. France had lost great power status as a result of military defeat by Germany in 1940. Defeated and occupied Germany was a mere object in the international system, and lost land in the east amounting to some 25 per cent of its pre-war territory. Italy was adjusting to the collapse of Mussolini's Fascist state. The huge cost of war was evident across a European continent described as 'a rubble heap, a charnel house, a breeding ground of pestilence and hate' (Winston Churchill, 1947). Some 17 million Europeans (excluding the approximately 20 million war dead in the USSR) had been killed as a result of the war. Enforced population movements including the expulsion of 10 million Germans from eastern Europe compounded the problems of early peacetime reconstruction. There were acute shortages of food and energy as Europe's agricultural output and coal production (the chief source of energy) were still 25 per cent below pre-war levels by the end of 1946. Meanwhile, European countries wrestled with the problems of restoring political order; only six west European states emerged from the war with their pre-war political institutions intact.

The spectacle of a politically and economically exhausted Europe prompted a widespread reaction: 'Never again'. Europe's recent history of war, nationalism and economic rivalries offered no model for constructing a prosperous, peaceful and free continent. Radical programmes of political and economic reconstruction were based on a general desire to break with the disastrous past, as if 1945 represented 'Year Zero'. The idea of European unity gave rise to one such programme.

Much support for European unity was founded on the belief that a new European community would permanently contain the dangerous force of nationalism, accommodate defeated states that might otherwise succumb to a deep-seated sense of aggrieved isolation, and render war 'not merely unthinkable, but materially impossible' (Robert Schuman, 1950). The common European experience of wartime defeat, occupation and humiliation seriously called into question the traditional conduct of inter-state relations in Europe. This second major conflagration on the European continent in less than a generation also fully exposed the inability of any single state to maintain peace or to protect its citizens in the event of war.

Besides the influence of internal European developments, extra-European conditions also contributed to the swelling tide of support for European unity. The rise of the two new superpowers, the USA and the USSR, highlighted the precarious position of the weak states of a balkanised Europe. At the same time the colossal economic power of the USA, which accounted for approximately 50 per cent of total world industrial production in 1945, inspired some of the original architects of the EC, such as Jean Monnet, to advocate the construction of a single European economy. The interaction of European and extra-European conditions was to be a feature of the process of European integration in later years, and was most immediately evident in the marked contrast between the visions of a united Europe and the realities of an increasingly divided continent. Clarion calls for a federal Europe found expression at the unofficial Congress of Europe at The Hague (May 1948). By this time, however, the possibility of realising expansive schemes for pan-European unity was fast receding. The mutual hostility (Cold War) of the two superpowers resulted in the division of Europe and of Germany which determined the geo-political dimensions of Europe for the next forty years.

The earliest post-war forms of cooperation between the west European states arose out of their extreme economic and military weakness in comparison with the superpowers. All European states to a greater or lesser extent faced considerable difficulties in financing their recovery programmes and lacked dollars (the 'dollar gap') to pay for imports. Secretary of State George Marshall offered American aid to assist the rebuilding of Europe (June 1947) and in the resulting four-year European Recovery Programme ('Marshall Aid'), $12,534 million was distributed. At American insistence the sixteen west European states in receipt of this aid coordinated their efforts and formed the Organisation for European Economic Cooperation (OEEC), the first major effort at post-war economic cooperation between these states. This pump-priming exercise helped to lay the foundations of sustained economic recovery and growth in western Europe over the next two decades. It also initiated long-standing American backing for west European integration in order to bolster the enfeebled west European economies, to secure a revived Germany within a stable European framework, and to create a more free, multilateral international economy in place of the highly fragmented European economy of the inter-war period.

Another important influence in promoting cooperation between the west European states was widespread fear of the Soviet threat to western Europe. International tension was particularly pronounced at the time of the first 'war scare' of the early post-war period when the Soviet-imposed Berlin blockade (June 1948 – May 1949) cut off all land routes between West Berlin and the West. In March 1948, Britain, France and the Benelux states (Belgium, the Netherlands and Luxembourg) formed the Brussels Treaty Organisation. This mutual security pact was born out of mounting Cold War tensions as the USSR rather than Germany was increasingly viewed in western circles as the principal adversary. It served as a catalyst for the North Atlantic Treaty (April 1949) which was signed by the USA, Canada and ten west European states. The idea of west European unity thus appeared partly as a by-product of the Cold War. At the time and later, however, the link between European unity and the enveloping Cold War was a contested one. Some states, like Britain, viewed any collective organisation of the west European states as a sub-system of the wider transatlantic alliance, while others, notably France, upheld the notion of a European 'Third Force' independent of the superpowers.

Early post-war west European organisations operated on the principle of intergovernmental cooperation with no loss of national sovereignty. This arrangement suited some states more than others and gradually produced a basic, enduring division over the organisation of western Europe. One set of states, led by Britain and including the Scandinavian countries, supported a limited, intergovernmental approach that opposed both federal political structures and proposals for a European customs union. Britain was reluctant to enter into any new, binding European commitments beyond those needed to organise west European defence cooperation, to qualify for European Recovery Programme aid and to ensure American support against the USSR. The Empire and Commonwealth as well as the restoration of the 'special' Anglo-American wartime relationship took precedence over Europe in the order of British external priorities. The Scandinavian countries were also disinclined to involve themselves too closely. The modest functions of their own Nordic Council (established in 1952) and the failure to create a Nordic customs union in the 1950s demonstrated their restricted interest in political and economic integration.

A second set of states, led by France, advocated a more closely integrated European grouping. France was particularly concerned to avert any future military threat from Germany in view of the German invasions of France in 1870, 1914 and 1940. After Germany's defeat in 1945, France initially aimed to maintain a weak, dismembered Germany. The onset of the Cold War, however, determined the more limited partition of Germany into two states, which included a potentially powerful, partially sovereign West Germany, the Federal Republic of Germany (FRG, 1949). France thus faced the unattractive prospect of FRG participation in the western international system without any specifically European controls.

The origins of the European Communities

Against this background Robert Schuman, the French foreign minister, presented a proposal to place all Franco-German coal and steel production under a common High Authority in an organisation open to other European countries (May 1950). France, the Benelux states, the FRG and Italy supported this plan, signed the Treaty of Paris (April 1951) establishing the European Coal and Steel Community, and thus as the 'Six' laid the first building block of the EC. Schuman and Jean Monnet, the author of the plan, launched the enterprise with the declared intention of eliminating Franco–German antagonism. The distinctive feature of the plan was the supranational High Authority with powers independent of the governments of the member states. The idea of integrating first just one sector of the western European economy promised a 'spillover' effect leading to the integration of other sectors and ultimately to political integration. This functional integration emphasised an incremental approach to European unity unlike the federalists' prescription for a far more comprehensive, deliberate political act to create federal institutions.

The adoption of the Schuman Plan reflected a wide range of national interests and concerns. France sought to anchor the FRG in a French-led European system that allayed fears of a revanchist Germany, enhanced France's status as a European power and challenged the prevailing notion of a British-organised west European bloc. Besides protecting French access to German coal, the plan established a longer-term trend linking the modernisation of the French economy to the idea of an economically integrated western Europe. West Germany's support was guaranteed by its first Chancellor (1949–63), Konrad Adenauer, whose immediate concern was to advance FRG claims for full sovereignty and equality without arousing the bogey of German nationalism. In his support for a west European federation, Adenauer established a connection between European integration and German interests that was to be maintained by his successors. Meanwhile, the Italian government aimed to restore the country's European credentials and to reinforce its authority in the face of a large, hostile communist party. The positive response of the Benelux states was predictable in view of their heavy dependence on the German economy and their support for close inter-state economic ties which had already led them to form the Benelux customs union in 1948.

The course of European integration 1954–61

The progress of western Europe towards integration has been marked by setbacks. For example, shortly after the launching of the Schuman Plan an American proposal for a major west European rearmament programme (September 1950), including the FRG, exposed the European states' mutual suspicions. France was determined to prevent the formation of a German national army and aimed to do so by proposing the creation of a European army including German troops (Pleven Plan, October 1950). This plan formed the basis of a supranational European Defence Community treaty signed by the Six (1952). In the event France was unwilling to surrender its national sovereignty and refused to ratify the treaty (1954). (It was not until the 1990s that the EU states seriously reconsidered the sensitive issues raised by this episode.) This major rebuff to the Community method of integration confirmed British doubts about the Six's unity of purpose and also provided an opportunity to reassert British leadership in western Europe. A British-inspired plan (1954) brought a sovereign, rearmed FRG into NATO and also into an enlarged version of the Brussels Treaty Organisation known as the Western European Union (WEU). In these seemingly unfavourable circumstances the Six embarked on the 'relaunching of Europe'. The Messina conference of foreign ministers of the Six (June 1955) opened negotiations that resulted in the formation of the European Economic Community (EEC) and the European Atomic Energy Community (EAEC) through the Treaties of Rome (March 1957). The failure of the EDC proposal was partly responsible for this successful initiative. The Community idea was no longer plagued by the issue of German rearmament and attention was refocused on the economic track to integration. During the period 1953–58, intra-Six trade was already rapidly expanding, at more than 10 per cent per annum. A distinct improvement in Franco-German relations also smoothed the path towards a new initiative. The formation of the WEU and British military guarantees helped to reconcile France to a rearmed Germany. The Saar settlement (1956) removed a contentious issue from Franco-German relations as this territory, under French supervision since 1945, was now reunited with West Germany. The subsequent rapport between de Gaulle (first president of the French Fifth Republic, 1958–69) and Adenauer resulted in the Franco-German Treaty of Friendship (1963), symbolising the post-war rapprochement between the two states. Meanwhile, the common market offered France an assured outlet for its mounting agricultural surpluses, and assisted the burgeoning export-orientated industrial production of the FRG.

The EEC was designed to form a common market with free movement of goods, capital, labour and services. Phased progression towards a customs union was a major goal, and the introduction of a common agricultural policy (CAP) also emerged as an immediate priority. The underlying political purpose – to create 'an ever closer union among the peoples of Europe' – accommodated different views about integration and avoided any specific reference to the supranational principle expressed in the ECSC treaty. The four main institutions of the EEC collectively expressed an assortment of emphases: the Commission as policy initiator represented the supranational dimension; the Council of Ministers as the decision-taking body was the organ of national governments; the Court of Justice established a new legal order independent of the member states; and the Common Assembly (later the European Parliament) was primarily a consultative body (see Chapter 4 for the institutional infrastructure of the EC/EU).

The successful negotiation of the Treaties of Rome sharpened and eventually formalised the division of western Europe into two trading blocs. Fears of a widening gulf between the Six and the rest of western Europe prompted a British attempt to devise a European free trade area including the Six. This proposal typified the strong tendency of British policy-makers at the time (and later) to underestimate the Six's seriousness of purpose and to overestimate British influence on the continent. It offered too little, too late to accommodate the Six and indeed was viewed by many of the EC's founders as an attempt to sabotage their project. At the same time, Britain was increasingly at odds with France and the FRG. British handling of the Suez crisis (October–November 1956) angered the French, while British support for negotiations with the USSR to reduce tensions in Europe conflicted with Adenauer's hard-edged Cold War policy. The emergence of a more assertive political leadership in France under de Gaulle (May–June 1958) and a further tightening of Franco-German bonds sealed the fate of the British proposal. France effectively strengthened its leadership of the Six while undermining British influence in Europe by terminating the free trade area negotiations (December 1958). The UK and six other states – Austria, Denmark, Norway, Portugal, Sweden and Switzerland – then established the European Free Trade Association (EFTA) in 1960 with no provisions for closer economic or political unification beyond a free trade area in manufactured goods. Western Europe thus entered the 1960s with a clearly institutionalised division between the core and the periphery.

The crisis of the 1960s

There have been many debates in the years since 1960 over the pace and direction of the EC's development. These have often focused on the relative importance of apparently conflicting goals: intergovernmental cooperation or supranationalism, limited or expansive visions of the EC's global identity, political or economic integration, enlargement of EC membership or deepening of its functional integration. Some would see the last two of these pairs of goals as complementary rather than conflicting.

During the 1960s divisions over these issues left a mixed record of achievements and failures. In its 'honeymoon period' the EC accelerated the tariff-cutting programme (1960), launched political union negotiations (1961), attracted applications for membership from three EFTA states – Britain, Denmark and Norway – and Ireland (1961), and concluded the first agreements on the CAP (1962). During the rest of the decade the most notable developments were the completion of the customs union, the full implementation of the CAP and the emergence of the EEC as a single actor in international trade negotiations. In the meantime, however, a series of crises dashed hopes of political union (1962), blocked enlargement (1963) and even threatened the EC's survival (1965–66).

These crises arose out of a clash between French policy under de Gaulle and the policies of the other member states. Gaullist emphasis on national independence involved intransigent opposition to supranationalism, and also presented a vision of Europe – 'from the Atlantic to the Urals' – freed from superpower rivalries. This 'European Europe' opposed the prevailing view of an integrated western Europe in the western alliance, and eventually led to France's withdrawal from NATO in 1966. The political union project collapsed as a result of irreconcilable differences between France and the other member states over NATO ties and the status of the EC relative to its member states. Enlargement plans were also blocked when de Gaulle unilaterally vetoed two British applications for membership in 1963 and 1967. Gaullist opposition to the Commission's supranational pretensions, especially its plan for automatic funding of the EC, resulted in a French boycott of all EC institutions (July 1965). The eventual settlement, the Luxembourg Agreement (January 1966), amounted to an agreement to disagree between France and the other member states about the right to exercise a national veto in the Council of Ministers. A further significant outcome of this trial of strength, however, was that the economic benefits of European integration to France were such that not even de Gaulle could contemplate permanent exclusion from the enterprise.

Renewal and recession 1969–84

Changing international conditions by the late 1960s – including de Gaulle's retirement in 1969 – gave renewed momentum to the EC. Pompidou, de Gaulle's successor, broke the log-jam on enlargement, allowing for the accession of Britain, Denmark and Ireland (1973) while the fourth applicant – Norway – rejected membership in a referendum. This reversal of French policy was due to mounting anxieties about West German economic power and strategic objectives which encouraged a greater recognition of the value of British membership as a counterweight to West Germany. While West Germany was still a 'political pygmy' (Willy Brandt) on the European diplomatic stage, it had emerged as Europe's economic superpower and not only accounted for some 20 per cent of total world trade but also possessed the strongest currency in Europe and acted as the EC's 'paymaster'. Changes in West German policy towards eastern Europe also alarmed Paris. The Ostpolitik (policy towards the east) of the Brandt government (1969–74) abandoned the previous policy of non-recognition of the east European states (Hallstein doctrine) and aimed for the normalisation of relations. This turn of events aroused French fears of a neutralist FRG drifting away from its western ties, all the more so in view of the impact of superpower relations on Europe. The Soviet invasion of Czechoslovakia (1968) shattered de Gaulle's ambition to loosen the grip of the superpowers on Europe and also administered the last rites to the idea of a 'Third Force' Europe between the superpowers. Meanwhile, the quickening pace of détente at the superpower level threatened to exclude European governments from a bargaining system dealing with European issues.

In this new atmosphere the Hague summit of EC leaders (December 1969) agreed to open negotiations with the applicant states, to develop new common policies, to forge a monetary union by 1980 and to explore the possibility of political cooperation. More difficult economic conditions during the 1970s, however, strained the European economies, blocked the more ambitious plans for integration emanating from the Hague summit, and subjected the EC's decision-making system to new pressures. The 'golden age of prosperity' and high economic growth rates in the 1950s and 1960s ended in 1973–74 with the quadrupling of the price of oil by the Organisation of Petroleum Exporting Countries (OPEC); the average annual growth rate (in GDP) of the leading four west European states slumped from 4.6 per cent (1960–73) to 2.2 per cent (1973–80). The consequent rise in inflation and unemployment undermined the economic aspects of the Hague programme and exposed problems of cohesion as the EC economies were very differently affected by recession. The economic and monetary union project (Werner Plan) was an early casualty of these new conditions, as the collapse of the dollar-based fixed exchange rate system (1971) resulted in floating currencies.

While economic and monetary union failed to materialise by 1980, the European Monetary System (EMS) of 1979 provided for closer cooperation in monetary policy. This Franco-German initiative developed out of a renewed emphasis on the Bonn/Paris axis at the centre of the EC; the French and West German leaders, Giscard d'Estaing and Helmut Schmidt, forged a close working relationship during the period 1974–81, in contrast to the preceding ten years of troubled relations. The EMS aimed to create a 'zone of monetary stability' in western Europe and survived to provide the basis for economic and monetary union plans in the 1990s.

The economic recession and the more protectionist climate of opinion, however, limited EC progress on other fronts and contributed to 'Eurosclerosis'. During the oil crisis of 1973–74 individual EC states mounted national efforts to safeguard their oil supplies. The planned progression from 'negative' integration (the removal of existing restrictions) towards 'positive' integration (new common policies) ran into increasing difficulties. The absorption of 80 per cent of the EC's budget by the CAP seriously impeded any new spending initiatives, while widespread government efforts to curb public expenditure created a further obstacle. The customs union survived, but non-tariff or invisible barriers continued to block the emergence of a common market.

Enlargement also presented the prospect of a weaker EC. Britain's protracted adjustment to membership occupied much time, as the Wilson Labour government conducted a 'renegotiation' of the terms of entry (1974–75) and the Thatcher governments of 1979–84 sought to reduce the UK's net contribution to the EC budget. Nevertheless, enlargement continued with the accession of Greece in 1981 and of Spain and Portugal in 1986, following the collapse of their dictatorships. The EC, originally dubbed 'little Europe', thus became more representative of western Europe, comprising some 90 per cent of western Europe's population and accounting for 88 per cent of the area's GDP.

The drive to closer union since 1985

The process of European integration since 1985 has produced more striking changes in the EC than in any comparable period since its formation. Landmark events such as the Single European Act (SEA) (1986), the Treaty on European Union (1992), the Treaty of Amsterdam (1997) and the launching of the single currency (1999) amounted to a decisive shift from the immobilism of the 1970s and early 1980s towards a greater degree of dynamism. During the same period the seemingly immutable division of Europe and of Germany unexpectedly and dramatically dissolved away in 1989–91 with the end of the Cold War, the unification of Germany, the disintegration of Soviet dominance in eastern Europe, and the collapse of the Soviet Union (see the Chronological Table for detailed coverage of these events).

The SEA aimed to create a single market by the end of 1992 and resulted in the largest frontier-free market in the advanced industrial world, accounting for 22.5 per cent of the world's GDP and 19.5 per cent of world exports (1991). Part of the impetus behind this initiative lay in the accumulating evidence of the EC's relatively poor performance in the global economy and its declining economic growth rate, especially in the wake of the doubling in the price of oil (1979–80). In the period 1973–85, when the EC's share of world trade in manufactured goods fell from 45 per cent to 36 per cent, the USA and Japan lengthened their technological lead over Europe while the new industrialising countries of the Far East posed a growing threat to large swathes of European industry.

Favourable conditions within the EC, however, were primarily responsible for the decision of the EC heads of government at the Milan European Council (June 1985) to convene an intergovernmental conference (IGC) on the EC's future that paved the way for the SEA. The settlement of the British demand for an EC budget rebate (June 1984) contributed to a rare burst of positive interest in the EC by Thatcher. Italy was characteristically determined to act as a pace-maker of further integration and was instrumental in obtaining a majority vote for an IGC at the Milan European Council, the first occasion on which the Council reached a decision by a show of hands. This outcome overrode the objections of Britain, Denmark and Greece, each of which continued to figure as part of the EU's awkward squad in the 1990s.

France and West Germany were the prime movers in rejuvenating the process of European integration. Renewed French interest in the EC partly arose out of a deep-seated fear of German detachment from the western alliance as a result of widespread support for the anti-nuclear peace movement in Germany during the early 1980s. More importantly, the chastening experience of the 'Socialist experiment' (1981–83) in the early years of Mitterrand's presidency and especially the massive fall in the value of the franc convinced Mitterrand that a strong franc (*franc fort*) necessitated a greater degree of monetary integration with Germany. France accordingly took and maintained the lead in pressing the case for economic and monetary union, calculating that a single European currency supervised by a central European bank was likely to be more susceptible to French influence than the German-dominated monetary regime of the EMS. Under Helmut Kohl's chancellorship since 1982 West Germany was also concerned to chart a new course for European integration. Bonn's main interest was to utilise the EC as a political entity and, as in the past, to advance German interests in a non-threatening way and particularly to protect the country's large investment in détente in the face of antagonistic superpower relations during the 'second Cold War' (1979–85).

The significance of the SEA for the future development of the EC subsequently gave rise to a fierce debate that left its mark on the EC in the 1990s. Some states, most notably the core or founding member states of the EC, saw the Act as a means of promoting further political, economic and monetary integration. This view was strongly championed by Jacques Delors, whose presidency of the Commission (1985–94) restored its role as a dynamic force in promoting new schemes, most notably a three-stage plan for full economic and monetary union (April 1989). The strongest counterblast to the Delors vision came from Thatcher. Her Bruges speech (September 1988) rejected the notion of a European super-state and denounced Delors' plans as creeping back-door socialism. By this time, however, Thatcher occupied a minority, often discounted position in EC councils and also increasingly within her Cabinet, where her handling of European policy eventually contributed to her downfall (November 1990).

This debate over the EC's future after the completion of the single market project intensified when the European Council (April 1989) agreed to convene an IGC on economic and monetary union and subsequently decided (June 1990) to establish an IGC on political union. These IGCs opened in December 1990 and culminated in the signing of the Treaty on European Union in Maastricht (February 1992). The centrepiece of this Treaty was the commitment to forge an economic and monetary union (EMU) by 1999 at the latest. The Treaty also included provisions for a common foreign and security policy (CFSP) that held out the possibility of a more defined, influential role for the EU in the international system.

The relationship between the making of this treaty and the impact of fast-changing conditions in Europe at large in the period 1989–91 reflected several features of the dynamics of European integration in this period. In many respects the treaty was born out of an unchanged European political landscape before the collapse of the Berlin Wall (9 November 1989) and the implosion of the East German state. The case for speedy progression from a single market to a single currency had already assumed a critical mass as a result of relatively buoyant economic conditions in the later 1980s and as the EU states demon-strated a far greater degree of convergence in their economic performances than at the time of the earlier, ill-fated attempt at economic and monetary union in the 1970s. Events on the wider European stage and especially the unification of Germany (October 1990) immediately reinforced and thereafter under-pinned progress towards the completion of the treaty.

Franco-German relations were of decisive importance in the making and implementation of the Maastricht Treaty's provisions for EMU. The prospect of German unification was a devastating blow to the French government. It por-tended a shift in the balance of power in Europe that threatened France's status, demolished its long-standing security interest in a divided Germany, and gave rise to alarming visions of Berlin rather than Paris as Europe's centre of gravity. Mitterrand's initial opposition to the prospect of a united Germany was lifted only by his insistence on closer ties between a united Germany and the EC. An integral part of France's long-established rationale for European integration was thus reasserted in 1990. Equally long-term considerations governed British reac-tions. Thatcher was also reluctant to concede the case for German unification, but was no more disposed than other British political leaders since 1945 to accept further integration as a necessary price for controlling Germany.

The most bankable German assurance for France was Bonn's support for EMU. In the period before the first elections of a united Germany (December

1990), however, this possibility was not a top priority for the Kohl government which was anxious to allay domestic fears about the possible loss of the Deutschmark (DM) and the Bundesbank, key emblems of German economic success since 1945. In the event Bonn accepted the principle of EMU but insisted on strict observance of convergence criteria. These were enshrined in the Maastricht Treaty and specified that any state wishing to proceed to the third and final stage of EMU had to achieve a budgetary deficit no more than 3 per cent of GDP, a maximum public debt ratio of 60 per cent of GDP, a stable exchange rate and a low rate of inflation.

After ratification of the Maastricht Treaty, Germany also played a prominent role in supervising progression towards EMU. For example, the German-inspired Stability Pact (November 1995) enivsaged a system of fines for single currency states that failed to abide by the Maastricht criteria. This measure aimed to assuage domestic opposition to the replacement of the DM by a weak, untested single European currency. The German financial establishment insisted that a hard core or optimal currency area had to exclude EU states with a profligate public spending record. Italy (which had a public debt of 124 per cent of its GDP in 1996) strongly resisted this view and was determined to be part of the first wave of single currency states, largely on the grounds of national prestige and as a founder member of the EC. As a result of French pressure the Stability Pact was turned into the Stability and Growth Pact (December 1996). This change of emphasis was indicative of the deepening economic recession and soaring unemployment (11 per cent of the EU labour force by 1996) which gripped the EU economies in the first half of the 1990s as the EU's average annual growth of 2.8 per cent in the 1980s dropped to 1.8 per cent (1990–98).

By the mid-1990s the fate of EMU hung in the balance as the EU economies were mired in recession and most states were failing to meet the convergence criteria. The political commitment of the French and German governments to the single currency, which was denominated the Euro (December 1995), was largely responsible for weathering the storm, as exemplified by the synchronised packages of economic measures introduced by the two governments (January 1996). Kohl, in particular, was unshakably committed to the successful introduction of the single currency and claimed (February 1996) that its failure would lead to an upsurge of nationalism and plunge Europe into new wars in the next century. This view summarised the experiences of a fast-disappearing generation of continental political leaders which had been scarred by the experience of the Second World War and strongly believed in the necessity of European integration to tackle the legacy of the 1914–45 period in European history. Chirac, the French president since May 1995, had reservations about the project. The rising tide of industrial unrest in France in late 1995 further exacerbated domestic opposition to the Maastricht Treaty which had been registered in the narrow majority for the treaty ('petit oui') in the referendum of September 1992. In the event the Chirac government held firm, fearing that any reversal or modification of the long-standing French commitment to EMU threatened a major diplomatic defeat and also entailed dire consequences for the franc on the money markets. The vast amount of political capital expended on the EMU by this stage virtually guaranteed its success. A fortuitous upturn in economic conditions in 1997 and in the first half of 1998 also ensured that all EU states except Greece qualified for the single currency zone by the time of the final decision on the composition of the zone (May 1998).

The fact that four of the fifteen EU states – Britain, Denmark and Sweden by choice together with Greece – were not part of the first wave of single currency states in January 1999 also contributed to the successful launching of the project. A key feature of the pattern of European integration in the 1990s, first evident in the Maastricht Treaty negotiations and in the Treaty of Amsterdam's provision for flexible decision-making, was acceptance of the idea of a 'multi-speed' Europe, which meant that the evolution of the EU was not governed by the slowest-moving member of the convoy of member states. In the case of EMU, for example, the distinction between the core and periphery states was registered in the making and ratification of the Maastricht Treaty when Britain and Denmark negotiated opt-outs from the final stage of EMU. Ideally, the British Conservative governments under John Major (1990–97) wished to remain in the slow lane to integration while directing traffic in the fast lane. Their inability to influence the course of events, however, became most apparent when sterling, which had entered the ERM in the closing stages of the Thatcher government (October 1990), was forced out of the ERM as a result of speculative pressures (September 1992). The increasingly rancorous debate over European policy in Conservative Party circles effectively ruled out British inclusion in the first wave of single currency states and also contributed to the Conservatives' massive electoral defeat (May 1997). The incoming Labour government under Tony Blair expressed support for the principle of British entry to the single currency. It insisted, however, that five economic tests had to be satisfied before this could take place, and thus left itself the same room for manoeuvre as the Thatcher governments had done in withholding sterling from the ERM in the period 1979–89.

A further significant feature of the making of the Maastricht Treaty was that it preceded the enlargement of the EU. The prevailing view among the EU states, with the notable exception of Britain, was that enlargement should be postponed until after the single market and the European Union had come into existence. The subsequent accession of Austria, Finland and Sweden (1995) was trouble-free, though Norway, as the fourth applicant, rejected membership for the second time. Unlike the new member states of the 1980s, Austria and Sweden brought additional financial resources as net contributors to the EU budget.

The far more problematical aspects of the enlargement issue concerned the EU's extension to include the former communist states of eastern Europe. In this field the EU states had no choice but to respond to the outcome of developments in the period 1989–91. Many east European states, spearheaded by the Visegrad countries (the Czech Republic, Hungary, Poland and Slovakia), clamoured for EU membership. In the event the EU made haste slowly and three of these states – the Czech Republic, Hungary and Poland – joined NATO (March 1999) long before they were likely to become EU members. It was not until

November 1998 that negotiations for EU membership formally opened with five east European states – the Czech Republic, Estonia, Hungary, Poland and Slovenia – and Cyprus.

The handling of the EU's eastward enlargement has been influenced by the strategic interests of individual EU states and in particular by considerations concerning the scale, cost and institutional implications of enlargement. Britain consistently pressed the case for enlargement in the hope that this process would act as a brake on the drive for political integration and in the belief that prior reform of the EU institutions was unnecessary. Under the Thatcher and Major governments, British distaste for EC institutional reform was rooted in a visceral loathing for any change likely to point the EC/EU in a more federal direction: the phrase 'federal goal' was struck from the proposed opening article of the Maastricht Treaty as a result of British objections. Germany has also been a keen supporter of enlargement, largely because of its strategic interest in stability beyond its eastern borders and also because of its industrial, financial and commercial stake in eastern Europe which far exceeds that of any other EU state (see Chapter 5). Unlike British governments, however, the German government acknowledged that a major overhaul of the EU's institutions was necessary to avert institutional paralysis in an enlarged EU.

Some EU states have been less enthusiastic about enlargement. French policy-makers, for example, have invariably envisaged a Europe of states organised in concentric circles, with the outer circle of east European states enjoying only association status with the core states. An underlying feature of the French emphasis on institutional reform before enlargement has been a reluctance to assist in the construction of what is perceived as an informal German economic empire in eastern Europe. Other EU states such as Greece, Ireland, Portugal and Spain have shared French reservations, largely because they stand to lose EU financial assistance as a result of enlargement.

The gross disparity between the EU and east European economies has also been a major stumbling to swift enlargement and has focused attention on the financial implications of enlargement. The first wave of enlargement will increase the EU's population by 28 per cent but will add only 3 per cent to the EU's GDP. This last figure indicates the relatively backward economic conditions in eastern Europe where, for example, per capita GDP in the Czech Republic and Slovenia is half the EU average, while Poland's is less than one-third and Estonia's one-fifth of the EU average (Eurostat 1997). The need for additional resources to facilitate enlargement was recognised in the Commission's document *Agenda 2000* (June 1997) which called for a fundamental restructuring of EU expenditure on CAP and regional funding that account for approximately 80 per cent of the EU budget. In the years from 1997 to 2000 the EU states engaged in much financial wrangling. This has involved demands for rebates by the major net contributors to the EU budget – Austria, Germany and Sweden, insistence by Britain on retaining the special rebate negotiated in 1984, opposition by Greece and Spain to cuts in assistance, and resistance by France to any reduction in agricultural subsidies. To date there have been only piecemeal changes, which suggests that the EU's first phase of enlargement in eastern Europe will be postponed for several years.

The collective responses of the EU states to international crises in the 1990s and most notably to the military conflicts surrounding the decaying corpse of Yugoslavia have done little to qualify the common portrayal of the EU as an economic giant but a political dwarf. The conflicting perspectives of the EU states were exposed during the deepening crisis in Yugoslavia in the early 1990s. In an echo of earlier Second World War associations, Germany strongly supported Croatia's independence, while long-standing ties with Serbia inclined France towards keeping the Yugoslav federation intact. In the event the Germans forced the issue by unilateral recognition of the independence of Croatia and Slovenia (December 1992). Other EU states fell into line but often against their better judgement and fearful of the consequences of the collapse of the Yugoslav federation. The subsequent failure of the EU's mediating efforts in the enveloping crisis in Bosnia and the eventual brokering of peace talks by the USA to end the war there (Dayton, Ohio 1995) further underlined the EU's weaknesses.

Throughout the multiple crises surrounding the disintegration of Yugoslavia, an enduring feature of the policies of the EU states has been their dependence on American leadership. Meanwhile, European integration has continued to be a partial process, highly developed in the economic sphere but far less so in the area of defence and security cooperation. A common foreign and security policy implies a further leap towards a more federal Europe. Whether the EU advances in this direction depends on how far the future determinants of European integration have similar unifying effects as the experience of the Second World War and of the Cold War had on an earlier generation of Europeans.

Further reading

Avery, G. and Cameron, F. (1998) *The Enlargement of the European Union*, Sheffield Academic Press, Sheffield.

Cornwall, M. (1996) 'Minority Rights and Wrongs in Eastern Europe in the 20th Century', *The Historian*, No. 50.

Crampton, R.J. (1999) *Eastern Europe in the Twentieth Century*, 2nd edn, Routledge, London.

El-Agraa, A.M. (ed.) (1998) *The European Union: History, Institutions, Economics and Policies*, 5th edn, Prentice Hall Europe, Hemel Hempstead.

Gowland, D. and Turner, A. (1999) *Reluctant Europeans: Britain and European Integration 1945–1998*, Longman, London.

Heller, A. and Fehrer, F. (1990) *From Yalta to Glasnost*, Blackwell, Oxford.

Middlemas, K. (1995) *Orchestrating Europe: The Informal Politics of the European Union 1973–95*, Fontana, London.

Lampe, J. (1996) *Yugoslavia as History. Twice there was a Country*, Cambridge University Press, Cambridge.

Swain, G. and Swain, N. (1993) *Eastern Europe since 1945*, Macmillan, London.

Urwin, D.W. (1995) *The Community of Europe: A History of European Integration since 1945*, 2nd edn, Longman, London.

Young, J.W. (1991) *Cold War Europe 1945–1989: A Political History*, Edward Arnold, London.

2 The palace and the shack: the wealth of Europe and its distribution

Introduction: Europe and the global capitalist system

For many centuries – from about 1400 to the beginning of the twentieth century – Europe (especially western Europe) dominated the rest of the world in power, in wealth, and in the organisation of commerce and the economy. In 1900, indeed, about 63 per cent of the world's industrial production was in Europe. Much of European thought has been based on the tactit assumption that here in Europe was the leading edge of the world's civilisation. Since 1920 – and especially since 1945 – this has ceased to be so. The USA is the most powerful and richest country in the world, Japan is close to the USA in economic output, and a swathe of countries on the Pacific Rim – the eastern side of Asia round to Australia – have economies which in spite of a serious recession in 1998 and 1999 seem still to be set on a medium-term growth pattern substantially greater than any others. This is not to say that Europe has switched from being dominant to being unimportant, but it is now just one of the major units in a world economic system.

Population

The population of Europe in 1996 was 728 million (13 per cent of world population), while the fifteen countries of the European Union (the EU) had 372.3 million people (6 per cent). By comparison the population of the USA and Canada was 293 million, Japan and South Korea 170 million.

We should take note of some population trends. The population of the world is increasing very fast. But in Europe growth in population arising from the existing resident population has virtually ceased, and indeed in some countries (especially in eastern Europe) has been replaced by a slow decline. Only in Turkey is there a strong natural increase. The decline is mainly due to a sharp drop in the birth rate. The average size of families has dropped well below the rate needed for replacement of the population (about 2.1 children per family) to about 1.75 in western Europe. In eastern Europe the effects of the dislocation of the economy and of society, combined in some cases with people postponing plans for children in order to acquire some of the material delights of the capitalist good life, have led generally to steep falls in the birth rate since 1989. In the CIS (the ex-Soviet Union) the fall was estimated at 9–10 per cent from 1992 to 1993 after a longish period of less dramatic decline. In the five *Länder* which once constituted East Germany the birth rate slumped by a startling 65 per cent between 1989 and 1993, and some demographers predict that the population of these *Länder* may sink by the middle of the twenty-first century from the 16 million of the 1980s to 9 million.

If the drop in birth rate is traced to the fertility rate – the number of births per woman of child-bearing age – we can clearly identify a downward trend common to all European countries other than Turkey. This began in different periods in different countries but has followed a similar pattern in each one from the decade in which it began. In the 1950–70 period the trend was most marked in the UK, Scandinavia (except Finland), northern and central Italy, and Germany, but it has since spread to France, and more recently, to Iberia, Finland, Greece, Poland and Romania. On this basis it is easy to predict that, leaving aside any effects of migration, the population will fall slowly in the next twenty years. It will fall rather faster in the UK and Germany, and probably faster still in much of eastern Europe (though not in Albania and Macedonia). The scale of this fall cannot be predicted with certainty, but it might be as much as 15–20 per cent from 1990 to 2020 in the UK and Germany, rather less in other countries of western Europe, but considerably more in eastern Europe and especially Russia and Ukraine.

It seems that conditions of family life in modern Europe, including readily available contraception, lead eventually to a fall in the birth rate to a level below that required for replacement. Whether this is inevitable in fully developed capitalist societies, or whether the impact of modernity can take different forms where cultures are different, is unclear; certain economically advanced Islamic countries seem so far to show a very much higher birth rate, and all underdeveloped countries show a much higher birth rate. Thus it is possible that the population of Europe may be maintained by a substantial immigration (official or illegal) from neighbouring Islamic countries.

But life expectancy has increased in modern European societies due to improved medical knowledge, health care and healthier living conditions. In 1995, life expectancy at birth in western European countries was 77. The effect is not sufficient to outweigh the fall in the birth rate. Rather, its effect is to increase the proportion of people over the age of 65 in the population. That proportion has increased in western Europe from 9 per cent in 1950 to 13.8 per cent in 1990 and will rise to about 16 per cent by 2010. In eastern Europe life expectancy is lower – 65 in Russia, 72 in Poland – but the proportion of over-65s will still be high because of the low birth rate. On seeing these figures one might jump to the conclusion that the large number of old-age pensioners in the society would constitute an unprecedentedly heavy burden on the working population who have to produce sufficient surplus to support them. (That conclusion is often touted by politicians trying to reduce health-care provisions and pensions.) But in fact the larger number of old-age pensioners is approximately off-set by the smaller number of children, so that there are fewer people under working age to support. The proportion of the population of working age remains about the same as at mid-century. And if the older people require a larger expenditure on health care, this may be partly counterbalanced by the smaller expenditure on education for the smaller number of children and students.

The effect of the continuing high birth rates in Turkey and the North African countries, however, may be considerable. This growing population already exerts a strong pressure to find outlets across the Mediterranean and the Bosphorus in the relatively rich European economies (see Chapter 14). In 1997 there were about 2.1 million Turks in Germany and about the same number of North Africans (Algerians, Tunisians and Moroccans) in France. Other west European countries also have substantial Turkish and North African populations. In the last ten years governments have sought to stem the inflow of immigrants, so the number has reduced somewhat, but the pressures of the surplus population so close to Europe's southern border will certainly grow, and it seems likely that legally or not there will be considerable migration from that area.

Europe and the world

Europe's relative significance in the global economy can be illustrated by reference to gross domestic product (GDP). This measure omits overseas earnings from trade, 'invisible earnings' and profits from capital invested overseas. The fifteen EU countries were expected to account for 19.8 per cent of world GDP in 1999, the USA for 20.4 per cent, Japan for 14 per cent. Alternatively, we might assess world significance by considering trade. The share of world international merchandise exports of the EU taken as a whole (i.e. ignoring trade between its members) was 14.8 per cent in 1997, larger than the USA (12.6 per cent) or Japan (7.7 per cent). If trade between its member countries is included, its share rises to about 38.4 per cent.

World trade is increasingly dominated by two major groupings of powerful economies – the European Union and the North Atlantic Free Trade Association (NAFTA, which consists of the USA, Canada and Mexico) – together with Japan. A less organised group of newly industrialised countries (NICs), comprising South Korea, Malaysia, Singapore, Brazil, is also significant. (China has huge potential significance and already has a large GDP, but its role in world trade is still small.) These groups organise their economies within common – or at least convergent – tariff structures. Clearly, there is a risk that trade between the groups might be so handicapped by tariffs that it diminished greatly, thus reducing also the efficiency and growth of the global economy; and the USA in particular has feared that the EU would act as a protectionist 'Fortress Europe' against global free trade. However, in 1993 in the Uruguay Round of GATT

(General Agreement on Tariffs and Trade, now the World Trade Organisation (WTO)), tariffs between the EU and the USA were reduced by about 50 per cent, which seems to confound these fears of European protectionism. But it is certainly true that finding agreements on tariffs and on acceptable constraints to preserve safety of goods, safety of the environment, acceptable conditions for workers, and verifiable quality without blocking trade between the groups (and so reducing economic growth) is difficult, and becoming increasingly so. In 1999 the supposedly neutral and authoritative assurance by the WTO that beef from American cattle which had been fed a growth hormone was safe for human consumption was called into question by EU experts. On such issues there is clearly much room for conflict, and no unquestionably neutral and authoritative arbiter of disputes could be found. But it seems likely that trade wars will be prevented by the powerful forces whose interests favour relatively free trade.

Prominent among these are the transnational corporations (TNCs), large companies whose activities and assets are spread across many different countries and continents, and in many cases span both NAFTA and the EU. A considerable proportion of the world's economy is now controlled by TNCs, including over a quarter of western European manufacturing. Thus there is little sense in supposing that the economic interests of Europe can be sharply distinguished from those of the USA or Japan, since the 'European' firms whose interests Europe might seek to protect may themselves be American or Japanese with factories in Europe. There has been considerable investment during the 1990s by such American-based or Japanese-based companies both in the EU and in eastern Europe.

The greater part of the world's population is not within these relatively rich groupings, and a different conception of 'Fortress Europe' would be that the EU and NAFTA together, as rich groupings protecting their own producers, disadvantage and exploit the heavily populated poor countries of the world. In fact, by the Lomé Convention of 1975 the EU has a policy of preferential trading arrangements (in manufactures and non-CAP agricultural products) for ex-colonies of European countries (mostly in sub-Saharan Africa, the Caribbean and the Pacific), but the effect of this seems to be slight. Nevertheless, the EU's attempt to defend its preferential tariffs for West Indian bananas against the USA (which wanted an open global market to allow into Europe the Latin American bananas produced by American companies) gave rise to the 'banana wars' of 1999, when serious threats were made of a range of American retaliatory tariffs on European goods, and a trade war threatened.

The core and the periphery

Within the EU itself, and more generally within Europe, a similar structure of unequal distribution of wealth can be discerned. We may distinguish regions where economic activity is at a high level and wealth is concentrated – the 'core' regions of Europe – from regions (generally further away from the centre) where wealth is much lower and the economy is more backward – the 'periphery'. From this point of view the 'Fortress' of Europe is the core within it, which tends to gather more of the wealth and economic activity by its own economic advantages.

We can regard the core of Europe as the broad belt of wealth, economic power, and development stretching from south-central England through Belgium and the southern and western parts of the Netherlands up the Rhine valley and into Switzerland, and continuing through Lombardy to the Mediterranean Sea at Genoa. It includes the cities of London, Brussels, Antwerp, the 'Randstad' of the south-west Netherlands (Rotterdam, Amsterdam, The Hague, etc.), Düsseldorf, Essen, Cologne, Frankfurt, Mannheim, Strasbourg, Stuttgart, Basel, Zürich, Milan, and Genoa. To this belt we should add extensions in the middle both westward and eastward: the city of Paris and its environs, Hamburg, and Bavaria around Munich. The core area is thus longish but rather fat in the middle; it has been called the 'Blue Banana'. A further strip of high development may arise on the western Mediterranean coast – the 'Sunbelt'. By contrast we may distinguish areas of relative poverty as the 'periphery', although there is no simple correlation between distance from the

Figure 2.1 The fortress of the rich
Source: *The Guardian*, 14 February 1994

core and deprivation (notably, parts of Scandinavia – especially the areas round Copenhagen and Oslo, central Sweden, and south Finland – are very prosperous). The regions which might be regarded as periphery in the EU (identified by the EU in 1998 as economically backward) are: Ireland (including Northern Ireland), the whole of Portugal, Spain (except for an area round Madrid, Catalonia and the Basque country of the north-east), Corsica and Sardinia, the southern part of Italy (the *Mezzogiorno*), and Greece.

Figure 2.2 The Eurocore: the Blue Banana, with the Sunbelt region of possible development

In addition a great many smaller regions within the core itself, scattered through the UK, Germany, France and Italy, are identified as industrial areas in decline – the old centres of heavy industries now mostly driven out of Europe by cheaper competitors in the Far East. With their ugly and polluted environments, few amenities, and large numbers of unemployed workers, they are unattractive to producer-service and high-tech industries. This is true, for example, of the north-east of England, parts of south Wales, the French Nord region and the adjoining Belgian coalfields, the Lorraine iron region and the Saar coalfield, and parts of the Ruhr coal and steel region, though other cities of the Ruhr (like Düsseldorf and Essen) have become successful core cities of international importance, partly because massive wartime damage made it necessary almost totally to reconstruct the urban environment after 1945.

But the relative poverty of these regions within the EU is nothing in comparison with the poverty of much of eastern Europe. There levels of GDP were already much lower than those of western Europe in the 1980s, their economies were in serious decline, and they suffered from extensive pollution from badly planned industrial development and the extensive use of readily available lignite (brown coal) for fuel. It was and is hoped that the establishment of a capitalist economy linked to the global economic system would jerk these economies onto a path to western levels of prosperity; but the immediate effect of the overthrow of communism in 1989 (or, in the ex-Soviet Union, in 1991), and the resulting disintegration of state planning with a major shift towards a capitalist economy, was a sharp drop in GDP.

It was not until 1993–95 that the downward fall of these economies was halted and replaced by a modest upswing. But that advance was achieved at the cost of a considerable increase in inequality, both between different countries and between different regions of particular countries. State industries were privatised and frequently found themselves unable to compete, their workers made redundant. Western firms were invited to establish plants in particular places on favourable terms, but the network of suppliers of parts and services for such plants frequently involved foreign suppliers, so that the injection of income tended to remain limited to the immediate area of these plants, while elsewhere unemployment soared. Thus the present inequalities within the EU will be greatly exacerbated if – as is intended for Poland, the Czech Republic, Hungary and Estonia in the first instance – countries with such relatively backward economies join the EU. But there is reason to hope that at least the more successful eastern European countries will have come somewhat closer to the economic levels of western Europe by the date such admissions might occur; the current growth rates of the more successful among them are quite high; e.g. Hungary 5.6 per cent, Poland 5 per cent annual growth of GDP at the end of 1998 (though these figures partly reflect merely the recovery from near-disaster).

Thus class inequalities in the capitalist system, which are discussed more fully in Chapter 3, may be expressed as 'spatial inequalities'. Some regions contain much of the wealth and economic power, while others are relatively powerless and poor. And it may be that the wealthier regions possess a built-in advantage in competition with poorer regions, in spite of their higher wage-costs. They tend to have more highly skilled labour available, better communications and more readily available ancillary producer services, and are themselves a desirable market for goods and services. In effect, the structure of contemporary capitalism works according to the biblical saying, 'Unto everyone that hath shall be given, and he shall have abundance, but from him that hath not shall be taken away even that which he hath' (Matthew 25:29); or, to use the jargon of geographical economics, it works (more or less) according to the *regional multiplier*. At least, that is so unless determined steps are taken to counter this effect.

The success of the core is partly determined by its central position, but partly also by the tendency of centres already established to continue to show a competitive advantage, so that the present pattern of the European economy can only be fully understood in the light of its history, even though some of the factors which were decisive for economic power in 1910, such as having coalfields fairly close, no longer apply. (See Figure 2.3. The wealth of major capital cities, however, continues.)

In the late twentieth century transport and communications have become much easier and cheaper, and though coal is still quite important much of it is used for the generation of electricity which is now easily transported over great distances. (The efficiency of electricity transmission has vastly increased since

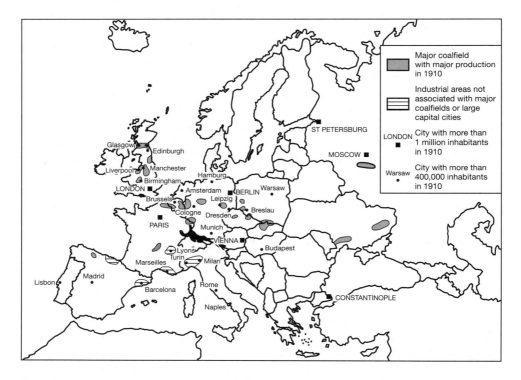

Figure 2.3 Europe: major centres of population in 1910, showing coalfields

1950.) Energy is also obtained from oil and gas, which can be transported very cheaply through pipelines or by sea in giant tankers, and from nuclear power stations producing electricity. So the main factors operative today in determining the location of wealth are rather:

1. *Labour*: different kinds for different purposes: professional for producer services and corporate management; skilled for high-tech and R and D (research and development), production and services; semi-skilled/unskilled for assembly-line production and consumer services. Attitudes and habits of the workforce are also important; managers seek hard-working, disciplined and cooperative labour, not prone to strikes.
2. *Major lines of communication* (especially significant where different lines of communication converge) for:
    (a) *Information*: telecommunications – including computer facilities for large-scale control of information traffic, postal services (which depend partly on air services);
    (b) *People*: passenger transport by air, rail and road (note the problem of congestion);
    (c) *Goods*: road, sea (where port facilities are vital), rail and air;
    (d) *Energy*: electricity supply grids, oil and gas pipelines, oil refineries, port and rail facilities for oil and coal.
3. *Proximity to markets* – especially for rapidly changing markets and markets with specialised kinds of demand.
4. *Proximity to producer services*, for example:
    (a) *Financial services*: banking, insurance, credit, security, management consultants;
    (b) *Information services*: computers and computer analysis, access to databanks;
    (c) *Research and design*: universities and science parks, specialised technical advice.
5. *Attractive living conditions* for the staff and for visitors, e.g. good infrastructure, pleasant climate, good urban conditions, good educational facilities.

In practice these factors tend to favour historically established core areas, especially capital cities. One may ask whether such inequalities are to be deplored, or whether they should rather be regarded as natural manifestations of economic progress, to be resolved, essentially, by people from the more backward regions moving to where the better jobs are to be found. And indeed there has already been a substantial migration of workers from eastern Europe (especially the Balkans) to the core in search of jobs. But national barriers to migrants, language differences, and a tendency to attachment to local communities make the response through migration to relative economic advantage fairly slow in Europe, whereas migration out of uncompetitive areas to the best jobs is much freer and quicker in the USA. Moreover, both national governments and the EU commit resources to preserving and assisting less successful economies (both regions and countries), which is, of course, a cost to the more successful. One aim of the EU is to bolster Europe's economic position in the competitive world economy by establishing a large single market to be the home market for European firms, and to promote efficiency and dynamism by encouraging open competition within Europe for this market, emulating in this way the success of the US economy. The single market was established in principle in 1992, but the structure of the European economy is still largely separated into the major national economies, with too many firms which by global standards are not big enough to compete for a world market effectively, and with many obstacles to open competition for the whole European market arising from differences in technical standards between different European countries and the protectionist efforts of national governments to help their own firms. The EU's competition policy is intended to dissolve these obstacles, but progress is only moderate, though there are increasing signs towards the end of the century that through mergers and takeovers the smaller and less successful companies are being absorbed into larger ones.

It is obvious that this drive to maximising efficiency tends to clash with the EU's regional policy, which seeks to build up the less successful with financial support at some cost to the more successful. And some economists argue that the continuing constraints in Europe to internal free trade put it at a persistent disadvantage compared to the USA and Japan. In the USA unemployment has been consistently lower than in the EU in the 1990s (4.4 per cent in 1999 in the USA and Canada, but 9.9 per cent in the EU). It has been argued that these figures reflect the way the USA's free movement of workers in pursuit of economic efficiency promotes a general dynamism of its economy, so that the USA is able to take full advantage of its large internal market; whereas in Europe – it is argued – the attempt to reduce inequality between different regions only reduces the growth of the economy and blurs the effect of the single market. But these claims are disputed. Though European unemployment is certainly high at the end of the 1990s, the rate of growth of GDP is slightly higher in the EU than in the USA. It is true that western European economists generally agree at least that the more effective the operation of the single market, the better for the competitiveness of Europe in the global market. However, it may be that the cost of an effective regional policy may not constitute a serious disadvantage to the more successful, while some extra sources of economic dynamism may arise from regions helped towards a position where they can themselves compete effectively. And the social damage which might otherwise arise could be very substantial.

A critical issue for the future of Europe (both within the EU and between the EU and the countries outside it) is whether these regional inequalities will tend to diminish as the periphery catches up with the core, or whether the unequal structure of modern world capitalism will reinforce itself, accentuating Europe's divisions. If they do so, it seems very possible that serious political conflicts may arise from the sense of injustice and envy in disadvantaged regions, leading to worsening problems of racism, crime, disease, uncontrollable movements of populations seeking work, and disruption of political structures. This would have consequences even for the core, since in a modern capitalist system social and economic pressures cannot be contained within a region.

These considerations are the rationale of EU policies of regional aid and of support for eastern European countries as possible applicants for membership, and also of some policies of intervention by national governments to establish new industries and to prop up existing ones by tax-breaks, provision of infrastructure, and direct but conditional subsidies. The fact that the infrastructure for a wealth-creating economy is so substantial and expensive implies that the loss of an established industry in a region will incur major wastage, which it is in the interest of a national government to avoid, and the social cost of such losses will also be considerable. In any case it is essential for a structure like the EU to keep a sense on the part of all its member countries that they all stand to gain by its development. Thus it remains the policy of the EU to work for cohesion of its different countries. This policy was reaffirmed by an amendment to the Treaty of Rome in 1987 (article 130a) as follows: 'In order to promote its overall harmonious development, the Community shall develop and pursue its actions leading to the strengthening of its economic and social cohesion. In particular, the Community shall aim at reducing disparities between the various regions and the backwardness of the least-favoured regions.' However, the practical application of this policy is limited by the limited funds available. The EU budget (of 85.5 million ECUs in 1999) is heavily committed by its agricultural support system, the European Agricultural Guidance and Guarantee Fund (EAGGP) (as determined by the Common Agricultural Policy, the CAP); support for agriculture takes 46.5 per cent of the EU budget, and while this sectoral support for agriculture does tend to help the backward regions it does not directly contribute to the diversification of their economies which is needed. For that purpose the EU's main weapon is the Structural Funds, taking 35 per cent of the EU budget in 1999, but it is doubtful if the effect of these funds is adequate for the economic prospects of the peripheral regions, though it is true that their current annual rates of growth are fairly good (e.g. Greece 3.5 per cent at the end of 1998, Portugal 2.7 per cent). Aid for eastern European countries outside the EU (devoted to technical and infrastructural aid) is much smaller even than these amounts; 4.25 billion ECU were spent by the EU on the PHARE aid programme in the five years 1990–95, compared with the Structural Fund's 18 billion ECUs in the single year of 1992.

Patterns of economic activity in Europe

The main cities of world trade and finance in America, western Europe and Japan, where the headquarters of the TNCs are mostly located, are in constant communication with each other. The leading ones have been called 'world cities' – the main financial centres, New York, London, Tokyo, Hong Kong, Paris, Chicago, Frankfurt, Amsterdam and Zürich. They need a host of sophisticated ancillary services – financial, legal and marketing – which add to their wealth and generate further needs, such as office space and office equipment, communications and transport, housing, food (though developments in information technology are now facilitating work at home in the leafy suburbs or even the Hebrides). High-tech developments tend to become established around these cities, and in the core regions generally (like those associated with the Cambridge Science Park close to London or the electronics of the area round Munich), while fashion industries are often located as close as possible to the richest markets. But there may be scope for some regions to take advantage of other kinds of locational advantage and build up high levels of wealth similar to the core. This can happen (and to some extent has happened) to capital cities like Madrid, Dublin, Prague, Warsaw, Budapest, Athens, which gather the producer services and the communicational significance of a whole country. They thus constitute a kind of mini-core for the surrounding areas.

In Portugal and Greece GDP per head is about one-third of that of the cities of the core, while the poorest regions within the eastern European countries generate a GDP per head equivalent to about one-twentieth of the EU average. But even quite close to major cities of the core there are areas of comparative deprivation, in northern Germany, north-eastern France, or Cornwall in England for example. Regions such as north-eastern Spain might be labelled the *semi-periphery*, since although quite distant from the core and lacking some of the economic power and sophistication of the core areas, they are nevertheless regions of rapid economic growth based on successful industrial development. They and other similar regions like north-east Scotland or the northern Czech Republic are essentially *branch-plant economies*, depending on factories set up by large firms whose central and controlling offices are elsewhere. Such economies are particularly vulnerable to downturns in world markets, since managers in a distant headquarters of the firm may determine working conditions or even shut down the branch to respond to the pressure of the international market. But it is not easy to take such decisions, partly because they may involve the loss of substantial investment and partly because the company needs to preserve its reputation in the area of its branch. Nevertheless, there is no doubt that the globalisation of the market and the greater mobility of capital has weakened the bargaining position of workers, and the risk of the closure of a large branch-plant with drastic effects on the regional economy is substantial.

A marked tendency is for the core areas to discard industry, and to focus instead on services, especially financial services (see Chapter 3 below). Outside the core, land and labour are cheaper and the transport of materials in and out of factories may be easier. So where production methods require substantial land, material and labour input, production is often set up outside the core, sometimes in labour-intensive 'sweatshops', sometimes in very large-scale automated factories. Both Volkswagen and Ford operate very large car-assembly plants in Spain, taking advantage of relatively low wage rates, while assembly-based production of silicon chips and other high-tech components may be located in East Asia or Latin America. Industry which remains in the core areas tends to be rather technical, requiring a highly skilled and educated workforce. Manufacturing firms are often linked as parts of networks of suppliers needing to keep in close contact with each other in a complex industry. Such industries are not usually large providers of employment.

Thus the global capitalist system at the end of the twentieth century is associated with *deindustrialisation in the core areas*. The major source of employment and wealth within them is *services*. In the UK, for example, 72.6 per cent of employees worked in services in 1997, compared with 69 per cent in 1995 and only 50 per cent in 1965; in France 71 per cent compared with 66 per cent in 1995 and only 43 per cent in 1965, and the figures for service employment would be much higher for the core cities of these countries. Indeed, even in the peripheral areas of Europe the proportion of employment in industry is falling, though in these areas there is an even stronger tendency to concentrate sophisticated services in capital cities. Portugal had 61.4 per cent employment in services in 1997, Italy 60.5 per cent, Spain 63.3 per cent. Even in smaller towns industrial employment is falling, because modern production methods use comparatively few people in the production process, favouring rather the control and speed provided by automatic machines. But it should be remembered that the service sector covers a very wide range of activities, from office cleaning and telephone call-centres and teaching to international financial negotiations and banking. In some peripheral areas a larger role may be taken by consumer services for tourists. In the core areas a key element is *producer services*, providing assistance to firms controlling production: advertising, banking, insurance, credit management, marketing, security services, computer services, personnel management, and so on. These services play a key role in the economy.

A feature of contemporary world capitalism is the *third agricultural revolution*: the development of agriculture – and especially food production – so systematically organised and scientifically controlled that it can be regarded as a branch of technical industry. Agribusiness needs very few workers and produces high-quality food on a very large scale. Crops and animals are kept in controlled conditions to optimise growth. They are looked after, harvested, packaged and prepared as foods, which are distributed for sale by largely mechanical operations and sold through large organisations, some of which are TNCs. This form of agriculture is so effective that Europe is now largely self-sufficient in foodstuffs, and the problem of agricultural policy in general is one of dealing with excess production. However, this industrialised agriculture exists alongside a very different kind of farming. Even in Europe many people in rural areas – especially in the peripheries and in the east – still work smallish farms by labour-intensive methods and live on the land. Their livelihood is threatened by industrialised agriculture which needs few workers. If the agricultural sector in Europe were completely uncontrolled, whole regions would be swiftly depopulated, and unemployment and dislocation would be enormous, with major political consequences.

The EU operates a system of controlled prices, quotas, and compensating support, and of payments for agricultural land taken out of production ('set-aside' land) in partial protection for rural areas, called the Common Agricultural Policy (CAP) (see the analysis of the CAP in Chapter 11). The cost of this policy (especially the EAGGP) is so large that it has always been highly controversial; countries with large peasant populations have tried to preserve it, those with

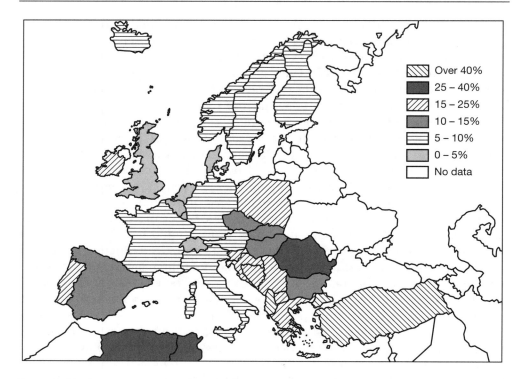

Figure 2.4 Percentage of workers employed in agriculture, 1989–1990

predominantly urban populations and with efficient large-scale agriculture have sought to reduce its cost and reform its structure. The cost increased sharply when Spain, Portugal and Greece were admitted to the EU and so became entitled to support for their (somewhat backward or anyway unprofitable) farmers on the same basis as the farmers of Normandy or the Mezzogiorno. But the cost of the CAP – if it continued on its present basis – on the planned enlargement of the EU to include Poland, the Czech Republic, Hungary, and possibly Slovenia and Slovakia would be huge, since farming there is a long way behind the efficiency of the best European farming. Thus it seems likely that a major reform of the CAP will be agreed before any further enlargement takes place. But it is also possible that a major agricultural revolution will take place in eastern Europe, sharply increasing its efficiency but causing massive rural unemployment there. The percentage of the workforce in agricultural employment is falling all over Europe (though in Turkey it is still over 50 per cent), but it is still large enough in most of eastern Europe for such a drastic collapse of rural employment to have very serious political effects (see Figure 2.4).

Energy

A major problem for any advanced economy is energy supply. Until 1963 Europe obtained most of its energy from coal (70 per cent in 1955), a growing proportion of which was converted into electricity. Only in Italy and Norway was there any considerable development of hydro-electric power. But it became apparent that energy from oil was considerably cheaper and it was easier to handle by automatic procedures. Consequently there was a great expansion of its use as a source of energy at the expense of coal. By 1972 oil provided 65 per cent of western Europe's energy needs and coal a mere 22 per cent. Nearly all this cheap oil was imported. After the 1973 Arab–Israeli War, however, the Organisation of Petroleum Exporting Countries (OPEC) (mainly countries of the Middle East) increased the price of oil more than fourfold; while in 1979–80 the price more than doubled again. (These traumatic events are known as the First and Second Oil Price Shocks.) But this did not lead to a return to coal; coal was still generally more expensive than several alternatives, and usually led to greater pollution of the environment. Moreover, the pattern of technologically advanced industrial production, and also of domestic appliances, led to a much greater demand for energy in the form of electricity, which could be produced either directly (primary electricity) from water power or nuclear power stations, or indirectly (thermal electricity) from any source of heat.

The governments of western Europe responded to the oil price shocks of the 1970s by trying to diversify the sources of energy so as not to be too dependent on any particular one, to diversify the countries from which oil was imported, to use energy more efficiently so as to need less of it, and to seek clean fuels and clean uses of power so as to reduce pollution. Taking advantage of Europe's own oilfields, especially those discovered in the 1950s beneath the North Sea (though others in the Atlantic and the Mediterranean have been discovered since), Europe developed its own oil production. It was also discovered that natural gas could be transported in pipelines (often in a double pipe carrying oil from the same region, since oil and gas are frequently found together) into Europe's core and used cheaply and efficiently. Gas was transported in this way not only from the North Sea but also from the Soviet Union and from North Africa. Finally, the use of nuclear power for electricity generation was greatly expanded, to produce 12 per cent of total EU energy consumption in 1985.

But in the 1980s the oil price fell once more, until by the mid-1980s it was again at the levels of the 1960s in real terms, and it has remained fairly low since then. The diversification policies have proved successful; oil and natural gas in 1999 produced within Europe (mainly from the North Sea) provided for 39 per cent of European energy consumption, and imported oil and gas came from three different major sources: Algeria and Libya, the Middle East, and the former Soviet Union. In all cases pipelines carried most of the oil and gas fast and efficiently, and diversity of transportation routes ensured effectively competitive pricing. It is worth noting, however, that certain countries are particularly significant for European energy supply because of their position as bases for actual or possible pipelines: Georgia, where an oil pipeline from Azerbaijan and the Caspian Sea now reaches an oil terminal from which supertankers can take oil to various ports, especially in Bulgaria and Turkey; Egypt, where pipelines from the Gulf and Saudia Arabia reach the Mediterranean, and from which future pipelines may take gas and oil direct to the Balkans; Turkey, where pipelines both from the Middle East and from the Caspian Sea pass into Europe; and Algeria and Libya, which export large amounts of oil by pipelines and supertankers across the Mediterranean. Both Algeria and Libya are troubled by difficult political relations with Europe and the USA, and in the case of the former, by serious civil unrest also. The fact that certain countries contain pipelines may well have importance for politics; for example, in relation to Turkey's application for EU membership.

Technical developments in the design of very large gas-fired power-stations emitting very small amounts of polluting gases make it likely that gas will become much more significant in European energy supply (it provided 21 per cent of the EU's total energy in 1996, an increase of nearly a quarter since

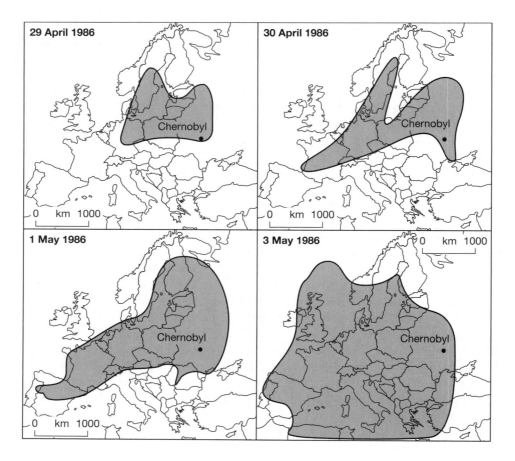

Figure 2.5 Radioactive pollution from the Chernobyl accident 1986

1990). Oil, however, remains important, mainly because of its use in transport systems (private cars etc.), and its proportion of total EU energy consumption has remained stable at 42 or 43 per cent since 1985. Only a future advent of cars run on concentrated gas seems likely to alter this situation, and some resulting air pollution seems inescapable even though proposed technical measures (if enforced) will mitigate it somewhat.

Eastern Europe's economies suffered greatly in the 1980s from the Soviet Union's decision (motivated by its own economic difficulties) to sell much of its oil and gas through pipelines to western Europe, reducing its previous supply of (uneconomically) cheap oil to eastern European countries. They responded (with Soviet help) by building numerous nuclear power stations (30 by 1989) and by maintaining their intensive coal production (which still provided 76 per cent of their energy in 1982). In the late 1980s and early 1990s their economies collapsed, partly because of the uneconomic structure of their arrangements for energy supply. It also became apparent that the years of cheap energy and relatively low technical expertise had led to grave pollution of the environment from inefficient power stations and vehicles, and – especially after the Chernobyl disaster of 1986 when a Ukrainian nuclear power station went out of control, spreading lethal contamination as far as Portugal – faith in the recently built nuclear power stations has plummeted. (These fears are widespread in the West, too, of course, and it seems likely that political pressures will lead to a general decline in nuclear power in Europe, especially if there is some further disaster.) Through the early 1990s the collapsing east European economy meant that demand for power was much reduced (dropping from 415 mtoe – million tons of oil equivalent – in 1983 to 340 in 1990 and 252 in 1996), but it shows a strong recovery in the late 1990s. This recovery, however, is based on the gradual absorption of the east European energy system into that of western Europe. Thus coal consumption dropped sharply to 50 per cent of total energy consumption in 1994, newer and technically more efficient and clean power stations are being built (including one new nuclear power station with western technology in Romania), and the outlook for a modernised energy system is good. (These remarks relate to eastern Europe outside the former Soviet Union. Within the latter area there are still major distortions of the economy and the energy system. Furthermore, some of the economies of the Balkans have been seriously disrupted by war in the 1990s.)

The major issue now confronting the European energy system is whether the great economies of scale which are now technically achievable (partly with improved power station technology and partly with efficient transmission) can be realised. The great obstacle to them is the national structure of the power supply and energy production systems in Europe. A regime of open international competition within Europe, thus promoting very large companies operating internationally in the energy markets (especially those for large industrial customers) would enable these benefits to be achieved, but currently many European countries preserve state monopolies within their own markets. Privatisation of these concerns, permitting subsequent mergers and takeovers, is thus the key to greater efficiency.

Structure of firms and industrial production

European industry in the period 1920–70 was especially characterised by Fordism – the mass production of standardised products by assembly lines in large factories. But such systems are inflexible, quality control in them is difficult, and the more technically complicated the products the more inefficiencies arise from trying to coordinate the production of the different elements. Moreover, large stores both of parts and of the products for future sale are necessary, as a result of the inflexible production system.

The advent of computerised information and control methods have made it possible to adapt the production process to demand, producing differentiated products to meet changing market demands and even individual consumer order, to bring parts to the assembly process as and when required, to coordinate supplies from a network of independent suppliers, and thus to reduce greatly the need to tie up capital in stored items. Such production processes are labelled 'just-in-time' systems (for production in immediate response to demand) and 'just-in-case' systems (for products adapted to the precise requirements of the customer). What makes them possible is (a) highly controlled production processes, often by robots or automated machine systems; and (b) rapid transfer of information and its linking to the production process itself. Computer-aided design tends to reduce the size and weight of moving parts of machines, and thus to minimise energy use in the production process itself. Such a process is called 'lean production', achieving maximum economies in the use of labour, materials, energy, and indeed capital (since very little capital is tied up in storage or waste). This kind of organisation encourages the separation of different elements of the production process, leading to a great increase in subcontracting. Flexibility is often obtained by the specification of standard components which can be assembled in different ways to make different products. Once the design has been determined, the firm may find it cheaper and more efficient to subcontract the work of making particular components to other firms. Thus interlocking contractual arrangements result in many relatively small firms producing components for other firms to assemble. The effect on the spatial distribution of industry is that different parts of a complex product may be produced in locations around the world and transported to the assembly site via a distribution centre. There are now many distribution centres for particular industries through the whole of the EU. Many of these are located in the Netherlands, because of its central position and its great port, Rotterdam.

Thus the production system is essentially an *information system*. It is the flow of information which determines the effectiveness of the production process and its link to the market; and this information system, in turn, is closely tied to the financial control of the firm. Such information systems may operate globally thanks to the speed and scale of modern telecommunications (using satellite communications for many of the greater-distance links). For example, the Tokyo headquarters of the Mitsubishi Corporation receives from and sends to its many branches all over the world more than 4.5 million words every day. Benetton of Italy produces clothes in precise response to a rapid, computerised flow of information from all its retail outlets in Europe. Obviously this kind of organisation, now becoming very common, makes fast and efficient communication vital for industry.

Such organisation might seem to favour the dispersion of industry, especially to those parts of the world where wages are lowest. In practice, the trend is rather for concentration of industry within regions (often in the core). Technical demands, the need to keep in touch with designers, suppliers and producer services favour keeping firms involved in any given industry within a not-too-distant range of each other. The production of a single European civil airplane, for example the European Airbus, involves the separation of its components into different parts produced in England at Manchester, Filton near Bristol, and Hatfield near London; in Belgium at Charleroi, in Germany at Bremen, Hamburg, Augsburg, and Laupheim near Stuttgart, in France at Nantes, Les Mureaux near Paris, and Toulouse; and in Spain at Madrid and Seville. Most of these sites are in the core. In these cities and regions similar kinds of high-tech production are under way, creating a network of highly skilled workers able to inform and influence each other. Furthermore, concentration of human resources to encourage technical development has become the policy of many European governments. Science parks linking universities and research institutes and industry have been set up to generate an impetus for technologically dynamic industrial development, adapting and applying discoveries as they appear, at Grenoble, Munich, Utrecht, Amsterdam, Cambridge, Sophia Antipolis (in the South of France), and in the development corridor along the M4 from London to Bristol.

Communications

This chapter has already shown very clearly how crucial communications are for modern Europe. This is even more true in view of the major obstacles to communication in Europe (as compared, say, with the USA or China): mountain ranges – the Alps, the Pyrenees, the Carpathians, etc., as well as more generally hilly country as in the Balkans, central Italy or much of Scotland; numerous sea inlets obstructing land communications; and in many parts land is already heavily occupied, making it difficult to acquire the land needed for major communication routes.

Ports

Economical movement of goods in bulk – an essential pre-condition for the advanced economic structures we have been describing – is achieved by the use of pipelines, giant tankers for liquids or gases, and containers for pre-packed units. For these, ports with special large-scale facilities are needed, which older ports did not possess. Those – like Liverpool – which have failed to adapt to these requirements are now of minor significance, while others – like Hamburg, Marseilles and Gothenburg – have abandoned their old port areas and constructed new facilities close by. Europe's leading port, Rotterdam, has successfully used its position at the mouth of the Rhine in a sheltered estuary where deep channels could be dredged, to build extensive port facilities and large factories and oil refineries to process some of its bulk products. Such facilities provide a growth-point for certain types of industry involving bulky goods. Like Rotterdam, most of the top 20 European ports, including the seven largest container ports, are located around the southern end of the North Sea, giving them direct access to the European core at a centre for land communications and close to major cities. For the Mediterranean trade, apart from Barcelona and Valencia, most of the big ports are at the head of the Ligurian Sea – Marseilles-Fos, Genoa, La Spezia and Livorno itself.

Air

The London airports are the largest international airport complex in Europe, with 60 million passengers in 1998, though Frankfurt carries more freight – over one million tons. Paris is some way behind London, then follow Amsterdam, Brussels, Rome, Copenhagen, Milan, Athens, Manchester, and Düsseldorf. Air transport is a prime example of the disadvantage which Europe suffers in the global economy from the political divisions of its economic systems. The European airlines escape to some extent the pressures of competition because their governments protect them; as a result, air travel in Europe is very much more expensive and more congested than in America. But these obstacles seem in 1999 to be on the way out. Encouraged both by commercial pressures and by the EU's competition policy, airlines are beginning to arrange cooperation and sharing of markets in ways which leave their separate identities formally intact. It seems likely that mergers will clarify the situation before long.

Road

The structure of industry and services described above is made possible by an open network of available communication by road; goods are transported by 44-ton lorries, people travel in all directions by road to negotiate with other firms or to get to work. Thus the suggestion that society could shift to a regime of reliance on rail transport such as it had in 1920 is quite incompatible with the shape of the economy and of the society that goes with it, at least in prosperous areas. The tonnage of goods carried by road is more than ten times that carried by rail, and western Europe is expected to buy 13.7 million new cars in 1999. Eastern Europe contains no such dense network of roads, and car ownership is very much less than in the west, though it is rapidly increasing (travel by car increased by 643 per cent from 1970 to 1991, nearly three times the increase in the west). Since the road network has been built by the national governments it is aligned more to routes inside the respective states than to integrated communication across Europe. Yet the latter is clearly what the single market requires for maximum efficiency. The EU has tried to promote major routes of international communication in Europe (mostly for rail rather than road), but success so far is not great. However, the major barriers to communication – the Alps and the Channel – have been considerably reduced by tunnels and by major road improvements in the Brenner Pass between Verona and Munich.

But the mobility which everyone loves so much and which very many Europeans see as essential to the fabric of their lives is seriously endangered by all the other road users, congesting the network of roads, damaging the environment, constricting the lives of children by the danger they pose, and rendering cities far less satisfactory as sites for interacting human life. Building more and wider roads only leads to greater traffic; building by-pass roads around major cities (as in the Boulevard Périphérique round Paris or the M25 round London) only leads to increasing blockages on them and at their exits. One response is to build more and more facilities – hypermarkets, leisure centres, industrial workplaces, offices, and of course homes – outside the city centres, or indeed to build new, spread-out cities. Another is to force cars out of cities (and lorries, with awkward consequences for the delivery of essential goods) by road taxes or shortage of expensive parking, and providing much improved public transport. But it is not easy to see how such policies could do better than stave off the worst of the tendencies to congestion of vehicles which are already obvious.

Rail

The EU's policy of promoting integrated European communications has focused mostly on high-speed trains – as with the French 'Trains de Grande Vitesse' (TGVs), which compete well with air transport for comfort and rapid travel between cities. But these were originally parts of national programmes for promotion of national economies, based on massive national investment, and the technical specifications (voltages, loadings, heights of tunnels, gauges, etc.) of different countries' systems do not necessarily match up. The EU plan of establishing a network of trans-European TGVs to promote integrated communication across the EU consequently proceeds slowly, though there are substantial developments, e.g. on the Paris to Cologne route through Amsterdam and from Venice through the Brenner Pass to Munich and Berlin. The transport of freight by rail is still considerable; however, its major disadvantage is that it fails to allow (without transfer from rail terminal to lorry) for transport in any direction through the dense network of firms located in the scattered way which road communication has encouraged. It therefore seems unlikely that it could take over the major freight-transport role in Europe from road.

Telecommunications

The network of telecommunications is developing extremely fast, facilitating the global intercommunication of masses of data (much of it to computers) which modern commercial organisation requires, providing for the world-wide web on the internet, and permitting the rapid expansion of international personal communication by mobile telephones, video-conferencing, etc. The investment required is boosted by the integration of this system with that required for television transmission, so that very large amounts of capital are being invested in laying a network of high-volume fibre-optic cable through urban areas and across continents and oceans and providing geo-stationary satellites with appropriate 'footprints' (areas of effective communication with the satellite). Much of the investment comes from large TNCs with bases both in the USA or Japan and in Europe. However, such investment is naturally more readily available for the richer areas where the larger markets and hence the best targets for advertising are to be found, so eastern Europe and parts of southern Europe are relatively poorly provided with these essential tools for full participation in the modern global economy.

Further reading

Atis, M. and Lee, N. (1997) *Economics of the European Union*, 2nd edn, Oxford University Press, Oxford.

Cole, J. and Cole, F. (1997) *A Geography of the European Union*, 2nd edn, Routledge, London.

Dent, C. (1997) *The European Economy: the Global Context*, Routledge, London.

The Economist, London. Relevant articles

El-Agraa, A. (1998) *The European Union: History, Institutions, Economics and Policies*, Prentice Hall Europe, Hemel Hempstead.

McDonald, F. and Dearden, S. (1999) *European Economic Integration*, Pearson Education Ltd, Harlow.

Pinder, D. (1998) *The New Europe: Economy, Society and Environment*, Wiley, Chichester and New York.

Schulze, M.-S. (1999) *Western Europe: Economic and Social Change since 1945*, Pearson Education Ltd, Harlow.

Somers, F. (1998) *European Union Economics: a Comparative Study*, 3rd edn, Pearson Education Ltd, Harlow.

Unwin, T. (1998) *A European Geography*, Pearson Education Ltd, Harlow.

3 European society: power to the people?

European society has been transformed over the last two centuries by a series of changes that have revolutionised the way in which we live and think. A largely rural society based on agriculture has become urbanised and industrialised and is now entering a new phase of deindustrialisation, as manufacturing jobs relocate to less developed countries. Europe today finds itself part of a new global economy, specialising in the provision of services for domestic and foreign consumption: banking, insurance, research, communications, education, health and welfare, tourism, arts and entertainment, etc.

This chapter begins by examining the changes that occurred in the initial transition to industrial society, especially the influence of economic development on social inequality and politics. It then explores the ways in which the social problems of mature industrial society are being tackled by governments as we approach the economic and social challenges of the future.

The rise of modern society

As the industrial revolution began to develop in the wake of the French Revolution a number of optimistic forecasters began to herald the arrival of a new society. In France, for example, Henri de Saint-Simon (1760–1825) and his acolyte Auguste Comte (1798–1857) proclaimed that science was replacing religion as the dominant thought pattern of the modern world. Advances in technology were solving the problems of production but the new economy would require a shake-up in our thinking about politics and society. The *ancien régime* of monarchy and aristocracy had been supported by the established church but, as science became the new currency of intellectual debate, both the Church and the class structure it supported would have to be replaced. They proposed to replace the Church by temples to Newton, where ordinary people would be exposed to the wonders of gravitational theory instead of the mysteries of religion! These new thinkers predicted that a new generation of scientifically trained leaders, drawn from the rising middle classes in commerce and industry, would assume power. By applying their

Table 3.1 Traditional and modern societies

	Traditional	**Modern**
Economic basis	Rural population mainly engaged in subsistence agriculture	Urban population mainly engaged in commerce and industry
	State and municipal regulation of economic life	Free trade based on market forces. Supply and demand balanced by price mechanism
	Traditional technology based on animal and water power	Advanced technology using mechanisation and fossil fuels
	Informal domestic units of production	Large-scale formal work organisations and wage labour
Social system	Closed communities isolated by poor communications	Urban cosmopolitan climate induced by improved transport and communications
	Status *ascribed* at birth. Authority inherited.	Status *achieved* by ability and education.
Political system	Rule by monarchy, aristocracy and landed gentry	Democracy led by professional experts
Belief system	State religion legitimises traditional rule of landed elite	Freedom of belief. Scientific explanations of nature and society
	War and military domination the basis of state policy	Free trade and peace replace war and civil insurrection
	Nationalism	Internationalism

science to the problems of society they would usher in a secular world in which old disputes about religion would fade away.

Although these 'Prophets of Paris' were overoptimistic about the prospect of avoiding social and political conflict, modern social scientists support many of their original claims. They were right to spot the revolutionary nature of the economic and intellectual transformations taking place. Modern societies are quite different from the traditional societies that preceded them. Table 3.1 summarises the contrasts often drawn between the two types of society.

Religion in modern Europe

However, the view of Saint-Simon and Comte that, with the rise of science, churches would go out of fashion proved to be mistaken. Although one could argue that the mass media and the modern educational system (apart from those schools still run by churches) tend to indoctrinate us with a scientific view-point it is hard to conclude that religion has simply faded away.

The French Revolution attempted to abolish the Catholic Church but subsequent generations saw it restored, despite fierce opposition from secularists. The religion that developed in the new industrial societies of Europe tended to become more fragmented than hitherto. Ruling classes tended to support their established national religion, although that differed from one country to another. The wars of religion that had preceded the modern period had broken up western Christianity into Catholic and Protestant states, as some monarchs declared national independence from Rome during the Reformation. The map of religious allegiance has remained fairly stable since (see Figure 3.1).

However, established state churches could not retain their hold over an urban industrial population which had escaped from the traditional social controls of the rural village. In Catholic countries the Church was regarded by radicals and socialists as a counter-revolutionary force, the opiate of the masses. Church control over education was strongly resisted by campaigners for secular education and freedom of belief. In countries such as England and Scotland, where the state church was Protestant, its opponents might include Catholic minorities (such as Irish immigrants) and Protestant dissenters such as the Quakers, Methodists and Baptists, as well as non-believers.

Thus, nineteenth-century religion was associated with social divisions and political conflict between those who supported the dominant, sometimes state, religion and those who opposed it, often for quite different reasons, yet could unite in a call for freedom of belief and the extension of full rights of citizenship to all. Some countries retained a plurality of beliefs and lifestyles; for example, in the Netherlands a complex division appeared, with supporters of the official Dutch Reformed Church opposed by more radical groups of Calvinists and by Roman Catholics and Socialists. Each of these communities developed their own separate social institutions: trade unions, political parties, schools and universities, sports and social clubs, even including a Catholic Goat Breeders' Association (McLeod 1997, p.18). Generally speaking, those who supported the political dominance of the dominant religion in a society became known as pro-clericalists and those who took an opposing view became known as anti-clericalists.

Pro- and anti-clericalism thus served to divide society, creating separate sub-cultures in local communities within the new industrial cities. While religion appealed more to the upper and middle classes than to the workers, and to women more than men, it remained as an important source of identification, complicating the economic and political struggles of modern society. It sometimes played an important part in rallying nationalist opposition to foreign domination, for example in the fight for Irish independence from British rule, and more recently in the emancipation of eastern and central European nations from the Soviet bloc. It has shown its uglier face in the subsequent ethnic conflicts in Yugoslavia and elsewhere.

As new waves of immigrants add to the social mix of Europe new religious communities continue to form, for example recently established Islamic

ICELAND

RUSSIA

FINLAND

NORWAY   SWEDEN

ESTONIA

LATVIA

EIRE   DENMARK

LITHUANIA

UK   HOLLAND   BELORUSSIA

POLAND

BELGIUM   GERMANY   UKRAINE

CZECH REP

FRANCE   AUSTRIA   SLOVAKIA

SWITZ   HUNGARY   MOLDAVIA

SLOVENIA   CROATIA   ROMANIA

PORTUGAL   BOSNIA &   SERBIA   BULGARIA

CORSICA   HERCEGOVINA

SPAIN   MONTENEGRO   MACEDONIA

MENORCA   ITALY   ALBANIA

IBIZA   MALLORCA   SARDINIA   GREECE

MOROCCO   ALGERIA   TUNISIA   SICILY

· · · · · ·   The divide between the Eastern Orthodox and the Western Latin Church

————   The Reformation divide between the Protestant and the Roman Catholic Churches

– – –   The divide between the former communist and the non-communist regimes

Long-established Islamic populations

Figure 3.1 The religious map of Europe
Source: T. Spybey (ed.) (1997) *Britain in Europe: an Introduction to Sociology,* p. 243, Figure 12.1

communities in Germany, France, and the UK. These have to be distinguished from the older Muslim communities left behind by the receding Ottoman Empire in the Balkans. Figure 3.1 also reminds us of the persisting ancient split between Roman Catholic and Eastern Orthodox branches of Christianity. Journalists report, for example, that Greek Orthodox businessmen are more successful than Roman Catholic or Protestant westerners in dealing with Russians because they share a common culture related to the Orthodox religion. But Orthodoxy does not completely unite its followers in the different countries of eastern Europe, where national traditions have diversified over the centuries.

Contemporary surveys reveal that religious observance has declined, even amongst the formerly more religious middle and upper classes. In many countries, fewer people now belong to any church, and some churches are having trouble maintaining their buildings and recruiting clergy. But religious beliefs seem to persist without regular church attendance and even some atheists continue to identify with the religious community from which they dissent. Science may have improved our understanding of the natural world and social science may have dispelled some of the mysteries of social and political life, but secular explanations can provide little spiritual comfort. Most people still seem to need something more to believe in, and some ritual celebration of the great turning points in their lives, such as marriage, the birth of a child, and the loss of a loved one. Sociologists of religion suggest that this search may lead them in new directions as new minority cults and exotic religions take root in Europe, for example some brands of evangelical Christianity introduced by West Indian immigrants into Britain or Asian mystic religions introduced into European cities by other immigrant groups. In a new society based on mass consumption religions may compete for 'customers' with differing tastes, and religious toleration may grow to reflect our greater respect for individualism over conformity to community traditions.

Theories of class and inequality in modern society

The change from a fairly rigid traditional status system to one related more to people's changing economic roles gave rise to two main interpretations. The *liberal view* was promoted by the rising middle classes who first challenged the agrarian elites which ruled Europe before the industrial revolution. Fighting against inherited wealth and power, liberals tended to champion the idea of equality of opportunity. In the capitalist economy that was sweeping across Europe, from the north and west towards the east and south, they saw the prospect of opportunity for all to compete on equal terms. A free labour market would allow workers to sell their talents to the highest bidder rather than be tied to a particular landlord. Although trade and manufacturing would create fortunes for some and penury for others the rewards would be fairly distributed on merit.

The *socialist view* was most potently expressed by Karl Marx (1818–83). He appreciated the material progress made possible by the development of modern industry. Eventually, he believed, the new methods of production would be harnessed for the benefit of all, but not under the system of capitalism which had ushered them in. Although capitalism was a necessary stage in human progress, it would have to be replaced by a socialist system before the full democratic potential of modern industrialism could be realised.

He thought that liberal capitalism was almost as oppressive as the feudal regimes it had replaced. In the past a minority ruling class exploited the mainly agricultural workforce by various forms of compulsion. When workers moved from the domination of their local landlord to make an apparently free contract to work for the factory owner they were entering a new form of 'wage slavery' from which they had little possibility of escape. Forced to accept whatever pay and conditions were on offer, they could not really be said to share in the new freedom enjoyed by their middle-class employers.

Marx predicted that, although overall living standards might rise under capitalism, the gap between the wealthy owners of capital and their workers would increase. Wealth would become concentrated in an elite, and small businessmen or independent craftsmen would be unable to compete with large monopoly companies. Skilled workers would be replaced by machinery and the working class would become a mass of unskilled and alienated drudges, struggling to survive on minimum wages. The horrors of the capitalist labour market, however, would force workers to organise, initially into trade unions and then into their own political parties to fight for reform. But reform would be blocked by the capitalist class who would dominate the state. Social inequality would be intensified by periodic booms and slumps. Social protests would escalate until the labour movement was strong enough to lead a revolution to sweep away capitalism and replace it by a socialist system based on common ownership.

Liberals and Marxists both recognised the international dimension of modern society. Marx lived long enough to see large-scale capitalist organisations encircling the globe, employing new means of communication to link together producers and consumers in many countries. Given such a powerful enemy, he argued that workers could not defeat it at local or national level. The socialist revolution might start in one country, probably in one of the most advanced capitalist societies, such as Britain or the USA, but it would have to spread throughout the world. Workers of the world would have to unite as effectively as the capitalists had done on an international scale. As one later sympathiser put it, capitalism was a tiger and it was impossible to tame it claw by claw!

Modern social scientists tend to enshrine liberal beliefs in their criticisms of Marx. Some, referred to as *functionalists*, argue that a complex industrial society is bound to develop inequalities because there will always be a need for leadership. Qualified experts in positions of authority have to be rewarded for exercising their talents and are bound to become the new elite. Functionalists point to what happened under the Soviet brand of state socialism where getting rid of capitalism did not prevent senior party members awarding themselves all sorts of special privileges.

Pluralists accuse Marx of oversimplifying the link between economic wealth, social status and political power. They prefer to follow Max Weber (1864–1920), who accepted that social class was a major cleavage in modern society but not the only one. They point to conflicts within classes, between one trade and another, or between rival regional, national, ethnic or religious groups, as in Northern Ireland, Italy, Spain, and various parts of eastern Europe today. While not believing in the classical liberal model of a society of competing individuals, they reject the two-class model and stress the plurality of social conflicts. Politics is not a simple football match between two sides, capital and labour. Political parties are seen as shifting coalitions representing constellations of interests all seeking a share of power. The parties have even been likened to firms competing for customers.

These rival theories of industrial democracy continue to offer different interpretations of the same facts. In the next section we will see how well the theories fit the available facts about social inequality in modern Europe.

Democracy adapts to modern industrialism

It is difficult to make neat generalisations about social inequality and conflict in twentieth-century Europe. The battle between, and sometimes within, the classes has taken place against a kaleidoscopic background of social upheaval induced by economic and political change. The First World War dealt a severe blow to hopes for the international solidarity of workers, as they rallied to their countries' flags. Their national loyalties may have been strengthened by social reforms conceded or promised by pragmatic governments. In the closing decades of the old century and the opening decades of the new, the extension of the franchise to all men and eventually, in most countries, to all women, was completed (see Table 3.2).

This period also saw the first phase in the establishment of state welfare systems. Many countries passed legislation introducing basic measures of social security to insure workers against such hazards as industrial accidents, ill health, unemployment, retirement in old age and the cost of rearing children. State expenditure on the provision of education, housing, health and other social services for the working classes steadily rose, although not yet to the more generous levels which were reached after the Second World War.

Some of these reforms were deliberately introduced by right-wing leaders like Bismarck to undermine the appeal of working-class radicals and were accompanied by attempts to crush growing labour movements. The gradual consolidation of trade unions and labour parties brought pressure on governments for further reforms, especially after the franchise was widened. Even employers and military leaders could see the sense of maintaining a healthy and better-educated citizenry to compete more effectively with rival nations in work or in war. Social legislation was also accelerated by the genuine concern of doctors, teachers and social researchers as they came face to face with the sufferings of the lower classes and revealed them to a wider public. By 1949 T.H. Marshall, a leading writer on social policy in Britain, saw the provision of welfare rights as the logical extension

Table 3.2 Introduction of universal franchise in Europe

Country	Universal male suffrage	Universal adult suffrage
Belgium	1894	1948
Netherlands	1918	1922
France	1848	1945
Italy	1913	1946
Germany	1871	1919
Ireland	1918	1923
UK	1918	1928
Denmark	1849*	1918
Norway	1900	1915
Sweden	1909	1921
Finland	1907	1907
Austria	1907	1919
Switzerland	1848	1971

* = With significant restrictions

Source: Extracted from C. Pierson (1998) *Beyond the Welfare State?*, p. 106, Table 4.3

of previously acquired civil rights to equality before the law and political rights to vote and hold office.

While Marxists argue that welfare provisions were won by class struggle, others claim that there was a functional necessity for such innovations in any advanced industrial state. The demands of urban living and exposure of families to the inherent risks of the labour market created new social problems for which new remedies had to be found. During the inter-war period, however, economic and social problems accumulated faster than many governments could learn to cope with them. The nineteenth-century faith in the efficiency of market forces began to be undermined. Pressure built up for governments to intervene on a wider scale, not just to deal with the casualties of economic collapse, but to prevent them occurring by more effective planning or steering of economic development. Governments of all persuasions began to intervene in the running or closer regulation of major industries and public services, directing resources to regional black spots and seeking to create employment by public works such as road building and electrification. Unfortunately, as each country erected tariff barriers to protect its own industries from foreign competition, the general effect was to reduce world trade and deepen the recession.

Class and capitalism since the Second World War

The two world wars and the unsettled economic and political circumstances of the period between them did not stop the process of modernisation. The whole of Europe continued along the path of industrialisation, although some regions followed generations behind the leaders. One way in which we can gauge the extent of development is by examining the shift in the occupational structure. As a country industrialises, workers are drawn from the land to work in industry and in the various private and public services necessary to support a modern society: government, financial services, social services, transport, communications, research and education, entertainment, and so forth.

At the more mature stages of industrialisation, technological progress raises productivity and the proportion of service jobs increases because fewer people are needed in manufacturing, and fewer still in agriculture. Figure 3.2 shows the shifting pattern of occupations for each of the geographical regions of Europe. It shows how the industrialisation began in western Europe and then spread to the northern, southern and eastern regions. By the 1990s agriculture occupied only 4 per cent of the western European workforce, with one-third working in manufacturing and nearly two-thirds in services.

It is not easy to translate these sectoral shifts in employment into changes in class structure. Broadly speaking, the increase in the service sector means more non-manual office jobs. But as manufacturing has become more technologically sophisticated it, too, employs many administrative workers and technicians who

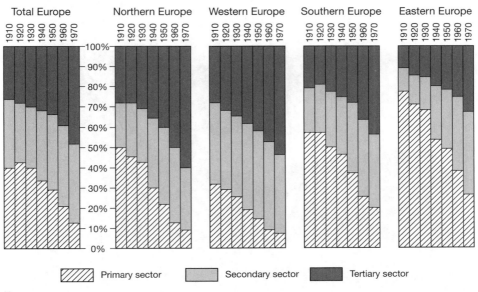

Key:

Northern Europe: Denmark, Finland, Norway and Sweden.
Western Europe: Austria, Belgium, West Germany, France, The Netherlands, Switzerland, Ireland and the UK.
Southern Europe: Greece, Italy, Portugal and Spain.
Eastern Europe: Bulgaria, Czechoslovakia, East Germany (GDR), Hungary, Poland, Romania and Yugoslavia.

Figure 3.2 Sectoral distribution of the working population by region, 1910–1980 (percent)
Source: extracted from G. Ambrosius and W. H. Hubbard (1989) *A Social and Economic History of Twentieth-century Europe,* p. 57, Figure 2.4.

are classed as non-manual. The services sector also includes many back-breaking jobs such as nursing, furniture removals and refuse collection, not to mention ballet dancing and all-in-wrestling. However, on balance, the shift from manufacturing to services increases the number of people who work with their heads rather than their hands.

These changes have tended to erode traditional class distinctions between the horny-handed sons of toil and the more genteel occupations. The entry of women into formerly male-only occupations has also upset the pecking order. Because women have traditionally received lower pay than men, the influx of women into office work has somewhat lowered its status. The traditional male white-collar worker has been increasingly replaced by a lower-paid 'white-blouse' worker.

Figure 3.3 The nineteenth-century image of the ruthless capitalist
Source: J. Vaizey (1971) *Revolutions of our time: capitalism* Weidenfeld and Nicolson, p. 38
This Dutch cartoon of *c.*1900 portrays Nathan Rothschild (1777–1836) in top hat rubbing his kid-gloved hands in glee as in the background workers are apparently being whipped into work in the factories.

Marxists focused on the male factory worker as the typical member of the working class, exploited by his class enemy, the ruthless capitalist (see Figure 3.3). They expected class inequality and conflict to escalate to the point of revolution. However, instead of the class structure polarising into a small elite dominating a mass of unskilled labourers, the middle ranks of the occupation structure have expanded. The mature industrial workforce is usually represented by a pyramid-shaped hierarchy of occupations graded by skill and responsibility and rewarded by appropriate pay and social status (see Figure 3.4).

This pyramid model is misleading in several ways:

1. The base is too broad. Unskilled jobs began to be eliminated by labour-saving machinery. The pyramid ought to be redrawn as a diamond or a pear.
2. There has always been some overlap in pay and status, with skilled manual workers, the 'aristocracy of labour', earning more than the lowest level of white-collar workers.
3. Such a diagram tends to imply that everyone is employed. It leaves out self-employed professionals or craftsmen, and the owners of corner shops or small businesses.

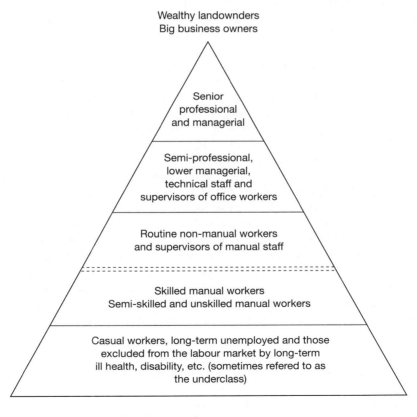

Figure 3.4 The modern hierarchy of occupations

4. It also ignores a significant minority, the 'idle' rich who could live off 'unearned' dividends from large fortunes, generally inherited. However, many of these hold well-paid directorships or even managerial posts in their own or other companies, so they tend to merge into the managerial class.

However, the pyramid model does convey well enough the large part played in modern society by white-collar workers at all levels, from junior clerical workers to senior managers and professionals. Non-manual employment increased during the twentieth century to meet the growth in the scale of organisations in the private and public sectors of all European countries. White-collar work grew from about a fifth of the workforce or less in the 1930s to around two-fifths or more in the 1980s. By 1990 professional, technical and related workers (not including routine non-manual workers) constituted nearly a third of the Swedish workforce, more than a fifth of the workforce in Finland, Denmark, Norway and the Netherlands, and more than a tenth in all other west European countries except Spain (9.6 per cent) and Portugal (8.5 per cent) (Spybey, *et al.*, 1997, p. 115).

These figures have to be read with some caution as there are regional variations within countries and different proportions of women workers in each country. In the UK, for example, recent figures reveal that a slight majority of men are still in manual jobs although over two-thirds of the female workforce is non-manual. This raises difficulties in categorising the social class of families where the husband is a manual worker and the wife or daughter an office worker. However, these complications apart, it is clear that the polarisation of society into two distinct classes has not occurred.

Many managers and professionals have savings and investments to supplement their considerable salaries and fringe benefits, and they clearly have a stake in the continuation of a system that rewards them so well. The argument has been extended to a wider group, including most white-collar workers and some of the higher-paid manual workers. With savings and investments, company pension cover, houses of their own, cars and other consumer durables, not to mention holidays abroad, these new beneficiaries of the post-war boom are hardly likely to be pining for a proletarian revolution. However, research on the so-called 'affluent manual workers' has revealed a continuing awareness of class differences and a willingness to support trade unions to defend their own interests. Their voting behaviour tends to favour labour parties but responds to government performance: they will support any party which offers them a better deal, providing they think it can deliver. Although broadly supportive of state welfare they are resistant to paying for it via heavier tax deductions from their own pay packets and opposed to 'welfare scroungers'. Their behaviour fits the pluralist model of competing interest groups better than the Marxist theory of class conflict.

Social mobility and equality of opportunity

One result of the expansion in the numbers of white-collar jobs was to make it more likely that the children of manual workers would end up in occupations considered to be superior in social status. With a shrinking demand for manual work in general, and unskilled work in particular, many children would need to acquire a more extended education to qualify for technical, supervisory and managerial posts. Modernisation has triggered off an explosion of educational provision at all levels.

Surveys conducted in the 1970s showed between a quarter and a third of the sons of manual workers obtaining white-collar jobs. In addition, especially in the newly industrialising countries, there was a considerable movement from agricultural families into both manual and non-manual jobs in industry, commerce and public services. However, children from middle-class families continued to have much better prospects than those from the lower classes and boys in every class had a slight edge over girls. There was some variation, with the most open society being Sweden, with its long history of labour governments, and the more closed being Germany, Italy, Spain and France, possibly as a result of their histories of more right-wing governments.

Study of entry into the very top elites of societies, as opposed to movement between lower- and middle-class occupations, revealed a much greater degree of social closure. Although there was more 'room at the top' in all societies and some sons (and, more rarely, daughters) of peasants or factory hands could find their way into comfortable managerial or professional occupations, there was not such easy access to the boardroom or to very senior government posts. Wealth, private education, and family influence still counted in the 'corridors of power' in capitalist societies.

The end of the post-war boom

The post-war boom from about 1950 to the early 1970s encouraged optimism amongst the aspiring lower classes that they or their children could 'get ahead'. Even for those who remained manual workers, most could look forward to full employment, improved living standards and the security of living in a welfare state.

Current prospects are less rosy. With slower growth since the mid-1970s, but continuing advances in productivity, mass unemployment at levels around 10 per cent seems to be becoming normal, even in the prosperous countries of the north and west. Young people's expectations are lowered but resentment is building up as more and more education and training is demanded for relatively humble career openings. Amongst those who fail to secure education or training, a pool of long-term unemployed is being created, some of whom have never had secure jobs. It has been suggested that this situation is a factor in rising rates of violence, crime, and drug-abuse.

Those lucky enough to find permanent jobs may continue to rise on merit thereafter, but the struggle to find work is fiercer. Added competition from migrants from other parts of Europe and beyond intensifies ethnic and racial conflicts. Demographic factors may ease the problem a little, as birth rates dip in the more advanced countries, but employment prospects may continue to decline in the peripheral countries of Europe, particularly in the former communist countries, unless they can improve educational provision and attract more inward investment. Within the EU countries, Spain, the southern parts of Italy, Portugal, Ireland and the former East Germany have much higher rates of youth unemployment than the rest. Eurostat figures for 1988 showed regional rates of youth unemployment in Spain ranging from 30 per cent to over 60 per cent. These rates are matched in the worst urban ghettos of large cities throughout Europe where immigrants are usually twice as likely to be unemployed as others.

In northern Europe, education or training continues for many beyond the age of 20. In the south, most have finished with schooling by the age of 17. Although state educational provision has expanded in most countries over the last couple of generations, the rate of take-up is still strongly influenced by home background, so that in most countries the working-class taxpayer effectively subsidises the further education of the middle classes. Even if access to education can be improved so that all able pupils gain their maximum level of qualification, in a tight labour market family influence may continue to tip the scales of justice in the allocation of jobs. Children of disadvantaged groups may have more chance of success in small business and other careers where formal qualifications are less important.

Social democracy and welfare capitalism

Before the end of the nineteenth century Marx's prediction of a socialist revolution was looking unrealistic. However, many believed that socialism might be achievable gradually by democratic means. Extension of the franchise allowed working-class parties to establish a considerable parliamentary presence. By 1920 they were securing 20–40 per cent of the vote and had shared in government in Austria, Belgium, Denmark, Finland, France, Germany, Portugal, Sweden and the UK. As the process of industrialisation gathered pace the working class was expected to keep on growing, giving labour parties an overall majority of votes. In countries that were taken over by fascism, or later by Soviet state socialism, this hope was dashed, as genuinely democratic trade unions and labour parties were brutally suppressed. But, where democracy was preserved or restored, why did labour parties not come to dominate modern politics?

We have seen some of the reasons already in the changing shape of the class structure. Manufacturing seldom accounted for half the workforce. The industrial working class stopped growing and even shrank as the services sector grew. Manual workers within the services sector were harder to recruit into trade unions (except for public service workers) and rural labourers often had a deferential or religious aversion to socialism. Even within the manufacturing sector, more workers became administrative, technical or managerial, seldom eager supporters of socialism. Labour parties failed to secure the allegiance of all industrial workers, although they received some compensating support from radicals in the middle and upper classes.

Labour movements were sometimes split into rival communist, social democratic, and other factions (especially in France and Italy) or into rival linguistic or religious groupings (as in Belgium and Holland). Right and centre parties could count on considerable support from industrial workers who shared their economic, religious or nationalist beliefs. The precise fate of working-class parties depended upon many variables: the array of left, centre and right parties available in each country and the shifting alliances between them, the system of voting and constitutional rules about the formation of governments, the success or failure of incumbent governments and the occurrence of crises or scandals, to say nothing of the personality of party leaders. Mitterrand, for example, was able to unify the normally divided French left to win power in the 1980s against a divided and discredited right.

Working-class parties were most successful when they broadened their appeal beyond the industrial worker, as the West German SPD did so dramatically after 1959, when they moderated their formerly Marxist aims. In the UK Labour were in power from 1945 to 1950, and again intermittently in the 1960s and 1970s but lost power for eighteen years until they moderated their policies and the country tired of the Conservatives in 1997.

The Swedish social democrats held power almost continuously from 1932 to the 1990s and led the way towards the development of welfare capitalism. They expanded state welfare services whilst nurturing a successful capitalist economy, combining full employment with an active labour market policy to phase out old industries and retrain workers for new ones. The growth of welfare services provided jobs for many women and helped others to get the education and child care they needed to work elsewhere.

The political basis of such welfare capitalism was a social contract between the state, employers' associations and trade unions, often labelled 'corporatism'. It allowed wages and prices to be held in check, employment and investment to be planned, and taxation and welfare expenditure to be agreed. Other western states attempted variations on this formula, even under conservative or liberal governments, but apart from Austria, few succeeded in maintaining the necessary degree of cooperation. Nevertheless, welfare states blossomed. From 1960 to 1975 the average country in western Europe increased its spending on welfare from 15 per cent to 27 per cent of GDP. Social welfare provisions were transformed, from minimal concessions to the poor into universal public services (including education, public housing, social security, health and social services) on which everyone might have to rely at some stage in their life.

Criticisms of the welfare state: from left and right

Marxists condemned social democracy as a sell-out. Although the workers benefited from improved social security and social services so did the middle classes. Employers were assured of a healthy, educated and well-housed labour force. Professionals gained well-paid state posts. There was no overall redistribution of wealth. The gulf between rich and poor remained. The state taxed the young and healthy in all classes to support the old and sick and other dependents.

New Right thinkers inspired Reagan and Thatcher to attack state welfare in the name of market forces. State spending was accused of pushing up taxes, creating bureaucratic inefficiency, and encouraging dependency. People were encouraged to fend for themselves, by purchasing their own houses, private education, health insurance and pensions. The state, it was argued, should provide only a minimal safety net, for those who could not afford private services.

Although few governments dared to cut back on welfare spending as harshly as the New Right advocated, there was a worldwide retrenchment, especially in the 1980s. Even socialist governments in France and Spain adopted Thatcherite policies. Social expenditure growth in the OECD countries, which had averaged around 8 per cent per annum from 1960 to 1975, slowed to about 4 per cent thereafter. Even Sweden, the citadel of social democracy, succumbed to periods of conservative government.

Beyond the welfare state: disorganised capitalism?

After the mid-1970s the post-war boom ended and the prospects for social democratic reforms worsened for a number of reasons. The return of mass unemployment reduced the tax base, putting pressure on government spending. Paying for millions on the dole without increasing taxes meant less money was available for other social policies. Demographic trends threatened a gradual increase in the elderly population, the main recipients of welfare spending. More had to be put aside to support them; but in doing so the state met with resistance from taxpayers.

Defenders of state welfare pointed out that, if the state did not raid our pockets, the private insurance companies would. Shifting the burden to the private sector did not diminish it, especially when allowance was made for the extra administrative costs and profit margins of private alternatives.

Unemployment and tighter labour laws weakened the trade unions throughout Europe after a generation of post-war growth. Members thrown out of work could not afford subscriptions and those lucky enough to remain employed grew less militant, afraid of victimisation. Some former strongholds of the union movement were especially hard hit by recession and government cutbacks or privatisation. The process went furthest in the UK with the privatisation of former nationalised industries such as coal, gas, electricity and steel, and a shift away from public provision in bus transport and even some social services. Unions lost bargaining power with employers and government. Apprenticeships gave way to state education and training schemes in which employers gained more influence. Young people remaining unemployed or in casual jobs had no opportunity to join a union and looked like becoming a 'missing generation' for the labour movement.

The globalisation of capitalism accelerated. Multi-national companies now switched investment around the world in search of cheap labour and sympathetic governments. States, even with socialist parties in government, could no longer tie employers down to corporatist agreements of the kind that once prevailed in Sweden. The proliferation of trading blocs such as the EU was interpreted as the political adaptation of capitalist nation states to new economic realities. There was little sign of the labour movement gearing up for effective international resistance: most unions were fiercely protectionist and suspicious of deals with fellow workers abroad, who they feared, rightly, might be after their jobs. The battles over the Social Charter in Europe were the first signs of a new continental labour politics which might attempt a reconstitution of corporatism on a continental scale. But the differences in living standards of workers throughout Europe made it difficult for labour to achieve international solidarity in negotiations with employers or governments.

New social movements were competing with class politics. Feminism, gay and lesbian rights, anti-racism, the peace movement, and ecological protest, could, sometimes with difficulty, be aligned with the left. Nationalism, regionalism and religious revivals were more likely to undermine such a 'rainbow coalition'. The far right was making ominous signs of appeal to the dispossessed or insecure by playing on racist tendencies.

Traditional class loyalties were weakened by the collapse of old industrial communities. Support for established class-based parties was weaker than at the height of the post-war boom. Although class was still one of the best indicators of how a person would vote, new divisions were appearing between those who depended upon the state (for employment or social services) and those who worked in the private sector and made private provision for transport, housing, health, education and pensions. However, splits in the working classes had occurred throughout its history without destroying all sense of unity. Polls showed continuing strong support for state health and welfare provisions.

It had been suggested that the more affluent workers might be tempted to support centre or right parties and to shun the so called 'underclass' of permanently unemployed or casual workers, and those kept out of the labour market by lack of skill, single parenthood, sickness or disability. The presence of immigrant minorities of different ethnicity might strengthen this tendency unless strong government action was taken to combat discrimination and racism. However, the notion of an underclass was condemned by the left as a rhetorical device that spun together many disparate tendencies in modern society. There was little in common between so many disadvantaged groups except the contempt which society showed them by applying such a label. The Marxist response was to argue that apart from a small elite we are all one pay cheque away from the dole queue and there was no difference between the underclass and the rest of us. Perhaps the social division between men and women was more important.

Gender and inequality

Although formal inequality between women and men was eroded by the move to universal adult suffrage (see Table 3.2 above) it took some time before women's new electoral strength was translated into a greater measure of social equality. Traditional gender roles tended to persist, especially in late industrialising countries or those with strong religious and legal support for male supremacy. In most countries women worked on the land and young unmarried women worked in industry, especially textiles, but at the start of this century most women would be expected, unless they were very poor, to devote their adult lives to motherhood and housework.

The cause of women's emancipation was taken up by a radical minority, often led by middle-class women who had struggled to enter the professions, but it was wartime experience which helped to loosen stereotypes considerably, as women took on formerly male occupations. Longer-term demographic trends towards smaller families, reinforced by the legalisation of abortion and advances in contraception, probably had a greater effect, freeing women at an earlier age from the burdens of child rearing and opening up prospects for a return to full-time employment. The spread of household equipment such as washing machines and vacuum cleaners may have helped but standards of housekeeping often kept pace, offsetting possible reductions in hours of housework. Changes in family law have improved women's property rights and made separation and divorce easier. The growth of state welfare benefits and services also makes it more feasible, though still not easy, for a woman to exit from an intolerable marriage, although there is still strong economic pressure to marry or remarry.

The post-war period has seen a general rise in the rate of economic participation in paid work by women, especially married women (Spybey 1997, p.137). By the late 1980s married women's employment had increased throughout the EU, but with considerable variation between countries: more than half of them were employed in Britain, France, and the Scandinavian countries (83 per cent in Sweden), but a third or less in Ireland, Italy and Spain. The sectoral distribution differed between men and women. There is much variation in women's employment between and within countries according to the stage of industrial development and the state of the labour market.

However, a common feature is for women to be concentrated in particular industries and occupations which echo their traditional caring roles: nursing, primary school teaching and social work, catering and cleaning, textiles, clothing, and hairdressing, for example. Even when employed in general office work they tend to be confined to junior posts serving the needs of male bosses – the secretary is sometimes jokingly referred to as the 'office wife'. These jobs are identified as 'women's jobs' and consequently carry poorer pay and promotion prospects. Even where women compete on equal terms with men, their domestic ties and male prejudice may prevent them getting top jobs. Women are also more likely than men to work part-time, a particularly pronounced tendency in the UK, and this often entails poorer pay and conditions and less chance of continuous employment and an occupational pension. However, the European Court of Justice has built upon the Treaty of Rome principle of equal pay for equal work to exert some pressure against such gender discrimination in employment and other spheres.

The impact of marriage on women's working life can be seen in Figure 3.5, which also shows the contrasting pace of change in Poland, West Germany, Sweden and Italy between 1950 and 1982. Whereas in Sweden in 1950 most women left the labour force on marriage, by 1982 they continued in work with participation rates almost as high as men's. The generous provisions of the Swedish welfare state no doubt support this trend: better education and child care, and a tax and benefit regime which encourages both parents to work full-time, and provides parental leave entitlement for fathers as well as mothers.

Women in communist countries were encouraged to perform paid work but the 'emancipation' of Soviet woman was not accompanied by the domestication of Soviet man, who expected his wife to combine a full-time job with all the duties of the traditional wife, made worse by the shortage of consumer goods in the shops and the need to spend hours in queues. State child care was provided, with East Germany and Hungary providing the best services, but provision often lagged behind demand and the collapse of the Soviet system has seen savage cut-backs as state spending is slashed. The revival of religion in some countries has tended to reverse some of the changes made under communism, such as more

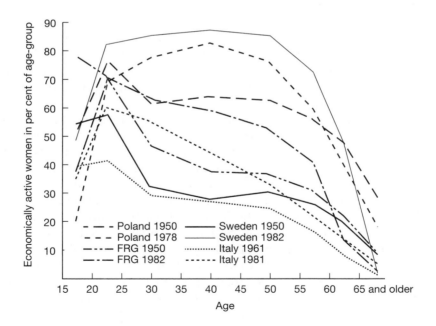

Figure 3.5 Age-specific female participation rates for various countries, 1950–1982 (percentage economically active persons in age-group)
Source: G. Ambrosius and W. H. Hubbard (1989) *A Social and Economic History of Twentieth-century Europe,* p. 51, Figure 2.2.

liberal provision of contraception and abortion facilities. There may be a tendency, for those who can afford it, to go back to more traditional gender roles. However, the prolonged economic crises in the east have thrown many out of work, with women more affected than men. Economic dislocation has resulted in a high divorce rate and some women have been driven into prostitution as their only means of support. It remains to be seen how long it will take for economic reorganisation to provide new jobs for all.

In the long term Europe will have to come to a new social consensus on the role of women, and men, in modern economic circumstances. If Europe recovers fully from the prolonged recessions of recent years, a real alternative to the male breadwinner/female housewife tradition could open up, one in which both men and women work, full-time or part-time according to their needs. The burden of care for young children and elderly relatives or other dependents could be shared equally between the sexes. However, we seem to be stuck halfway to this new regime, with women more involved in paid work outside the home, but men not yet reciprocating by taking more responsibility for housework and caring tasks, which are still regarded as 'women's work'. It is hard to envisage a time when a 'working husband' (or 'career man') could feel comfortable phoning his boss to tell him (or her) that he must take the day off because his children are ill, or he has to attend to a sick parent whilst his wife is on a business trip abroad.

The dual career household is, in any case, unlikely to be a universal phenomenon. Surveys of work patterns suggest that couples in which both partners have secure jobs constitute a fortunate group, to be contrasted with other cases in which both partners are unemployed. Moreover, the children of couples in work are more likely to find employment themselves. Employment, and unemployment, seem to run in families, leading to a greater polarisation of the workforce into the 'haves' and 'have nots'.

An egalitarian family structure would require considerable changes in social policy. The state would have to introduce new patterns of taxes, welfare benefits, and social services at affordable cost to support two-earner families as well as single parents who wish to work. It would also have to monitor occupational training, recruitment, promotion, pay and pensions, to ensure equality of opportunity between the sexes. As most of our existing welfare states were built in the 1940s, when the male breadwinner was the norm and sexist assumptions widespread, there is much rethinking to be done. So far, the UK seems to differ from most of its continental neighbours, relying on women taking part-time jobs, and failing to deliver sufficient child care facilities to allow them to compete with men on fair terms for full-time careers. However, social attitudes and practice vary considerably throughout Europe. The only consistent feature is that women are generally under-represented in positions of power, in politics as well as at the workplace.

There is a protracted debate amongst feminists about where private enterprise stands on the gender equality issue. Some maintain that capitalist employers are 'gender blind' and will hire whatever labour is cheapest, most flexible and adequately skilled. Others argue that capitalism takes advantage of older patriarchal traditions, continuing to pay women less than men, and using them as a pool of reserve labour that can be drawn on in a boom and expelled in a recession. The role of trade unions is somewhat ambiguous. They have a long history of male domination which has sometimes caused them to see women as unwelcome competition for skilled jobs. More recently, especially as unions have fought hard against declining membership, they have taken a more progressive attitude. However, because women are more likely to work part-time, and often for small employers, they are harder to recruit into trade unions. Their domestic commitments make it harder to attend union meetings or hold office, even if they are bold enough to outface male prejudice.

More women will be needed in government, industry and trade unions before their needs are fully embodied in social policy. The EU has accepted the principle of equal opportunities for men and women but it remains to be seen how effectively such a principle can be implemented, given the competing pressures of legislation, public opinion and market forces. In the UK, the Labour government's introduction of minimum wage legislation, which protects workers in low pay industries, may improve the position of women, who tend to be concentrated in those industries.

The revival of social democracy in western Europe

In late 1980s and early 1990s labour parties in western Europe confronted two major obstacles. In the west the New Right seemed to be winning many of the economic arguments, convincing the public that free markets were more efficient than state planning or state ownership. In the east the Soviet regimes were crumbling, their centrally planned economies having clearly not delivered the goods to their own consumers. However, by the later 1990s, a remarkable recovery had taken place in the fortunes of moderate socialism. At the end of the millennium we find social democratic governments in power in 12 countries (see Table 3.3).

Elsewhere in western Europe labour parties had a share of power in coalition governments in Luxembourg and Switzerland and provided a strong opposition in Spain. Only in Ireland and Belgium were right-wing parties securely in power in the late 1990s.

What had happened to bring the centre-left back into power in so many countries? In most cases they had radically revised their policies to meet the criticisms of the neo-liberals, 'chasing the Lady' (Margaret Thatcher) in a move towards the New Right. Plans for extending state ownership in the economy were repudiated and socialism was redefined as being compatible with a market economy. Even privatisation of social and government services was acceptable if it could be shown to deliver more efficient use of taxpayers' money. Labour parties moved away from their close alignment with trade unions and began to pay as much attention to consumers as to producers of public services.

Table 3.3 Social Democratic victories in western Europe in the late 1990s

Country	Date of election	Social Democratic share of vote (percentage)	Social Democratic prime minister or equivalent
Finland	Feb 1994	26	Paavo Lipponen
Portugal	Oct 1995	44	Antonio Guterres
Austria	Dec 1995	38	Victor Klima
Italy	Apr 1996	21	Massimo d'Alema
Greece	Sept 1996	42	Kostas Simitis
UK	May 1997	44	Tony Blair
France	June 1997	24	Lionel Jospin
Norway*	Sept 1997	35	Kjell Magne Bondevik
Denmark	Mar 1998	36	Poul Nyrup Rasmussen
Netherlands	May 1998	29	Wim Kok
Sweden	Sept 1998	36	Goran Persson
Germany	Sept 1998	41	Gerhard Schröder

* = not a member of the EU

Source: Collated by the author from Wilfried Derksen, *Elections around the World,* website http://www.agora.stm.it/elections/election/geo-euro.htm. December 1998

Their return to power had little to do with traditional socialist promises to increase taxation in order to provide improved benefits and services to the poor. 'Tax and spend' policies were dropped. Deregulating the economy would encourage industrial investment and create more jobs. This would be accompanied by supply side policies such as improving training and education, especially for unemployed youth. Post-war social democracy had been refashioned to meet the new circumstances of a post-industrial Europe competing in a global market. Keynesian demand management at the level of the national economy no longer seemed to be sufficient so European or international solutions were sought.

But the new left went beyond neo-liberalism. In 1998 the former German finance minister Oskar Lafontaine re-endorsed the German SPD's belief in the welfare state and emphasised its contribution to maintaining full employment and economic demand. Conscious of the challenge of unemployment he accused the New Right of abandoning politics and surrendering to the free play of market forces. 'Wage dumping, tax dumping and welfare dumping are not our responses to the globalisation of markets!' he declared, and he attacked policies which aimed at lowering welfare benefits and employment rights.

But Lafontaine recognised that labour markets could no longer be managed on a national level and European standards would have to be agreed. Among the rights that he and other socialist leaders were eager to defend were the rights to a decent minimum wage, a maximum number of working hours per week, equal opportunities for men and women, part-time as well as full-time, humane working conditions for all, including migrant workers, representation by free trade unions, environmental protection, and adequate provision of education, social services and welfare benefits. At the Twentieth Congress of the Socialist International (SI) a Declaration on the World Economy proclaimed the need to accept the global economic revolution but make it serve the people. The Congress also committed the socialist and social democratic parties to the search for full employment.

But the implementation of these broad aims, summed up by the SI slogan 'To Regulate Globalization and to Globalize Regulation', has not proceeded very far and is likely to face continuing differences of interpretation. Tony Blair, having been praised by his German and French colleagues for signing the Social Chapter and showing a greater willingness to cooperate at the European level than previous Conservative leaders, has continued to argue John Major's case for preserving the greater flexibility of the British labour market. As he urges continental countries to deregulate their labour markets further and to lower direct taxes, he wins more approval from conservatives than from social democrats, who are seeking to harmonise taxes by getting UK tax rates raised to the levels prevailing across the Channel.

European socialists came back to power with promises not to raise taxation. But without doing so, how can they raise the investment required to improve education, training, infrastructure and employment, even within their own countries? The exploitation of migrant labour can best be rooted out by providing more jobs in their home countries. But the last conservative government in Germany lost power partly because of resistance to taxes levied to provide government help for the reconstruction of the East German economy after reunification. How would German taxpayers respond to extra taxes to pay for enough economic aid to poorer regions of eastern Europe and Turkey to make would-be economic migrants stay at home? Western leaders are still squabbling about how to distribute the bill for the existing EU agricultural and regional budgets, even before the Union is enlarged.

Liberty, equality and fraternity appeal more to conference delegates than to taxpayers. The task of spelling out to the average voter in western Europe the case for redistribution on a global scale may not be achievable within the limitations of domestic electoral politics. This is all the more difficult to achieve in an age when the average voter for a left-of-centre party bears a larger portion of the tax burden than he or she did in the mid-twentieth century, when taxes fell most heavily on the middle classes. Tax resistance is now a working-class phenomenon that any labour party ignores at its peril. It is possible that solidarity amongst social democratic governments could achieve a tax regime in the EU that would shift the burden to corporation taxes or at least to less visible forms of personal taxation. But the room for manoeuvre is limited since too much taxation on corporations could discourage inward investment. Although a case could be made for deliberately engineering this to help less-developed countries gain investment, such a ploy would be unlikely to win much favour with European voters.

Conclusion

We have seen that social inequality in Europe has taken directions which nineteenth-century liberals and Marxists were unable to predict. The 'middle way' of social democracy seemed to offer a compromise between capitalism and socialism until the 1970s, since when it has been on the defensive. In the early 1980s there were still predictions of a convergence between east and west, as a reformed eastern Europe appeared to be heading in the social democratic direction. The sudden collapse of the Soviet system seemed for a time to have inspired the abandonment of any 'ism' with 'social' as a prefix. Russia and most of the former Soviet states took the plunge into the icy waters of market capitalism, in which increased social inequality seems to be the price of economic dynamism. If this proves too bracing there may be a turn to the left, but perhaps more likely to the far right. Meanwhile the future of social democracy in the west is still being debated, with as much attention to gender and race as to class, and in an international context that poses fresh challenges to economic growth and social stability.

Further reading

Ambrosius, G. and Hubbard, W. H. (1989) *A Social and Economic History of Twentieth-century Europe*, Harvard University Press, Massachusetts.

Bailey, J. (ed.) (1997) *Social Europe*, Addison Wesley Longman, Harlow.

Bairoch, P. (1988) *Cities and Economic Development*, Mansell Publishing Ltd, London.

Breen, R. and Rottman, D.B. (1995) *Class Stratification: a Comparative Perspective*, Harvester Wheatsheaf, Hemel Hempstead.

Cochrane, A. and Clarke, J. (eds) (1993) *Comparing Welfare States: Britain in International Context*, Sage, London.

Esping-Andersen, G. (ed.) (1996) *Welfare States in Transition; National Adaptations in Global Economies*, Sage, London.

Eurostat (1997) *Europe in Figures*, 4th edn., Office for Official Publications of the European Communities, Luxembourg.

Giddens, A. (1998) *The third Way: the Renewal of Social Democracy*, Polity Press, Cambridge.

Hamilton, M. and Hirszowicz, M. (1993) *Class and Inequality: Comparative Perspectives*, Harvester Wheatsheaf, Hemel Hempstead.

McLeod, H. (1997) *Religion and the People of Western Europe, 1789–1989*, Oxford University Press, Oxford.

Pierson, C. (1998) *Beyond the Welfare State?*, Blackwell, Oxford.

Sassoon, D. (1997) *One Hundred Years of Socialism: the West European Left in the Twentieth Century*, Fontana Press, London.

Spybey, T. (ed.) (1997) *Britain in Europe: an Introduction to Sociology*, Routledge, London.

Theobald, R. (1994) *Understanding Industrial Society: a Sociological Guide*, Macmillan, Basingstoke.

Vaizey, J. (1971) *Revolutions of our time: capitalism*, Weidenfeld and Nicolson.

van Kersbergen, K. (1995) *Social Capitalism: a Study of Christian Democracy and the Welfare State*, Routledge, London.

Wise, M. and Gibb, R. (1993) *Single Market to Social Europe*, Longman, Harlow.

4 Composition of an unfinished symphony: the European Union

Europe has experienced much sustained and heated debate in recent years on the subject of the EC/EU. Unfortunately, much of it has been ill-informed and more concerned with internal partisan politics than with the real issues. British governments, in particular, have consistently presented themselves as valiant defenders of British interests fighting to prevent the loss of more sovereignty to 'Brussels'. This impression has little to do with reality, and obscures a situation which appears complex but is basically quite simple. The purpose of this chapter is twofold: to enable readers to understand what the EU is and how it works, and to try to give an objective summary of the situation after the Treaty of Amsterdam.

Some simple points should be clarified first. 'Brussels' is far too complex a term to be used, as it so often is, as a catch-all phrase to cover anything emanating from the EU. Those who praise or blame 'Brussels' for a decision may in fact be referring to the European Commission which made the proposal, the European Parliament committee which examined it, the Council of the European Union which took the decision, or the officers in a Directorate-General which actually put it into operation; all too often it is a vague derogatory term of general application, aimed at the Community as an entity. It is very important to remember that the decision is finally taken by ministers of all the member states in the Council of the EU, in most areas now in conjunction with the European Parliament. So, if governments and elected MEPs represent people, in that sense 'Brussels' is us.

A second term that is bandied about too easily is 'sovereignty', which has almost opposite meanings when used in an internal or international context. Internally – i.e. applied to a nation-state – it means the seat of final authority, on behalf of the people in whom that authority may be theoretically vested. That means a hierarchy of authority, in which order is maintained and sanctions applied by governmental authorities, in theory on behalf of a sovereign people who in practice are subject to those government authorities. In international terms, though, sovereignty means a state's right to act according to what that state's government perceives as its own interests, and without regard to others. That means in theory that every state, large or small, rich or poor, is the equal of every other state, and has the right to behave accordingly. So whilst in international society 'sovereignty' means a community of equals, with individual states behaving according to self-interest, in a nation-state it means a pyramid of authority to which the individual is subject. If we applied the international definition of sovereignty inside the nation-state it would be called anarchy.

In practice, of course, states cannot behave just as they like. In reality there is an inevitable interdependence between states, which forces them to develop various forms of cooperation; one of the most advanced and complex of these is exemplified by the EC/EU.

The six founder members of the EC set out to establish common markets in coal and steel, economics, and atomic energy. A common market implies a great deal more than the removal of internal tariffs and quotas and the erection of a common external tariff. Its declared aim of removing all barriers to trade and ensuring the free movement of people and capital as well as goods and services takes it into non-economic areas. People cannot move around freely in the common market if they need work permits or visas for another member state, or if a mining engineer's British, Dutch or German degree is not recognised in Belgium. That means getting rid of internal passport controls and reaching agreement on the content of degree courses, so there is a strong and inevitable integrationist tendency which attracts the idealists as well as the economists. Eventually, the degree of cooperation inherent in a common market leads naturally to consideration of a common foreign and security policy and a common currency. This is the stage we reached with Maastricht, which brought together the economic, idealistic and defence considerations in one treaty. The new Treaty of Amsterdam completed much of the unfinished business of Maastricht.

The usual classification of international organisations into intergovernmental, supranational and non-governmental is unhelpful for analysis, and certainly needs further refinement if we are to analyse the EU properly. It is more accurate to speak of intergovernmental and supranational elements inside organisations than to label the organisation as a whole. Similarly, whilst any organisation formed by means of a treaty signed between states (governments, *de facto*) is in that sense an intergovernmental organisation, it may well have institutions or offices whose officials do not belong to or represent governments, and whose powers, within defined limits, override those of the national member governments and therefore have to be regarded as supranational elements within the organisation. There may be others which are simply intergovernmental, with no supranational or internationalist elements at all, and yet others where the treaty was signed by governmental representatives but which are in practice non-governmental, carrying out most or all of their work at the technical and professional level. In any case, we really need one extra label to define those bodies which do not, in the main, see themselves as representing national interests, and certainly not the interests of their governments. In this chapter, we shall use the term 'internationalist' to describe such bodies. In the Community and the Union, the intergovernmental organ is the Council of the European Union (hereafter referred to simply as 'the Council'), whilst the European

Commission (hereafter 'the Commission'), the European Parliament and the Court of Justice each dispose of some supranational powers. In addition, the Commission must be regarded as an international and independent body, serving the Community as a whole, whilst the European Parliament certainly sees itself as having a collective role which is internationalist.

This perception by each institution of its own, and others', roles stems from, interprets and develops the clear constitutional statements about institutional powers and duties laid down in the treaties. The ink is hardly dry on the documents before the institutions start interpreting them in the light of their own role-perception, sometimes culminating in a Court of Justice ruling and not infrequently in a revision or an agreed interpretation. It is through this constant synthesis of ideas and interpretations that institutional power and procedure are refined and developed, and to understand it we therefore have to examine the major institutions and their powers and duties. It would be very neat and tidy if we could study first the institutions and then the procedures, but the two are so intermingled that it really is not possible to separate them. What should stay with the reader, at the end of the day, is an impression of institutional interdependence, and that is a very accurate reflection of both the Community and the Union.

The organisational structure of the European Community

(For the following section, it may be helpful to refer to Figures 4.1 and 4.2.)

The organisational structure of the European Coal and Steel Community formed a model which was followed closely, seven years later, by the European Economic Community (EEC) and the European Atomic Energy Community (EAEC). Each Community had a Council of Ministers and an Executive (the High Authority for the ECSC, Commissions for the other two) but they shared a Court of Justice and the parliamentary body known as the Common Assembly. In 1967 the three Communities were merged, so that although the three treaties and the three Communities still existed inside the EC, the Merger Treaty created one Commission and one Council of Ministers alongside the Common Assembly and the Court of Justice. The same four institutions thus served all three Communities.

This organisational pattern reflected the demands, on the one hand, of the basic philosophies of the six parliamentary democracies which made up the original membership, and, on the other, of the requirements of political and organisational reality. Though democratic theory predicated some representation of the peoples of the member states through the Common Assembly (later European Parliament), political reality meant that nothing would really happen unless the governments were able to discuss issues and come to an agreement; hence the Council of Ministers. But the international nature of such a complex organisation demanded an international executive, the Commission, and an independent and international Court of Justice was obviously necessary so that

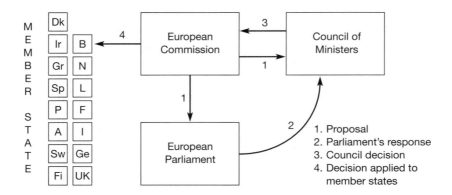

Figure 4.1 The European Union: the decision-making process

there could be some means of settling disagreements arising from the Treaty. As we shall see, the Treaty was essentially a constitutional document for a political system, which had misleading similarities to the political systems of the member states but was in fact significantly different.

Until the Treaty of Maastricht, the basic organisational relationship of the four major institutions could be stated quite simply. The Commission put forward the ideas, the European Parliament gave its opinion on the proposal, the Council of Ministers took the final decision and the Commission was responsible for putting the agreed policy into effect and monitoring its progress. The Court of Justice was not, and is not, directly involved in the decision-making circuit but is vital to its operation; without it, there would be no final and authoritative interpretation of the Treaty and the powers of the institutions. This explanation is oversimplified, but it embodies an important basic fact – that this is a power-sharing structure in which each institution has particular powers and cannot, in the main, proceed without the others.

The principle of power-sharing and an institutional balance has survived to the present day, creating a political system in which power is shared between governments, elected representatives and an independent executive, with a Court of Justice able to settle any question which might arise concerning the extent of the powers and duties of any institution. But the institutional balance has shifted, basically because the treaties of Maastricht and Amsterdam placed an important qualification against the power-sharing principle; Maastricht's new areas, common foreign and security policy (CFSP) and justice and home affairs, were kept outside the power-sharing structure and were effectively reserved to the Council of Ministers, and even the Court had no jurisdiction over them. The 'old' areas – the common markets – were left under the Community structure.

The amended structure after the Treaty of Amsterdam

After the Maastricht treaty the EU was therefore composed of three 'pillars' – first: the EC; second: foreign policy, security and defence; and third: justice and

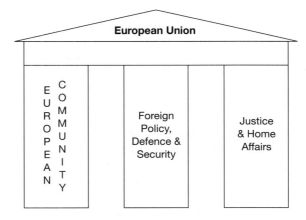

Figure 4.2 The European Union: after the Treaty of Maastricht

home affairs (police and judicial cooperation, customs, immigration and so on). After five years' experience of these arrangements the Treaty of Amsterdam amended the 'pillar' structure in various ways, notably with the transfer of much of justice and home affairs to the first 'pillar' under a new Title IIIa, which gave the Community competence to adopt measures relating to free movement, visas, asylum, immigration, judicial cooperation in civil matters and related issues. This transfer has therefore led to a restructuring of those aspects of police and judicial cooperation which remain in the third 'pillar'.

The post-Amsterdam situation could therefore be summarised as shown below.

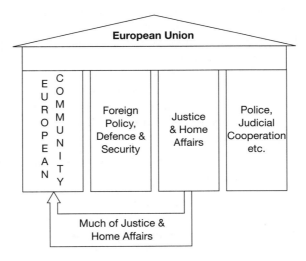

Figure 4.3 The European Union after the Treaty of Amsterdam

The Community area (the first 'pillar'), Title II of the Treaty on European Union (changed to Title IIIa after the Treaty of Amsterdam)

The whole of the Community structures, including the areas such as economic and monetary union, agriculture and employment policy, are covered by the Community's power-sharing procedure, changed after the Amsterdam Treaty to strengthen the European Parliament's role. The Commission has a sole right of initiative and most decisions are now taken by legislative co-decision between the Council and the Parliament. In nearly all cases the Council votes by qualified majority voting (QMV). The jurisdiction of the Court of Justice is final. The one clear exception to this system is the decision-making arrangement for the transferred areas of asylum, immigration etc., which lays down an intergovernmental procedure for the first five years followed by the possibility of a switch to classical Community institutional involvement after 2002.

Common foreign and security policy (CFSP – the second 'pillar'), Title V of the Treaty on European Union

The new treaty reinforces the intergovernmental nature of the title, with a continuation of unanimous voting in the Council, though it is now possible for neutral countries (Austria, Denmark, Ireland and Sweden) to refrain from undertaking action through the use of a mechanism called constructive abstention – which effectively means their abstentions are not counted, thus allowing for a 'unanimous' vote. When actual implementation of an agreed common strategy is debated QMV is possible, provided that the decisions do not include military implications, but an emergency brake mechanism in the form of a veto by a member state could still apply. The Secretary-General of the Council becomes, in addition, the High Representative of the Union and will negotiate on behalf of the Union with other states. A Planning Unit is established in the Council in an attempt to provide early warning of CFSP developments; effectively, therefore, in-house bodies have been established to serve the Council in the matter of CFSP, doing the sort of work that in the first pillar would be done by the Commission. The Community institutions have only a limited role. The Commission 'shall be fully associated with the work', the European Parliament is merely 'informed' while the Court of Justice still is not mentioned at all in the new provisions.

Police and judicial cooperation in criminal matters (the third 'pillar'), Title VI of the Treaty on European Union

This title aims to provide citizens with a high level of safety within an area of freedom, security and justice by developing common action among the member states in the fields of police and judicial cooperation in criminal matters. The objective is to prevent crime, particularly terrorism, trafficking in persons and offences against children, illicit drug-trafficking and arms trading, corruption and fraud. The Commission and the Council have joint rights of initiative, but the Parliament and national parliaments are only to be consulted, and the

Council decides, always by unanimity. The Court, however, is given a considerable degree of jurisdiction over Title VI for the first time.

Anatomy of the European Union

The inter-relationship of the four major institutions

The Council of Ministers (since 1993 the Council of the European Union) is the meeting place for the governments of the member states. Each government is represented by one minister, served and supported by a delegation of national civil servants and an international secretariat. Unlike national governments, however, the Council is not the author of the proposals it considers. That role is reserved for the European Commission, an executive body originally appointed by the governments acting together but thereafter independent of them. The European Parliament, directly elected by the people of the member states since 1979, does not see itself as representing states or governments; individually, Members of the European Parliament (MEPs) see themselves as representatives of their electors, and collectively as the body which has the democratic oversight of the EU as a whole. These three institutions, as we shall see, effectively share the decision-making power of the Union between them. The fourth major institution, the European Court of Justice, takes no direct part in this power-sharing structure, but is nevertheless vital to its operation. Although appointed by joint action of the governments in the first place, the Court is a totally independent body composed of jurists of the highest international reputation, and its ruling on any dispute – which might include an argument as to the limits of an institution's powers – is final.

The Council of the EU

The Council is composed of one minister, relevant to the subject under discussion, from each member state. The General Affairs Council (composed of foreign ministers – the 'senior' council), the Finance Council (ECOFIN, composed of finance ministers) and the Agricultural Council rank higher than others and meet more frequently. There are in fact 20 councils in addition to the above: the Energy Council, Education Council, Social Affairs Council and so on, plus the 'special' councils that meet from time to time – but they are all referred to collectively as 'the Council'. Whatever form it takes, the Council is the crucial element in the final decision-taking of the Union, considering and deciding, mostly now in conjunction with the European Parliament under the co-decision procedure, on proposals which have been made by the Commission.

The Presidency of the Council is held by each member state for six months at a time, rotating between the member states in alphabetical order in their own language. The first six months of the year always provides much more opportunity of getting things done, since August is not a working month and the

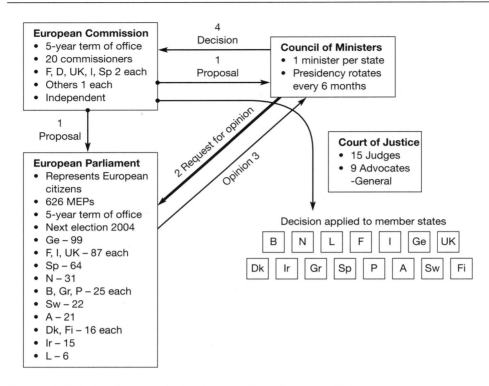

Figure 4.4 Relations between the institutions of the European Union

holidays tend to spill over to some extent into July and September, so since 1993 the cycle has reversed pairings of countries to ensure that states get a summer Presidency and a winter Presidency alternately. The Presidency country takes the chair of the Council and of its committees and working groups, and is generally responsible for leading and facilitating the Council's work during the period of its Presidency. Considerable political and diplomatic skill is involved, since the Presidency has to try to reconcile the positions of 15 member states, which may have widely differing positions on an issue. Time will always be a problem; Presidency countries naturally want to be able to point to some definite achievements after their term in office, and six months is really a very short time to conclude matters of importance. This obviously poses questions which will have to be addressed as the Union expands: even with 15 members there is already a seven-and-a-half year period before a state once again becomes the Presidency country, which is really too long, but shortening the time for which the Presidency is held would provide too little time in office.

Note that the Council is not a European government or cabinet; it could hardly be, since the ministers round the table come from different political systems and political parties. Seven of the 15 member states are monarchies (if one includes Luxembourg) and eight are republics. Their governments are of varying political persuasions.

It is important to notice that while the Council has decision-making powers, which since the Treaty of Amsterdam are largely shared with the European Parliament, it does not formally have the power of proposal. Almost all of the time it has to work on proposals from the Commission, which it can only change by unanimity, though in practice many of the Commission's proposals are based on a Council 'recommendation' – effectively a hint that the member states would look sympathetically on a proposal on the subject. Thus, although media commentators frequently say that the real power (of decision) lies with the Council, the exercise of that power depends absolutely (with some exceptions – mainly foreign and security policy) on the complementary roles played by the Commission and the Parliament, with the Court in the background to make sure that nobody pretends to a power not given by the Treaty. The Union, and especially the Community, therefore has to be seen as a power-sharing system, which is arguably more democratic than the political systems of some of the member states.

It may now help to list the sort of legislation that emanates from the Council, as far as the Community area is concerned. These instruments may be regulations, directives or decisions:

- *Regulations* are directly applicable in all member states. They are binding in their entirety – that is to say, both as to the end to be achieved and the means by which it is to be achieved.
- *Directives* are binding as to the end to be achieved on all member states to whom they are addressed, but the means is left to each member state.
- *Decisions* are binding in their entirety on those to whom they are addressed – i.e. both ends and means.
- The Council can also make *Recommendations* and express *Opinions;* these have no binding force, though depending on the circumstances they may have considerable influence and may lead, as we saw above, to Commission proposals.

A great deal of anguish, especially in Britain, has been expended on the system of voting in the Council. Originally, most decisions required unanimity, which effectively meant that each country had a veto; if all states did not vote in favour, the motion was lost. Difficult enough with six states, this became more and more difficult as the Community expanded until it virtually brought things to a standstill. To try to speed things up without reluctant states being steamrollered by the majority, a system known as qualified majority voting (QMV) was introduced, weighting the votes in the Council roughly in proportion to the size of the member state (see Table 4.1). Which system of voting is used in the Council on a particular matter depends on the legal base – i.e., whatever procedure is laid down in the Treaty. For some things (accession of new members, for example) unanimity is required, but for others, including most matters concerning the Internal Market, QMV is specified.

QMV provides the Council with a means of coming to a conclusion without being hampered by the need for unanimity but with safeguards to prevent the contentious and divisive atmosphere which could result from a simple majority with seven states against and eight in favour. As can be seen, the number of votes is in proportion to the size of the state; in addition, however, 62 votes in favour are required for a successful vote, whilst any coalition of ministers assembling 26 votes can stop the decision being taken. A simple calculation reveals the sophistication of the QMV. It can be seen that the five biggest countries voting together cannot carry the day; that only amounts to 48 votes, so another 14 votes are needed – which means three more states. Conversely, two big states plus two of the smaller states, or a variety of other combinations, can put together 26 votes and block the decision. Concern about being 'outvoted in Brussels' should be evaluated against this background. There was prolonged wrangling amongst governments about the QMV formula after the unification of Germany and upon the accession of other states, but it was eventually settled by the Ioannina Compromise at the Corfu meeting of the European Council (March, 1994). The Treaties specify the circumstances in which Council is required to act unanimously or by qualified majority vote.

Table 4.1 Qualified majority voting in the Council of the European Union: how the votes are weighted.

Country	Number of votes	Weighting
Germany, France, Italy, United Kingdom	10	40
Spain	8	8
Belgium, Greece, Netherlands, Portugal	5	20
Austria, Sweden	4	8
Denmark, Finland, Ireland	3	9
Luxembourg	2	2

In qualified majority voting, Commission proposals must receive 62 votes out of a total of 87 in order to be approved. To amend a Commission proposal without the Commission's consent, unanimity among Council members is required.

In practice, the Council always tries to obtain as broad a consensus as possible before acting.

It would be misleading if this account of the Council gave the impression that only ministers were involved. Ministers, after all, have important and time-consuming jobs to do in their own countries, and meetings of the Council which actually involve ministers last only for a day or two at a time. In any case, as a permanent institution, the Council needs staff of its own to arrange the meetings, provide agendas, take the minutes and generally see to it that the affairs of the Council are provided for while the ministers are not in Brussels. The permanent staff of the Council in the Council's Secretariat-General do this. Ministers need deputies, too; the Council could not do its work if everything had to be left till the ministers themselves met, so each member state maintains a Representative Delegation, under an Ambassador to the EU and a Deputy Ambassador.

Collectively the delegations are known as COREPER (from the initials in French) or the Committee of Permanent Representatives. Officials from all fifteen delegations meet in working parties to try to hammer out as much as possible in between ministerial meetings. These are national civil servants following the policy of their governments, so to a considerable extent they are able to act on behalf of the ministers; by the time the ministers actually meet, the agenda has been reduced to only those matters which could not be agreed by the civil servants, if necessary by consultation with their head office. This machinery obviously throws civil servants of different nationalities together, and there are some useful side effects, the most obvious of which is that people discover that 'foreigners' are not aliens from another planet. In addition, since many countries have similar problems, civil servants from one state learn that others are solving the problems in quite different ways, so there is a mutual exchange of ideas. The overall structure of the Council is summed up in Figure 4.5.

There is one other body in the diagram which has not yet been explained – the European Council. This is the Council meeting at Heads of Government level, popularly termed the European Summit, which meets at least twice a year. The role of the European Council has grown, particularly in providing general

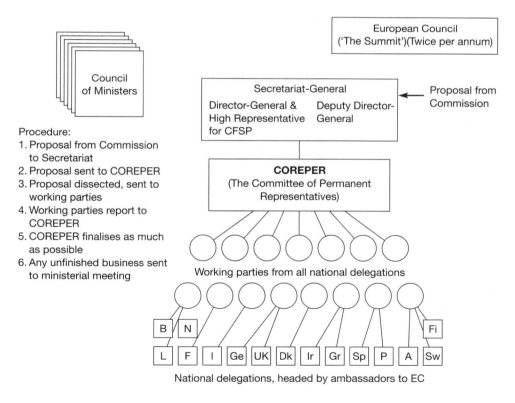

Figure 4.5 How the Council of the EU works.

guidelines as to the direction in which the member states wish to see the Community (and now the Union) develop. In practice, the treaty requirement of two meetings per annum is now usually exceeded. Even in the course of a (half-year) Presidency three or four meetings are not uncommon.

The Commission

The Commission has four roles: as guardian of the treaties, as initiator of proposals, as the executive in putting decisions into effect, and as international negotiator for the Community on external economic relations. 'The Commission' is the title of the collegiate body of 20 commissioners, but is also used to describe the whole of the bureaucracy, organised in 23 Directorates-General, over which the commissioners preside. There must be at least one national from each member state amongst the commissioners; in practice there are two from each of the larger states (France, Germany, Italy, Spain and the UK) and one from each of the others. A tempting analogy would be to say they are international civil servants, but that is misleading in the British context because each commissioner is finally responsible for his own portfolio and does not work to a minister, whilst collectively the commissioners have a joint responsibility for the collegiate decisions of the Commission as a whole. Commissioners therefore are a cross between a British permanent secretary and a minister; like a permanent secretary, they head and administer one or more departments (the Directorates-General) but, like a minister, they have the final responsibility for their policies and they are overtly political in the interests of their own Directorate-General and of the Commission collectively. The Commission meets weekly, taking its decisions by simple majority. It has to publish annually a General Report on the activities of the Community, not later than a month before the opening of the European Parliament session, so that Parliament can in effect debate and comment upon the overall activities of the Community in addition to the specific controls set out below.

There is a President of the Commission, who is responsible for the general direction and oversight of the work of the Commission as a whole. Though this is a position of considerable power and influence, it does not enable the President, even together with the Commission, to 'rule Europe from Brussels'. The Commission is just one institutional facet of the Community's procedure; it cannot do anything without the input of the Parliament and the Council, and would be subject to the judgement of the Court should it grow too big for its boots. Certainly the President himself cannot 'go it alone', though inevitably the impact of a particular President is what the incumbent is able to make of it; Jacques Santer's predecessor, Jacques Delors, maintained a high profile and had a considerable impact upon the European scene, one effect of which was to provide the Euro-sceptics with a bogey-man and scapegoat around whom to weave the often fanciful stories about the evils of 'Brussels rule'. Partly, no doubt, with this in mind, Jaques Santer kept a lower profile, though in fact his powers were increased by the Amsterdam Treaty. The President now has more power over the choosing and reshuffling of commissioners, and the Commission as a whole now works under his political direction, strengthening the Commission's position somewhat in a structure which member states' governments are always keen to dominate through the Council.

The term of office of the Commission was extended from four years to five, so that it is now coincident with that of the Parliament, whose powers and duties relative to the Commission have been emphasised in other ways. Under the terms of the Treaty of Amsterdam, the member states' governments will still nominate the President of the Commission, but in common accord with the Parliament. The whole Commission as a collegiate body needs a vote of approval by the Parliament before it is actually appointed (Article 158.1), and the Parliament immediately interpreted this to mean that it should consider each commissioner separately, even if the vote that followed was to approve the Commission as a whole. The President appointed in 1994, Jacques Santer, was almost rejected by the vote of the Parliament, and the closeness of that vote certainly strengthened the Parliament's position with regard to future appointments. This new power indicates the way in which the Community develops. The Parliament lobbies for and gains an addition to its role, incorporated formally in a Treaty, and, from that point on, interpretations of what that amendment actually means push the frontiers a little further still. The Parliament retains its power to require the resignation of the whole Commission via a motion of censure carried on a two-thirds majority of the votes cast (Article 144). This power has never been used, though there was a good deal of sabre-rattling during the fraud and inefficiency allegations of January 1999, and the subsequent resignation of the whole Commission[1] on March 15 was largely due to the furore generated by the Parliament's enquiry and debates.

The European Parliament

Over the last ten years the Parliament has evolved from a consultative body to something much more like a legislative body, increasingly sharing the decision-making role with the Council. Members of the European Parliament (626 MEPs) have been directly elected by the citizens of Europe since 1979 so they are representatives of the people, not of states. Before 1979 the Assembly was appointed, theoretically by and from member states' Parliaments and generally in proportion to party strengths within those Parliaments. Even the appointed Assembly, however, exuded a robust internationalism which put pressure on member states and the Council to strengthen the Community, in particular by giving more power to the European Parliament. It was the appointed Assembly which eventually forced the Council to institute direct elections for a Parliament with a fixed term of office of four (now five) years, though that Parliament has not yet succeeded in forcing through a standard system of election for all the member states. The most glaring anomaly is the UK, which was until 1999 the only state not using a proportional system; the result is that until the 1994 election all but one of the British MEPs were Labour or Conservative, despite the

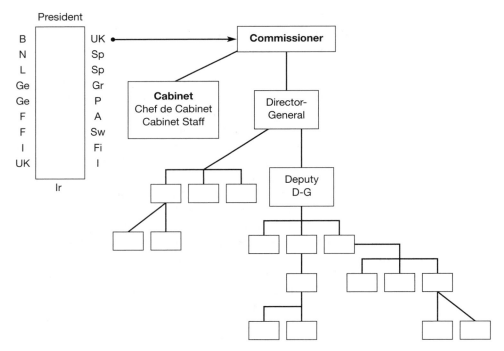

Each Commissioner is responsible for one or more Directorates-General. Commissioners do NOT represent the country of origin, or anything else. Their oath of loyalty is to the Community alone

Figure 4.6 The European Commission

fact that other parties polled percentages that would have won them seats in any other member state.

The membership of the Parliament is roughly in proportion to population size, though a glance at Table 4.2 will show that the big states were determined to prove that they were all equal! After the unification of Germany, however, this position was no longer tenable (though the big states have retained a more than proportional representation) and of course numbers had to be altered after the accession of Austria, Finland and Sweden. Since it is obvious that numbers cannot go on expanding indefinitely as new states accede, the Parliament wanted a limit to be set, and the Treaty of Amsterdam set the ceiling at 700 members. Turnout in the five-yearly elections has been disappointing, and has declined all over Europe in recent years, reaching its nadir in the elections of 10 June 1999. This suggests that the Community and Union have not yet been established in the average citizen's mind as an issue of major importance in everyday life. However, this is partly attributable to the way the governments of the member states have used both the Union and elections to the European Parliament as a political football in the national political arena when it suited them.

The seating plan is a semicircle, with the focal point the President's chair and the Party Groups occupying segments of the semicircle. On the President's right

Table 4.2 European Parliament results 1999

	PSE	PPE	ELDR	UPE	GUE/NGL	V	ARE	I-EDN	NI	?	Total
Austria	7	7	–	–	–	2	–	–	5	–	21
Belgium	5	6	5	–	–	5	2	–	2	–	25
Denmark	3	1	6	–	1	–	–	4	–	1	16
Finland	3	5	5	–	1	2	–	–	–	–	16
France	22	15	–	–	6	9	–	13	5	17	87
Germany	33	53	–	–	6	7	–	–	–	–	99
Greece	9	9	–	–	5	–	–	–	–	2	25
Ireland	1	4	1	6	–	2	–	–	–	1	15
Italy	17	32	1	9	6	2	7	–	5	8	87
Luxembourg	2	2	1	–	–	1	–	–	–	–	6
Netherlands	6	9	8	–	1	4	–	3	–	–	31
Portugal	12	9	–	2	2	–	–	–	–	–	25
Spain	24	29	2	–	4	–	2	–	–	3	64
Sweden	6	7	4	–	3	2	–	–	–	–	22
United Kingdom	30	36	10	–	–	2	2	1	1	5	87
Total	180	224	43	17	35	38	13	21	18	37	626

Source: Compiled by Richard Bullard, Brussels, June 1999

Note: The final composition of the parliamentary groups will not be known for certain until 20 July 1999, after we go to press. Consequently the above table has been compiled on the assumption that newly elected MEPs will go into the parliamentary group that held MEPs of the same persuasion before the election – e.g. the British Conservative MEPs have been counted as members of the EPP group. The final composition of the parliamentary groups will not be quite the same.

Key

PSE or PES: Group of the Party of the European Socialists; PPE or EPP: Group of the European People's Party; ELDR: Group of the European Liberal, Democrat and Reform Party; UPE or UFE: Group Union for Europe; GUE/NGL or EUL/NGL: Confederal Group of the European United Left/Nordic Green Left; V or G: The Green Group in the European Parliament; ARE or ERA: Group of the European Radical Alliance; I-EDN or I-EN: Group of Independents for a Europe of Nations; NI or IND: Independents?: Candidates listed hereby have not yet declared an alignment to a specific political group.

the front seats of the semicircle are for the Commission; on his left, for the Council, since both of these groups can have representatives in the Chamber to explain their points of view on the matter under consideration. The Council representative answers questions for an hour at every session, the President of the Council gives an account of a 'summit' after the meeting, and the President of the Foreign Affairs Council outlines his Presidency's programme at the start of a Presidency and reports on it at the end. Commissioners have the right to speak, to explain and defend the proposal under discussion, and to answer questions, but neither the Commission nor the Council has the right to vote in the Parliament.

The European Parliament differs from any National Assembly in one very important respect. It does not support a government. There is no European government drawn from the majority party in the European Parliament, so there is not the same compulsion to maintain party discipline. A vote against the motion before the House does not bring down a government or induce an election. It could not do this, in any case, because the term of office for the European Parliament is fixed, at five years. There are other factors which weaken the tendency to toe the party line which is the norm in the UK; the semi-circular design of the chamber itself does not encourage confrontational or nationalistic politics, nor does the seating plan. MEPs sit in party Groups – not necessarily with the same names as national party groups – and in alphabetical order within those groups. Stemming from the lack of compulsion to maintain party discipline and the fact that they do not sit together by nationality, bloc voting as a national group is quite rare – and difficult to detect if it does happen, as a member state's MEPs will be distributed over a number of Party Groups. Within those Groups, voting discipline is also weaker than in the UK Parliament. There is a whip, but it is difficult to enforce and there is really little attempt to do so, because there is no 'government' or 'opposition' party to support. Obviously it is also more difficult to agree upon and enforce a 'party line'. In the Socialist Group, for instance, which is composed of MEPs from every member state, the brand of socialism varies sufficiently to make it more difficult to find binding agreement on a party line. The fact that the Group is not supporting or opposing a government also makes the point of having a 'line' less obvious. So in the European Parliament we should note:

- Weaker Group discipline
- Commonality of interest – the Parliament sees itself as having a purpose and corporate role much more clearly than, say, the UK parliament. It tends to be an institution which tries to push the development of the Community forward, and therefore has more in common with the Commission than with the Council.
- Weaker national identification
- Voting tends to be on the merits of the question

The European Parliament works roughly on a four-week cycle shown opposite:

Strasbourg is now officially the seat of the Parliament, though Group and committee meetings are in Brussels. Although the Parliament's strong preference to centre everything in Brussels has so far foundered on the self-interest of

Table 4.3 Meeting-cycle of the European Parliament

Week 1	Week 2	Week 3	Week 4
Group meetings	Plenary session	Committees	Constituency

France, which does not wish to lose the status and economic spin-off that result from being the site of a major institution, some Directorates-General have now been transferred to Brussels and there is now a parliamentary Chamber there.

The European Parliament's work is focused on its 21 committees, though this is not a number fixed by statute. Proposals go to the committees before they come to be considered in plenary session, which has the considerable advantage that all proposals have been dissected and examined in detail before the Parliament as a whole considers them. The committee appoints a *rapporteur*, whose job is to draft the report of the committee on the proposal it is considering in a way that reflects the committee's view. The committee votes on the report (by simple majority) and it is that report, with the committee's recommendations, which then goes before the Parliament in plenary session, where the committee spokesman presents it and outlines the committee's views. The report is then debated and voted upon. Voting is by show of hands or, if requested, electronically, via buttons on every MEP's desk in the Chamber to record the votes. The Parliament is then able to notify the Council of its position and carry the process of legislation a step forward. Where the legal base is Article 189b, the Parliament's position is much stronger, since under that procedure it is a co-decision maker with the Council, and this area has been expanded considerably by the Treaty of Amsterdam.

This method of procedure, together with the system of voting and the lack of need for partisan support, means that the flow of business is incredibly fast to anyone used to the Westminster pace of life, and the European Parliament gets through a lot of work in a session. The other profound difference between the European and British Parliaments is that whereas in the UK MPs virtually always vote with their party, MEPs feel much less compulsion to do so, and issues tend to be examined and voted on according to their merits.

The extent of the Parliament's control over legislation stems from the Treaties and covers four areas. The phrase 'The Council, acting on a proposal from the Commission and after consulting the European Parliament, shall decide...', summed up the original relationship between the institutions. Although four decision-making procedures still exist (assent, co-decision, consultation and cooperation), the Parliament's power has been considerably strengthened and the co-decision procedure with the Council has now become the most widely used. Coupled with the comparative absence of partisan voting, these procedures mean that the European Parliament effectively exerts more control over Community legislation than the House of Commons does over the British government. One example which may be cited is the budget; both Parliaments have to pass the respective budgets before they are legal, but whereas the Westminster parliament makes a lot of fuss and then votes loyally on the party line, the European Parliament has thrown the budget out completely on two occasions.

Until the Amsterdam Treaty the Parliament tended to have a natural affinity with the Commission in trying to push the Union forward, and has had a tendency to view the Council with, at best, a stance of armed neutrality. Governments and governmental bodies do not like to see obstacles placed in their way, and since the Parliament as the watchdog of Community interests does not shrink from such obstructive activity, the increase in parliamentary powers has usually been achieved after conflict with the Council. There has been an increase in dialogue between the two bodies, for example, about the budget; and since 1981 this has become the Trialogue – the Presidents of the Council, the Parliament and the Commission. This meeting has actually negotiated an inter-institutional budget agreement which all three institutions then approved; the practice has now been extended outside the budgetary field, with similar agreements in other areas. The relationship is evolving, however, and the extension of the co-decision procedure established by the Amsterdam Treaty means that the Parliament and the Council have to view each other as legislative partners, so more of an affinity may develop between them.

The Court of Justice

We have seen that while the Court of Justice does not take part in the decision-making cycle of the Community, its existence is essential to the system. Some authoritative and final ruling on interpretations of the treaty, and settling disputes between institutions, member states, commercial organisations and other interested parties (and/or any permutation of these bodies), has to be not only available but accepted by all parties if the system is to work at all. In its absence, the whole structure would grind to a halt or malfunction as a consequence, let us say, of an argument over the right of the Council to come to a decision after it had asked for, but before it had received, the opinion of the Parliament. Such a dispute did actually arise, and the Court's judgement substantially affected the balance of power in the Community in favour of the Parliament.

The Court is composed of 15 judges and nine Advocates-General, each of whom must be qualified to hold the highest judicial office in his or her own country or be a jurisconsult of recognised competence, whose independence and impartiality are beyond doubt (Article 167). They are appointed by 'common accord' of member states, but once appointed they are totally independent of governments or other institutions of the Community. The statute of the Court provides for the immunity of judges in the performance of their duties, requires them to take an oath of impartiality, forbids the tenure of any political or administrative office, and provides when appropriate for their retiral and, *in extremis,* removal. As can be seen, therefore, great care has been taken to make this institution a completely independent and impartial body.

The main points of Article 177, which lays down its jurisdiction, show how important the Court is to the operations of the Community:

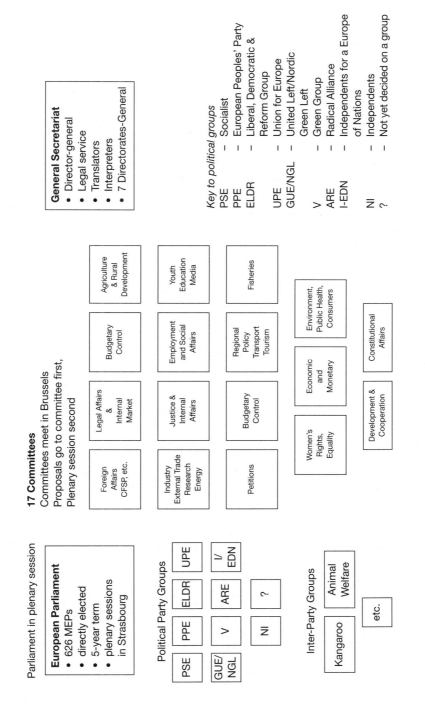

Parliament in plenary session

European Parliament
- 626 MEPs
- directly elected
- 5-year term
- plenary sessions
  in Strasbourg

Political Party Groups

PSE	PPE	ELDR	UPE
GUE/NGL	V	ARE	I/EDN
NI	?		

Inter-Party Groups

| Kangaroo | Animal Welfare |
| etc. | |

17 Committees
Committees meet in Brussels
Proposals go to committee first,
Plenary session second

Foreign Affairs CFSP, etc.	Legal Affairs & Internal Market	Budgetary Control	Agriculture & Rural Development
Industry External Trade Research Energy	Justice & Internal Affairs	Employment and Social Affairs	Youth Education Media
Petitions	Budgetary Control	Regional Policy Transport Tourism	Fisheries
Women's Rights, Equality	Economic and Monetary	Environment, Public Health, Consumers	
Development & Cooperation	Constitutional Affairs		

General Secretariat
- Director-general
- Legal service
- Translators
- Interpreters
- 7 Directorates-General

Key to political groups

PSE	–	Socialist
PPE	–	European Peoples' Party
ELDR	–	Liberal, Democratic & Reform Group
UPE	–	Union for Europe
GUE/NGL	–	United Left/Nordic Green Left
V	–	Green Group
ARE	–	Radical Alliance
I-EDN	–	Independents for a Europe of Nations
NI	–	Independents
?	–	Not yet decided on a group

Figure 4.7 The European Parliament

- It may interpret the Treaty, in cases of doubt as to its meaning.
- It may rule that the action of an institution is, or is not, valid and within its powers; if the institution has exceeded its powers, the Court can declare the action void.
- It may (and under some circumstances must) hand down a ruling on request from a court or tribunal of a member state, if that court or tribunal considers it needs such a ruling to enable it to give judgment.

The Court's judgments are enforceable under Article 187, and a state found wanting will inevitably comply, albeit after a certain amount of huffing and puffing to satisfy whatever internal political pressures caused it to offend in the first place. The Court is in fact available to 'any natural or legal person' – European institutions, governments, companies, EU staff, and even an ordinary citizen of a member state – providing that a breach of the Treaty is alleged. There have, in fact, been a number of successful actions by citizens against their own governments under these provisions.

Three examples will show why the Court is so important to an understanding of the way the Community works. They illustrate how a state or an institution can be called to account if a breach of the Treaty is alleged; one concerns an institution purporting to have a power which it did not have, one a state in breach of treaty regulations, and one a state whose internal regulations breached treaty provisions.

In what came to be called the 'Lamb War', the French government halted consignments of English lamb at the Channel ports. This would of course be illegal under common market regulations had it been done to protect French agricul-

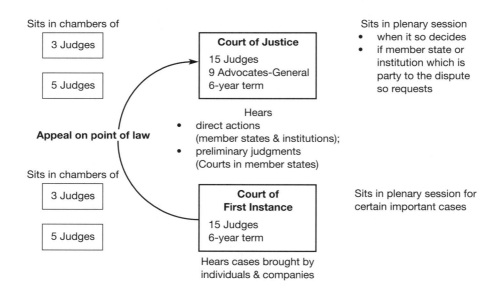

Figure 4.8 The European Court of Justice

tural interests, though in truth that was the real reason for the French action, in response to heavy political pressure from the French lamb farmers. The French government, however, maintained that it was acting in the interests of public health and hygiene, and had a responsibility to inspect the lamb to make sure it was fit for Gallic stomachs, which was not illegal. By the time some sample lorry-loads of lamb had been unloaded from their refrigerated trucks, taken to laboratories some distance away, tested and returned, the whole consignment had, of course, gone off and could not be sold. There was outrage in Britain, fanned by the tabloid press, whose three-inch headlines screamed indignation and abuse ('Hop Off You Frogs' was one tabloid's contribution), whilst the French press expressed mild surprise at the British lack of concern for public hygiene. The Commission and the British government therefore took the French government to Court, alleging a breach of the Treaty, and were successful. The French government was ordered to desist, and did so after a certain amount of blustering. Some months later the British government found it necessary, of course in the interests of public health, to stop and inspect imports of French apples; this time the seven-centimetre headlines were in French papers, whilst the British gave precedence to the football results, but the outcome was the same and this time the British government had to back down. Both incidents illustrate the degree of national chauvinism lurking below the surface, if somebody chooses to stir it up. The Community can be a useful and convenient scapegoat to take electors' minds off the internal political situation if a government is suffering adverse criticism.

The other two cases are perhaps even more important. In the Marshall case a British woman maintained that the Treaty had been breached by the British government because British women were required to retire at the age of 60 whilst men could go on to 65, which effectively breached the equal pay provisions. The Court held in her favour and the British government was obliged to re-examine its legislation on the retirement age; it took a long time, but finally the British government settled retirement age at 65 for both sexes. The case illustrates the circumstances in which Community law can cause a change in national law where the two are in conflict, and also provides an example of an individual citizen taking her own government to Court.

The Iso-glucose case, on the other hand, is an important example of an inter-institutional dispute between the Council and the European Parliament. The Council purported to enact a regulation imposing a levy on glucose; it did so after asking for the opinion of the European Parliament, as it was required to do by the Treaty, but without waiting to receive it. The Council maintained that whilst the Treaty required that the European Parliament should be consulted, it said nothing about having to wait for the opinion. The Court, however, held that the meaning of the Treaty was that the opinion had to be asked for and received before the Council could proceed, and annulled the regulation. The power of the Parliament was thus effectively enhanced. Since the Council could not proceed without its opinion, it could drag its feet when faced with a regulation or directive it disliked, thus putting pressure on the Commission and Council to compromise if they wanted to get the instrument passed.

The single European currency and the advent of the Euro

The one part of the Maastricht Treaty that was unequivocally supranational was the section proposing the creation of the single currency, because the controlling body, the European Central Bank (ECB), broke new ground in the Community and the Union by being completely independent. It was to be responsible to nobody, on the model of the Bundesbank; not the member states, not the Council, and not the Parliament, though Parliament would receive reports and no doubt its debates on those reports would not be without some influence. The ECB was to be under a Board of Governors made up of one governor from each national central bank, with the proviso that each of those banks must also be independent. Since strict conditions were set to make sure that all participating states would not present economic problems for a single currency community, it was recognised that not all the 15 member states would be ready to join at the set date. In the event 11 countries adopted the single currency provisions from 1 January 1999. It is worth noting that the adoption of a single currency is the natural concomitant of a single market. If the objective of a single market is the 'level playing field' and the elimination of all obstacles to trade, then the maintenance of separate currencies and exchange rates set by individual central banks or governments was the largest remaining barrier.

Whilst one can understand that people might see the adoption of a single currency and the consequent disappearance of the familiar mark or franc as a leap into the unknown, this is a process that has been going on throughout history. Were it not so, a merchant in the south of England engaged in trade with Scotland would be paying commission on the changing of Anglo-Saxon groats into Scottish bawbees, and Andalucians shipping sherry into England would probably want to be paid in gold. Whilst this is not the place to examine in detail the economic effects of the single currency, the political effects on the Union and the member states are clearly relevant. The big question in most minds is whether monetary union will lead to political union; whilst that is a convenient label which can mean as much or as little as a politician wishes, not surprisingly it has been represented as the end of national identity and the beginning of a United States of Europe. It is strange that this question looms so large, not only because Europe was once a collection of smaller kingdoms each possessing its own currency but also because there are plenty of examples to hand of nations with a common currency which have certainly not lost their identity. Luxembourg has been in a currency union with Belgium since the 1920s, but is still manifestly a separate state. There are many countries which have been in political union with others but have not lost their national identity. The traveller would have no difficulty in recognising a different culture as he or she passed from Baden-Württemberg into Bavaria, or over the border from England to Scotland. In any case, most politicians in member states would rather swim in the national puddle than in the European ocean, and are much too jealous of their national status to let it go. But perhaps there are natural limits to any sort of European Union; the problems of conducting Europe-wide elections for one

Parliament for the whole of Europe, from which a European government would be drawn, would be insuperable. The lamps of nationality will not be going out in Europe in our lifetime, nor in that of our great-grandchildren many times removed. What will happen is that we shall have to recognise that national governments alone cannot solve problems like pollution, which require a pan-national approach. For that, the European Union provides a natural solution.

Enlargement of the Union

Enlargement of the Union presents a problem on which successive European 'summits' have simply equivocated, because it presents them with a dilemma. On the one hand the Union, as an outstanding proponent of the principle of the free market, cannot refuse to expand. To do so would invite the scathing rebuke that it was merely interested in advancing the interests of a small group of states. But with every new accession the difficulties grow – even the smallest new state will add one minister, one commissioner, one judge and some MEPs to the relevant institutions, and more to other non-institutional bodies like the Committee of the Regions and the Economic and Social Committee. A limit to the total number in the Parliament has now been set at 700, but every solution creates a problem. Once there are 700 MEPs, the addition of any new states will mean that the number of MEPs per state will have to be reduced, thereby reducing citizens' access to their elected representatives. There has been as yet no solution to representation in the other institutions, though the Commission has been warning for some time that it is already larger than it needs to be. The five big states are, of course, reluctant to give up one of their two commissioners, and even if they did the problem would get worse as soon as another state joined. The Commission's own preference would be for a ten- or twelve-member Commission, and it has already started an internal reorganisation, aimed at increasing its efficiency, which may force the issue. But it is difficult to see how a limit can be placed on the Council, based as it is upon the equal representation of every state, and the simple truth is that gaining agreement in a large Council obviously becomes more difficult than in a small one. Six ministers round the table would mean that in a two-hour meeting each minister would be able to make up to 20 minutes' contribution to the debate, whereas 15 would only have eight minutes – and 26 members are envisaged in the near future.

The new institutional balance: an analysis of some of the effects of the Treaty of Amsterdam

There were those who considered right from the start that expecting 15 governments to sit round a table, generate intelligent ideas for dealing with exceedingly complex foreign policy and security issues and come up with agreed solutions was not a realistic scenario. Similarly, it was apparent to a number of analysts that justice and home affairs needed so much day-to-day cooperation at a sub-government level that it could not practicably be controlled by the Council if an acceptable level of democratic control over these sensitive areas were to be maintained. Predictably, the Treaty of Amsterdam restored the Commission's powers of proposal and execution, the democratic oversight of the Parliament and the jurisdiction of the Court in much of this area. However, as far as CFSP was concerned the governments proved implacable; foreign policy must remain a government matter, and the Council kept a tight hold on it. For the time being at least, the self-interest of member states has been maintained over the humanitarian aspects of the many problem areas in Europe. This is not good for the image of the EU, which appears to be blundering, incompetent and insensitive, and disastrous for those strife-torn areas where people are dying and communities are being ripped apart. But this is an intractable problem; on the one hand foreign policy is almost the last area in which states will be willing to allow any form of supranational control, and on the other it is quite evident that no state is willing or capable of dealing with these issues alone, or even in conjunction with others. Had CFSP been under the power-sharing structure of the first pillar, there would at least have been independent proposals from the Commission which would have had to be considered and which would have been in the public domain, but even then member governments' publicity machines would have been hard at work putting their own slant on the situation and if necessary holding 'Brussels' up for more criticism.

Governments do not have to *have* a definite and identified interest in some extant issue in foreign affairs; the fact that they *might* have such an interest in future, in some field which has not yet become an issue, is enough to ensure that they want to keep their hands firmly on the reins. The history of the development of international cooperation has always revolved around the stubborn insistence of governments that they can control things by themselves and the eventual grudging admission that in some areas they cannot. The most interesting facet of European development at the moment is that it is becoming very apparent that areas which governments cannot control by themselves (such as pollution, drugs, international crime and the environment) are developing alongside areas which national governments do not need to control, because it can be done better at a lower level. On the one hand this implies more pan-European cooperation, and on the other more devolution to sub-governmental levels.

As we have seen, over the years the Commission's virtual monopoly as policy-proposer has become somewhat diluted, but it has grown stronger as the Union's executive, whilst over the last ten years the Parliament has evolved from a consultative to something more like a legislative body, now sharing an increasing decision-making role with the Council. But the Council's emergence from the Maastricht Treaty in sole control of the new competencies, even after the transfer by the Amsterdam Treaty of much of justice and home affairs to the Community's power-sharing structure, has strengthened the Council and consequently the governments of the member states *vis-à-vis* the other institutions. With the exception of the single currency arrangements, especially the supranational Central Bank, the overall effect of both Treaties was to enhance the role of the member states, notwithstanding the improvements in the position of the European Parliament. In foreign policy especially little more has been achieved than an apparatus for intergovernmental consultation reminiscent of a continuous Congress of Vienna, and the shortcomings are apparent in the total lack of a decisive policy in the Balkans.

It might seem from the above that the power balance has shifted markedly towards the member states and their institutional organ, the Council of the European Union. On closer examination, however, it might be more accurate to conclude that whilst member governments are struggling to maintain their alleged control over events, in practice they are having to admit that increasingly those events demand more international cooperation and hence an increase in the role of the other institutions. Certainly, the provisions of the two treaties have brought about a significant and continuing change in inter-institutional relationships, perhaps more than was foreseen at the time. There is clearly a need for an independent policy-proposing body free from the political considerations which motivate the governments of the member states, which means enhancing as much as possible the original role of the Commission. There also needs to be more democratic oversight of, and participation in, the decision-making process, plus, of course, the exposure of all the machinery and policies to judical review.

Although it was said earlier that the Commission's proposal-making role had been somewhat diluted, the pendulum has begun to swing back a little since 1997 with the Commission's shared right of initiative with the Council on the transferred areas of justice and home affairs, and restoration of its sole right of initiative being at least envisaged after the five-year period. Perhaps, therefore, the need for the independence of the policy-proposing body is being recognised, if only because it is becoming obvious to governments that the Council is not a realistic way of coming up with firm proposals.

Political realism dictates that the governments of the member states should be heavily involved in decision-making, but also that the inevitable loss of control by national parliaments over their governments which is a by-product of international cooperation of this degree of complexity needs a matching increase elsewhere. The very obvious way of doing this has always been by increasing the powers of the parliament, but unfortunately national Parliaments have tended to be jealous of the European Parliament and have not been sympathetic to increases in its powers. However, its powers have increased over the years, and, in particular, the extension of the European Parliament's powers to include more co-decision making with the Council helped to increase democratic oversight. At the same time this envisages an alteration in the relationship between the Council and the Parliament. Whilst the Parliament was excluded from any real role in the decision-making process, it tended to regard the Council very warily. Now, however, the Council looks more like a legislative partner, and the whole process more like a bi-cameral legislature. The Parliament's relationship with the Commission must evolve, especially when one considers the extra power given to the Parliament over the choice of the Commission in the first place.

There are, however, more disturbing tendencies in the offing. In the autumn of 1998 the Parliament refused to discharge the 1996 budget[2] because of irregularities which had been shown up by its own procedures or the Court of Auditors. At this stage there was no suggestion of any fraud, but the media seized on the Parliament's refusal, smelt numerous rats and sent the terriers in to flush them out. Digging for dirt anywhere always succeeds in finding something, and very soon Europe was awash with stories of fraud, mismanagement, incompetence and 'cronyism'; national politicians and political parties beat their breasts and seethed with righteousness, member governments saw a chance of cutting the Commission down to size and talked of 'root and branch reform', and suddenly the Union was in the middle of a crisis. Even the Parliament, though very properly setting up a three-man committee to investigate the allegations fully, was not entirely disinterested in its motives, for here was a golden opportunity to demonstrate its role of citizens' watchdog. In the event the enquiry found little in the way of fraud, but did find sufficient irregularities and poor management to give the Euro-sceptics a field day, and on 15 March 1999 the whole Commission resigned.[3]

On the surface, Parliament flexed its muscles and demonstrated to the Commission and the Council – and to the world – that it was not to be trifled with, and certainly the affair will ensure that the other institutions will regard it with a new respect. On the other hand, in these debates Parliament was split as never before – internal divisions within party groups, and fierce fighting between groups which normally manage to come privately to a compromise in order to present, in public, a united *parliamentary* front to the outside world and, in particular, to the other institutions.

In some cases at least, there also seemed to be some conflict between the MEPs of a particular nationality, across the party groups, and their national governments, with the government usually emerging victorious. Until very recently Parliament had resisted robustly (as the Treaty, by implication at least, requires) any attempt by national governments to dictate the behaviour of MEPs from a member state. But in this case the Spanish and Portuguese MEPs, whatever party group they belonged to, appeared to vote as a national bloc on the 'advice' of their governments, and the British Labour MEPs similarly seem to have been influenced by the British prime minister. British governments, at least, had made spasmodic – and, it has to be said, unsuccessful – attempts over the years to bring the British MEPs closer to the system of party discipline that prevailed at Westminster. If member governments should ever succeed in exerting control over MEPs, it would gravely endanger the whole supranational basis of the Parliament and therefore the Union as a whole. Parliament's great strength has been that since there was (and is) no European government there was no need for a strong disciplinary system, and therefore, unlike most national parliaments, it could consider proposals on their merits and not in relation to their partisan origins. Any increase in the tendency of MEPs from across the party spectrum to vote together as a national bloc would give the governments of the member states – whose input many analysts consider is already too great – far too much power.

The behaviour of the governments – always uneasy in a system where power has to be shared, and therefore jealous of the other institutions – left much to be desired. Even at the birth of the Economic Community and the Atomic Energy Community, member governments took the opportunity when creating the two new Commissions to give them less power than had been enjoyed by the High Authority of the Coal and Steel Community, and every subsequent revision of the treaties has been a battle between those who wanted to advance the role of the Community and member governments trying to keep power to themselves. National politicians, after all, were seen as significant men and women because their *national* electorates had elected them to power, and inevitably therefore what was happening in Europe was seen by ministers round the Council table through the distorting lens of national public opinion. British governments in particular have been guilty of judging European issues by the yardstick of internal politics within their own party, and have provided an interpretation of events in Brussels to the eager British media which has sometimes had little to do with reality. Consequently, there was a good deal of private glee in the corridors of Westminster and Whitehall when the Commission was accused by the spin doctors and the media of a wide range of crimes. After the resignation of the Santer Commission, the usual reference in even the more serious sections of the British media was to the 'disgraced Commission'. But in fact the impression given – that most, if not all, of the commissioners had been caught with their fingers in the till – was far from the truth. Only one of the commissioners, Edith Cresson, was actually found to have transgressed, by installing friends and relatives in positions of profit, whilst Jacques Santer himself was guilty only of not keeping a close enough eye on such activities. If these were the standards by which executive bodies were to be judged, there would have been 'disgraced' governments all over Europe in the last decades of the twentieth century.

In the event, however, there were some benefits for the Community as a result of the 'fraud and cronyism' accusations. The flood of objections and tide of ridicule which might have been expected to flow from the sight of nearly all the 'disgraced' commissioners remaining in their posts until a new Commission took up office on 20 September 1999 did not materialise, and the Commission tried to use the time by setting about the overhaul of procedures and machinery to ensure that what *was* wrong did not give rise to problems in future. Inevitably, the Commission's relationship with the Parliament was re-appraised the Parliament's committees will rank rather higher as segments of the institutional machinery in future and Neil Kinnock's nomination as Vice President-Elect with responsibility for relations with the European Parliament was a visible signal to that effect. But inevitably, also, the affair affected the confidence of the Commission and led to something of a political vacuum; the Commission issued a statement after the mass resignation to the effect that the commissioners did not intend to put forward any political proposals during their 'caretaker period', since that might compromise the integrity of the new Commission. Similarly, whatever the Commission had been doing to review its internal machinery was compromised.

At the time of writing (June 1999) it seems quite probable that when Romano Prodi becomes President he will feel it is necessary to examine the whole structure of the Commission, or at least take credit for internal reviews of structures and procedures which have already been done and parade them as evidence of his determination to 'run a tight ship'. Though the member states' governments will be responsible for appointing the new Commission, the Parliament will have to ratify the nominations, and that ratification will now be taken very seriously. But herein lies a danger for the Union. Governments may again be tempted to pressure their MEPs to support the their nomination(s) to the Commission.[4] If so, they are likely to have a fight on their hands – the Parliament had a long struggle to win the right to ratify the nominations, and will not easily abandon it. The governments have agreed on a new President-Elect, chosen, like so many before him, in the expectation that he would be more amenable. As so often in the past, that expectation seems unlikely to be fulfilled, to judge by Prodi's speeches since taking office.

The Council has gained by other post-Amsterdam developments unconnected with the Commission crisis. Its hold on CFSP has been strengthened, by the appointment of the Secretary-General as High Representative, who will conduct matters concerned with CFSP on behalf of the Union. His normal work as Secretary-General will now be carried out by the incumbent of a new post of Deputy Secretary-General, so the Council is consolidating its already tight hold over CFSP.

The future development of the Union will revolve around the resolution of two opposing forces – the reluctance of governments to release their grip on *anything*, and the growing number of problems that cannot be solved except by supranational means. As this chapter has tried to show, for natural and inevitable reasons the odds in the long run are against the governments. There are a growing number of issues which national governments simply cannot deal with on their own – pollution, international crime, drugs, foreign policy, defence – and which can only be solved by international cooperation, whilst there are others which no longer *need* to be dealt with at national level and are probably better dealt with at sub-national level. So as we move into the twenty-first century we shall see a growing amount of internationalism and a continuation of devolution from the centre, not by choice but by natural progression. It remains to be seen how far into the twenty-first century we shall have to go before there is a general political recognition that this is the case.

Further reading

Clesse, A. and Vernon, R. (eds) (1991) *The European Community after 1992: A New Role in World Politics?*, Institute for European and International Studies, Association Luxembourg-Harvard, Luxembourg.

Commission of the European Communities (1994) *Treaty on European Union*, Office for Official Publications of the European Communities, Luxembourg.

Commission of the European Communities (1997) *Treaty of Amsterdam amending the Treaty on European Union, The Treaties establishing the European Communitities and certain related acts*, Office for Official Publications of the European Communities, Luxembourg.

European Parliament (1992) *Maastricht: The Treaty on European Union. The Position of the European Parliament,* Office for Official Publications of the European Communities, Luxembourg.

Freestone, D.A.C. and Davidson, J.S. (1988) *The Institutional Framework of the European Communities,* Croom Helm, London.

George, S. (1991) *Politics and Policy in the European Community,* 2nd edn, Oxford University Press, Oxford.

Nicoll, W. and Salmon, T. (1994) *Understanding the New European Community,* Harvester Wheatsheaf, Hemel Hempstead.

Williams, A.M. (1991) *The European Community,* Blackwell, Oxford.

Notes

1. Technically, all the commissioners resigned individually, since there was no provision in the Treaty for the resignation of the entire Commission except in pursuance of Article 144, following a vote of censure by the Parliament.

2. 'Discharge the budget': this is the process whereby the Parliament examines the last (completed) budget to see that all the expenditure involved was in conformity with the budgetary proposals it had agreed to in the first place – effectively, approving the accounts. In this instate the Parliament found irregularities and refused to discharge the budget for 1996 until these had been investigated.

3. In fact, since there was no provision in the treaty for the resignation of the whole Commission except pursuant on a vote of censure by the Parliament, which had not happened, technically every commissioner resigned individually. The unfortunate President, Jacques Santer, became the chief whipping boy of the media, which was ironic since it was the Santer Commission which had started in 1995 a systematic review of the management and procedures of the Commission. One commissioner, Edith Cresson, was found to have appointed friends and relatives to positions of profit, but no-one else was found guilty of fraud or 'cronyism'.

4. At the time of writing, the Conservative leader in Britain, William Hague, is trying to force his MEPs out of the European People's Party. To their credit, they are resisting.

5 European security: structures, challenges and risks

The Cold War period

The Cold War period of 1945–90 constituted a unique episode in the history of security arrangements amongst the states of Europe. For over forty years most of the continent was divided into two spheres of political and military influence, institutionalised by the foundation of the North Atlantic Treaty Organisation (NATO) in 1949 and the construction of the Warsaw Treaty Organisation (WTO) in 1955 in response to West Germany's impending membership of the Atlantic Alliance later that same year. The division of Europe ran vertically through Germany and also through its old capital, Berlin, marooned deep inside East Germany (GDR). The political division of Europe was reinforced by its military division on the ground. On either side of the inner German border two large armies, the strongest and most sophisticated the world had ever seen, faced each other for decades. In no other part of the world were American and Soviet forces directly opposed to each other across a land border. That one of these armies was extra-European added to the uniqueness of the arrangements. The most powerful actor in the European security regime of the Cold War was the United States, and its usurpation of a role Moscow felt ought properly to be its own added to the tension.

There was no blueprint at the end of the Second World War for a geo-strategic equilibrium between two rival alliance blocs led by the United States and the Soviet Union. The inability of the victorious powers in 1945 to reconcile competing ideological and strategic interests in Europe led, incrementally, to the familiar European security framework of NATO balanced by the WTO, with a few neutrals scattered around the fringes. The military strength of both blocs, not least the impressive strategic nuclear capabilities of the superpowers, created a condition of mutual deterrence which made the security structure very stable. However, this military balance of terror inhibited political flexibility. Political change across the continent, especially in authoritarian eastern Europe, came only very gradually. By 1970, by default rather than by any astute long-term planning, divided Europe had become one of the most secure and stable regions of the world. The mutual respect for spheres of influence meant that crises, such as the WTO suppression of a more liberal brand of socialism in Czechoslovakia in 1968, could be ridden out without undue panic or the prospect of inter-bloc war. In contrast, elsewhere in the international system (for instance the Middle East and South East Asia) instability appeared endemic and brutal wars occurred regularly. In Europe the political division of the continent was a cultural tragedy, and personal freedoms were severely limited east of the inner German border, but the real prospect of international war was less than at any period in Europe's history stretching back centuries.

A divided but stable Europe was not pre-ordained. Throughout the late 1940s and the 1950s, there were expectations in both blocs that the goals of the great 1945 wartime summits at Yalta and Potsdam – namely, a unified Germany and a peaceful, harmonious continent – would eventually be achieved. There was a sense that the division of the continent both by ideology and by actual barbed wire and concrete was unnatural and temporary. By 1970 such sentiments had largely evaporated and there was a reluctant but apparently realistic acceptance of Soviet hegemony in eastern Europe balanced by a separate liberal-democratic regional system in western Europe under American strategic protection. Diplomatic moves began to regularise these arrangements and drain away some of the Cold War hostilities. Since its foundation in 1949 the West German state (FRG) had adopted a deeply hostile attitude towards the GDR and those communist states which supported it. The FRG viewed the GDR as illegitimate, as it did those other boundaries unilaterally imposed by the Soviet Union throughout easten Europe. Successive West German governments argued that these border arrangements deprived it of territory and people legitimately part of Germany before the Second World War, and that there had never been any treaty validating Moscow's actions. To keep the FRG in the Western camp and as a compliant member of NATO – indeed, its front line member – the West supported the West German position. However, in 1970, in the spirit of détente, the Brandt government began moves to ameliorate the situation. From the philosophical basis that the FRG was more concerned about German people than German borders, Chancellor Brandt initiated the new *'Ostpolitik'* which led to a normalising of relations between the FRG and eastern Europe. Between 1970 and 1974 the FRG agreed a clutch of treaties with the USSR, Poland, the GDR and Czechoslovakia which put relations on a more cordial, working basis. The *Ostpolitik* removed a major impediment to East–West relations in Europe, and opened the way for West German political and economic influence throughout the region, much of which was aimed at improving conditions for German people in the GDR and elsewhere. The Soviet Union and its client states cautiously accepted the German initiative because the bargain delivered Western acceptance of the international arrangements imposed on half of Europe by the Red Army a generation earlier. It also delivered large West German economic credits to the East.

At the same time an ongoing process of negotiations known as the Conference on Security and Cooperation in Europe (CSCE) complemented Brandt's *Ostpolitik* by establishing widespread acceptance of Europe's division.

Negotiations between 1973 and 1975 resulted in the Helsinki Final Act. In the summer of 1975, 35 countries – all of Europe (except Albania) and the United States and Canada – met in Helsinki at Heads of Government level. The document signed was called an Act rather than a Treaty as it did not have the status of international law. Nonetheless, it contributed to the evolutionary framework of European security which reinforced the balance between East and West in Europe. CSCE was presented as embodying one Europe from the Atlantic to the Urals, but in reality the whole procedure was an exercise in political recognition of the realities of post-war power. There were three elements or 'baskets' to the Final Act. The most important was 'Basket I' on security relations between states. This renounced the use of force to settle international disputes and declared the frontiers of all European states to be 'inviolable'. Although this was not quite legal recognition, it constituted *de facto* recognition of the Soviet arrangements throughout the region. The Soviet Union had been seeking such an acceptance from the West for thirty years. By 1975 the West was merely accepting the reality of the situation. 'Basket II' covered economic, cultural and scientific cooperation across Europe. In carefully controlled ways, that was already happening. 'Basket III' clauses on human rights were what the Soviet Union yielded in return for 'Basket I'; it assumed that the communist states could control any domestic liberal movements encouraged by the Final Act declarations on matters such as freedom of information and movement. Amongst Western conservatives there was some despondency that the Final Act gave too much to the Soviet bloc in return for ineffectual human rights promises. However, the unfulfilled expectations created by the human rights clauses, coupled with the removal of the German revanchist threat accomplished by the Brandt *Ostpolitik,* played major roles in the delegitimisation of the corrupt, inefficient communist regimes during the 1980s.

After these CSCE negotiations, there were supposed to be disarmament discussions, and indeed Mutual and Balanced Force Reduction (MBFR) talks were held in Vienna between NATO and the WTO from 1973 until 1989. But the participants really aimed rather at arms control to cement the functioning deterrent balance between the two blocs rather than at disarmament which might risk instability. Intermediate-range nuclear missiles, with ranges between 500 and 5000 kilometres, were seen as particularly destabilising by both sides, so the superpowers agreed to their removal from the European theatre in the Intermediate Nuclear Forces (INF) treaty of 1987. Stability between the two blocs required their removal, but the other arms control agreements in Europe concerned confidence-building measures rather than disarmament.

One irony of this feature of Cold War European security was that its limited achievements reached a peak as domestic political developments were making the military prowess of the eastern bloc irrelevant. The Helsinki Final Act allowed for some very limited confidence and security-building measures between the two military blocs. Very occasional inspections of each other's military exercises became possible. In the early 1980s it was decided to enhance these non-threatening arms control measures to reinforce the stability of mutual deterrence. The 1986 Conference on Disarmament in Europe (CDE) extended mutual inspection privileges in numbers and scope, increasing the transparency of each alliance's forces and further diminishing anxieties about surprise attacks. The Conventional Forces in Europe (CFE) treaty of 1990 deepened and extended the transparency set in place by CDE even further and set sub-regional limits to alliance forces throughout the European theatre. The CFE treaty, the result of long and hard negotiations, was signed at the November 1990 Paris CSCE Conference when the Cold War was declared over by the Charter of Paris. The Berlin Wall, physically dividing the city since 1961, had fallen a year earlier, Germany had unified economically in July 1990 and politically in October 1990, much of eastern Europe had shaken off communist rule, the USSR was teetering on the verge of disintegration, and the Red Army was slowly but surely withdrawing from its 45-year occupation of eastern Europe. Large elements of the CFE treaty were redundant as it was being signed, and the European security equilibrium it was designed to sustain was being transformed at that very moment.

Security architecture after the Cold War

The political and economic strain of waging a global Cold War brought about the collapse of the communist system in eastern Europe and the disintegration of the USSR in 1991. The command economies and totalitarian political systems of the Soviet bloc were not flexible enough to compete with the democratic, advanced industrial societies of the West. In the age of the microchip and information technology the communist systems could not maintain the pace of their rivals nor address the consumer expectations of their people. Inept efforts to reform, or to stifle dissent, led to implosion and collapse. In 1989 and 1990 east European communist regimes lacked the will and the resources to fight to stay in power, particularly when Soviet president Gorbachev made it clear that the Red Army would remain in barracks this time and not assist in quelling revolution as it had done so effectively in Hungary in 1956 and Czechoslovakia in 1968. The discredited nature of the old communist regimes, especially among the younger generation, facilitated a remarkably quick and relatively bloodless transformation. Perceptions of Germany as no longer the historic threat portrayed by the communist governments also allowed change. The east European regimes had been tolerated by the people for much of the time since the Second World War because the communists did at least provide security against the German threat which had twice in forty years wrought havoc throughout eastern Europe. By the 1980s the notion of a real German threat had disappeared as a factor legitimising communist rule. As Soviet policy-makers began to contemplate the possibility of withdrawal from eastern Europe, the prospect of strategic partnership with the United States and club membership of the Western advanced industrial community were held out to the political leadership of a traumatised Soviet Union and its likely successor state, the new Russia.

North Atlantic Treaty Organisation (NATO)

This transformation of Europe's Cold War security arrangements prompted some celebration in the liberated societies of east Europe, but over much of Europe the shock of change induced a prevalent mood of uncertainty, caution and a sense that risks should not be taken. NATO was recognised as the security mechanism which could be credited with winning the Cold War and, most importantly, linking the United States into European security arrangements. Most of Europe, except Russia and France, supported the continuance of NATO's role and its adaptation to post-Cold War circumstances. Russia was anxious that NATO would be used to project American and German influence into eastern Europe, and France was hoping that some form of integrated European defence organisation would overtake NATO as the primary European security institution.

The Cold War bequeathed to Europe a clutch of multilateral institutions with core or auxiliary security functions. NATO is the primary institution. The Western European Union (WEU) and the Organisation for Security and Cooperation in Europe (OSCE) are also institutions devoted primarily to security but in practice have been secondary to NATO at least to the end of the twentieth century. The European Union (EU) looked forward to a major security role amongst its other many functions, but as yet can only aspire to a practical security role and has to restrict itself to political gestures. The respective roles of these institutions, and how they relate to each other, is commonly described as the architecture of European security. In post-Cold War Europe this framework constitutes a flexible model, subject to challenge and change. This new security environment is much less conducive to multilateral cohesion and collective action than was the Cold War. Across Europe the security stakes have been much reduced from the worst that could have happened during the Cold War. But while the worst threat has disappeared for the time being, lesser threats, such as local ethnic conflicts or international terrorism, have multiplied. However, because they are lesser threats and are not equally vital to all states with interests in European security, there is a much wider element of choice in how to respond and less prospect of purposive consensus.

In this transformed environment NATO has remained the leading security institution. Until 1991 NATO performed its collective duties and responsibilities well, and to the international acclaim of the liberal, democratic world. For over forty years its core task was to stop something happening. Through the successive application of deterrence-based strategic doctrines and the deployment of capable military forces alliance cohesion was sustained, and Soviet influence in the North Atlantic and European region was contained within the limits it had reached when the North Atlantic Treaty was signed in 1949. Throughout the Cold War NATO's core security objective was clear enough, and anxiety over national security was high enough to sustain fundamental political harmony amongst the member states within the large treaty area despite all the strains and stresses of the era. This was no mean accomplishment for an alliance as widely spread as NATO, and with member states as disparate as Norway and

Portugal and as potentially opposed as Greece and Turkey. Externally, the Alliance was under perpetual challenge from an impressive Soviet military machine, complemented by disconcerting and contrasting waves of seductive and aggressive diplomacy over many years. Internally, it was often buffeted by periodic arguments over nuclear strategy, burden-sharing, and out-of-area issues. France left the integrated military structure in 1966, and Greek–Turkish problems required sensitive management. Yet NATO survived and prospered. It is not unreasonable to claim that in 1989, the year of its fortieth anniversary and the collapse of the Berlin Wall, NATO was the world's most successful multilateral peacetime alliance in modern history.

With the Cold War over the Alliance's central task was done, but by the 1990s it had become a political institution as well as a military alliance. Sentimentality, institutional self-preservation, and natural political caution created a deep reluctance to disband it. There was a feeling that NATO had accumulated capital which was worth strenuous efforts to protect, and that it would be foolhardy to dismantle such a successful security organisation. Attractive but secondary by-products of the Alliance's Cold War experience were elevated into compelling reasons for sustaining NATO, even though the core objective which spawned these by-products no longer applied. Arguments regularly deployed for continuance of NATO included inhibiting the growth of separate national directions of defence policies, not least Germany's; keeping the USA involved in European security and perpetuating Washington's large contribution to the European defence burden; maintaining transatlantic solidarity against the (admittedly unlikely) prospect of revived Russian expansionism in Europe; maintaining the military force inter-operability built up by decades of effort (which could be important for future tasks); sustaining an organisation which could be a vehicle for a wider European collective security; utilising a standing mechanism for transatlantic armaments cooperation; and having an effective military alliance in place for traditional defence tasks (as yet undefined). However, while NATO does fulfil these functions, not all European states are enthusiastic about all or even many of these Cold War by-products.

So there was a search for a grand purpose to keep NATO alive and relevant to the modern world. But this search immediately revealed a fundamental weakness in the enterprise. Viable alliances should not need to search for a *raison d'être*; that core purpose should be obvious, driving states to pool their defence resources in support of a vital common interest. Instead, NATO's core mission is vaguely envisaged as that of a military agent of the 'international community' – a term often used but rarely explained – ready, and in the Balkans attempting, to stem post-Cold War instability by providing forces for humanitarian and peace-keeping tasks.

This mission has emerged from a set of amorphous objectives announced at the landmark NATO summit in Rome in November 1991. NATO's 'New Strategic Concept' announced at Rome contains one six-line paragraph detailing the Alliance's purpose in the most general terms. There NATO's purpose is said to be 'to safeguard the freedom and security of all its members by political and military means in accordance with the principles of the United Nations Charter' and 'the establishment of a just and lasting peaceful order in Europe'. This 'New Strategic Concept' is really about creating some kind of political role for NATO. NATO is seen as the centre of a 'framework of interlocking institutions'. There are, it is claimed, three mutually reinforcing elements to the 'New Strategic Concept': dialogue, cooperation, and collective defence capabilities. Notice that the military purpose of this military alliance comes third to certain ambitious political objectives, defined only in broad and imprecise terms. Examination of the Rome Declaration of Peace and Cooperation for a specific *raison d'être* for NATO will also be in vain. The document describes NATO as an 'agent of change, a source of stability and an indispensable guarantor of its members' security', 'playing a key role in building a new lasting order of peace in Europe: a Europe of cooperation and prosperity'. It also talks about meeting 'any potential risks to our security which may arise from instability or tension'. It is difficult to divine any concrete political purposes from the rhetoric of these statements, and fundamental questions about the role of NATO remain unanswered.

Though NATO has survived as an institution, the years from 1991 to 1998 were difficult and disappointing. Efforts were made to imbue the Alliance with a sense of purpose and activity. A multilateral Rapid Reaction Corps was created and the concept of a Combined Joint Task Force (CJTF) agreed. The notion of a distinctive European Defence Identity within the Alliance was firmed up, and France moved closer to the integrated military structure it had left in 1966.

But the decision to expand NATO membership taken at the 1997 Madrid summit is of much greater significance, since the frontiers of any member state are guaranteed by the Alliance as a whole. NATO agreed to allow the Czech Republic, Hungary and Poland to join by 1999. This extends formal alliance commitments deep into east Europe and gives the impression of a dynamic organisation confident about its interest and goals. To reassure Russia (which always feared an extension of NATO power into eastern Europe) a NATO–Russia Founding Act was also agreed in 1997, allowing a permanent Russian liaison unit at NATO's headquarters with rights of frequent consultation on a wide range of NATO's core tasks. (NATO also agreed a charter with Ukraine, which, though it allows a permanent mission at NATO headquarters, is much less comprehensive than the NATO–Russia agreement.) NATO had already in 1994 established bilateral 'Partnership for Peace' arrangements with several other east European countries regarded as still unsuitable for NATO membership, giving them assistance and advice on a wide range of defence-related issues conducive to participation in a cooperative, democratic Europe. In 1997 a European–Atlantic Partnership Council (EAPC) was formed with them (replacing the North Atlantic Cooperation Council (NACC) which functioned from 1991 to 1994), thus providing a forum for political dialogue between NATO and most of the rest of Europe.

Any possibility of actual military action by NATO always depended on American willingness to commit its forces. In the early 1990s the disintegration of Yugoslavia presented a possible case for NATO action if it were to safeguard

European peace by its power. But since the USA was not prepared for such action it did nothing effective for several years, preferring to hope that UN guarantees might suffice. Though it was the world's most powerful military alliance, NATO thus showed itself relatively ineffective. In a search for military relevance, the NATO foreign ministers agreed in December 1992 that NATO had a worthwhile role as a peace-keeping agent for the United Nations, the CSCE or other international organisations. Unquestionably, NATO's operational and training experience make it capable of the projection of power to a crisis point. But its operational capabilities were not backed by political confidence about the wisdom of deploying them. When in 1994 the Bosnian Serbs sacked Srebrenica despite the UN's guarantee of its inhabitants' safety, the USA and NATO were finally prodded into airstrikes against the Serbs, thus decisively shifting the military balance against them. This restored a military balance to Bosnia, and the exhausted local belligerents agreed at the Dayton Peace Accord of 1995 to a peace guaranteed by NATO. Only thus did NATO assume a peace-enforcement role in 1996, protecting, not the *status quo*, but a local political system very different from that in existence when the conflicts began in 1992.

Until the Kosovo (Kosova)[1] conflict in 1999, the powers which make up NATO did not wish to use NATO's military power unless such action were approved by the United Nations. But this gave that body, and thereby non-NATO countries such as Russia and China, influence over the use or non-use of NATO forces at the point of crisis. The Kosovo crisis represented a turning-point for NATO. Fears that the Serb regime was about to embark upon further genocide against the majority Albanians of the Kosovo province, with disastrous implications for human rights and the stability of democracy in neighbouring states, finally led the NATO powers to embark on a major campaign of airstrikes. A further factor was the realisation that NATO's credibility might collapse if it simply did nothing. For the first time NATO had launched an attack on a sovereign state without UN backing. One lesson of the Kosovo conflict was that for domestic political reasons the USA was reluctant to deploy ground forces in this area except in a peace-keeping capacity. NATO's strategy therefore combined heavy air assault upon Serb forces with logistical support to ethnic Albanian fighters of the Kosovo Liberation Army (KLA) on the ground. An air attack with the help of NATO's more sophisticated technology incurred smaller risks, and NATO had launched such an attack against the then dominant Bosnian Serb forces in 1994. In 1999 NATO demanded a settlement guaranteed by NATO troops in Kosovo, which was legally a part of Serbia. In this way it gave controversial substance to its peace-making and humanitarian mission, originally announced at Rome in 1991 and reiterated in an 'updated' strategic concept at the fiftieth-anniversary summit at Washington in April 1999.

Organisation for Security and Cooperation in Europe (OSCE)

The CSCE Charter of Paris (1990) attempted to set up the CSCE (renamed the OSCE in December 1994) as a leading post-Cold War European security actor. It was mooted as a possible successor to NATO, and a future institution for Europewide collective security. A secretariat was put in place in Prague, an electoral data office in Warsaw, and a conflict resolution office in Vienna. But the large membership of OSCE (over 50 members) implied a wide divergence of national interests within it. It can act only with the unanimous agreement of its members, with a rotating chairmanship, so it is unable to act effectively. Moreover, OSCE covers an impossibly ambitious geographical area. In the Helsinki conference of 1992 held to address these problems, Germany proposed a CSCE Security Council on the UN model. This proposal received little support; Britain was especially cool. Few states wished to see the CSCE's real institutional power changed more than marginally. Many have policy interests in which the intrusions of a pan-European security organisation would not be welcome; for instance Russia in its relations with some of its constituent republics, and Britain in relation to Northern Ireland. So the 1992 Helsinki Accord rules out enforcement action by the OCSE itself, permitting it only to cooperate with the UN, and to call upon NATO or WEU to provide troops for peace-keeping. Any OSCE-backed peace-keeping operation may only go ahead given the unanimous support of all the foreign ministers and of 'all parties concerned', and if NATO and WEU then agree how best to fulfil the task.

The Western European Union (WEU) and the European Union (EU)

By the 1980s the WEU was viewed as a partner of NATO and in the longer term its potential successor in some European political quarters, though not in London, and thereby as a mechanism through which the EU could acquire a defence function. It was not, of course, conceived in 1954 with that role. It was, rather, created to control German rearmament and to reassure West Germany's uneasy NATO European partners that a rearmed Germany could be securely managed, and for thirty years its role was negligible. But during the 1980s some Europeans came to see the WEU as a vehicle for west European defence cooperation independently of the USA. This was partly due to tensions associated with the Reagan administration's Strategic Defence Initiative (Star Wars 1983) which arose between some European members of NATO and the USA; disputes centred on shares of the defence burden and on arms control. Some Europeans also wanted the EU to organise a common defence and security policy within the framework of the WEU. Such a policy could build upon the existing Franco German-led 'Eurocorps', sometimes thought of as an embryonic European army (see Figure 5.1).

The Maastricht Treaty did indeed foresee a more concrete role for the WEU as a defence agency alongside the EU, perhaps leading to absorption by the EU. But disagreement remained between and within west European governments on this issue. The USA has, of course, been hostile to any serious challenge posed by WEU to the basic integrity of the transatlantic defence relationship. The 1997 Amsterdam Treaty did not make any progress on this issue, and left the WEU without the institutional clout and strong integrated military structure of NATO.

Figure 5.1 The German troops would recall to older French people the sight of German troops parading down the Champs Elysées after conquering France in 1940

Source: *The Independent*, 31 January 1998 (Dyclos-Merilon-Turpin/FSP)

NATO's Washington summit in 1999 announced plans to give the EU (rather than the WEU) access to NATO planning capabilities and assets for EU-led operations.

To date the EC/EU has had one broad political-security role – incorporating German power-potential into an integrated West European framework. But the EU has had no official defence or security functions. In the Maastricht negotiations, the French government wanted the EU to be empowered to *instruct* the WEU to 'elaborate and implement decisions and activities of the Union which have defence implications', thus making the WEU subordinate to the EU, but Britain successfully insisted that the EU be empowered only to *request* such action. Thus the EU remains essentially an economic and social organisation, and its members have a poor track record of cohesion on foreign policy matters. In many ways the wars in ex-Yugoslavia gave a new impetus to the EU's search for security competence. In 1991 Jacques Poos, Chairman of the EC foreign ministers, declared: 'If there is any problem Europe can solve, it is Yugoslavia.' The sense in the EC was that if the EC was to show itself capable of dealing with an external security crisis, then one directly in the backyard of the new Europe presented an ideal oppurtunity for doing so. Yugoslavia was in receipt of considerable EC aid, and the EC was a major trading partner. If military force was required to back up EC mediation, then NATO military forces in Italy and on the Mediterranean would be readily available. But delays, uncertainty, and prevarication in 1991 obliged the EC to turn to the United Nations, and hand prime responsibility for any initiative to tackle the escalating crises to the old patron power, the USA. Both opponents and advocates of a common EU foreign and defence policy drew lessons from this: on the one hand some concluded

Table 5.1 Membership of international organisations addressing European security, 1998

NATO	WEU	EU	EAPC
Belgium	Belgium	Austria	NATO
Canada	France	Belgium	+
Czech Republic	Germany	Denmark	
Denmark	Greece	Finland	Albania
France	Italy	France	Armenia
Germany	Luxembourg	Germany	Austria
Greece	The Netherlands	Greece	Azerbaijan
Hungary	Portugal	Ireland	Belarus
Iceland	Spain	Italy	Bulgaria
Italy	UK	Luxembourg	Estonia
Luxembourg		The Netherlands	Finland
The Netherlands	**Observer status**	Portugal	Georgia
Norway	Austria	Spain	Kazakhstan
Poland	Denmark	Sweden	Kyrgyzstan
Portugal	Finland	UK	Latvia
Spain	Ireland		Lithuania
Turkey	Sweden		Macedonia
UK			Moldova
USA	**Associate members**		Romania
	Iceland		Russia
	Norway		Slovakia
	Turkey		Slovenia
			Sweden
	Associate Partners		Switzerland
	Bulgaria		Tadjikistan
	Estonia		Turkmenistan
	Latvia		Ukraine
	Lithuania		Uzbekistan
	Romania		
	Slovakia		

OSCE			
Albania	Estonia	Liechtenstein	Slovakia
Andorra	Finland	Lithuania	Slovenia
Armenia	France	Luxembourg	Spain
Austria	Georgia	Macedonia	Sweden
Azerbaijan	Germany	Malta	Switzerland
Belarus	Greece	Moldova	Tadjikistan
Belgium	Hungary	Monaco	Turkey
Bosnia-Hercegovina	Iceland	Netherlands	Turkmenistan
Bulgaria	Ireland	Norway	UK
Canada	Italy	Poland	Ukraine
Croatia	Kazakhstan	Portugal	USA
Cyprus	Kyrgyzstan	Romania	Uzbekistan
Czech Republic	Latvia	Russia	The Vatican
Denmark		San Marino	Yugoslavia*

* Membership suspended

that effective unified action in security matters by the EU powers was impossible, on the other that it was essential, and that the institutions needed for bringing it about must be established.

Threats, challenges and risks for the twenty-first century

The character and shape of European security in the near future is difficult to predict. Certain key features of the contemporary environment will determine international stability and peace over the next few years. The first phase of NATO enlargement will leave many countries of eastern Europe in a strategic limbo between NATO security guarantees and Russia. Many countries not included in the first phase have serious concerns about the security of their frontiers. EAPC does not provide any firm security commitments by NATO and will live in the shadow of the special NATO–Russia Permanent Joint Council established in Brussels by the 1997 Founding Act.

Tensions continue to exist between the USA and some of the European members of NATO. For example, the USA sought in the 1990s to contain Iran and to pressurise Libya by economic sanctions. But France, Germany and Italy have strong and valuable trade links with these states and are not prepared to follow the American lead. Libya imports about $8 billion in goods and services, mostly from France, Germany and Italy. Libya and Iran provide almost 20 per cent of Europe's oil imports. The Iranian market is worth about $25 billion in 2000 to European and Japanese industry. The American Iran–Libya Sanctions Act made non-US firms with assets in the United States liable to fines and other legal action in American courts if they invest $30 million or more a year in Libyan and Iranian oil and gas projects. The EU had already officially described the Act as 'completely unacceptable'. It has filed a challenge against this American Act with the World Trade Organisation (WTO). Another instance of challenge to American influence is France's policy of making NATO less dependent on American government policy, by seeking a reform of NATO structures. France has pressed for a European commander rather than an American one for Allied Forces South (AFSOUTH) at Naples, a general reduction in the importance of NATO's regional commands, and an elevation of the political decision-making authority of the NATO Council.

Since 1994 the USA has set the pace on NATO enlargement, and relations between the USA and Russia will continue to influence this process. Individually, the great powers have the capacity to create high tension and crisis. The national security policies of each of the Great Powers all contain elements of uncertainty and unpredictability, and are subject to many contradictory pressures and strains. The USA is under pressure to devote more resources to Middle Eastern and East Asian security than to European security. Russia's mounting concern with its decline as a world power has resulted in great volatility. Germany is increasingly torn between its economic and political interest in eastern Europe and its political and economic axis with France. France has difficulty reconciling its European security and defence identity goals with the apparent necessity of closer cooperation with NATO. The UK juggles its potentially conflicting relations with the USA and with Europe. Such states are the crucial, 'bell-wether' great powers, and the outcome of any of the pressures described above will deeply affect European security in the years ahead.

NATO may be enlarged, but for the Great Powers it is less likely to be 'deepened' (i.e. organised to tie down its members to collective action only). Future alliance action is likely to depend on cooperation amongst like-minded states, in particular areas and for particular contingencies, as in the Gulf War of 1990–91 and in the deployment of the Dayton forces in Bosnia since January 1996. The difficulties encountered by NATO in agreeing a military strategy acceptable to all 19 members when the air attack was launched against Serbia in March 1999 supports this view. The concept of a NATO Combined Joint Task Force (CJTF) is one whereby some member states use alliance assets to address security contingencies beyond NATO boundaries but not all NATO members become involved. This could be a formula for the assertion of national interests and *ad hoc* coalition, rather than deeper defence integration. It is clear that the end of the Cold War removes a very strong pressure for a collective defence policy encompassing Europe and the USA; and it may well be that collective security institutions like NATO or the WEU will come to lose their effective grip. But others believe that in the new situation the European states (perhaps with the USA) need to use their power to guarantee European peace and stability in the interest of long-term economic development.

It is a paradox that while the Great Powers are reasserting national interests and shaping the future of the institutions, it is other lesser states which pose the most numerous threats to European security. There is a range of very fragile states, mostly but not exclusively in eastern Europe, which are susceptible to ethnic and religious conflict, civil war, and political and economic disintegration. The territory of the former Soviet Union has been the location of many post-Cold War conflicts in the 1990s, and could be so again in the twenty-first century.

While most risks and challenges arise from actual or prospective civil or ethnic conflicts, these are relatively low-level conflicts. The threat least likely to contemporary European security, but most dangerous should it occur, is that of traditional, large-scale inter-state war between great powers. In this regard the greatest challenge – not yet a threat – to European security is the German–Russian relationship. The enduring, crucial, strategic importance of this relationship to European security arrangements constitutes a major condition determining the prospects for European security. Russia's European policy attaches a top priority to transforming NATO from a collective defence organisation to a much weaker collective security organisation, ideally answerable to the OSCE. Such developments would dilute American power and German influence in European security arrangements and enhance Russian influence. Since the collapse of the Soviet Union, German influence in eastern Europe – especially economic influence – has been dominant. More than half of eastern European trade with the EU is with Germany, and twice as much German private investment is now going to eastern Europe than to western Europe. The German–Polish border area, where low-cost labour advantage is maximised by western capital, is one of the most active investment spots in the world. By 1996 Poland's trade with Germany was valued at over DM 26 billion; the Czech Republic's trade with Germany reached DM 25 billion, and Hungary's trade with Germany stood at DM 15 billion. In 1996 Germany was the leading export and import trading partner of all three of the former Soviet satellite states. Russian political influence is attempting to stage a comeback in parts of the old WTO, and a political offensive is in train. German national political and economic interests are being drawn ever more towards that more traditional marketplace, source of raw materials and cheap labour, and arena of political competition between the German and Russian borders.

A crucial factor affecting European security arrangements will be the nature and extent of US involvement. There are two aspects to this: whether the Europeans will continue to see US involvement, and indeed leadership, as both necessary and desirable, and whether the USA will continue to commit resources to European security arrangements. Within Europe there are those who argue that US involvement is essential and that the USA has demonstrated in two world wars and the Cold War that no other state has either the political or military capabilities to mediate successfully between the continental great powers while reassuring the rest of Europe that their liberties and conditions are safe. Against this, others argue that an organisation such as NATO, in which American leadership has been evident, had its roots in the Cold War and the perceived threat of a mighty Soviet empire. That threat is now gone and new security arrangements, involving post-communist Russia, are more appropriate for the new Europe; indeed, it might be said that the time has come for Europe to stand on its own feet and acquire the political and institutional capabilities to guarantee its own peace and stability. Moreover, given the political, cultural and ideological divergences between Europe and the USA and the fact that European and US economic interests sometimes clash, it might be argued that it is undesirable for Europe always to play 'second fiddle' to the USA in matters of security and foreign policy.

Within the USA, it may be difficult to persuade the US Congress and people to perpetuate security guarantees to Europe when no direct ideological or military threat to the United States from Europe exists. In the mid-1980s surveys indicated that more than 66 per cent of Americans supported the deployment of American military forces to defend western Europe from aggression. In 1994 the figure had dropped to nearly 50 per cent. Conservative commentators argue that it may be even more difficult if western Europe is seen to be reluctant to support US interests outside continental Europe, and that the United States will increasingly measure NATO's value by what NATO does to assist in safeguarding Washington's Atlantic security interests from the Barents Sea to the Indian Ocean.

Since 1993 American defence-planning has been predicated on the priority to deter or fight two major regional conflicts almost simultaneously, unilaterally if necessary. The regions which the USA sees as the focus of its military machine are East Asia and the Middle East; not Europe. The Clinton administration declared in 1994 that nowhere was 'the need for continued United States engagement more evident' than in East Asia. The United States also has enduring interests in the Middle East, including guaranteeing the security of Israel and maintaining the free flow of oil at reasonable prices. A range of crises in recent years does seem to have vindicated the perspective in American foreign and security policy of two major regional conflicts. In October 1994, at the same time as sensitive negotiations between the United States and North Korea over its nuclear weapons programme, Iraq moved large military forces towards the Kuwait border. Within 72 hours the United States had heavy ground forces in Kuwait with a further 150,000 troops poised for deployment if necessary. In March 1996 at the same time as the Arab–Israeli peace process was in deep crisis over terrorist outrages inside Israel, two US carrier battle groups were moved to Taiwanese waters to counter belligerent behaviour by China.

In global security, the strategic priorities for NATO's European member states are in central and eastern Europe and the Mediterranean littoral, particularly North Africa. For the United States the strategic priorities are the Middle East and the Gulf, East Asia and Russia. There is some overlap but there is also considerable divergence. There is little agreement beyond rhetoric in 1999 on prioritising and constructing a strategy to counter terrorism, to inhibit the proliferation of weapons of mass destruction, and to achieve security objectives. Regardless of old ties and allegiances, the national interest criterion is now pervasive in American foreign policy circles. The future good health of European security arrangements may involve a number of possible scenarios, such as the EU evolving strong common foreign and defence policies with clear institutional clout, or security organisations which are rooted in the Cold War era being replaced with new arrangements involving both the EU powers, the states of eastern and central Europe and Russia, or alternatively the west Europeans making it evident to Washington, especially the Congress, that it is in the strategic self-interest of the United States to sustain NATO (and through it, the USA's involvement in European security arrangements). Valuable as NATO's contribution to the protection of American political and economic interests on the European continent may be, it is the threat to American interests outside Europe that captures the attention of US policy-makers in transatlantic relations. If western Europe refuses to play 'second fiddle' to American strategic policy in the Middle East, any residual, sentimental affection for NATO will be vulnerable.

Conclusion

The first decade of the twenty-first century will be very important for European security. NATO, the vehicle for American commitment, may be at risk unless the capable western European states show the political will to bear a wider military burden alongside the United States. NATO could also be eclipsed if collective defence in the traditional alliance format is exchanged for pan-European collective security or the relegation of NATO below the OSCE as the primary European security institution. Occasional state collapse in the post-communist societies, as in the Soviet Union, Yugoslavia and Albania, would seem to be a likely prospect in some of the poorer countries unsure of national identity or economic prospects. Distressing as such incidents may be, most potentially dysfunctional states do not occupy positions of continental, strategic significance in the modern era. Contemporary European security arrangements have an incomplete quality to them but, to a large extent, they reflect the geo-strategic realities of the post-Cold War years. Such arrangements look set to continue for some time.

Further reading

Bown, C. and Mooney, P. (1981) *Cold War to Détente 1945–1980*, Heinemann, London.

Brown, M. (1995) 'The Flawed Logic of NATO Expansion', *Survival*, 37(i) pp. 34–52.

Gaddis, J.L. (1987) *The Long Peace. Inquiries into the History of the Cold War*, Oxford University Press, Oxford.

Gordon, P. (1997) 'Does WEU Have a Role?', *Washington Quarterly*, 20(1) pp. 125–140.

Kissinger, H.A. (1995) *Diplomacy*, Simon and Schuster, London, Chapter 30.

Wyllie, J.H. (1986) *European Security in the Nuclear Age*, Blackwell, Oxford.

Wyllie, J.H. (1997) *European Security in the New Political Environment*, Longman, London.

Note

1. The province's name is Kosovo in Serbian, Kosova in Albanian.

6 The major democracies of western Europe: France, Italy, Germany, and the United Kingdom

Introduction

Since 1945 the four major democracies of western Europe have confronted similar problems and challenges: democratic consolidation and economic reconstruction; the building of political and social consensus; urbanisation, modernisation, and changes to the social structure; the impact of recession and economic crisis since the 1970s, and in particular the growing burdens on the welfare state; the increasing internationalisation of both politics and economics, and the challenges of European integration. All of these developments have been associated with major transformations in cultural and social life – for example, the decline in the social and political influence of the main churches through widespread secularisation; the move from large-scale and labour-intensive manufacturing industry to light industry, computerisation, and the service sector, with a concomitant decline in traditional working-class sub-cultures and in the relationship between social class membership and political behaviour; the political impact of feminism with challenges to patriarchal privilege; the changing ethnic and racial composition of societies; and the momentous challenge posed by the growth in the power of the mass media and the impact of new forms of marketing and communications upon politics.

More recently, the collapse of communist rule in eastern and central Europe, and the reopening of old and seemingly intractable ethnic conflicts, as well as the eastern countries' need for economic aid, have added to the debate about the future of European democracy. Traditional parties and ideologies have been forced, with varying degrees of enthusiasm and success, to respond to new political agendas, centred on ecological concerns, race and ethnicity, regionalism, and gender politics, for example; and to organise around new socio-political cleavages, many of which are as yet only semi-formed. Whereas some parties have sought to transform their ideologies and structures totally, others have been content to adapt to change more slowly. New political forces have sought to enter the mainstream – the Greens, for example, but also, most dramatically in the 1990s, a resurgent extreme right in several countries. The major

European democracies face mounting evidence of voter volatility and unrest. It is possible that, in the absence of successful institutional and political renewal, the future stability and health of European democracy may be threatened.

This chapter presents a synopsis and analysis of the main contours of political developments in each of the four major western European democracies since 1945. It examines each country in turn, before turning to a comparative analysis of the challenges confronting the major democracies at the start of the new millennium.

France

The experience of war, occupation, and liberation left deep scars upon the French body politic: in 1945 the country was divided between those who had resisted the Nazis and those who had collaborated either actively or passively. This political dichotomy was compounded by divisions within the victorious resistance movement between a nationalist right wing, loyal to General Charles de Gaulle, and a Communist-led left wing. The French Communist Party (PCF) emerged in elections held in October 1945 as the biggest single party with 26 per cent of the popular vote. However, the political life of the Fourth Republic – inaugurated in October 1946 – was to be dominated by a series of shaky coalition governments, often led by the moderate and pro-Western socialist party (SFIO); and both the Gaullist and communist movements were to experience marginalisation, following de Gaulle's withdrawal from active politics in 1946 in disagreement with the new constitution and the PCF's removal from the post-war government in 1947. Importantly, the wartime experience had discredited those substantial sections of the French right which had collaborated with the Nazi occupation, and which adhered to an almost pre-revolutionary creed which conflated racial purity with 'true Frenchness', and national glory with respect for hierarchy. Although such sentiments would resurface in the 1950s in the far right Poujadiste movement, and even in some parts of the Gaullist movement, and again in the 1980s in Jean-Marie Le Pen's *Front National*, for the most part the post-1945 French right would embrace a conservative variant of the democratic republicanism of 1789.

A key priority of the governments of the Fourth Republic was economic reconstruction. From 1945 to 1947 the National Resistance Council nationalised many key industries and banking and insurance concerns. Although the pace and direction of nationalisations changed after 1947, state intervention and direction remained a cornerstone of the French drive to rebuild and modernise the economy. A modernisation plan was launched by Jean Monnet in 1945, based on the premise that the only way to catch up with countries such as the UK and USA was through development of large corporations which could introduce technological innovations and benefit from economies of scale. From 1946 governments sought to raise investment and production in the private sector by the assistance and encouragement of mergers. A series of five-year plans from 1947 prioritised industrial growth, to be achieved initially through the development of French industry behind the barriers of protection. Politicians such as Pierre Mendès-France and Guy Mollet sought to speed up modernisation throughout the 1950s. Industry grew rapidly, living standards rose, and from 1952 increased urbanisation began dramatically to change the social structure. On the negative side, rural depopulation saw many small farmers forced off the land, small businesses suffered from the policy of industrial and commercial concentration, and the new city-dwellers frequently suffered from urban congestion. Moreover, the planning process was entrusted to civil servants and technocrats who were often accused of top-down and authoritarian management. The *dirigiste* foundations of French-style corporatism were laid in this period, pre-empting later Gaullist tendencies to bypass traditional interests and elites by dealing with sympathetic professional associations.

The Fourth Republic was politically unstable. A strong parliament, inclusive of all shades of opinion through proportional representation, had been envisaged. However, parties within parliament remained deeply polarised. Weak governments, unable to straddle the great political cleavages, further reproduced chronic instability. France had no fewer than 25 governments and 15 prime ministers between 1945 and 1958. Even more worrying, from the point of view of the political establishment, was that by 1951 nearly half the electorate was voting for parties – communist or extreme right – which rejected the post-war political system; indeed the 1950s saw a rise in support for the right-wing Poujadiste movement which appealed to those lower middle classes adversely affected by economic restructuring.

It is possible that the Fourth Republic might have endured longer, but for the crisis which erupted in Algeria in 1954. The outbreak of a violent and bloody colonial war there had a profound effect upon French society, polarising the country between supporters and opponents of French imperial rule. By 1957–58 it was clear that elements of the French military were out of control and willing to resort to open rebellion and threats of assassination against cabinet ministers; France's moral standing in the world was collapsing as reports of torture of Algerians reached the outside; and right-wing terrorist groups at home were targeting opponents of the colonial war. Fears rose that the civilian authorities were in danger of losing power to the army in a coup.

When a coup came, in May 1958, it did not inaugurate a military-style dictatorship. Rather, Charles de Gaulle, helped by his wartime prestige and by the fact that he had stood above the chaos of the Fourth Republic, took power, promising a new constitution for a Fifth Republic. That constitution, promulgated in September, introduced a strongly centralised presidential democracy with a directly elected head of state (de Gaulle became president in December). The powers of parliament *vis-à-vis* the executive were reduced. De Gaulle consolidated his position by removing the military threat to democracy, and ended the war in Algeria, granting that country its independence.

The Gaullist decade saw substantial elements of continuity in economic policy. State direction of private sector operations through technocratic planning continued to act as a motor force of development. With the foundation of the EEC in 1957 the French economy was opened up, step by step, to greater competition; however, caution and compromises with those business interests which felt threatened by international competition were necessitated by political as well as economic criteria. In 1963 a new regional planning agency was created – DATAR – with the intention of further by-passing local elites and developing the more backward areas of the country. Its operations also tended to undermine political parties and reinforce the irrelevancy of parliament as a forum where regional problems could be aired and resolved. Throughout the 1960s the regime sought to strengthen industry by encouraging mergers and shutdowns which led to mounting unemployment and a lengthening of the working week – the longest in western Europe by 1968.

Economic modernisation was not accompanied by a modernisation of social structures. Indeed, Gaullism exuded paternalism and populist appeal to traditional morality, patterns of social behaviour and respect for authority. The combination of rapid economic growth with social stagnation created several sources of powerful discontent. Workers, especially the newly urbanised, were angered by rising unemployment, low wage increases, and public spending cuts on health and housing after 1963. Students railed against a university sector in which numbers had expanded rapidly without a corresponding increase in spending on education. Small farmers were alienated by the effects of land clearances. These grievances came to a head in May 1968 when France was rocked by virtual revolution. Tens of thousands of students and workers occupied universities and factories, and for a period it seemed as if the Fifth Republic would fall. Eventually, de Gaulle called a general election which was won by the right-wing parties, capitalising upon the fear of revolution and chaos. However, the regime had been badly shaken, and in April 1969 de Gaulle resigned the presidency, being succeeded by Georges Pompidou after elections.

May 1968 represented a revolt against the stifling paternalism of post-war French society. In the early 1970s French governments moved to introduce a number of changes, including greater trade union rights, educational reforms, and progressive social legislation including the legalisation of abortion and freer access to birth control. However, under both Georges Pompidou's presidency (1969–74) and that of his successor, Valéry Giscard d'Estaing (1974–81), France remained a highly centralised state.

During the 1970s a number of important developments changed the nature of political competition. On the right of the political spectrum the remains of the Gaullist movement had to compete with a non-Gaullist right which saw itself as more modern, liberal, pro-European and less nationalist. Such forces were organised by Giscard d'Estaing into the Union for French Democracy (UDF), a centre-right coalition which supported his presidential bid in 1974. Gaullist forces, reorganised by Jacques Chirac into the Rally for the Republic (RPR) in 1976, would have to both compete against, and cooperate with, this new centre-right in order to hold on to power.

In 1972 the Communist and Socialist parties signed a Common Programme of the Left which facilitated greater cooperation from which the Socialist Party

(PS) of François Mitterrand would emerge as the main victor. Despite a flirtation with the more open-minded and liberal positions of 'Eurocommunism' during the 1970s, the French Communists, under Georges Marchais, had reasserted their hard-line and sectarian reflexes by the end of the decade and were unable to compete with Mitterrand's PS. It was the PS, preaching social modernisation, regional reform, workers' self-management, and redistribution of wealth, which benefited most from the post-1968 change in atmosphere.

Positive election returns for the left in 1978 were followed by Mitterrand's election in May 1981 as the first Socialist president of the Fifth Republic. The PS then achieved a majority in parliament and a government which included four Communist ministers took office.

The early Mitterrand government had many radical innovations to its credit, including: strengthening workers' rights and raising the wages of many workers; attempted reflation of the economy through increased public spending; increases in social welfare provision; the introduction of legislation to increase women's rights in the economic and social spheres; and long-overdue regional reforms – named after the minister responsible, Gaston Defferre – which, though criticised in their implementation, provided for democratically elected regional authorities for the first time and represented a step away from the old tradition of centralising all power in Paris.

By early 1983 the reform programme was in trouble. The international climate worked against radical economic policies which depended upon increased borrowing and higher taxes, and in 1983–84 Mitterrand rejected Keynesian economics in favour of austerity. Realisation that the government could not deliver socialism whilst ignoring external pressures also led to a greater enthusiasm for European cooperation and integration. In July 1984 the Communists resigned from government, Mitterrand replaced his prime minister, Pierre Mauroy, with the young technocrat, Laurent Fabius, and the administration moved towards the centre. Elections in 1986 returned a right-wing parliamentary majority and a period of cohabitation between a right-wing government (with the Gaullist, Chirac, as prime minister) and a Socialist president began. Although the new government carried out some privatisations, the ground had already been prepared by the Fabius administration, and the U-turn was less dramatic than might have been expected.

Mitterrand's re-election in 1988 brought the PS back to office. But this time there was little of the earlier idealism; the Communists – reduced to less than 10 per cent of the vote – remained firmly in opposition; and Mitterrand included several centre-right figures from the UDF in his new, pragmatic administration. His appointment of a succession of moderate prime ministers – Michel Rocard, Edith Cresson, Pierre Bérégovoy – seemed to confirm to some commentators that French politics was undergoing a process of de-ideologisation, with centre-left and centre-right agreeing on the fundamentals of policy. To others, the impression was created of a Socialist Party unsure of how to react to the country's economic problems or (after 1990) the challenge of a united Germany.

A wild card in French politics was a resurgent extreme right in the form of the racist *Front National* (FN), led by Jean-Marie Le Pen. Benefiting from the persistence of mass unemployment, and the decline of the PCF as an effective vehicle for the protest vote, the FN, preaching hostility towards immigrants and calling for social authoritarianism, was to achieve 10–15 per cent of the vote in elections from the mid-1980s. Its rise succeeded to some extent in setting the political agenda in the early 1990s, tempting politicians such as Chirac and Cresson to pander to anti-immigrant sentiments. The FN also sought to exploit growing fears of a loss of national sovereignty which it claimed was inherent in the Maastricht Treaty on European Union; the Treaty was only very narrowly approved by the French in a referendum in September 1992 following a campaign against ratification by the FN, the PCF, and some Gaullists.

Although a mass anti-racism movement was formed in response to the FN, a clear turn to the right in French politics was apparent in the early 1990s, and this was confirmed by the election of a right-wing government in March 1993, under the Gaullist Edouard Balladur. Another period of co-habitation began. The socialists had fallen to around 19 per cent of the popular vote in the 1993 elections, their worst performance in over 20 years, and had suffered a rout in terms of parliamentary seats. Nevertheless, the volatility of the political situation meant that by the end of 1993, the new government had already been forced to stage two humiliating retreats in the face of popular opposition to its education reforms and its plans to reduce the wages of young workers. Local elections in early 1994 which saw a modest left-wing revival confirmed the impression of volatility.

In May 1995 the Mitterrand era finally came to an end when the Gaullist Jacques Chirac was elected president. By now Mitterrand was terminally ill with cancer and his last years in office had seen growing unease with the moral and political behaviour of members of his entourage, and a widespread feeling that his regime had run out of ideas. This reflected badly on his Socialist Party, as did the party's failure to stem the tide of rising unemployment during the 1988–93 period. Nevertheless, the PS presidential candidate – the widely respected Lionel Jospin – did much better than expected in 1995; he actually topped the poll in the first round of the presidential elections and polled an impressive 45.8 per cent in the second, running Chirac a close second. The outcome allowed Jospin to establish his control over the notoriously fissile PS party machine and to prepare the ground for a post-Mitterrand PS revival.

He did not have to wait long. By late 1995 the tide had already turned against the right and Chirac and his Gaullist prime minister, Alain Juppé, were embroiled in the worst period of social unrest France had seen for nearly 30 years. A programme of drastic public spending cuts – which included lowering pensions, cutting social services, reducing the rail network, and privatising telecommunications – provoked trade union and student anger. Opinion polls saw Juppé's popularity ratings slump to an all-time low. Chirac's argument that the cuts – and increased taxes – were needed to qualify for European monetary union cut little ice in a country where Euro-scepticism was growing, and where pride in France's welfare state transcended the usual left/right divide. By April 1996 the PCF (under its new leader, Robert Hue) had explicitly ditched its hardline stance and was seeking a new government alliance with Jospin's Socialists and other centre-left forces.

In early summer 1997 President Chirac made a disastrous tactical blunder by calling a general election. A left-wing alliance of PS, PCF, Greens, Radicals and the tiny Citizens' Movement scored an impressive victory over the right-wing coalition of Gaullists and centrists. The left won 319 seats in the National Assembly to the right's 257 and Chirac had to appoint Jospin as prime minister at the head of a government which included two Communist ministers and Dominique Voynet, the young female Green leader, as environment minister. A third of Jospin's cabinet were women – a very significant advance for women at the top of French politics.

The first two years of the Jospin government saw many tensions within the left: over European monetary union, to which the PCF and the Citizens' Movement were opposed; over increases in pensions and welfare contributions; over the speed with which the government was moving to reduce France's dependence on nuclear energy (a key Green party demand); and, of course, over whether proposals to tackle unemployment went far enough. However, the willingness of the government partners to make compromises and to hold together was impressive, and was helped, perhaps, by the gradual transformation of the PCF into a more moderate force. Party leader Robert Hue pledged his strategic commitment to the government in October 1997, determined not to repeat the PCF–PS internecine feuding of the 1978–83 period; coincidentally, the death of his hard-line predecessor, Georges Marchais, in November 1997 seemed to symbolise the passing of the communist old guard. Not even PCF dismay over France's support for NATO's bombing of Yugoslavia in 1999 undermined the PCF's commitment to the government.

Jospin's government was also helped by a near-miraculous recovery of the French economy in late 1997: a boost in French exports and tourism receipts and a pick-up in domestic demand helped the government cut the budget deficit and so meet the Maastricht criteria for entry to the single currency without the sort of drastic social spending cuts which might have destabilised the left. A relatively painless 1998 budget meant that, despite continuing protests over France's 3.2 million unemployment figure, Jospin's popularity and the unity of his government both remained high. It was also possible for Jospin to keep his promise to his Green and Communist allies to introduce a phased move to a 35-hour working week, which it was hoped would help create new jobs.

The election of a Labour government in Britain in May 1997 and of a sympathetic left coalition government in Germany in September 1998 boosted French hopes of a centre-left agenda across the EU which prioritised the fight against mass unemployment and social inequality. Ironically, it was the UK Labour government, which had gone much further than its French or German comrades in accepting neo-Thatcherite strictures on curbing public spending, which was most reluctant to embrace French proposals here.

As the 1990s drew to a close the French government looked relatively stable and the prospects of a strong left-wing challenge in the 2002 presidential elections looked better than for some time. Two big problems remained for the left. First, there was the central question of mass unemployment and whether the centre-left parties across the EU could succeed in injecting new urgency into the struggle to create jobs. Second, there was the political question of whether the PS's smaller coalition allies – especially the PCF and the Greens – could continue on a 'moderate' path without abandoning key principles or losing their separate identities and their appeal to their voters. But perhaps the biggest advantage which Jospin and the left enjoyed was the obvious and total disarray on the right of French politics. A bitterly divided right – divided over European integration, over racism, over economic and social policies, and over how to manage the period of 'cohabitation' between Chirac and Jospin – saw several new parties appear and disappear in the 1990s; the Gaullists split over whether or not to change the party's name and profile; the centrist UDF split over alliances with the FN. The FN itself suffered a damaging split when Le Pen's deputy, Bruno Mégret, led a sizeable section of the party in revolt against the old leader. As Chirac strongly endorsed European monetary union and attacked racism, his party tried to avoid collapse by abstaining on the question of the Euro, and Chirac found himself estranged from Charles de Gaulle – the former president's grandson – who announced he was willing to accept nomination as an FN candidate in the 1999 European elections.

Politics and society in France at the end of the twentieth century were diversified and fragmented with the potential for unforeseen challenges to the major parties being launched by new forces seeking to mobilise around the big issues of unemployment, Europe, and immigration. Although the logic of presidential elections has once again reinforced competition between right and left alliances, French society is scarcely less fragmented politically than in the days of the Fourth Republic.

Italy

From Mussolini's downfall in July 1943 – after which he fled behind German lines, presiding in name over a Nazi puppet regime – until final liberation from fascism on 25 April 1945, Italy was involved in civil conflict, although the increasing domination of the Germans over the remnants of Italian fascism allowed the conflict to be articulated by the anti-fascist side as a war of national liberation. Both the communist and Christian Democrat wings of the Italian resistance movement were to emphasise the patriotic nature of the anti-fascist struggle. Democratic patriotism was seen as a useful way of constructing a new Italian national identity which was not merely post-fascist but decidedly anti-fascist, thus denying the hard right patriotic legitimacy in post-1945 Italy.

Whilst such political myths played a positive role in binding some of the wounds of the previous 20 years, the reality was a lot more complex. An extreme right, nostalgic for Mussolini's rule, remained an enduring force in Italian politics; reorganised in December 1946 as the Italian Social Movement (MSI) in order to circumvent the constitutional ban on the old Fascist Party, it would wait for nearly 50 years until the collapse of the Christian democrat system of power in the early 1990s gave it an opportunity to expand its social base, entering the Italian government in May 1994 with five cabinet ministers.

The Italian people voted in June 1946 to abolish the monarchy. A new consti- tution established Italy as a democratic republic. The Christian Democrats (DC), under Alcide de Gasperi who became prime minister in December 1945, engi- neered (with Washington's approval) the expulsion of the Italian Communist Party (PCI) from the post-war government in 1947, and in 1948 the long period of Christian democratic dominance began in earnest when the party won gen- eral elections with nearly 50 per cent of the vote. The DC would remain in power, at the head of a series of mostly coalition governments, until its collapse amid massive corruption scandals in 1993–94.

Italian economic policy after 1945 sought regeneration through integration with the world capitalist economy. An 'open-doors' policy was pursued which emphasised competition in external markets. Northern Italian industry was encouraged to take advantage of low wages paid to southern migrant labour, and to act as the motor force of a growth drive led by exports. This policy neces- sitated internal migration from south to north, heavy external emigration of 'surplus' workers, weakened trade unions, and relative neglect of agriculture, especially the notoriously inefficient southern agricultural sector.

After 1953 the DC felt that political circumstances necessitated greater state intervention in the economy. Elections in 1953 saw the DC slide to 40 per cent, and the PCI increase its vote to nearly 23 per cent, eclipsing the Socialists on the left. Having failed in an attempt to manipulate the electoral law in its favour, the DC moved to entrench itself in power against the danger of an eventual left-wing victory at the polls by exploiting the full potential for patronage of giant state corporations created during Fascism – such as the Institute for Industrial Reconstruction (IRI) – or instituted by the DC – such as the State Hydrocarbons Corporation (ENI). Public works programmes contributed to the economic boom in the 1950s and 1960s. The DC under Amintore Fanfani brought the state and semi-state sectors under party control, patronage becoming a mainstay of the party's system of power. Public sector jobs were increasingly awarded on the basis of political loyalty rather than merit.

In the period from 1957 to the mid-1960s high growth rates transformed Italy into a modern industrial economy. But serious social and economic problems were exacerbated during the 1960s. In the cities appalling conditions and low wage rates prevailed for many of the hundreds of thousands of newly urbanised poor. The long-standing imbalance between the rich north and the underdevel- oped south became, if anything, even more critical as Italy emerged as a major economic power. Unemployment in the 1950s reached four times the European average. Social problems were neglected – provision of public housing was negli- gible and no national health service existed until the late 1970s.

From the mid-1960s when wages began to pick up, trade unions became more vocal. The DC responded to a rise in PCI support by seeking to isolate the Communists through incorporation of the Socialist Party (PSI) in coalition govern- ment from 1963. This move was facilitated by the election of a more liberal-minded

Pope, John XXIII, in 1958; his predecessor, Pius XII, had vigorously opposed any opening by the DC to the PSI. The new coalition merely encouraged expectations of social reforms which the PSI was unable to deliver whilst the DC controlled the purse-strings. In the longer term the PSI was drawn into the web of patronage and corruption which came to characterise the Italian ruling elite, a process which was facilitated by Bettino Craxi's election as PSI leader in 1976.

By 1969 the economic miracle was in trouble. Attempts to buy social peace and political stability by expanding the numbers in higher education and in the state bureaucracy, and by paying hidden subsidies to dependent social groups (in the form of 'invalidity' payments to semi-employed small farmers, for example) could not prevent a social explosion in 1969. The so-called 'Hot Autumn' of that year saw massive industrial unrest, with more hours lost in strikes than in any other country in the developed world.

The early 1970s saw some social reforms which strengthened workers' rights, establishing a new institutionalised role for the trade unions. The perceived shift in the balance of power towards the labour movement, together with continuing good election results for the PCI, provoked an extreme right-wing backlash: neo-fascist terrorists bombed civilian targets from 1969, hoping to provoke political chaos and calls for an authoritarian government, and both far-right and far-left terrorism plagued Italian politics during the 1970s and 1980s.

The 1970s saw social change. Despite opposition from both the DC and the Vatican, a majority of Italian voters approved the legalisation of divorce (1974) and abortion (1981) in referenda. Together with evidence of falling attendances at church services, these developments highlighted the widespread secularisation of Italian society. The election of a conservative Pope, John Paul II, in 1978 failed to reverse the trends. During the 1970s a large and vocal feminist movement campaigned successfully for changes in family law and in the laws on rape, which had effectively condemned women to second-class citizenship. However, it was to prove more difficult to change societal attitudes, especially in the conservative south.

In the wake of the social and economic change which characterised the early 1970s, electoral support for the Italian left grew impressively. The PCI scored more than 34 per cent in elections in 1976, within 4 per cent of the DC. The PCI, pioneers of independent-minded reform-communism long before Gorbachev, called for an 'historic compromise' with the DC. A powerful array of forces – the economic and financial establishment, the Church, the DC and its allies, the security services, the American embassy, the Mafia, and the shadowy far-right masonic lodge known as P2 (to which nearly 1,000 of the most influential figures in Italian public life belonged) – opposed the election of any left-wing government. According to PCI leader Enrico Berlinguer, a successful democratic reform of the Italian state, to tackle corruption and the Mafia and to strengthen democratic institutions, could not be undertaken by the Communists alone in the face of such opposition. It required the two big parties to work together. If the DC would commit itself to political reform, the PCI would agree to postpone socialist measures. A period of 'national solidarity' opened during which the DC, under Giulio

Andreotti, continued to exclude the Communists from government, but obtained their support in parliament in return for consultation. Such a formula caused considerable tension within both parties: the right wing of the DC resented and opposed any 'legitimation' of the Communists; and the left wing of the PCI feared that their party would simply be used by the establishment to undermine the gains of the labour movement, and then be cast aside. The murder in 1978 of leading DC reformer Aldo Moro, an advocate of dialogue with the PCI, was followed by a turn to the right. Moro was kidnapped and murdered by the left-wing terrorist group, the Red Brigades. Subsequent revelations suggested that elements of the state security services and some of his own DC colleagues were implicated in the events leading to his death.

The 1980s opened with the PCI back in opposition and very much in isolation. The party's loss of any sense of strategic direction was bitterly exposed after the tragic death of its leader, Berlinguer, in 1984; thereafter, open factionalism gradually robbed the party of its once proud unity. The party's defeat in a referendum on wage cuts in 1985, and its inability to halt job losses or privatisations, was followed by an electoral set-back in 1987, when the PCI share of the vote fell back to 26.6 per cent.

In 1983 the DC agreed to the appointment of Socialist leader Bettino Craxi as prime minister, although Christian Democrats continued to dominate the cabinet. Craxi had led the PSI steadily to the right, acquiring a reputation for fierce anti-communism and ruthless pragmatism. He sought to project the PSI as a decisive force for change, attractive to the young professionals and middle classes and contemptuous of socialist ideology and political moralism – which he associated with the PCI. Under his leadership, the Socialists played a double role in government. They claimed to be a more modern alternative to both the Communists and Christian Democrats, yet cooperated closely with the latter in keeping the former isolated. They demanded economic rationalisation, yet became ever more embroiled in the system of corruption and patronage with which they came to be as closely associated as the Christian Democrats. Craxi's party succeeded in winning wealthy backers, such as the media mogul Silvio Berlusconi. Nevertheless, for all its new influence and powers of patronage, the PSI was unable to exceed around 15 per cent of the popular vote.

By the early 1990s the Italian political system was showing signs of considerable strain. No real change of government had been achieved since 1947. The Mafia remained a powerful threat, not only to democracy and the rule of law, but to the very survival of the Italian state. The system of political patronage, based upon high levels of public spending, was difficult to sustain in times of economic recession and Italy entered the 1990s with the highest level of public debt in western Europe. The decision of PCI leader Achille Occhetto to rename and relaunch the party as the post-communist Democratic Party of the Left (PDS) in February 1991 was intended as an initiative to break the log-jam and create a new centre-left majority. In the event the party split, with radicals leaving to form the Communist Refoundation Party, and a divided left suffered further losses in elections in 1992.

Meanwhile a revolt against government corruption got under way in the north. The populist Northern Leagues, centred in wealthy Milan and led by the outspoken Umberto Bossi, exploited the well-documented connections between government parties and the Mafia to accuse Rome of draining the north of resources and pumping them into the south, where the Christian Democrats had their power base. The Leagues veered between calls for a new federal Italy, and threats of outright northern secession. Appealing to the self-interest of the northern middle classes, but capturing working-class support also with a heady mixture of regionalist fervour and hostility towards 'immigrants' from the south, the Leagues won nearly 9 per cent of the total national vote in 1992.

In 1991–94 investigations into political corruption by a number of outstandingly brave Italian magistrates – their resolve strengthened, if anything, by the Mafia's assassination of several of their colleagues – revealed massive networks of bribery and theft of public funds and ensnared hundreds of leading politicians. Virtually the entire ruling political elite was exposed as corrupt. Left-wing hopes of a thorough democratic revolution, perhaps involving a move to the left, were dashed by a growing exasperation with all politicians and with politics in general – expressed in a longing for a 'saviour' from without who would smash the old system. A popular referendum on electoral reform in June 1993 produced a massive majority in favour of a move away from proportional representation – seen as leading to weak and corrupt cabinets. Serious discussion of the implications of various reforms tended to get brushed aside by a tidal wave of negative feeling towards the entire political class.

Local elections in November 1993 produced victory for a left-wing alliance, led by the PDS. However, a huge increase in the neo-fascist vote was also recorded; the neo-fascist MSI was visibly replacing the crumbling Christian Democrats as the main right-wing force in the south of the country. The DC was now disintegrating, with a rump renaming and relaunching itself early in 1994 as the Italian Popular Party (PPI), and several other factions giving birth to smaller right-wing parties.

In February 1994 Silvio Berlusconi launched a new political movement, *Forza Italia,* with the intention of blocking an anticipated left-wing victory in general elections scheduled for March. The movement was aggressively right-wing, preaching free market economics, business success, anti-communism, and promising instant cures to the country's economic and political crises. It benefited from the backing of Berlusconi's vast media and business empire. Although Berlusconi was associated with the old regime – a member of the P2 masonic lodge, and a friend to many of the disgraced political elite – he managed to project an image of success and dynamism. In alliance with the Northern Leagues and the neo-fascists, his movement harnessed a popular mood of weariness with political squabbling, desire for strong government, and longing for economic prosperity, to inflict a heavy defeat on the left-wing alliance in March; Berlusconi subsequently became prime minister.

His cabinet was the first in any European country since 1945 to include fascist ministers, causing concern in many European capitals. Moreover, it represented an unprecedented concentration of political, economic, and media power in the hands of one man. Ultimately, the contradictions of this position were to lead to Berlusconi's fall from office after less than one year – when the Northern Leagues withdrew their support. An interim government of non-party technocrats, led by Lamberto Dini, was appointed by President Scalfaro to lead Italy from the end of 1994. Berlusconi was subsequently implicated in a series of corruption and bribery scandals, all the time alleging that he was the victim of smears by 'communist' judges and public prosecutors – and refusing to relinquish the leadership of his increasingly volatile *Forza Italia* movement.

In April 1996 a centre-left coalition of parties led by the PDS – the so-called Olive Tree – won elections. Italy's first government including former communists in senior ministerial positions was formed, although the PDS offered the prime minister's job to a moderate and highly respected former Christian Democrat, Romano Prodi. Over the next two years the Prodi government chalked up considerable success in preparing Italy for entry to the single European currency, beginning the slow reform of the Italian bureaucracy and, to a lesser extent, tackling the reform of the country's bloated pensions system. It relied, however, for its parliamentary majority on the small Party of Communist Refoundation (PRC). The price the PRC exacted was a commitment to move towards a 35-hour working week (French-style) and a watering down of social spending cuts which the PRC feared would hit the poor and the vulnerable. Never that enthusiastic about the European single currency, the PRC saw its role as ensuring that the price of preparing Italy for the 'Euro' did not fall on the shoulders of the working class.

In 1997 the PDS leader Massimo D'Alema persuaded his party to move towards the centre, attacking trade union leaders and proclaiming his ambition to lead a 'Blairite' moderate, centrist party. In early 1998 the PDS changed its name to the 'Left Democrats' (DS), replaced the hammer and sickle symbol with a red rose, and even encouraged speculation that its ultimate ambition was to unite all moderates in a US-style Democratic Party.

In October 1998 D'Alema achieved a major step forward towards his ambition for his party when he replaced Prodi as prime minister. He headed a coalition government which, though based on the previous Olive Tree forces, was broader in its appeal – including both former conservatives led by ex-President Francesco Cossiga, and a group of Marxists who had broken away from the PRC over that party's opposition to the centre-left government. As the 1990s ended, further splits and realignments in Italian politics were inevitable before the DS could realise its long-term goal of constructing a large centrist party which subscribed to a Italian version of Tony Blair's 'Third Way' for the centre-left (see below).

Federal Republic of Germany

After the defeat of the Nazi regime in 1945, Germany found itself under the military and political sway of the four liberating allied powers – France, the UK, the

USA, and the USSR. Although the preservation of German unity remained on the agenda in the immediate post-war period, Western reluctance to accept Soviet demands that any united Germany should be neutral and demilitarised, together with the dynamics of the Cold War which soon developed, effectively sealed the division of the country.

The new Federal Republic of Germany (FRG) adopted a Basic Law in May 1949. This provided for a parliamentary democracy, with a cabinet government, accountable to parliament. The country was divided into states, or *Länder*, governed by their own parliaments and enjoying considerable powers. At the federal level, a two-chamber parliament consisted of a lower house *(Bundestag)*, directly elected every four years by the people, and a much smaller upper house *(Bundesrat)*, comprising representatives of the various state governments. A federal president is elected every five years by the lower house of parliament, augmented by an equal number of *Länder* representatives. The head of government, the chancellor, enjoys considerable authority. A dual electoral system provides for half the seats in the *Bundestag* to be filled on the basis of a constituency-based vote, and half on the basis of a party list system. However, parties polling less than 5 per cent of the total national vote are excluded. This measure, it was claimed, would ensure stability and governability; it also penalises smaller parties and narrows the range of views which are represented in parliament.

One of the first tasks to be faced by the FRG was de-Nazification – the removal from positions of authority and bringing to justice of those guilty of crimes under the Nazi dictatorship. However de-Nazification soon fell victim to the logic of the Cold War. Although some 13 million people had been screened by 1949, less than 2,000 were considered major offenders. As the USSR came to be regarded as the new enemy, and the FRG as being on the front line of the new East–West potential conflict, fierce anti-communism, rather than thoroughgoing catharsis *vis-à-vis* the Nazi past, came to characterise the political life of the FRG. The Communist Party of Germany (KPD) was banned in 1956 – although it soon resurfaced under a new name, the DKP.

Until 1969 the political life of the FRG was dominated by the Christian Democratic Union (CDU) and its conservative ally in Bavaria, the Christian Social Union (CSU). The CDU/CSU was a centre-right force, firmly committed to the Western alliance under American leadership and strongly anti-communist. Although it embraced capitalist economic rationale and was committed to private sector-led economic growth, it also sought a measure of social partnership between employers and trade unions, and articulated the concept of a social market economy. This was in essence a kind of paternalistic capitalism, in which the state assumed some responsibility for regulating prices in the housing and farm sectors, for social insurance, and for offering protection to the lower income groups.

The CDU leader Konrad Adenauer was chancellor from September 1949 until October 1963. The period witnessed the consolidation of CDU supremacy as the party led the FRG through a sustained economic boom. The model of economic management adopted allocated huge powers to an independent central bank, the Bundesbank, which was charged with keeping inflation under control at all costs.

A strongly centralised trade union movement, the DGB, was enlisted by the state to assist in guaranteeing labour discipline in return for a recognised place at the negotiating table; collective bargaining over wages was regulated by law.

The period of economic success and capitalist stabilisation and the growing consolidation of CDU power forced a historic rethink within the ranks of the main opposition party, the Social Democratic Party (SPD). Moving towards the centre, the SPD dropped its support for widespread nationalisation of the economy, accepted the capitalist market economy, and abandoned its militant secularism, accepting religious instruction in schools. This process came to a head at the SPD congress in Bad Godesberg in 1959, when the party turned its back on Marxism and embraced reformism. The following year saw the SPD effectively accept the main outlines of Adenauer's foreign policy.

In 1960–66 the CDU governed in coalition with the centrist Free Democrats (FDP). As elsewhere in western Europe, the decade saw considerable social and cultural change, which presented a challenge to the CDU. In 1963 Adenauer was succeeded as chancellor by Ludwig Erhard. Policy divisions within the government, the growing confidence of the SPD (which elected Willy Brandt as its leader in 1963), and the easing of the Cold War in the 1960s all contributed to a CDU loss of confidence in 1966 which was followed by a period of 'grand coalition' between the CDU–CSU and the SPD. In 1969 the popularity of Brandt's policy of improved relations with the East *(Ostpolitik)* saw the SPD clinch victory. An SPD–FDP coalition followed with Brandt as chancellor. The SPD remained in power until 1982, Brandt being succeeded as chancellor by Helmut Schmidt in 1974. The 1970s saw substantially improved relations with the USSR and eastern Europe, including the GDR.

Whilst consensus amongst the main parties, political stability, and mounting acceptance of the FRG internationally, combined with substantial economic recovery, represented a success story, there was of course another side to West German life. Revolt against the stifling conformism and orthodoxy of politics and society was commonplace in the late 1960s and early 1970s amongst young people, and especially students. In its most extreme manifestation, this led to urban terrorism by far left groups, such as the Baader-Meinhof gang. The heavy-handed response of the authorities included much-criticised police measures, and the introduction of notorious laws banning left-wing radicals from holding public sector jobs. Such measures caused concern amongst intellectuals and civil liberties groups about the extent to which authoritarian impulses still characterised the official response to political dissent.

In the 1970s the FRG, in common with its partners throughout western Europe, suffered the effects of the oil crisis and recession. A nuclear energy programme was one response to this situation. Opposition to nuclear energy, to growing involvement in NATO, and to the environmental pollution caused by industrial growth, produced a vocal Green movement in the early 1980s. The Greens soon established a reputation as amongst the most politically effective and formidable of European environmental movements, heralding a new brand of politics which soon found echoes in other European countries. Mobilisation against NATO plans to modernise nuclear weapons on FRG soil gave the Greens a popular cause, and in 1983 they entered the national parliament.

In 1982 the FDP moved to the right, responding to a combination of circumstances – the ascendancy of 'new right' ideas elsewhere, the renewed Cold War following the Soviet invasion of Afghanistan and martial law in Poland, and clashes with the SPD over the funding of welfare programmes. As a result, the FDP brought down the SPD-led government and returned the CDU, under Helmut Kohl, to power. The new government reduced social welfare spending and increased incentives to the private sector. Throughout the 1980s the Kohl administration's primary objective was to maintain the country's economic standing in the face of international recession and mounting unemployment at home. The FRG had established itself as a highly successful exporter, dominating the markets of its neighbours. Not surprisingly, the Kohl governments would display support for the completion of a unified European market, and by the end of the 1980s European political union had become a key and strategic policy goal.

The collapse of the GDR presented the FRG with unanticipated challenges and opportunities at the beginning of the 1990s. Economic union of the two Germanies in July 1990 was followed by political union in October. Kohl's promises of instant economic improvements to the people of the former GDR, the prestige he enjoyed as the man who presided over unification, and the hesitancy and uncertainty of the SPD in the face of unification, all contributed to a CDU victory in all-German elections held in December 1990. In the early 1990s the SPD moved somewhat to the left, voicing well-founded (but at the time unpopular) concerns about the pace and direction of German unification, and fielding the socialist SPD party chairman, Oskar Lafontaine, as candidate for the post of federal chancellor in 1994. In the event Kohl, still buoyed by his image as the architect of both German and European unification, led the CDU and its allies to another victory, although their parliamentary majority was slashed. Despite that success, it was becoming clear that united Germany faced a number of difficulties which were to blight the last years of Kohl's reign.

Unification has plainly not involved a fusion between two equal partners; rather it has resembled a takeover of the GDR by the FRG – symbolised by the simple extension of the FRG's Basic Law to cover the GDR, rather than the promulgation of a new Constitution for the united Germany. The impression of West German arrogance and insensitivity led to resentment amongst those strata in the former East Germany which suffered most economically. A backlash in the east against perceived neglect by Bonn has seen a steady level of support for the former GDR Communists, now renamed the Party of Democratic Socialism (PDS). In early 1994 the PDS scored impressive local government gains. In general elections in September 1998 (which ended Kohl's period in power), they not only retained a level of support in the east of above 20 per cent, but surprised the political establishment in Bonn by exceeding the 5 per cent barrier on a national level and winning more than 35 seats in the *Bundestag;* they followed this within weeks by re-entering the government of an east German *Länd* in coalition with the SPD, establishing a considerable measure of legitimacy for the PDS. The heavy-handed approach of Kohl and the CDU to the former Communists during the 1990s, involving threats to proscribe the PDS and repeated insults to their electorate, had clearly backfired on the CDU. This, combined with the failure of the promised economic miracle in the east, resulted in heavy losses there for the CDU in 1998.

Moreover, unification imposed heavy economic costs on the German economy at a time of recession. Many Westerners were unwilling to pay higher taxes or suffer reductions in living standards in order to help subsidise the recovery in the east. Reports of resentment towards Easterners, stereotyped as lazy or parasitical, underlined the enormity of the effort required to build a truly unified nation.

Unification also saw an alarming rise in neo-Nazi violence and racist propaganda, with an escalation of murderous attacks upon immigrants, Jews, homosexuals, and other vulnerable groups, calling into question the willingness or ability of the authorities to respond decisively to right-wing violence. Whilst electoral support for the far right remains as yet slight, the potential for such groups to exploit economic hardship in order to undermine democracy clearly exists.

Finally, the costs of unity have cast a shadow over German enthusiasm for European union. The period 1993–98 saw a significant drop in public support for the single European currency, the Euro – Chancellor Kohl's most cherished project. Although Germany remains fully committed to European economic, monetary and political union, the growing sense of uncertainty engulfing Europe and the growing economic burden at home mean that it will calculate carefully whether it can afford to foot the bill for European union. Germany, for example, made a net contribution of around DM25 billion (£10 billion) to the European Union budget in 1994 – a figure which could treble if poorer states in the east become full EU members.

All of these problems and concerns, plus a general sense of weariness with the ageing Kohl after so long in office, contributed to a spectacular turnabout in fortunes for Germany's left-wing parties in federal elections held in September 1998. The SPD had prepared the way for its resurrection by endorsing as its candidate for chancellor the media-friendly and moderate regional party leader, Gerhard Schröder. He fought a clever campaign, promising modest reforms and coining the slogan 'the New Centre' to signify his moderate credentials. He also permitted speculation of a possible post-election deal with the CDU to form a so-called Grand Coalition to grow, distancing himself from the scaremongering on the right wing about the effects of a 'Red–Green' government between the SPD and the Greens (or possibly even the east German PDS). In the event the scale of the CDU's defeat saw the SPD and Greens win a comfortable overall majority in the *Bundestag*, with the PDS also doing well.

The new government took office in October 1998 on a centre-left platform, but one with many radical elements. It should not be forgotten that this was the first time ever that the SPD had gone into government with a coalition partner which was not to its right in terms of ideology. Oskar Lafontaine, the left-wing chairman of the SPD, became finance minister and immediately began calling for interventionist policies to tackle mass unemployment and social injustice.

Joschka Fischer, Green Party leader and an enthusiastic European federalist, became minister for foreign affairs. The government's platform pledged that every economic policy would be judged on whether it reduced unemployment. Tax reform aimed at reducing the burden on low- and middle-income families and at making the rich pay more as many tax write-offs were removed. Germany's citizenship laws were to be changed to allow millions of immigrants to acquire new rights, and the country was to receive its first ever anti-discrimination law. All nuclear power stations would be shut down, gradually but irreversibly, and green taxes on petrol, electricity and gas were pledged. A new partnership with unions and employers to fight unemployment was promised. In summary, it was clear that Germany had taken a clear move to the left.

Needless to say, the new government also faced huge problems. In the face of massive unemployment, a budgetary situation inherited from Kohl which Schröder described as 'a mess', and continuing social malaise, the centre-left was rather less united on firm policies than on rhetoric. The clear preference of the finance minister, Lafontaine, for Keynesian-style interventionist policies designed to boost jobs and tackle social injustice presaged a struggle with not only the Bundesbank but also the powerful European Central Bank. Lafontaine, speaking for many of the centre-left in Europe, called for the statutes of both to be redrafted so that they had an obligation to tackle unemployment and marginalisa-tion – and not merely, as at present, to seek low inflation regardless of the social costs. The bankers dug their heels in at the start of 1999, refusing to budge and accusing the politicians of 'interference'. The fact that such strictures seemed to have the backing of the more 'moderate' or Blairite wing of the SPD itself (includ-ing Schröder) meant that divisions with the new German government over basic policy and ideological issues were almost inevitable from the outset. In Spring 1999 Lafontaine paid the price for this radicalism; publicly chastised by the chan-cellor for his outspokenness, he resigned from all government and party posts. His resignation dismayed the SPD left and seemed a major victory for the bankers.

Secondly, tensions were present from the beginning within the Green Party. Joschka Fischer had always represented the more pragmatic wing of the Greens – the so-called 'realos', who had faced continuing internal opposition from the Greens' fundamentalist wing, or 'fundis'. Fischer's embrace of compromise and moderation alienated many Greens; for example, many were unwilling to accept a long-term timetable for the elimination of nuclear power and were resolutely opposed to Germany's membership of NATO and to the deployment of German troops in peace-keeping operations abroad (both policies which Fischer, in his capacity as foreign minister, would be personally responsible for overseeing). Fischer's support for NATO's bombing of Yugoslavia in Spring 1999 led to much protest and soul-searching within the Greens. Nevertheless, most Green MPs seemed to believe that the price for bringing the government down over this issue would be electoral annihilation.

Thirdly, tensions were perceptible from the beginning over European policy. On the eve of Germany's EU Presidency in January 1999, Fischer, a European federalist, outlined an ambitious plan for a democratic and federal, socially just and ecologically friendly, European Union with a single constitution, government, army and foreign policy. Undoubtedly, many in the German government share this vision. Nonetheless, Schröder has sought on occasions to rein in his more idealistic colleagues and tone down talk of a single European state. Partly for tactical reasons, and partly because of his own innate pragmatism, he has preferred to stress national advantage over strategic vision. Whilst assuring Germany's allies that he has no intention of allowing the country to become semi-detached from the European project or to turn inwards on itself, it seems likely that a more pragmatic and self-confident approach to European policy will characterise Schröder's government, with politicians such as Fischer providing elements of ideological impetus and moral conscience.

Finally, the continuing resilience of the east German PDS provides both a parliamentary focus for opposition to the Schröder government, should it stray too far towards the centre, and a point of pressure on the government should it fail to deliver greater prosperity in the east.

United Kingdom

Alone among the major west European democracies, the United Kingdom entered the post-war era without having to embark on the search for new political institutions. The UK had experienced neither fascist dictatorship nor enemy occupation (apart from the Channel Islands). Nor, for that matter, had it experienced a far-reaching democratic political revolution in modern times; a hallmark of the UK political system has been its gradualist evolution, embracing democratic reforms without ever fully shedding its aristocratic and elitist origins. The UK, for example, does not have a written constitution; the upper house of its two-chamber parliament is an unelected House of Lords; and although its constitutional monarchy is politically powerless and largely symbolic, the prime minister, or head of the executive, can exercise considerable powers of patronage and decision-making in the name of the Crown prerogative (i.e. outside parliamentary accountability). The political system has been praised for stability and durability, but criticised for secrecy, elitism, and centralisation of power.

In 1945 the UK had entered an era of long-term decline as a world power, although the extent of this was only to become apparent later. Although Conservative prime minister Winston Churchill presided over victory in the Second World War, the radicalising and levelling effect of the war upon British society, and the enormous hopes raised for social progress in the post-war era, delivered election victory in 1945 to the Labour Party, led by Clement Attlee. Committed in theory to wholesale nationalisation of the economy, Labour in practice followed a much more moderate course, embracing the mixed economy but dedicating itself to social amelioration through welfare provision and wealth redistribution. The Labour government carried out a number of major social reforms, including, most famously, the foundation of a National Health Service to provide free and comprehensive health coverage to all. In many respects Labour was building on earlier reports produced by the national coalition government of the war years (and enjoying Conservative and Liberal support) which had recommended the formation of a welfare state to provide health care and education, and insurance coverage 'from the cradle to the grave'. The Attlee government also strove to deliver full employment.

Inevitably, the cost of such measures forced a devaluation of the currency in 1949 and a reduction in the UK's overseas and defence commitments. The period from 1945 through to the 1960s saw the UK withdraw from, and preside over the dismantling of, its empire. Decolonisation, and close and growing dependence on the USA, tended to dominate British foreign policy. The UK mostly stood aside from efforts at European cooperation in the 1950s.

Internal divisions within the Labour Party over cuts in social welfare spending and foreign policy led to the return of the Conservative Party to power in 1951. Four subsequent Conservative prime ministers – Churchill (until April 1955), Anthony Eden (April 1955–January 1957), Harold Macmillan (January 1957–October 1963) and Alec Douglas-Home (October 1963–October 1964) – presided over administrations which followed consensus politics – accepting the welfare state, pursuing stability and partnership between government, employers, and the trade unions, and seeking to build upon economic growth. Realisation that industrial growth necessitated entry to European markets led to an application to join the EEC in 1961, which was vetoed by France until 1969.

Following the collapse of the Conservative government in 1964, amid economic woes and moral scandal, Labour returned to power. The new prime minister, Harold Wilson, captured the imagination of the country with a call for a scientific-technological revolution. The 1960s saw far-reaching social change. The rise of a youth culture and the challenge of the feminist movement confronted old, traditional values. The so-called sexual revolution saw greater access to birth control, while a consumer boom partially transformed the nature of domestic labour for many women by bringing labour-saving machinery within their budgets. Educational reforms included the foundation of the Open University, extending the possibility of participation in third-level education.

Despite a generally favourable economic situation, Labour lost in 1970 and a Conservative government, led by Edward Heath, took office. The 1970s were to prove a disastrous decade for the UK economically. Recession and the impact of the oil crisis forced power cuts and the introduction of a three-day working week in late 1973; wages and prices were temporarily frozen. Conflict with the trade unions over Heath's 1971 Industrial Relations Act culminated in a miners' strike which eventually brought his government down in 1974.

Back in power between 1974 and 1979, Labour faced mounting economic problems. High inflation, faltering productivity, rising unemployment, and the widespread perception that trade unions enjoyed too much power bedevilled efforts at recovery. Labour was forced increasingly to borrow heavily from the International Monetary Fund and to plead with the unions for social peace. By 1979 the Labour government had ceded effective control over its economic policy to the IMF, and had to introduce monetarist policies which bitterly divided the

Labour Party. The Conservatives then fought an aggressive campaign which returned Margaret Thatcher to power as the country's first woman prime minister.

Until her removal from office in November 1990, Thatcher, a free market right-winger, presided over a series of governments which set out to change the face of the UK, abandoning consensus politics. In her economic policy she sought to reduce public ownership, embarking on a sustained programme of privatisation of nationalised industries; she cut income tax, raised indirect taxes, and removed controls on prices and wages, leaving the free market to determine their levels. A monetarist policy saw public spending attacked and efforts to control the money supply prioritised. The trade unions were targeted by measures which sought, for example, to reduce their right to secondary picketing and to regulate their internal affairs.

Politically, Thatcher earned a reputation as a British nationalist and a centraliser of power. Hostile to demands from Scotland and Wales for regional devolution, she considerably reduced the powers of local government. Engaging in fiercely nationalistic rhetoric, she attacked the threat to UK sovereignty allegedly posed by the European Community. Returned to power in 1983, following victory over Argentina in the Falklands War, she cultivated strong personalistic leadership. Calls for a return to 'traditional family values' and attacks on the rights of homosexuals and other groups brought forth accusations of moral authoritarianism. However, the rhetoric and the reality were not always matched. By the end of the 1980s the economy was again in recession. Manufacturing output had decreased considerably, and evidence suggested that both regional and social class imbalances had grown. Inflation had indeed been reduced. The trade unions had been greatly weakened (perhaps her most lasting achievement). But nothing like the promised economic miracle to restore lost national greatness had materialised. Unemployment, which had stood at one million in 1979, had by 1990 reached between three and four million.

Thatcher fell from power when her own party became convinced that the vastly unpopular poll tax, which she had introduced to finance local government, would cost it the next election. Her successor, John Major, retained power with a much reduced majority in 1992. His government continued with Thatcherite policies in most spheres, but was plagued by indecisive leadership, splits over policy (especially on European unity), various moral and political scandals, and a general air of incompetence and loss of direction. The Conservatives' share of the vote fell to 27 per cent in local government elections in May 1994, and they suffered serious losses in European Parliament elections the following month when their 28 per cent vote was their worst national election result for more than a century. The next three years saw the Major government practically paralysed by growing internal party splits over Europe, mounting corruption and sleaze allegations against Conservative MPs and government ministers, and apparent mishandling of important policy issues such as food safety and the fate of British agriculture. In the general election of May 1997 the Conservatives faced a resurgent and revitalised Labour Party, and were undermined in some constituencies by defections to the fiercely Euro-sceptic

Referendum Party, founded by the millionaire businessman, Sir James Goldsmith. As Labour swept to power with its biggest ever parliamentary majority, the Conservatives lost nearly half of their House of Commons seats, failing to win a single seat in either Scotland or Wales. In the aftermath of the defeat, and a divisive leadership battle, John Major was succeeded as party leader by the young and decidedly uncharismatic William Hague. Hague further alienated moderate Conservatives, such as former cabinet ministers Kenneth Clark and Michael Heseltine, by shifting the party to the right, pledging opposition to the European single currency. This was precisely the sort of Euro-sceptical policy which pro-European Conservatives felt had lost them the 1997 election by ceding the centre ground in politics to Labour.

The 1980s was a traumatic decade for Labour. In the early 1980s, under the influence of its left wing, the party embraced policies such as opposition to membership of the EEC and support for unilateral nuclear disarmament which proved unpopular with the electorate. Internal divisions culminated in a split in 1981, when several Labour right-wingers formed the breakaway Social Democratic Party (SDP). This short-lived phenomenon eventually merged with the Liberals to form the Liberal Democrats in the late 1980s. However, the split certainly damaged Labour. Under first Neil Kinnock (1983–92) and then John Smith (1992–94), Labour sought to modernise and moderate its image and programme, supporting European integration, accepting that an immediate reversal of all Conservative economic changes was not feasible, and seeking to appeal to the middle classes. Defeat in 1992 was a bitter blow to the hopes of Labour's modernisers, but by the mid-1990s under its new leader, Tony Blair, it appeared a more credible party of government than it had done for many years.

By the time a new Labour government took office in May 1997 the UK faced several formidable challenges. While some of the country's severest economic problems – such as endemic mass unemployment – could be said to reflect international realities, in several other respects the UK was falling behind its partners and competitors: for example, in education and training, investment in public transport and infrastructure, and provision of social services. The Conservatives, kept in power due to their dominance in the heavily populated south of England and never polling more than 43 per cent of the vote since 1979, had bequeathed a highly centralised political system from which many people felt alienated, especially in the north of England and in Scotland and Wales. The new Labour government was determined to honour its election pledges to devolve power to regional assemblies in Scotland and Wales, as well as to strengthen local government in England, before a build-up of frustration might threaten the unity of the UK. Labour also faced demands for modernisation of the British political system, including the difficult issue of electoral reform. Meanwhile, in Northern Ireland, murderous sectarian violence, which had first erupted in 1969, had abated somewhat in the period 1994–97 as dialogue between the British and Irish governments, Northern Irish politicians, and some of the terrorist organisations involved in the conflict had got under way.

When Labour came to power this so-called peace process was looking increasingly fragile. The prime minister, Tony Blair, made the search for a agreed settlement of the province's conflict a top priority of his government. Indeed, the urgency and energy with which Blair addressed the crisis in Northern Ireland won him respect. In April 1998 a peace agreement was finally signed between the Irish and British governments, the two main Northern Ireland political parties – SDLP and Ulster Unionists – representatives of Sinn Féin (political wing of the IRA) and of Loyalist political parties, and several other minor parties. This agreement provided for a directly elected NI assembly, a power-sharing executive led by a first minister and including all democratic parties which agreed to implement the agreement in full, a strong north–south dimension, and a Council of the Isles involving the British and Irish parliaments and the assemblies of Scotland, Wales and Northern Ireland. Opposed bitterly by hard-line republicans and unionists, the agreement was ratified by clear majorities both north and south of the Irish border in May 1998. The moderate attitude of the Ulster Unionist leader, David Trimble, had been crucial in securing the support of most Ulster Protestants for the agreement, and Blair and the then Northern Ireland secretary of state, Mo Mowlam, had played key roles in securing Trimble's support. Pro-agreement forces won a majority of seats in the new Northern Ireland assembly in elections held in June 1998. The peace process, however, faced horrendous obstacles. A brutal bomb attack by renegade IRA members in Omagh, Co. Tyrone, in August 1998 left 29 people dead and over 300 injured; although the bombing failed in its immediate purpose – to derail the peace process and provoke renewed sectarian conflict – it underlined the need for decommissioning of terrorist arms before admitting their political wings to the new Northern Ireland government. On this point, the peace process repeatedly stalled in late 1998 and early 1999; and the early release of terrorist prisoners from prison, under the agreement, further increased suspicion and unease in the province. The Labour government had nevertheless achieved a huge amount in moving the process forward in just 18 months and Blair's personal commitment to making the peace agreement stick remained high.

In many other policy areas the Blair government was to prove a government of contradictions. A cornerstone of 'New Labour' thinking was that the party had finally won office by appealing to the centre ground – a centre ground which had allegedly accepted the privatisations, anti-union policies, and reductions in personal taxation of the Thatcherite years but wanted a more caring version of capitalism. Yet it was far from clear how policies which mounted a real challenge to poverty, inequality and social exclusion could be pursued if the government was unwilling to raise the revenue to pay for them; and Labour's acceptance of the spending constraints of its Conservative predecessor was to lead to much disillusionment on the part of its traditional supporters. It was also part of the New Labour mantra that the party had lost four successive elections partly because of indiscipline on its own part, the hostility of the tabloid media, and its loss of touch with the public mood. Yet Blair's attempts to ensure that such perceived shortcomings were not repeated were also to expose contradictions at the heart of government. By the end of its first two years in office the Blair government faced accusations of top-heavy centralisation of power and decision-making within the Labour party; too cosy a relationship with the (traditionally) right-wing press, especially those papers owned by media mogul Rupert Murdoch; too close a relationship to big business, as Labour apparently tried to supplant the Conservatives as the favoured party of the rich and powerful; and a tendency towards government by 'spin doctors'. The contradictions and problems the government faced can be illustrated by a brief look at some policy areas.

Labour had come to power promising to be a radical and reforming government which would modernise and democratise Britain's rather outdated constitution. Commentators were soon able to point to hesitations and contradictions. The party sought to reform the House of Lords – Britain's unelected second chamber – but whilst legislating for the abolition of hereditary peers' voting rights in the face of Conservative opposition, it drew back from proposing a democratically elected Senate. Blair's strong personal support for the monarchy meant that any republican views of Labour politicians were fully reined in. Deeply divided on electoral reform, Labour did legislate for forms of proportional representation for the Scottish and Welsh assemblies and for European Parliament elections; but its insistence on a closed party list system for the latter provoked criticism of centralised control over the party's candidates and a desire to stamp out dissent. In government, the party moved with less speed to introduce freedom of information legislation and other measures to promote 'active citizenship' than had been promised when in opposition.

Perhaps the government's most undeniable achievement in constitutional reform was the establishment of a Scottish parliament with tax-raising powers and a Welsh assembly with narrower legislative powers. Both proposals were approved by voters in Scotland and Wales in referenda held in September 1997 – by an overwhelming majority of Scots and by a slender majority of voters in Wales, which had always been more closely integrated with England. Both bodies came into being in 1999, following direct elections in May. Labour also promised a directly elected mayor for London and the possibility of directly elected mayors for other large English cities, and of regional assemblies. However, once again the party drew back from more far-reaching proposals. The Welsh assembly was relatively toothless. The party fought shy of suggestions from the Liberal Democrats and others that democratic decentralisation logically necessitated introduction of an English parliament and a fully federal system of government. And, in the face of growing Scottish nationalism, Blair sought to impose centralised control on the Scottish Labour Party and to seek ways of drawing back from the full implications of devolution.

On economic and social policy the government also faced some contradictions and hesitancies. Its attempts to reform the welfare state smacked of a mixture of truly radical measures, such as proposals designed to make it easier for single parents to enter the labour force, and to encourage young workers to find jobs, and penny-pinching proposals which even the Conservatives had not sought to introduce, such as making it harder for many people to claim social welfare benefits. It could boast of increased spending on health and education and a reduction in hospital waiting lists; but also stood accused of authoritarian social impulses and 'nannying'. For example Blair's personal advocacy of Christian morality and talk of 'family values' left many libertarians and feminists outraged and worried. In September 1998 Blair published a pamphlet advocating his so-called 'Third Way' in politics – essentially a rejection of many of the key tenets of traditional social democracy or democratic socialism and an embrace of a Clinton-style blend of free market economics and 'caring' social policies. Rejected by many European socialists as a surrender to Thatcherism, this 'Third Way' was significant as an indication of the Labour government's economic thinking. Blair praised Thatcher's privatisation programme and anti-union legislation as 'necessary acts of modernisation' and pledged to move beyond the so-called Old Left's alleged support for 'state control, high taxation and producer interests'. In essence, this represented wholesale acceptance of key tenets of Thatcherite free market ideology, and the Labour government gave every sign of regarding its remaining links to the trade union movement as an embarrassment.

On Europe, too, the heavy hand of previous Conservative administrations could be felt. Labour's instincts are undoubtedly more pro-European than the Conservative Party's. And Blair had pledged to place Britain in the driving seat of European affairs. Although his election was widely welcomed in Europe, his government was soon adopting a cautious note. Wary of offending the Euro-sceptical Murdoch press, it refused to commit Britain unequivocally to membership of the single currency while indicating that in principle it favoured joining. What this meant in practice was that the UK would not join in the first wave; but would almost certainly join afterwards – however, a feeling that the single currency was being introduced by stealth in order to avoid a national debate on the issue which might damage the Labour Party was hard to avoid. Blair's government also adopted a strident defence of what it perceived as Britain's national interests – refusing to agree to common tax policies, for example; suggesting that aspects of the Social Chapter to the Maastricht Treaty might be watered down in practice; and disappointing its centre-left allies in France and Germany by refusing to agree to higher public spending by the EU to tackle unemployment.

Halfway through its first term it was becoming clear that Blair's government was one of the most right-leaning of Europe's social democratic governments and shared neither the spirited defence of the welfare state nor the whole-hearted European federalism which were joint hallmarks of most of its centre-left allies. Of course, these are matters of emphasis. Blair's government contained ministers who were traditional social democrats and European federalists, just as the governments of Jospin, D'Alema and Schröder contained ardent admirers of Blair's 'Third Way'. But, in general, it was fair to say that the fundamental shift to the right in British politics which had occurred with Thatcherism still left its mark on British political thinking at the start of the new millennium.

Into the new millennium: the challenges facing the major multi-party democracies in comparative perspective

Western Europe's four biggest democracies, in common with their smaller neighbours, face a number of considerable challenges in the years ahead.

The European economy has undergone a period of prolonged recession, which may be intensified in the short to medium term by uncertainty about the pace and outcome of European monetary and economic union, and the demands of less developed countries in eastern and central Europe. A key factor undermining economic security for many has been mass unemployment, which is estimated at 18 million in the European Union in 1998. Of course, Europe in the post-war period has known economic restructuring and upheaval before – the 1950s and 1960s were decades of rapid economic change when millions of people were uprooted. Then, however, the problem was one of the imbalances caused by societal modernisation and economic growth; the mood was generally one of optimism for the future, and politicians could point to the promise of future rewards. Now, no easy solution to mass unemployment seems at hand – indeed, for many people no solution at all seems possible. Not since the 1930s has economic insecurity and uncertainty so greatly coincided with political pessimism.

Economic crisis is accompanied in many countries by a growing sense of political crisis. The main parties of both left and right face the consequences of the perceived failure of their ideologies to explain or make sense of reality. The growing complexity of policy-making and the globalisation of economic processes contribute to a sense of parties being unable to deliver their election promises. Although centre-right parties which are prepared to 'go with the flow' of the international markets are perhaps less immediately challenged by such developments than left-wing parties which see their dreams of radical social change through controlled economic management implode, in the longer term all democratic parties must struggle to convince the electorate that democracy can still deliver in sufficient measure for people to feel that they have a stake in its defence and preservation. Cynicism and nihilism are directed at politics in general and there is mounting evidence of voter alienation, volatility, and protest voting.

The secularisation of society, the rise of a market-based consumer culture, and the erosion of long-standing political identities and sub-cultures, are spreading a sense of loss of identity and of moral values. It is perhaps those social groups adversely affected by economic decline that are most vulnerable to moral panic.

This combination of circumstances creates a potentially lethal cocktail of resentment, despair, and sullen alienation on the part of millions of Europeans which extremist groups with no share in the values of liberal democracy seek to exploit. The spectre of communism may no longer haunt Europe, but the spectres of racism, neo-fascism, and intolerance would appear to be back. Neo-fascist parties have scored considerable electoral success in France and Italy; in Germany and in the UK there has been a marked increase in extremist violence against minorities. The search for scapegoats is on.

At the end of the twentieth century centre-left governments held office for the first time ever in all four of western Europe's major democracies simultaneously. The common problems they faced were matched by a common set of values and of priorities – tackling unemployment, overcoming social exclusion, reinvesting in health and education, reforming the welfare state without dismantling or undermining it, and building a European Union which was not just a free market but also a community in which the left's traditional values – solidarity, social justice and full employment – could find expression. But on many of these questions, the centre-left forces were critically divided in terms of their strategic vision and ideological outlook between those who were inspired by Blair's pragmatic 'Third Way', with its embrace of free market capitalism, and those who looked to the radical, feminist, Keynesian and ecological strands of centre-left thinking which were articulated by many within the German and French left parties. There was always the danger that such divisions would paralyse the centre-left at a pan-European level and render powerless their potential challenge to the monetarist ideology of the European Central Bank as the single currency was introduced. A failure to deliver real change might, in turn, lead to further voter disillusionment and a strengthening of the extreme right.

Of course it does not pay to be too pessimistic. The political culture of the major European democracies has proved very resilient. Europeans have fought and died for the values of pluralism, democracy, solidarity, and individual and collective liberties, and those values will not be surrendered easily. But the challenges facing the major democracies are obviously great.

An overriding concern must be the popular feeling, evidenced by opinion polls, that political systems are remote from the lives and concerns of ordinary people. This may be related to the declining ability of national governments to deliver desired policy outcomes whilst, at the same time, the business of building a European Union remains very incomplete, fraught with obstacles, and insufficiently engaged with the peoples of Europe. One possible response, as argued in Chapter 14, could be greater regional decentralisation, though this might, of course, spark off a nationalist reaction. Another response would be political reforms aimed at increasing citizen participation and involvement in politics, strengthening civil society, improving accountability of decision-makers to society, and harnessing new forms of political communication. The reform of Germany's citizenship laws by Chancellor Schröder's government is an example of this.

Western Europe's four major democracies have considerable achievements to their credit in the post-war era, not least the attainment of greater security for the mass of their citizens, the preservation of basic civil liberties, and the acceptance of norms of at least minimal social justice and social responsibility. The struggle to defend and build upon those achievements may well be the overriding priority in the coming years.

Further reading

Coxall, B. and Robins, L. (1998) *Contemporary British Politics,* 3rd edn, Macmillan, Basingstoke.

Dunleavy, P., *et al.* (1997) *Developments in British Politics 5,* Macmillan, Basingstoke.

Gildea, R. (1997) *France Since 1945,* Oxford University Press, Oxford.

Gundle, S. and Parker, S. (eds) (1996) *The New Italian Republic,* Routledge, London.

Hancock, M.D., *et al.* (eds) (1993) *Politics in Western Europe,* Chatham House, London.

Jones, B., *et al.* (1997) *Politics UK,* Prentice Hall, London.

Lewis, D. and McKenzie, J. (1995) *The New Germany: Social, Political and Cultural Challenges of Unification,* University of Exeter Press, Exeter.

Mény, Y. (1993) *Government and Politics in Western Europe: Britain, France, Italy, Germany,* Oxford University Press, Oxford.

Perry, S. (1997) *Aspects of Contemporary France,* Routledge, London.

Richards, C. (1995) *The New Italians,* Penguin, Harmondsworth.

Sassoon, D. (1997) *Contemporary Italy: Politics, Economy and Society,* Longman, London.

Smith, G., Paterson, W.E. and Padgett, S. (eds) (1997) *Developments in German Politics 2,* Macmillan, Basingstoke.

Stevens, A. (1996) *The Government and Politics of France,* 2nd edn, Macmillan, Basingstoke.

7 The Nordic countries: peripheral Europeans?

Introduction

Since the publication of a book by Toivo Miljan (1977), the phrase 'reluctant Europeans' has been closely associated with the Nordic countries in one form or another. At the time the book appeared, one of these states – Denmark, the original 'reluctant European' – had already joined the EEC (1973). The main thrust of the author's argument was that the remaining states of the region were slowly but inexorably being propelled in the same direction as Denmark by powerful economic forces. The states in question were Finland, Norway and Sweden: the fifth and last state in the region – Iceland – was left out of the reckoning as a special case. In each of these states there were considerable political and cultural obstacles in the way of following Denmark's example. Obstacles of this kind had, however, been present in Denmark before its accession to the EEC and they had not been able to outweigh the force exerted by economic factors. Since the book was written two of the remaining states, Finland and Sweden, have joined the EU (1995) after holding referenda on the issue. Iceland and Norway remain outside. Let us take a closer look, starting with a brief survey of some of the key characteristics of the Nordic region.

The Nordic region lies on – or, in the case of Iceland, off – the north-western periphery of continental Europe. The combined total population of the five states does not reach the 25 million mark (see Table 7.1). Three of the five states achieved their independence this century: Norway in 1905, Finland in 1917 and Iceland in 1944. It is not surprising, then, that the preferred course of all of these states in the realm of foreign policy during the twentieth century would have been to stay out of disputes between the great powers. During the First World War they were able to manage it, though Finland suffered a short but bitter civil war in the wake of the Bolshevik revolution. But during the Second World War the Danish position as the stopper in the bottle of the Baltic, and Norway's strategic importance for Atlantic trade routes, ensured that both countries fell under German occupation. Similarly, Iceland was occupied by the Allied forces, while Finland was embroiled in two major wars with the Soviet

Union. So only Sweden managed this time to stay neutral. The different states eventually evolved varying security policies in the light of their experiences. But they worked out these policies with consideration for their regional neighbours' defence worries and established what came to be known as 'the Nordic Balance' as a result. The gist of this was that Denmark and Norway joined NATO but rejected military bases on their territory unless tension between East and West escalated dangerously. They also refused to have nuclear weapons on their soil. The intention was to try to minimise Cold War tensions in the region and to avoid shifting the balance to the detriment of Finland and Sweden.

The prevailing political temper of this region is pragmatic. There is a strongly marked preference for the functionalist rather than the federalist approach in the field of international cooperation. Nordic politicians (with the possible exception of the Finns) therefore tend to be much more than halfway sympathetic to the cautious and non-rigid British attitude towards ambitious initiatives coming out of the EU. They are mistrustful of the pursuit of principles to their logical conclusion, and also tend to hold to the maxim 'If it ain't broke, don't fix it!'

Table 7.1 The Nordic countries

Country	Population (000)	Area (1,000km²)	Population density (per km²)
Denmark	5,251	43	121
Finland	5,117	338	17
Iceland	268	103	3
Norway	4,370	324	14
Sweden	8,838	450	21
Nordic	23,943	–	–

Source: *Yearbook of Nordic Statistics (1997)*, OECD (1997)

Note: Figures for 1996.

This cast of mind can be clearly illustrated by reference to the creation of the Nordic Council in 1952. Sweden in 1949 proposed a Nordic Defence Pact which would have brought Denmark and Norway into a non-aligned military alliance. This seemed to the latter two powers to offer considerably less security than NATO membership, which would guarantee supplies of defence equipment under the powerful American shield. So when the project failed, Denmark took the initiative in creating a new regional organisation designed to multiply grass-root contacts between the regional states, based purely on the principle of close regional cooperation for the advantage of all the members. Foreign policy and defence policy were excluded from the competence of this Nordic Council.

Because of this, it was possible for Finland, which always had to keep a wary eye on the security worries of the Soviet Union next door, to join the other four states in the organisation in 1955. The calculation was that a steady flow of carefully thought-out but unspectacular initiatives would create a network of interdependencies knitting the states of the region ever more closely together – 'cobweb integration'. But if this meant creating a new politically integrated regional grouping, it was never feasible. The defence and security policies of the member states diverged too sharply to foster political integration. Moreover, national feelings ran too strongly for any political merger to be in question. The appropriate metaphor is probably one of a family of states with each member jealous of its independence but conscious of a fellow feeling with the others. Meanwhile, the Nordic Council has brought about a modest improvement in the levels of human happiness within the region. It has, for example, created a passport union between the member states, carried out a reciprocal extension of social security rules and introduced a common regional labour market. These are no small matters for the inhabitants of the five states, and they have been annually buttressed by further examples of mutually advantageous agreed cooperation, especially cross-border cooperation at grass roots level.

Linguistically, Finland is the odd state out within the Nordic region and its language is unintelligible to the other states. What makes Finland, nevertheless, a genuine and non-artificial member of the region is historical circumstance and cultural inheritance. From the fourtenth century until 1809, Finland was predominantly a province of Sweden. From 1809, when Sweden lost a war with Russia, the country came under the rule of the Russian Tsars until it won independence in the aftermath of the Bolshevik revolution in 1917. Throughout the long period of Russian rule, however, the country maintained the legal and administrative institutions which it had inherited from Sweden so that its political inheritance in the twentieth century can certainly be called western democratic rather than eastern/autocratic. It also has a small but significant Swedish-speaking minority – currently about 6 per cent of the population – of impeccable democratic credentials; this has declined from its mid-nineteenth-century position of a dominant political and business elite to become roughly a centrist force in Finland's political scales.

The other four countries of the region are linguistically akin. Icelandic, the closest to Old Norse, is the remotest in more senses than one, and spoken Danish, for example, is not so easy for the average Swede to understand. But the written languages have a close similarity, and written Danish, Norwegian, and Swedish present no great difficulties for mutual comprehension.

Three of the states – Denmark, Norway and Sweden – have constitutional monarchies. Finland and Iceland are republics. The monarchies are purely symbolic and dignified parts of their political systems. It is of more political significance that all five have deeply entrenched liberal democratic values. Finland got off to a shaky start in this respect with a bitter civil war between 'Reds' and 'Whites' in the early months of 1918 and a briefly threatening spell of right-wing extremism a decade or so later (the 'Lapua Movement'). Subsequently, however, the country totally accepted the democratic norms of its neighbours to the west. All five states operate one form or another of proportional representation electoral systems at the national and local level. This has resulted in multi-party political systems with many coalition governments, most commonly in Denmark, Finland and Iceland, but much less so in Norway and Sweden. This, in turn, has tended to produce political progress, so to speak, in a straight line – free of the reversals of course associated with adversarial politics in a predominantly two-party political system. The main dysfunction has perhaps been that the political elites have sometimes established so cosy a relationship between themselves as to provoke an occasional explosion of electoral anger, as in the Danish general election of 1973. However, the Danes have the most strongly developed sense of humour of any of the Nordic peoples, and it was reflected in the conduct and programme of their main protest party in 1973, the Progressives.

The multiplication of parties has not led to weak and ineffective government in the Nordic region because their political and electoral systems are underpinned by a strong social cohesion with the partial and temporary exception of inter-war Finland. The Norwegian national day, for example, is 17 May which commemorates the adoption of the Eidsvoll constitution of 1814. This constitution was approved by a genuine national assembly in a brief interlude before Norway fell under Swedish rule until winning independence finally in 1905. It is still the basis of the country's fundamental laws. Similarly, Denmark's national day, 5 June, marks the adoption of a strikingly liberal constitution on that date in 1849 and also the adoption of the present constitution in 1953. The symbolism is significant and unifying. Similarly, ordinary citizens of all five countries fly their national flags in their gardens to a degree unimaginable in a country like the UK.

National sentiment, then, cements. But, in addition, the advent of democracy in the Nordic countries in the early twentieth century was antedated by the growth of vigorous grass-roots popular movements which were self-governing and spontaneous. These included temperance societies, which developed a strong input into the self-improvement of working people through education; agricultural cooperative movements, which encouraged rural populations to self-help and to participation in democratic processes; folk high schools, and most of all, trade unions which increasingly mobilised the working class in the pursuit of political influence.

The dominant parties in much of the region in the second half of the twentieth century have been social democratic, most clearly so in Norway and Sweden, increasingly so in Finland, at or near the centre of gravity of the political spectrum in Denmark, and a significant (though far from dominant) player in Iceland (see Table 7.2). Sweden holds the record: here the Social Democrats have been the natural governing party since 1933. Everywhere the Social Democrats have been concerned to build up and to preserve the welfare states which have become almost synonymous with the region. It is part of the fascination of studying the political life of the Nordic states to see how they have coped with the impact of economic recession. But here we begin to touch on the economic dimension which Miljan said would exert an inexorable pull on all these states to join the EU.

A brief survey of the Nordic countries

Denmark

Denmark is unique in the Nordic region in never having been ruled by any of its neighbours. On the contrary, it has ruled them. From 1397 until 1523 Denmark held sway over Norway and Sweden in the Kalmar Union. Gross misrule led to the revolt of the Swedes in 1523 under Gustav Vasa and to the emergence of Sweden as a major European power for a long period under the Vasa dynasty. Norway continued under Danish sovereignty until 1814, when the Danes were forced to relinquish control. But this long period of Danish ascendancy meant that the official Norwegian language – *riksmål* – was strongly influenced by Danish and that Copenhagen was the cultural centre for Norwegians seeking higher education until 1813, when the University of Christiania (later, Oslo) was founded. Iceland continued to be a Danish dependency until 1918, when it achieved home rule, and 1944, when it became fully independent. Greenland and the Faroe Islands continue to be home rule territories whose foreign policy and defence are conducted from Copenhagen, though Greenland was permitted to opt out of the EC (1982) with a consequent sharp reduction in the EC's surface area but a minimal drop in its population.

In 1863–64 Denmark lost a war against Prussia and Austria, and since then its foreign policy has been based on an acute consciousness of military weakness and on a search for the option which represents the least of the evils. The country is geographically an extension of the north German plain and is hence virtually indefensible against an overland attack from the south. It was therefore occupied, almost without resistance, by Hitler's Nazi troops on 9 April 1940, although passive resistance, obstruction and sabotage became an increasing strain on the occupying power from 1943 onwards. Not surprisingly, in the immediate post-war period many Danes were apprehensive about closer contacts with Germany. So the opposition to joining the EC campaigned in terms of this being 'a new 9 April'. The opposition failed, but it is no accident that, since joining the EC/EU, Denmark has been one of the members most reluctant to agree to proposals for closer economic integration, as evidenced in particular in the Maastricht and Amsterdam Treaties. Equally, it is no accident that Denmark has perhaps the most stringent set of parliamentary controls of any member state over proposals emanating from Brussels.

The Danes finally settled almost a century of vexed disputes with the Germans over minorities on their southern border by treaty in March 1955 and in 1970 they reached agreement with the FRG on the division of the continental shelf. They may be described as being Scandinavian by instinct, European by necessity. Denmark does not regard its Scandinavianism and its Europeanism as mutually exclusive. On the contrary, it regards itself as the bridgehead between the two of them, as exemplified by its constant and eventually successful pressure to have a bridge built to Sweden across Öresund. This major engineering venture, agreed in 1991, is due to open to traffic in the year 2000. The impact in linking the Scandinavian economies more closely into

Europe is likely to be considerable. But at the same time the Danes are haunted by the fear of a gradual erosion of their national distinctiveness within a Europe dominated by the major EU states.

On the domestic front, Danish prime ministers since 1945 have more often than not been Social Democrats (see Table 7.2). Thus, the present holder of the office, Poul Nyrup Rasmussen, has been in post since 1994 and has ensured himself a further term through winning (just) the general election of March 1998. However, the Social Democrats – or any other party, for that matter – are never strong enough to rule alone. So government in Denmark is overwhelmingly a matter of seeking coalitions, cross-party agreements and consensus. In such an atmosphere 'give and take' politics are mandatory.

Finland

Finland had never been a nation-state in its own right before achieving independence from Russia (1917). Once it did become independent it had to manage its international affairs in the knowledge that it shared a 800 mile-long border with its increasingly formidable neighbour to the east, the Soviet Union. Its preferred course of action in the inter-war years was to stay out of great power conflicts in Europe while if possible strengthening its ties with the Nordic states to the west, especially with Sweden. Unfortunately, however, Finland's strategic position, guarding the approaches to Leningrad (now St Petersburg) from the west and north, eventually exposed it to security demands from Stalin which it felt it could not concede. The upshot was the Winter War (November 1939–March 1940), which Finland fought solo against the mighty Soviet Union. Then, in a vain attempt to recover the resultant losses of territory (ceded as a result of Finland's defeat), the country joined Germany in its attack on the Soviet Union in June 1941. Finland was a belligerent on a strictly limited front until forced to pull out in September 1944 and bloodily to expel all German forces on Finnish soil.

The lengthy ensuing period of the Cold War between East and West thus saw Finland in the most exposed and vulnerable position of all the Nordic states. During this time, the term 'Finlandisation' came into use to signify a creeping erosion of the country's sovereignty through pressures exerted upon it from successive rulers in the Kremlin. The reality was more complex and more subtle. The peace treaty signed by the Finns in Paris in February 1947 severely limited the size of the country's armed forces, levied heavy reparation payments and required the cession to the Soviet Union of some 12 per cent of Finland's territory. The April 1948 Treaty of Friendship, Cooperation and Mutual Assistance (FCMA) between Finland and the Soviet Union required the Finns to fight to repel any attack from Germany or any state allied to Germany and, furthermore, to consult with the Soviets whenever there was the threat of any such attack.

The crucial points in respect of Finno–Soviet relations throughout the entire period of the Cold War, therefore, were as follows:

Table 7.2 Nordic governments since the 1980s

Year	Prime minister	Party composition
Denmark		
1982	Schlüter, P.	Conservatives, Liberals, Christian People's Party, Centre Democrats
1988	Schlüter, P.	Conservatives, Social Liberals, Liberals
1990	Schlüter, P.	Conservatives, Liberals
1994	Rasmussen, P. Nyrup	Social Democrats, Social Liberals, Christian People's Party, Centre Democrats
1998	Rasmussen, P. Nyrup	Social Democrats, Social Liberals, Radicals & Unity List
Finland		
1982	Sorsa, K.	Social Democrats, Democratic League Centre Party, Swedish People's Party
1982	Sorsa, K.	Social Democrats, Centre Party Swedish People's Party
1983	Sorsa, K.	Social Democrats, Centre Party Swedish People's Party, Rural Party
1987	Holkeri, H.	Conservatives, Social Democrats, Swedish People's Party, Rural Party
1990	Holkeri, H.	Conservatives, Social Democrats, Swedish People's Party
1991	Aho, E.	Centre Party, Swedish People's Party, Conservatives, Christian League
1995	Lipponen, P.	Social Democrats, Left Alliance, Swedish People's Party, Greens, Conservatives
1999	Lipponen, P.	Social Democrats, Left Alliance, Swedish People's Party, Greens, Conservatives
Iceland		
1980	Thoroddsen, G.	Splinter from Independence Party, Progressive Party, People's Alliance
1983	Hermannsson, S.	Progressive Party, Independence Party
1987	Pálsson, T.	Independence Party, Progessive Party, Social Democrats
1988	Hermannsson, S.	Progressive Party, People's Alliance, Social Democrats
1989	Hermannsson, S.	Progressive Party, People's Alliance, Social Democrats, Citizens' Party
1991	Oddsson, D.	Independence Party, Social Democrats
1995	Oddsson, D.	Independence Party, Progressive Party
1999	Oddsson, D.	Independence Party, Progressive Party

Table 7.2 Continued

Year	Prime minister	Party composition
Norway		
1981	Brundtland, G. H.	Labour Party
1981	Willoch, K.	Conservatives
1983	Willoch, K.	Conservatives, Centre Party, Christian Democrats
1986	Brundtland, G. H.	Labour Party
1989	Syse, J. P.	Conservatives, Centre Party, Christian Democrats
1990	Brundtland, G. H.	Labour Party
1993	Brundtland, G. H.	Labour Party
1996	Jagland, T.	Labour Party
1997	Bondevik, K. M.	Christian Democrats, Liberals, Centre Party
Sweden		
1981	Fälldin, T.	Centre Party, Liberals
1982	Palme, O.	Social Democrats
1985	Palme, O.	Social Democrats
1986	Carlsson, I.	Social Democrats
1988	Carlsson, I.	Social Democrats
1990	Carlsson, I.	Social Democrats
1991	Bildt, C.	Conservatives, Centre Party, Liberals, Christian Democrats
1994	Carlsson, I.	Social Democrats
1996	Persson, G.	Social Democrats
1998	Persson, G.	Social Democrats

Notes: The party of the respective prime minister is denoted first.

- Finland, unlike other neighbours of the Soviet Union further to the south, notably Czechoslovakia, Hungary and Poland, was allowed to retain its liberal democratic system unscathed in all essentials.
- The country was aided in this respect because the most influential authors of the post-war foreign policy, Paasikivi (president of Finland, 1946–56) and Kekkonen (president, 1956–81), were acutely aware of the basic needs of Soviet security policy. It probably helped also that Kekkonen originated from tough rural stock and was capable of outlasting his Soviet hosts when it came to the consumption of hard liquor!
- Finland became expert in the practice of 'trade-off' politics with the Soviet Union. For example, it renewed the FCMA treaty in 1955, long before its expiry date, and in return secured the withdrawal of Soviet troops from the Porkkala base ten miles from the Finnish capital, Helsinki. Or again, Finland

was allowed (partially) to join the European Free Trade Association (EFTA), through a special arrangement (FINEFTA) in 1961, because it agreed at the same time to equivalent parallel concessions for the USSR in respect of manufactured goods. Similarly, in 1973 it was permitted to sign a free trade agreement with the EEC in return for the early renewal of the FCMA treaty.

The ending of the Cold War removed these constraints on Finnish foreign policy and eventually opened the way to EU membership (1995). A distinctive feature of the country's political system in the Nordic context has been the considerable amount of power and influence vested in the presidency (chosen by electoral college before 1994, now by direct election). Thus, the president has the capacity to be a leading player in questions of foreign policy and also to play a crucial role in the complex business of government formation in a parliamentary system where many political parties have representation. President Kekkonen exploited the potentialities of his office to the full. As a Centre Party man, he was, more or less, at the balancing point of the parliamentary seesaw anyway, and on occasion he used his 'clout' with Soviet leaders to influence domestic politics in the direction he desired, though never to the detriment of the basics of the liberal democratic parliamentary system. So, for example, he played a big part in bringing the 'Popular Front' wing of the Communist Party back to government in 1966 and at intervals again thereafter (a unique phenomenon in the Nordic lands). Since he left the scene through ill-health in 1981, however, the presidency has become an office whose powers have been exercised more modestly, and Finland has approximated more and more closely to the spirit of the political systems of its western neighbours. Indeed, the official powers of the Finnish president in foreign policy matters will be curtailed under the new Finnish constitution due for parliamentary ratification in 1999 with some responsibilities transferred in practice to the prime minister.

Iceland

With a population of 270,000 and an area of roughly 103,000 square kilometres, Iceland can be regarded as one of the smallest of the European 'small states' or as a very large 'micro-state'. Despite its geographical position – perched precariously astride the Mid-Atlantic Ridge – the fact that the island was first settled by the Vikings in the ninth century ensured that Iceland has been ensconced within the Nordic region.

While Icelanders share similar ethnic origins to their Scandinavian counterparts, it is problematic to apply many of the stereotypes associated with social democratic Scandinavia to Iceland. The Independence Party and the agrarian Progressives have been key coalition partners in the formation of governments and substantial alternatives to the Social Democrats in the eyes of Icelandic voters. Part of the explanation for this lies in the fact that Icelandic traditions of nationalism include a substantial cultural element. Icelanders have stressed their Viking heritage and their Old Norse dialect which enables them to read the centuries-old 'Sagas' first hand and helps to set them apart culturally from the other Nordic peoples. On top of this, democratic principles were operational in the country well before the achievement of an independent Iceland. For instance, a separate consultative assembly, called the Althingi after its ancient predecessor, was inaugurated in 1845. The independence movement in this country was also well developed by the twentieth century, progressively achieving incremental home rule from the Danes in the period 1904–18. This helped ensure that the (new) Independence Party became an active participant in electoral proceedings (by 1929), articulating a form of Icelandic nationalism that was essentially different from the Nordic mainstream.

Iceland clearly maintains an 'Atlanticist' orientation. The link with Denmark was finally broken by the April 1940 German invasion of Denmark and the country's strategic location prompted the island's occupation by British (initially) and (later) US troops from May 1940. The achievement of complete Icelandic independence (1944) therefore took place at the time when the post-war international order was being laid and was associated with a close relationship with the Americans and not just the Europeans; a point not lost on the Icelanders ever since. To this day, the country maintains no armed forces of its own, having 'sub-contracted' its defence to NATO through its membership of the organisation and relying on the presence of the US base at Keflavik.

Iceland is also singled out from its Nordic brethren by its unusual economic structure (see Table 7.3). Although fisheries are an important activity in some of the other Nordic countries (such as Norway), it is the primary economic activity in the Icelandic case, accounting for three-quarters of the country's merchandise exports and 55 per cent of foreign currency earnings. Not surprisingly, Iceland regards fisheries as central to the country's economic well-being, helping to ensure high standards of living (see Table 7.3). Fisheries' issues have been the source of several key disputes with European neighbours (1952–56; 1958–61; 1972–73 and 1975–76 – the latter two known as the 'Cod Wars'). Indeed, fisheries have shaped Iceland's attitudes towards European integration and provided the main reason for Icelandic refusals to join the EC. Iceland objected to the Community's Common Fisheries Policy (CFP) and has been content with membership of EFTA (which it joined in 1970). Hence, Iceland has been a member of the family of European nations, but prefers to be on the periphery jealously guarding its cultural heritage and new-found political independence.

Norway

Norway is the only Nordic country to have rejected joining the EC/EU in a popular vote (1972 and 1994). The reasons have much to do with Norwegian geo-political structure. Opposition to joining has continued to be especially strong in both the north and the south-west of the country. These are regions of many small, scattered and fiercely independent local communities. From their perspective, even rule from Oslo has caused resentments, not to mention rule from Copenhagen (before 1814) or Stockholm (before 1905). By the same token, rule from Brussels appears almost infinitely remote and potentially suffocatingly bureaucratic.

Table 7.3 Economic profile of the Nordic countries

	Denmark	**Finland**	**Iceland**	**Norway**	**Sweden**
GDP*	20,002	16,543	20,376	21,080	17,386
Unemployment rates (%)*	8	20	4	5	8
Employment distribution (%)*					
– **Agriculture**	5.1	8.3	9.4	5.6	3.4
– **Industry**	26.8	26.8	26.1	23.1	25
– **Services**	68.1	64.9	65.2	71.3	71.6

Source: *Yearbook of Nordic Statistics (1997)*, OECD (1997)

Notes:
*   Gross Domestic Product at market prices per person in purchasing power standards (PPS). Figures for 1995.
** Unemployed people aged 16–64 as percentage of active people 16–64. Figures for 1996.
***Distribution as percentage of total civilian population (TCE). Figures for 1996.

The primary sector of the Norwegian economy has declined by half (from 12 per cent to 6 per cent) between the two referenda but its political clout continues to be disproportionate to its economic strength. So the country's fishermen, agitated by fears about the impact of the CFP on their livelihood if Norway acceded to the EU, have been resolutely determined to keep the country out. The same has been true of the farmers, fearing economic disadvantage from the impact of the CAP. In addition, the country is more insulated than its neighbours from pressures to join the EU by virtue of its extensive, highly profitable, largely state-controlled North Sea oilfields and also because of its markedly more Atlanticist orientation than that of its immediate Nordic neighbours.

In this latter connection, the size and importance of the Norwegian mercantile marine is a weighty factor. During World War II, for instance, Norwegian merchant ships played a crucial part in bringing supplies to Britain during the anti-U-boat 'Battle of the Atlantic'. They constituted the fourth largest merchant fleet at the disposal of the Allied Powers. The continuing importance of trade in Norwegian merchant carriers has meant that the country has a global outlook and a particular interest in free trade arrangements on a worldwide scale.

This outlook eventually led Norway to decide to seek its security in NATO and to rely for its defence on the American nuclear shield rather than seek refuge in a Swedish-led Scandinavian Defence Pact. The bitter experience of occupation and Nazi repression during the Second World War set the Norwegians apart from the Swedes and made neutralism an unattractive foreign policy option.

The most important party on the Norwegian political scene since the severe economic depression years of the 1930s has been the Labour Party. Its early years were marked by an exceptional degree of radicalism and for most of the 1920s, its majority, alone among all its sister parties in western Europe, attached itself to the Communist Third International. It first achieved real governmental power, however, in 1935 as virtually a social democratic party. Its main centres of strength are in Oslo and in the northern part of Norway. Opposition to EU membership has, as mentioned, been persistently most marked in north Norway and in the (predominantly non-Labour) territory of the mountainous south-west. The tilting of the balance against membership has owed much to the divisions within the Labour Party on the issue in the Oslo region. Objections to what was perceived as a conservatively orientated and capitalist edifice bulked large in 1972. In 1994, defence of the large Norwegian public service sector against possible encroachment from Brussels weighed in the scales.

Sweden

Present-day pacific Sweden was not always so. The Vikings from the Roslagen area, the Rus, gave Russia its name; prison bars were known as 'Swedish curtains' in German-speaking Europe when Gustavus Adolphus ravaged the area during the Thirty Years' War. But the Swedes have not been involved in serious fighting since they lost the war of 1809 at the hands of the Russians and with it, Finland and their Gustavian dynasty. With the exception of some skirmishes with the Norwegians, when the latter sought in vain to resist Swedish rule in 1814, the Swedes have enjoyed almost two centuries of peace. By the mid-twentieth century, their watchword in foreign policy was 'freedom from alliances in time of peace, neutrality in time of war'.

Their neutrality, one cornerstone of their security policy, rested not on formal international recognition but on a careful calculation of the risks involved in the country's geographical position in Europe. The Swedes were primarily concerned with reducing ever-changing potential threats to their independence; namely:

- when Germany and the Soviet Union were heading towards conflict in the 1930s;
- when the Nazi Third Reich became temporarily dominant in Europe from 1940–43. During this period, when Norway and Denmark were both under Nazi occupation, Sweden walked a tightrope but used limited concessions (in respect of allowing German troop movements and supplying iron ore) to avert the threat to its independence; and
- balancing the security interests of the superpowers in the Nordic region during the Cold War.

A second cornerstone of Swedish security policy has been to maintain a modern and effective military capacity at considerable cost. The Social Democrats (SAP), who dominated the domestic political scene for 44 years at a stretch after achieving power in 1933, followed a different path from their Danish and Norwegian sister parties in this respect. Instead of securing NATO membership, Sweden's security was to be underpinned in the post-war years by the building of a 'total defence' capability, which would reinforce Sweden's claims of being a neutral state and deter superpower military intervention. This tradition of having an independent defence capability can still be seen in the 1990s, with Sweden's commitment to building its own modern multi-role fighter, the Gripen, and not to go for the cheaper option of purchasing arms from abroad. To join the EC was thus not an option for Sweden as long as the Cold War lasted because of the fear of losing control over security policy. By the same token, the ending of the Cold War opened up the possibility of EC/EU membership for the first time.

Other, less crucial, factors have also coloured the Swedish attitude to Brussels. Perhaps the most significant one was the pride of the Social Democrats in the famous 'Swedish model' welfare state which they had painstakingly created, along with many ingenious innovations in economic management. It was feared that this would be put under threat by any close association with Brussels as voiced by the (then) prime minister, Tage Erlander, in his landmark speech to the powerful Metalworkers Union in 1961. Pride in the achievements of the welfare state was a central component in Swedish nationalism. The dominant party could not believe that its quasi-Keynesian reforms would have been possible in a predominantly conservatively orientated EEC. Now, of course, economic adversity has clouded the picture. The severe recession of 1990–93 in Sweden and the need for welfare cuts and tighter fiscal management by government went hand in hand with the changes in attitude towards joining the EC/EU as this Swedish pride began to evaporate. At the same time, the parties of the moderate left have become more and more powerful within the EU. So the force of these arguments against entry was greatly weakened.

A subsidiary objection to membership was the fear that Sweden would not be able to pursue its ambition to become a model power for the provision of aid to underdeveloped countries of the world within the confines of a policy made in Brussels. This was a genuinely idealistic strand of Swedish foreign policy-making not only among the supporters of the Social Democratic Party, but across a wider political spectrum.

In conclusion, the Social Democrats continue to be the largest and most influential party within the Swedish political system despite experiencing several spells out of office since 1976 (see Table 7.2, on page 153). They have been greatly helped by divisions between the non-socialist parties and also by support from the Left Party to the left of them on the political spectrum. The only major exception to this is on EU-related issues, where the Left Party, along with the Greens, are openly against Sweden's continued membership of the Union. Long experience of office has in addition enabled the Social Democrats to establish a generally good working relationship with the leaders of industry and commerce in the country.

The Nordic countries and European integration

For a considerable time, the Nordic countries had a cautious attitude towards supranational European organisations and European integration. These countries, often for differing reasons, preferred more limited intergovernmental forms of European cooperation, all finding sanctuary in the Nordic Council (1952) and some of them (Denmark, Norway and Sweden) as founders of EFTA. Their official rationales for staying outside the more ambitious attempts at European integration by the EEC Six are well documented. For Finland and Sweden, security policy considerations were paramount. The Swedes opposed any open-ended participation in matters with security or defence implications and quite correctly argued that the EEC's customs union would require the Swedish government to adopt the Community's common commercial policy (CCP) on third countries, so indirectly compromising the country's neutrality. In addition, the governing Social Democrats also disliked the 'capitalist', essentially Catholic and continental European basis of the Community. For Finland, the neutrality arguments against joining the Community were crystal-clear. As long as Finnish foreign policy was restricted by the confines of the 1948 Treaty on Friendship, Cooperation and Mutual Assistance (FCMA) with the USSR, and the Soviets continued to regard the EEC as little more than the 'economic arm of NATO' then full membership of such an organisation was out of the question. For the Danes, Icelanders and Norwegians, membership of any organisation that might compromise the 'Atlanticist' nature of their security policies was to be resisted.

However, there were also striking similarities in Nordic attitudes towards European integration. First and foremost, none of the Nordic countries subscribed to a federal Europe. Second, one of the main considerations of these countries (especially in terms of commercial policy) has been the high levels of international trade between themselves and with Britain. In the early years, the governments of these countries were unanimous in 'shadowing' the attitudes of the British government and shared similar preferences for intergovernmental cooperation and limited trade liberalisation. So the Nordic countries were instrumental in the creation of EFTA, which brought together those nations (including Britain) that preferred more limited forms of European cooperation.

The sea change in Britain's attitude towards joining the EEC prompted some of the Nordic countries to consider EEC membership more seriously from the 1960s. After the Macmillan government's decision to apply for full membership in 1961, the Nordic countries adopted differing approaches to the Community. Denmark and Norway, for example, followed the British and submitted full membership applications in 1961 (Denmark) and 1962 (Norway) and 1967 (Denmark and Norway), along with the UK. Little progress was made, for the Danes and the Norwegians were insistent that their applications were tied to Britain's and met a similar fate in both 1963 and 1967 due to French refusal to allow Britain to join the Community. The Swedish government, conscious of the costs of loosening ties with Britain, but restricted by the policy of 'active neutrality', applied for associate EEC status in 1961 and later even proposed an 'open' application in 1967 to consider new ways that might allow neutral Sweden to accede to the Community. Finland and Iceland remained 'non-candidates', choosing not to consider EEC accession as a viable option.

The early 1970s marked an important watershed in Nordic relations with the Community. Once French objections to Britain's membership were removed in the early 1970s, the prospect of accession by some of the Nordic countries became a distinct reality. Denmark joined the Community, while Norway nearly did so but ultimately rejected the invitation in a 1972 referendum (by 53 per cent). For the first time, the Nordic region was split, with all save Denmark preferring not to join. Denmark assumed a significant leadership role as a 'bridge-builder' between the Community and the Nordic countries that chose to remain outside. As an indirect outcome of forthcoming British and Danish accession, the remaining Nordic countries each signed bilateral free trade agreements with the Community in 1972. In effect, the Nordic countries had, for the first time, secured formal, structured trading relationships with the Community and guaranteed market access for their exports into Community markets.

The Norwegian rejection of full membership in 1972 was a bitter one and the issue of the Community was long to be taboo in Norwegian politics because of the deep schism the referendum debates had made in Norwegian society. Yet, to a large degree, the Nordic countries (other than Denmark) were content to monitor their growing trading relations with the rest of Europe, principally through EFTA, which remained the main vehicle for trade liberalisation between the Nordic countries (Iceland finally joined in 1970 and Finland in 1986). In 1984, the Nordic countries participated through EFTA in the 'Luxembourg Process', promoting closer cooperation with the EC.

However, the peripheral status of the Nordic countries was illustrated by the fact that changes in governmental attitudes towards European integration in the 1980s were prompted by external pressures. By 1985 the Community was beginning a more dynamic phase in its development and started in 1987 on the road towards completing the Single European Market (SEM). The Nordic governments, experiencing ever-growing levels of international trade with the Community, responded forcefully to the SEM programme, perceiving it as a challenge that needed to be met and contained. In particular, the Nordic governments were fearful that the SEM could turn into a 'Fortress Europe', excluding their exports, and undermining the economic stability that was so essential to the continuation of their welfare states.

The economic challenges posed by the SEM were, of course, not exclusive to the Nordic countries, and along with their Alpine EFTA colleagues, they agreed a common EFTA reply. In response to the 1989 initiative by the European Commission President, Jacques Delors, all the Nordic governments were enthusiastic about developing a 'half-way house' arrangement that would allow them access to the SEM, but did not require Finland, Iceland, Norway or Sweden to join the EC. For neutral Finland and Sweden, the proposed arrangement would theoretically allow them to maintain their non-aligned security policies, whilst at the same time developing even closer economic relations with the EC. The outcome, the European Economic Area (EEA), proved to be a disappointment to the Nordic governments. On the one hand, the Nordic EFTA countries accepted a degree of supranationalism in order to allow for the SEM to be extended to the Association's territories. On the other, they failed to gain a full decision-making input into the formulation of the EC's future SEM legislation, putting themselves at a disadvantage. Several of them therefore moved quickly to consider full membership, even before the EEA came into operation. Sweden, for example, grappling with a severe recession and heartened by the strategic changes affecting eastern Europe, was actively considering the merits of full membership application by 1990.

Once Sweden applied (July 1991), the floodgates opened to the rest of the Nordic flotilla. The Finnish government, led by prime minister Esko Aho, followed the Swedish lead, taking comfort in the fact that neutral Sweden now deemed non-alignment and EC membership as compatible, and that the 1948 Finno-Soviet treaty had dissolved along with the Soviet Union. The Finns applied in March 1992. The Norwegian Labour government, led by Gro Harlem Bruntland, was confident that the return of the EC membership issue to the forefront of Norwegian politics would not lead to its electoral downfall and followed in quick succession (November 1992). It argued that if the rest of Scandinavia (and 80 per cent of the Nordic population) would eventually be within the Community, full membership would be in the national interest. This left Iceland as the only country that still considered full membership as unattractive. Iceland's obsession with the perceived negative impact of the CFP meant that accession continued to be resisted.

The Nordic EC membership flotilla, like the arduous Arctic convoys of the Second World War, was susceptible to a few torpedo scares, dangerous rocks and unforeseen political icebergs. In particular, there remains a clear 'elite versus populace' divide on questions of European integration in nearly all the Nordic countries. Traditional north–south, urban–rural, liberal–conservative divisions in Nordic society have, to a large degree, been re-emphasised by domestic attitudes towards the EC/EU. In May 1992, for example, the domestic difficulties for Nordic governments in convincing their publics of the benefits of EC membership were only too apparent. Denmark was placed in the embarrassing situation of seeing its population narrowly reject the Maastricht Treaty (see Table 7.4). The situation was only redressed after the Danish government had secured numerous opt-outs and put the revised deal to another public referendum in June 1993 which approved the Treaty by 57 per cent. Danish enthusiasm for European integration remains less than wholehearted, although the Danish public eventually went on to approve the Treaty of Amsterdam by 55 per cent (see Table 7.4).

Similar difficulties were to be evident in the domestic debates on full membership undertaken in Finland, Norway and Sweden during the referendum campaigns of 1994. Although Finland approved full membership by 57 per cent, this was only after vocal opposition from the northern provinces and farming communities had caused considerable discomfort for the Finnish government led by an agrarian Centre Party prime minister. Shortly after, the Swedes faced similar soul-searching on European questions. The final vote was very close, approving membership by only 52 per cent. Norway was once again to reject full membership in its referendum with a similar majority to that polled in 1972 illustrating how slowly the country's attitudes to the EC have changed (see Table 7.4).

Table 7.4 Results of public referenda on EC/EU issues

Issue/Year	'Yes' (%)	'No' (%)	Turnout (%)
Denmark			
EC membership (1972)	63.4	37.6	90.4
Single European Act (1986)	56	44	75
Treaty on European Union (1992)	49.3	50.7	82.9
Treaty on European Union (1993)	56.8	43.2	86
Treaty of Amsterdam (1998)	55.1	44.9	74.8
Finland			
EU membership (1994)	57	43	74
Norway			
EC membership (1972)	46.5	53.5	79.2
EU membership (1994)	47.8	52.2	87.9
Sweden			
EU membership (1994)*	52.3	46.8	83.3

Notes: In the Swedish referendum, 0.9 per cent of voters submitted blank protest ballots.

It seems clear then that the peripheral status of the Nordic countries as small states on the northern frontiers of Europe will ensure that they continue to be cautious participants in closer European integration. High levels of domestic EU-scepticism, traditions of nationalism and attachments to Nordic identities will probably guarantee that it will be a considerable time before the Nordic region is united inside the boundaries of the EU. Only Finland (of the three Nordic EU members) has felt able to participate in stage three of the EMU timetable aimed at establishing a single currency. Indeed, the single currency has revived controversy within these states concerning supranational European integration. It has also encouraged divisions between some Nordic states.

Conclusion: the challenges of the 1990s

The 1990s represent an era of change for the Nordic countries as they adapt to a number of underlying trends and external pressures. Like the rest of Europe, the Nordic countries are gradually reorienting their foreign and security policies to take account of the changing post-1989 security environment in Europe. For Finland and Sweden, this means a revision of their once strictly neutral status to incorporate a more flexible definition of non-alignment and to allow for closer cooperation with other western powers. Sweden, for example, has contributed forces to the peace-keeping operations in Bosnia in spite of the fact that these are under NATO command, an act that would have been impossible in the heady days of 'active neutrality'. In similar fashion, the upheaval in Europe since 1989 has enabled Denmark, Iceland and Norway to re-examine their ties within NATO, although this security structure will continue to provide the main framework guaranteeing their security needs.

These essentially strategic challenges to the Nordic countries have been accompanied by larger economic and political dynamics. The Nordic countries, once renowned for the stable, prosperous economies underpinning their social democratic welfare states, are no longer as vibrant as they once were. Structural problems, such as declining industrial productivity and spiralling labour costs, which were beginning to appear in the 1980s, were accelerated (in the Finnish and Swedish cases) by the onset of severe recession in 1990–93, estimated by the OECD to be two of the hardest economic downturns to be experienced by any state in the developed world in the post-war period. Furthermore, the economic cycle of the Nordic region has become more diverse, asymmetrical and unpredictable since the discovery of large oil reserves by the Norwegians in the 1970s. Norway has joined Iceland in operating on a more or less separate economic cycle from the rest of Scandinavia. Norway, buoyed by its large oil exports, has been relatively immune from (or at least able to postpone) the economic problems which Sweden and Finland experienced in the early 1990s.

Greater instability is now an integral part of the economic performances of the Nordic countries. A financial crisis, for example, spurred on by the deregulation of financial services and a consequent credit boom, brought the banking sectors in Finland, Norway, and Sweden to the point of bankruptcy in the early 1990s. For the first time in living memory serious questions were asked about the future viability of these countries' generous welfare states and the success of social democratic-inspired economic policy. Indeed, the (then) Swedish Conservative prime minister, Carl Bildt, claimed in 1991 that the 'Nordic model was now dead' and that the Nordic countries would have to join the rest of the European fold in preaching the virtues of deregulation, austerity and tight governmental fiscal management.

Certainly, major elements of the economic and political 'model' associated with Scandinavia, the so-called 'middle way', have been abandoned in several of the countries. Nationally organised centralised, collective bargaining of wage increases were, for example, terminated in Sweden from 1990. Harmonious industrial relations are no longer a constant feature associated with the Nordic countries – witness the strikes in Denmark in 1998. The principles of universal entitlement and citizenship underpinning the social democratic welfare states have been selectively abandoned and reinterpreted as Nordic governments have reduced welfare services in order to control public expenditure. High taxation, deemed an essential pre-requisite for supporting high levels of social services, has become more politically sensitive. Large Swedish firms (such as the telecommunications giant, Ericsson), threatened to move their production facilities outside the region recently unless lower taxes were introduced. To a degree, the social democratic-inspired consensus underpinning these 'consensual democracies' is now coming under greater threat.

The solution for some of these countries has been to seek and attain EU membership as a means of providing 'complementary medicine' for the process of economic restructuring, liberalisation and deregulation already taking place in some of these countries. Yet this solution has in itself been fraught with political difficulties. All of the states (whether EU members or not) include high levels of public scepticism (and in most cases outright opposition) towards the EU. This situation looks unlikely to disappear in the near future, especially since there is strong public opposition to the Euro single currency in Denmark and Sweden (and even in Finland, which has adopted the Euro). Yet there are few viable alternatives open to these states. Nordic cooperation has to all intents and purposes been supplemented by a wider Baltic-based phenomenon which includes the independent Baltic states of Estonia, Latvia and Lithuania. Given that these states have applied for EU membership (1995), the most probable scenario is that a Nordic, or more accurately Baltic, dimension for future international cooperation will emerge within an enlarged EU. Nevertheless, the Nordic EU members have enjoyed some success in influencing the EU's agenda to reflect Nordic priorities. They were, for instance, responsible for the appearance in the Amsterdam Treaty of issues such as transparency and openness, and an employment chapter.

Most probably then, the Nordic countries will continue to be 'peripheral Europeans': part of European integration, but preferring where possible to sit on the sidelines, able selectively to choose when and where to participate in developments taking place in continental Europe. Their scepticism on the idea of a federal Europe and their general reluctance (with the possible exception of Finland) to move towards wholesale European integration continues to show itself, but now within the EU rather than just outside it. Hence, their role as 'reluctant Europeans' may have moved into differing forums and venues, but their status as 'peripheral Europeans' remains as constant as ever.

Further reading

Archer, C. and Sogner, I. (1998) *Norway, European Integration and Atlantic Security,* Sage, London.

Elder, N., Thomas, A.H. and Arter, D. (1988) *The Consensual Democracies?,* revised edn, Blackwell, Oxford.

Heclo, H. and Madsen, H. (1987) *Policy and Politics in Sweden,* Temple University Press, Philadelphia.

Karvonen, L. and Sundberg, J. (1991) *Social Democracy in Transition,* Dartmouth, Aldershot.

Kirby, D. (1979) *Finland in the Twentieth Century,* Hurst, London.

Lyck, L. (1992) (ed.) *Denmark and EC Membership Evaluated,* Pinter, London.

Miles, L. (1996) (ed.) *The European Union and the Nordic Countries,* Routledge, London.

Miles, L. (1997) *Sweden and European Integration,* Ashgate, Aldershot.

Miljan, T. (1977) *The Reluctant Europeans,* Hurst, London.

Nelsen, B.F. (1993) *Norway and the European Community: The Political Economy of Integration,* Praeger, Westport.

Nordal, J. and Kristinsson, V. (1996) *Iceland – The Republic,* Central Bank of Iceland, Reykjavik.

Pettersen, P.A., Jenssen, A.T. and Listhaug, D. (1996) 'The 1994 Referendum in Norway', *Scandinavian Political Studies,* vol. 19, no. 3.

Tiilikainen, T. (1998) *Europe and Finland,* Ashgate, Aldershot.

8 Escaping from the jackboots: Spain, Portugal, Greece

Introduction

During the mid-1970s Spain, Portugal and Greece emerged from periods of right-wing dictatorship. Spain and Portugal had been governed by authoritarian regimes since the victory of General Franco in the Spanish civil war in 1939, and the ascent to power of the Portuguese dictator, Salazar, in 1926; in Greece, a military dictatorship which seized power in 1967 had been preceded by almost two decades of quasi-democratic rule during which entrenched discrimination against left-wingers – the losers in the civil war of 1946–49 – was commonplace.

Although factors particular to each country were important in their respective democratic transitions, similar processes of social and economic change contributed to the dictatorships' downfall. Moreover, the fact that all three embarked upon the transition within a three-year period (1974–77) can scarcely be coincidental: the international context exerted an influence. The concept of southern Europe as a distinct regional sub-system has facilitated comparative analysis of the emergence and consolidation of new political systems. Aspects of this regional sub-system which have been highlighted include: relative economic underdevelopment, delayed political modernisation, cultural distinctiveness, and particular exposure to international influences.

Relative economic underdevelopment is manifest in late and partial industrialisation, with the southern European countries remaining more rural and technologically backward than northern Europe. Some writers have argued that their economies are distorted by chronic unevenness and structural dependency.

At the political level southern Europe was a latecomer to mass democracy: Spain's brief experience of democracy was stamped out by Franco's victory in 1939; Portugal and Greece only really achieved the status of functioning pluralist democracies after 1974. Moreover, all three countries have exhibited weak civil societies, with a relative lack of a participatory culture, the persistence of traditional elites and of pre-modern forms of political organisation, and entrenched clientelism – the exchange of favours by politicians in return for the procurement of political support. Efforts at creating strong and autonomous interest groups and social movements have been patchy; and parties tend to remain relatively weak in terms of their roots in society and their effective articulation of societal interests. The line between party and state is frequently traversed: for example, a party membership card often facilitates a job in parts of the public sector.

Culturally, southern Europe has continued to be more influenced by forms of traditional religion – although Spain, in particular, has recently undergone substantial secularisation. This point refers not simply to the fact that southern Europe tends to be Roman Catholic (or in the case of Greece, Orthodox) whereas northern Europe tends to be more Protestant; rather it refers primarily to the traditional and more mystical forms which Catholicism takes in Portugal or Spain, as opposed to Catholicism in, say, Britain or the Netherlands. Attention has also been paid to another cultural aspect with clear political implications: the greater importance of the family (including the extended family) in social life. Although rapid urbanisation in recent decades has disrupted traditional patterns of family life, the economic importance of the family as a buffer against unemployment and poverty in societies with relatively underdeveloped social welfare systems remains significant.

Finally, southern European countries are weaker powers which have been increasingly vulnerable to economic and cultural penetration in the latter half of the twentieth century and to the political influence of stronger powers. Throughout the immediate post-war decades the United States exercised a clearly decisive influence over Greece, especially; more recently the EU has probably replaced the US as the primary external political influence throughout the region. External influences can crucially condition the options available to political and social forces.

Having embarked upon the transition to liberal democracy within a few years of each other and having joined the EU during the 1980s, these three countries can be seen as sharing a common path and facing similar challenges.

The crisis and downfall of the dictatorships

Portugal

The Portuguese dictatorship, overthrown in April 1974, had been in power since 1926 when it replaced a parliamentary, but not democratic, republican regime (1910–26). Antonio Salazar was the regime's strong man until September 1968. He was succeeded by Marcelo Caetano, whose attempts to preserve power through controlled liberalisation ended in failure.

Salazar's advent to power represented a triumph for the landowning class over more urban and modern strata. The regime attempted until the 1960s to preserve a conservative, Catholic Portugal based on the economic power of large landowners. Ideologically, it reinforced itself by reference to myths of rural purity, anti-communism, Roman Catholic beliefs and morals, and Portuguese nationalism. It was opposed to modernity and reflected a curious blend of rural nostalgia and fundamentalist Catholicism.

It would be wrong to think that Salazar possessed no industrial policy. Behind tariff barriers, modest but important industrial growth was encouraged in the 1930s and 1940s. State investment in public works provided employment and laid the basis of an infrastructure which was to permit the economic U-turn of the 1950s and 1960s. During the 1950s the economy was gradually permitted to take advantage of favourable world conditions. In the 1960s an economic take-off, partially financed by inflows of foreign capital, transformed Portuguese society. Urbanisation and modernisation rendered the regime ideologically bankrupt and politically isolated.

It has been argued that the attempt to create the so-called New State *(Estado Novo)* came to an end in the early 1960s. At the start of the decade Portugal was still a largely rural society with nearly half of its labour force employed in agriculture. Compared to northern Europe, high levels of illiteracy and low standards in health care and provision of basic sanitation prevailed. Political repression weighed heavily, with containment of dissent entrusted to the secret police. Throughout the 1960s three developments contributed to worsening social tensions: increasing integration with the world economy (above all with northern Europe), the mounting burden of colonial wars in Africa, and a growing crisis of ideology and of legitimacy.

The dictatorship had negotiated EFTA membership in 1958. This marked the beginning of a retreat from protectionism and isolation. It has been estimated that almost one million people – one-eighth of the total population – emigrated (mostly to northern Europe) during the 1960s. The outflow of people was matched by a huge increase in inflows of foreign capital; by 1970 foreign capital invested in Portugal had increased by nearly thirty-fold. Colonial wars added to the pressure for change. Liberation struggles against Portuguese imperialism began in Angola, Guinea-Bissau, and Mozambique in the early 1960s. The dictatorship answered with a military build-up which resulted in a largely conscript force of almost 250,000 by the early 1970s. In relation to the country's population, this military machine was surpassed only by North and South Vietnam and by Israel. One in four men of military age ended up in an army which was increasingly enmeshed in futile and brutal colonial wars. The burden on the exchequer was vast. Spending on the military consumed half of total public expenditure by the late 1960s.

As the regime sought to improve living standards in order to maintain both its own legitimacy and support for the war effort, a programme of bringing in foreign capital became essential. The structural reorientation of the economy was radical. A small, protected home market gave way to emphasis on export-centred manufacturing industry, with foreign companies taking advantage of low wages and a union-free environment. Emigration and conscription soaked up potential unemployment and emigrants' remittances helped with the balance of payments. The country was increasingly dependent on foreign capital and on northern Europe. By the 1970s employment in agriculture had dropped to one-third of the labour force.

Ideologically, the project of a rural, Catholic, anti-modern and isolated Portugal was dead by the late 1960s. However, the regime had no new vision to put in its place. A new urban working class had emerged. It was poorly paid and badly housed, its working conditions were harsh, and it was denied trade union rights. In a sense, society was undergoing a profound identity crisis. Uncontrolled economic growth both raised expectations and created new problems of pollution, poor sanitation and housing conditions, and growing income inequality.

From September 1968 until April 1974 the regime veered shakily between controlled liberalisation and bouts of increased repression. Some exiles (including the future president, Mario Soares) were permitted to return home, and a 1972 trade agreement with the EC encouraged the regime's technocratic advisers to hope for full EC membership. Realisation that this would be facilitated by a transition to democracy increased pressure from within for further change. In 1973 Caetano resorted to repression in the face of industrial unrest. This coincided with discontent within the military where younger officers had founded a radical Armed Forces Movement (MFA). War-weariness by now united broad sectors of society, including many conservatives. In April 1974 the MFA seized power, ending nearly 50 years of dictatorship. The new government ended the wars in Africa, granting independence to the colonies. On virtually every other issue, however, both army and society were divided. For the next two years politics swung back and forth between left and right.

Between April 1974 and the summer of 1975 the Portuguese Communist Party (PCP), the best organised opposition force in the dying days of the old dictatorship, sought to capture the leadership of the revolution. It supported the appointment of a left-wing army officer, Vasco Goncalves, as prime minister in July 1974, and the formation of a Revolutionary Council in early 1975. This body nationalised banks and insurance companies, broke up the large landed estates and distributed land to the peasants. It was envisaged that the Revolutionary Council would guard against capitalist or fascist restoration.

From mid-1975 events moved against the left. Whilst the majority of Portuguese had welcomed the demise of dictatorship, many – especially in the Catholic north – remained conservative. Moreover, there was a widespread fear that the pro-Soviet PCP would simply replace one form of dictatorship with another. The PCP's tactics earned it the hostility of the Portuguese Socialist Party (PSP), led by Mario Soares. Pro-Western technocratic elements within the power structures, together with moderate army officers, began to regroup. Elections to a constituent assembly were held on 25 April 1975 and disappointed the communists, who won just 12.5 per cent of the vote. The PSP emerged as the only really national party with 37.9 per cent; conservatives took 34 per cent. In April 1976 the PSP won general elections and in July the period of revolutionary turmoil ended when Mario Soares became prime minister.

Spain

In many ways the path of the Spanish dictatorship is strikingly different. In power since 1939, Franco imposed a highly centralised and authoritarian regime. He shared with Salazar a hatred of socialism, communism, and liberalism, and was also concerned with repressing every sign of social or ethnic pluralism. Ethnic groups such as the Basques and Catalans bore the brunt of a repression which drove their languages and cultures largely underground. The Spanish dictatorship drew upon the support of rural landowners and the Catholic Church. It also appealed to the army's self-image as the protector of a unified and centralised Spain and its hatred of regional autonomy. The army was used to repress those who had supported the democratic government in the Spanish civil war and the divisions of that war were effectively institutionalised.

Franco's regime, although the most classically fascist of the three dictatorships, represented a coalition of forces which was riddled by contradictions. Monarchists, fascists (the *Falange*), rural landowners, technocrats, nationalist soldiers, and Catholic clerics, coexisted sometimes uneasily inside the National Movement, the regime's political party. Franco, proclaimed *Caudillo* (Leader), presided over this coalition, mediating between its often warring components. It was the *Falange* which provided the fascist trappings – a uniformed mass movement complete with Roman salute, quasi-corporatist doctrines of social organisation, and authoritarian nationalism. But the *Falange* was never more than one part of the movement.

From 1939 until the mid-1950s the regime pursued economic and social policies similar to those followed in Portugal. Trade unions were smashed and replaced by fascist corporations; political repression was employed to keep workers in line; low wages and high food prices meant that the spending power of most people was limited and little existed by way of demand-led growth. The power of the big landowners was reinforced and agriculture remained notoriously inefficient. Marshall Aid was not offered in 1947 and Spain remained isolated internationally.

By the early 1950s problems were mounting, with shortages of food and technology necessitating imports. An economic debate divided the ruling party between opponents and advocates of the development of free market capitalism. The latter won through; economic and military agreements with the US in 1953 were followed by membership of the International Monetary Fund in 1958. A Stabilisation Plan in 1959 aimed at attracting foreign investment and modernising the economy whilst retaining political repression.

As in Portugal, the 1960s and early 1970s witnessed growing involvement with foreign markets, penetration by foreign capital, and moves to draw closer to the EC. Spain requested associate EC membership in 1962. The regime hoped that full membership could eventually be achieved without democratisation. Growth rates rose dramatically in the 1960s, especially in the north. This rapid and uneven development generated social and economic problems – above all the uncontrolled growth of urban centres as people flocked from agriculture into industry with consequent hardship for the newly urbanised workers.

Four important contradictions surfaced during the decade. First, a growing urban working class began to find its voice. The illegal but active trade unions organised strikes from 1962. The regime's ability to keep workers passive depended on rising living standards. However, a reformist path was opposed by those who had reluctantly conceded the economic U-turn when assured of growing army representation in government and increased repression to avoid political change. Second, the balance of forces within the National Movement shifted away from the landowners and *Falange* towards an alliance of more internationally inclined forces – technocrats, bankers, and financiers. Third, attempts at limited reform in the mid-1960s with a slightly relaxed press law simply encouraged the underground opposition forces to organise against repression. Finally, as society became secularised, with falling rates of church attendance in urban areas, the Catholic Church began to distance itself from the regime. Progressive priests and bishops condemned torture and repression of workers' rights. In 1971 the Church actually apologised to the Spanish people for the support hitherto given to Franco.

As the 1970s got under way the regime's backers were hopelessly divided. Two broad groups emerged. Hard-line falangists favoured continuing repression; reformists favoured controlled liberalisation and an opening to the opposition forces. This latter group included Adolfo Suárez, who was to preside over a new centre-right political formation in the mid-1970s, the Democratic Centre Union, and was to be prime minister of democratic Spain. Some of the regime's leading members veered between repression and reform. These included Manuel Fraga, who later emerged as founder of the Popular Party (PP), the main conservative party in present-day Spain.

In 1969 the ageing Franco appointed as his successor Prince Juan Carlos, son of King Juan in whose name Franco had ruled. Political instability and street protests increased in 1973, when the assassination by Basque gunmen of the regime's second-in-command, Admiral Luis Carrero Blanco, prompted reformists within the regime to move into dialogue with the (still illegal) opposition parties. Following Franco's death in November 1975, Juan Carlos was crowned king and the way was cleared for a democratic transition. Adolfo Suárez became prime minister in 1976, and despite opposition from hard-liners, political parties were legalised from February 1977. The moderate tactics of the opposition parties – including the communists – were decisive in enabling a transition to democracy, without anything like the rupture which occurred in Portugal. Democratic elections in June 1977 gave victory to the centre-right UCD with 34 per cent; the socialists, led by Felipe González, gained 28 per cent; the communists, led by Santiago Carrillo, won 10 per cent; and Fraga's conservatives won 8 per cent.

Greece

The short-lived Greek military dictatorship came to power at a time when the international climate was less tolerant towards such regimes than it had been in the 1920s and 1930s, and it had little time in which to consolidate its authority. Nevertheless, the Greek dictatorship enjoyed the support of the USA, which was more concerned with securing a solid anti-communist ally in an area judged vulnerable to Soviet influence than in defending democracy inside Greece.

In 1945 the Allies had agreed that Greece should belong to the western sphere of influence. Stalin did little to help the Greek Communist Party (KKE) when it attempted to seize power in 1946. The communists had played a leading role in the anti-Nazi resistance movement and resented signs of a conservative restoration under British–American influence. British military intervention helped to secure the defeat of the communists and the imposition of a conservative regime after a bitter and bloody civil war (1946–49). The civil war left deep wounds on the body politic and helps explain the highly partisan nature of political alignments ever since. From 1949 anti-communism was adopted as an instrument of state policy and the KKE was banned.

Although Greece was formally a parliamentary regime, real power lay outside parliament. Alongside the fairly liberal constitution of 1952, a largely unwritten code operated, which accepted the army as the guarantor of the established social order. Repressive laws were directed against those suspected of communist sympathies. The civil service and the teaching professions were purged. Suspected left-wingers could be deprived of a passport, a driving licence, or a public sector job. In administering this system of discrimination, the police built up a huge network of spies.

Power was exercised by a triarchy of monarchy, army, and the parliamentary right. Any attempt to open up politics to the centre-left risked jeopardising this balance and calling into question the role of the army as custodian of the *status quo*. (This is what happened in the mid-1960s, prompting the military coup in 1967.) After 1952 British influence was superseded by US influence. The Greek economy was opened up to foreign (largely American) capital much earlier than the economies of Spain or Portugal. Greece joined NATO in 1952. Its vulnerability to outside influence was intensified by the situation in Cyprus where extreme Greek nationalists were pushing for union with Greece and where violence exploded in the mid-1950s.

In the 1958 election a reviving left braved discrimination to poll 25 per cent of the vote. More significant was the formation of a Centre Union in 1961 under the leadership of George Papandreou and his son, Andreas. The Centre Union combined elements of political liberalism, economic Keynesianism, radical popular nationalism and old-fashioned clientelism. It posed a real challenge to the dominance of the right. Elections in October 1961 returned the right, led by Constantine Karamanlis, to power. An association treaty with the EC in 1962 was intended to anchor Greece in the western camp. In November 1963 elections returned a centrist government led by George Papandreou, and Karamanlis left for voluntary exile in Paris.

Further elections in February 1964 gave Papandreou a clear mandate for change. Social reforms followed, including raising the school age from 12 to 15 and launching a campaign against illiteracy. Keynesian intervention in the economy sought to raise wages and boost demand. Political prisoners were released. It seemed as if the centrists were moving towards full democracy by opening up the political system to the lower social classes and overcoming the civil war divisions. However, such changes alarmed the military and powerful business groups.

In the summer of 1965 King Constantine II forced the government's resignation, to appease the military. A right-wing cabinet was installed, presiding over mounting social unrest before agreeing to hold new elections in May 1967. To forestall these elections the military seized power on 21 April 1967. A junta led by Colonel George Papadopoulos suspended human rights, banned political parties and strikes, proclaimed martial law, and sent thousands into internal exile.

Although ferocious anti-communist rhetoric was a hallmark of the junta, there is no doubt that their real target was the centrists; the military feared any threat to their privileged position. From 1967 to 1974 traditionalist values were extolled, but the corrupt lifestyle of the military leaders – soon enjoying the 'good life' on luxury yachts donated by grateful Greek shipping tycoons – belied their pious, moralistic propaganda.

The junta's contemptuous attitude towards all politicians alienated the traditional political establishment and even the king, who attempted an unsuccessful counter-coup in late 1967 before fleeing to Rome. Thereafter, all power was concentrated in military hands. The regime was isolated and discredited; it lacked internal unity or ideological coherence; and it was concerned with little more than its own privileges. It stumbled on with American support until 1974. Repression kept opposition contained until March 1973 when Athenian students staged an uprising. A further uprising in November was brutally repressed; 34 students were killed and scores wounded. Soon afterwards, a hard-line coup inside the junta brought intensified repression.

In April and May 1974 the junta staged a military escapade in Cyprus, apparently hoping that conflict with Turkey would shower it with patriotic honours. On 20 July Turkey invaded Cyprus, the island was divided into two zones, and the Greek army retreated in shambles. The junta lost US sympathy: Washington certainly had no desire to see two NATO allies at war. On 23 July the junta withdrew from politics in disarray. Karamanlis, who created a new centre-right party called New Democracy (ND), returned from Paris to preside over a transition to democracy. This time, the measures which had enshrined military power in the 1950s were ended, the communists were legalised, and full parliamentary democracy under civilian rule was achieved.

Dynamics of the democratic transitions

None of the democratic transitions in southern Europe was the outcome of a spontaneous mass revolution. In all cases, the actions and interactions of key elite groups, social and political forces (including parties, trade unions, and churches), and state institutions (especially the army) significantly determined the nature of the transition. It is essential, therefore, to study the social and political context which shaped these actors' perceptions of what was desirable and possible.

It is clear that sections of the old regime in Spain came to embrace the need to enter into dialogue with opposition forces and to abandon repression. By the early 1970s technocratic and business elites were beginning to accept the need for a democratic transition, although they often disagreed on how far democratisation should go. The dictatorship in Greece isolated itself from traditional conservative elites, and apart from key business backers, such as the shipping tycoons, had a limited support base. In Portugal the loss of military confidence in the dictatorship was decisive.

So why did the dictatorships disintegrate from within? Economic change since the 1950s involved greater dependence on foreign trade and foreign capital. Potential conflicts between manufacturers geared to supplying the restricted needs of a protected home market and multinational corporations and bankers and financiers had intensified. The suppression of trade unions and opposition parties alienated the workers, and the absence of channels of communication and negotiation dented support from business groups. The dictatorships did not permit real representation of diverse interests even within the ranks of their own supporters. Conflicts intensified and industrial relations deteriorated. A section of the dominant economic elites came to recognise the need for at least a limited pluralism. This was necessary both to achieve social and political stability, and to allow renegotiation of the alliance between the component parts of the ruling bloc. But even a limited pluralism was thwarted by the elimination of genuinely representative parties and interest groups. Attempts at half-hearted reform floundered, as the regimes realised that they risked losing everything once reform got under way. This, in turn, helped to convince some elites that only a transition to liberal democracy could secure stability and economic growth.

External pressures were also important. The incentive of EC membership seemed to offer a guarantee of greater prosperity, less dependence on US capital and influence (especially in Greece), and political stability through anchorage in the family of established western European democracies.

The relative weakness of mass opposition reduced the likelihood that the dismantling of the dictatorships might threaten the capitalist order and undermine the power of existing elites. Popular pressure from below for change certainly existed in all three countries – as was shown by strikes and demonstrations. Certain social groups in particular gave vent to this pressure – workers in Spain, students in Greece, young soldiers in Portugal. But there was never any real threat of left-wing revolution, except perhaps from sections of the Portuguese military. Pressure from below for change conditioned the actions of elites, but rarely set the agenda.

Mass opposition was probably strongest in Spain where the complex interactions of parties, trade unions, employers' organisations, political elites and the army was of critical importance. The moderate tactics adopted by the left-wing parties helped to reassure business groups and to facilitate a smooth transition to democracy. The Spanish Communist Party (PCE) found itself electorally and politically weakened by the dynamics of subsequent democratic consolidation, but its moderation and pragmatism were crucial in strengthening the hand of reformists such as Adolfo Suárez and in reducing military opposition to the transition. Similarly, the unions were prepared to demand sacrifices of their members and enter into agreement with the employers to guarantee the conditions for democratic stability.

The role of the military was decisive everywhere. The Spanish military had been interwoven into the fabric of the Franco dictatorship, enjoying a privileged position since the civil war, and regarding itself as the defender of Spanish unity. In Portugal, the military's involvement in colonial wars was to prove the catalyst of the dictatorship's downfall. Only Greece approximated to a pure military dictatorship. Although the military possessed its own concerns, it also exhibited many of the tensions and contradictions present in society. Nowhere was the military to prove a monolithic bloc. In Portugal internal divisions rendered the post-1974 army an unstable political instrument; the PCP, for example, found its attempts to use the Revolutionary Council to push for more radical transformations of society frustrated by the inability of the military to act cohesively. In Greece military divisions forced the dictatorship to withdraw from the political stage. Even in Spain many younger and better-educated officers perceived their role as a force of modernisation rather than crude repression. A Military Democratic Union was formed in 1974 to push for changes. The number of senior officers favouring legalisation of the PCE rose from 5 per cent to 30 per cent in 1975–76. The lesson from southern Europe seems to be that in times of rapid social and economic change precipitating a crisis of political legitimacy the military can become an site of internal struggle. Much depends on the strength of civil society, the tactics and strategies of social and political forces, and external pressures.

The consolidation of new political institutions

Clearly, a distinction exists between transitions to democracy and the subsequent consolidation of new political systems. Admittedly, it is not always easy to state where transition ends and consolidation begins. Nor is it clear what time scale should be adopted. Moreover, the struggle to defend and reinvigorate democracy is a continuous one which every generation faces. Bearing this in mind, it might still be argued that a qualitative step forward has been taken on the road away from authoritarian regimes when the values and ground rules of the new democratic political system gain widespread acceptance and new political institutions begin to function smoothly.

Democracy can be consolidated only through a number of processes. The powers and role of the state must be delineated, allowing an autonomous civil society to flourish. The new constitution must be accepted by a majority of citizens and political actors. The different interests and views in society must be effectively represented by parties which are independent of the state and accountable to citizens. Governments must be formed on the basis of a majority, and power must alternate peacefully between government and opposition. The party system must be stabilised, and anti-democratic parties must become marginal, preferably through lack of support. The armed forces must be subordinated to the democratic civilian authorities. Channels of communication and negotiation must be established between the state, parties, and major interest groups. A civic culture must be established in which the concept of citizenship rights and obligations is accepted and understood.

Spain, Portugal, and Greece have come a long way in achieving democratic consolidation. Civilian dominance over the military has been established. This happened relatively early in Greece, where the military discredited itself comprehensively; attempts to plot against the new government in 1974–75 floundered when a large majority of the officer corps remained loyal to the elected authorities. In Portugal the military continued to play a significant role in politics into the 1980s; nevertheless, the Revolutionary Council was disbanded in 1982 and in February 1986 a civilian – Mario Soares – finally became head of state. In Spain the civilian authorities had to make considerable concessions to secure the military's withdrawal from politics. These included increasing defence spending and soft-pedaling on regional reforms. An attempted military coup in February 1981 collapsed following the personal intervention of the king. Since then the military has stayed out of politics, although threats to Spanish unity can still provoke its unease.

Relatively stable party systems now function in all three countries. The only really 'anti-system' party in the region is the Basque *Herri Batasuna* (political wing of the ETA terrorist organisation). Support for far-right or neo-fascist parties has been insignificant up to 1999. The communist parties all operate within the democratic system. In Portugal a short-lived Democratic Renewal Party was founded by elements close to the military in 1985 but collapsed in 1987. Political competition since has been between four relatively stable forces: centre-right liberals (PSD), centre-left socialists (PSP), conservatives (CDS) and communists (PCP). During the 1990s the Portuguese communists have contested elections as part of a coalition with Greens and others which is known as the United Democratic Coalition (CDU). In Spain considerable turmoil in the mid-1970s has given way to a three-party system – socialists (PSOE), conservatives (PP), and communists and allies (United Left – IU). The remaining 20 per cent of voters support regional parties which mostly accept the Spanish constitution. In Greece there is a similar three-party system of conservatives (ND), socialists (PASOK), and communists – although the communists are divided into two rival groupings. Signs of upheaval within the Greek party system appeared with a split within ND in spring 1993 leading to the formation of another right-of-centre party called Political Spring. Led by Antonis Samaras, it benefited from an upsurge in Greek nationalism following international recognition of the Former Yugoslav Republic of Macedonia (FYROM). It saw its support fade in the late 1990s as ND reasserted itself on the right.

Survey evidence suggests that popular support for the new political systems is relatively high. Moreover, the recourse to referenda to abolish the monarchy and establish a republic (as in Greece in 1974), or to approve legalisation of parties (as in Spain in 1976) helped to confer legitimacy.

Nevertheless, a number of negative phenomena threatening the consolidation of democracy can be observed. The persistence of charisma as a key political asset is a double-edged sword. Whilst the enormous popularity of certain leaders has helped to stabilise democracy, it may mean that some parties find it difficult to survive intact after the death or retirement of their leaders. The extreme factionalism with New Democracy after the retirement and subsequent death of Constantine Karamanlis is an example. The personalisation of politics can also accentuate rivalries and feed the tendency towards demagogic leadership and towards dynasties. The election in March 1997 of Costas Karamanlis, nephew of the party founder, as leader of New Democracy in a bid to restore party unity is again an example. Parliaments remain weak and executives retain a considerable degree of autonomy from parliamentary supervision; this, however, is a problem common to all European democracies. The weakness of civil society manifests itself in a number of ways. Parties are seldom mass organisations, despite the use of state patronage. Trade unions remain numerically weak – only 10–15 per cent of the labour force in Spain and Portugal – and plagued by political rivalries. Employers' organisations lack internal coherence. The relative weakness of channels of communication and negotiation between the state and the main interest groups has meant that industrial relations have recently been plagued by conflict. Finally, evidence of corruption has come to light. The main parties in Spain and Greece on both left and right have been repeatedly embroiled in scandals involving allegations of embezzlement of state funds and massive use of patronage to reward their supporters. Although the multi-faceted crisis of parties is a feature of all western democracies, the distinction between party and state in southern Europe has arguably been blurred to a greater extent than in northern Europe. Some writers detect a degeneration of political parties into little more than rival parasitical clans. Other writers argue that most examples of clientelism, as distinct from corruption, are fairly harmless and may even have helped to secure the new democratic systems.

Party competition since the transition to democracy

Party competition in southern Europe since the mid-1970s has been characterised by: the dominant role of conservative and socialist parties, the deradicalisation of the socialist parties, the struggle of the conservative parties to modernise, and the decline of the communist parties, split everywhere between reformers and traditionalists.

The socialist parties were the dominant force in Spain and Greece during the 1980s, and to a lesser extent in Portugal from the mid-1970s until the mid-1980s. As the 1990s drew to a close, the socialists were again in power in Greece and Portugal. In Spain the Socialist Workers' Party (PSOE) won elections in 1982, 1986 and 1989, polling between 40 and 48 per cent of the vote. PSOE returned to power as a minority government with 38.8 per cent in June 1993, despite losing seats and votes. It was finally ousted by the conservative PP in March 1996 when PSOE polled 37.5 per cent. In Greece the Pan-Hellenic Socialist Movement (PASOK) was founded by Andreas Papandreou in 1974 and won power in 1981 with 48 per cent of the vote. PASOK held office until June 1989, and won elections in 1993 and 1996. In Portugal the PSP has been less successful electorally; but it held the premiership in 1976–78 and 1983–85, has held the presidency since 1986, and won general elections in October 1995.

The character of the socialist parties has changed enormously. Early radical aspirations have been abandoned in favour of moderate social democracy. PSOE dropped its commitment to Marxism in 1978, thereafter evolving steadily into a centrist party in terms of economic policy. During the 1980s it was even accused of favouring Thatcherite economics. At the end of the 1980s the trade unions accused PSOE of betraying the unemployed through its deflationary policies. Unemployment has remained the weak point of the party's record and, together with corruption scandals, probably helps to account for its recent electoral losses. The Spanish economy has grown under PSOE direction but monetarist policies have brought about this growth. Even if the retention of the state's controlling share in many industries renders the charge of Thatcherism less than accurate, few would deny that the results achieved have little to do with socialism as the party once envisaged it. In foreign policy too Felipe González abandoned former socialist policies in 1986, and secured NATO membership and entry into the EC. PSOE's most radical achievements in government have perhaps involved reducing the Church's influence in education and introducing social reforms such as divorce and abortion legislation. By the mid-1990s PSOE was embroiled in a series of damaging scandals and accusations of involvement in an illegal 'dirty war' against suspected Basque terrorists, which had seen some suspects abducted, tortured and murdered. It was perceived as having run out of ideas and as no longer the force for modernisation, attractive to young voters, which it once was. Its attempt to cling on to power in 1996 by branding the conservative PP as unreconstructed Francoists who would threaten both democracy and the social security system failed and it went into opposition. In June 1997 González resigned as PSOE leader but refused to rule out a future comeback. His erstwhile protégé Joaquín Almunia, was elected as leader and other moderates dominated the party executive, routing supporters of Alfonso Guerra on the left and prompting Guerra's resignation as deputy party leader.

In Greece PASOK in opposition called for withdrawal from NATO and opposed EC membership. It advocated an independent foreign policy sympathetic to Third World causes, social reforms aimed at achieving gender equality, comprehensive health and education programmes and widespread socialisation of industry and financial institutions. The first PASOK government attempted many reforms, but was forced to moderate its foreign policy stance, especially with regard to the American military presence and membership of the EC. Papandreou made much of renegotiating the terms of EC membership so as to obtain a better deal for Greece, but achieved little by doing so; moreover EC aid probably created a dynamic of dependency. In the mid-1980s PASOK adopted austerity measures which weakened trade unions and effectively shelved Keynesian-style spending plans. Back in government from 1993 its fate was tied up with Papandreou's declining health. From November 1995 PASOK was torn with factionalism between Papandreou's supporters and those of the technocrat,

Kostas Simitis, who pledged to dismantle clientelism and introduce monetarist reforms which would prepare Greece for European monetary union. Papandreou's highly personal and populist style and his refusal to allow the nomination of a potential successor had deepened party divisions. In January 1996 Papandreou was succeeded as prime minister by Simitis and in June he died. Simitis became party leader after a bitter internal battle with interior minister Akis Tsokhatzopoulos, a Papandreou loyalist. Simitis was strengthened by success in elections held in September 1996 when he led PASOK to an unexpectedly comfortable victory, polling 41.5 per cent of the vote. Although the election saw some PASOK voters transfer their support to the communists and other left-wing parties, Simitis could claim a mandate for his technocratic and pro-European policies which were soon to provoke opposition from within both PASOK and the trade unions.

In Portugal the PSP has sought to project itself as the party of EC-sponsored modernisation. In practice this entailed reversing many of the nationalisations of the early revolutionary period and implementing measures to attract foreign investment. The party has been open to coalition with the centre-right PSD, which supported Soares' presidential re-election in 1991. When the PSP returned to power in 1995, under António Guterres, it was on a platform of modernisation and opposition to corruption, rather than radical social change.

A number of factors explain the rightwards move of the socialist parties. The 1980s saw the rise of New Right ideas internationally and the vulnerable position of the southern European economies left the socialists exposed. There was a strong temptation to embrace the free market modernisation promised by the EC as the only basis upon which to build for future prosperity. Moreover, there was a need to reassure dominant economic and social groups that democracy would not result in upheaval and revolution. Once the task of democratic consolidation was perceived as vital, a move away from radicalism was inevitable. The socialist parties all had fairly weak links to organised labour, which reduced internal organisational resistance to the rightwards move. The parties were centralised machines in which a cult of leadership facilitated policy U-turns. Papandreou, for example, regularly purged the PASOK leadership almost at will and bequeathed it a legacy of personalised factionalism and bitterness. It is true that resistance in PSOE to González's policy changes has sometimes been forthcoming from a populist wing associated with Alfonso Guerra. Nevertheless, in March 1994, González was able to orchestrate a leadership reshuffle which reduced Guerra's influence; and in June 1997, even after his own resignation from the party leadership, González was able to marginalise Guerra and the PSOE left even further. Finally, socialists have faced weak competition on their left flank.

A balance sheet of the socialists' performance in southern Europe must record a number of substantial achievements: democratic consolidation, EU membership, extension of civil liberties and women's rights, and economic growth. But the socialists' loss of any clear radical or reforming commitment now poses identity problems, as does their growing involvement in scandals and clientelist politics (although they are not unique in this).

The socialists' move towards the centre and embracing of market-led economics has compounded the identity problems of the right-wing or conservative forces. In both Spain and Greece conservative parties played the dominant role in government during the 1970s but lost power in the early 1980s. The right was more successful electorally in Portugal during these years.

In Greece ND, in power from 1974–81, embraced welfare policies and a consensus approach to industrial relations; it enjoyed business backing whilst speaking of the need for social democracy. However, the moderate image was not accepted by all its members and a backlash by right-wingers intensified after it lost power in 1981. During the 1980s ND moved further to the right, calling for privatisation of state-owned industries and strict control of the money supply. Greece's crippling burden of debt, allegations of abuse of state funds by PASOK, and the perceived need to meet EC conditions for aid, all created a climate in which calls for fiscal rectitude gained a receptive audience. (Ironically these themes were to be taken up by Simitis after he became leader of PASOK in 1996, leaving ND without a clear message of its own.) ND defeated PASOK in June 1989, but without gaining a majority in parliament. A year-long coalition with the communists – to tackle corruption – ended when ND gained a one-seat majority, ruling on its own until October 1993.

In the early 1990s ND's economic policies provoked industrial and student unrest. The party backed down in 1991 in the face of opposition to its education reforms. It was forced to abandon plans to pardon the imprisoned leaders of the old military junta, and was placed on the defensive over the crisis in Macedonia. A split in 1993 showed how vulnerable it was to internal party conflict. Defeat by PASOK in October 1993 was followed by the election of a new leader, Miltiades Evert, a moderate who had previously clashed with the right wing of his own party. Evert, however, found it increasingly difficult to compete with the pro-European policies of PASOK, especially after Simitis succeeded Papandreou as prime minister in January 1996. From September 1996 Evert's leadership was fatally undermined by electoral defeat and internal party feuding. His party had lost business support to PASOK in elections held in September. In March 1997 in a desperate bid to restore unity, ND elected Costas Karamanlis (nephew of its founder) as its new leader.

In Spain two main rightist formations emerged during the mid-1970s: the centre-right UCD, led by Suárez, and the more conservative PP, led until 1990 by Manuel Fraga. Political polarisation during the early 1980s badly squeezed the UCD and permitted the rise of the PP. Paradoxically, this may have sealed the electoral fate of the right throughout the 1980s, for many Spaniards were clearly unwilling to trust the PP, given some of its leaders' past associations with the dictatorship.

In the early 1990s the PP suffered from factionalism, a failure to modernise its image and ideology, and difficulty in adapting to social change. It was unable to attract any significant working-class support and was thwarted by the fact that many conservative voters continued to favour regionalist parties. The election of Jose Maria Aznar as leader in 1990 heralded a serious attempt to address these concerns. Aznar pushed through reforms in February 1993 aimed at increasing the PP's appeal to women and young people, and introduced mandatory dismissal for corrupt office-holders. A concerted drive in June 1993 to project the PP as a modernising, young, and attractive alternative to a tired socialist government failed to produce immediate results. In 1993 the PP polled a mere 34.8 per cent of the vote, 4 points behind PSOE, and was again condemned to opposition. However, the growing crisis of the socialist government through involvement in scandals allowed Aznar to fight elections in March 1996 on a platform promising renewal and moderation. The PP returned to office as a minority government, supported by regional parties. It polled 38.9 per cent of the vote to PSOE's 37.5 per cent. Aznar's cabinet, however, was strongly conservative and Catholic. Although the PP reversed its opposition to regional reforms, it played to traditional conservative themes of austerity and privatisation. Budget cuts, to prepare Spain for the European single currency, resulted in renewed unrest and civil service strikes in 1996 and 1997.

In Portugal the centre-right PSD dominated politics from the mid-1980s to the mid-1990s, balancing a neo-liberal, market-led approach to economics with the pursuit of consensus with the socialists. Led by Anibal Cavaco Silva, the PSD held power from 1987 to 1995. Nevertheless, it faced a challenge from the more right-wing CDS – a party with between 10 and 14 per cent of the vote. The PSD in power has not always been as willing to push through the privatisation as its rhetoric had suggested. Critics have sometimes alleged that the patronage potential of the public sector is one reason why this is so; another may be an unwillingness to face deteriorating industrial relations. Indeed, corruption scandals and the perceived arrogance of Cavaco Silva both contributed to the PSD's defeat in elections in October 1995. In March 1996 the PSD elected Marcelo Rebelo de Sousa as its leader, in a bid to restore badly shaken party unity and morale.

The record for the southern European conservatives is mixed. Nowhere has the right achieved real political dominance, although in Portugal it came close in the late 1980s. In Spain conservatives continued to suffer from association with the authoritarian past although victory in 1996 confirmed that this is easing as time passes. In Greece the right resembles a shaky coalition of potentially divergent interests. The dilemma everywhere is clear: should the right pursue consensus with the centre-left or aim for dominance, through conflict if necessary? Consensus may be a safer option, guaranteeing social stability and democratic consolidation. However, it threatens to erode the distinctive identity of both the socialist and conservative parties in southern Europe, given the similarity in their policies now, and to reward whichever can appear most competent at implementing a (largely) shared agenda. This, in, turn may increase the temptation to hurl accusations of corruption and incompetence at each other, exaggerating such differences as still exist.

The third main political force in the region has been the communists, although several such parties have now evolved into post-communist parties. The communist parties all resisted the old dictatorships, and the Iberian parties especially were important actors during the democratic transition. Since then, however, they have faced marginalisation. Two types of response have been characteristic. The first has involved a reformist strategy which prioritised demo-cratic consolidation, isolation of the extreme right, and establishment of the democratic credentials of the communists themselves. The second has involved an attempt to move the transition process along quickly, under communist lead-ership, in the direction of socialist revolution.

The majority of the Spanish communists chose the first response, contribut-ing to democratic consolidation but paying an electoral price. Disappointing election results, the top-heavy leadership style of PCE boss Carrillo, and direct interference from Moscow, all contributed to a severe internal party crisis in the early 1980s. The PCE split into several factions, sank to a mere 3 per cent of the vote and almost disintegrated in 1982–86. The Greek communists had split as far back as 1968 into a pro-Soviet hard-line KKE and a moderate minor-ity faction which took a democratic line. The Portuguese party remained wedded to Soviet orthodoxy.

Until the early 1990s the PCP and the KKE maintained an electoral presence of around 10 per cent, a strong trade union base, and a loyal working-class fol-lowing. However, since the collapse of the USSR these parties have struggled to come to terms with the implosion of their ideology. Severe internal splits led to expulsions from both parties in the early 1990s. Not even the election of new leaders – Carlos Carvalhas (PCP) in 1992 and Aleka Papariga (KKE) in 1991 – has stemmed the haemorrhage of voters, members, and influence. In October 1993 the KKE saw its share of the Greek vote fall to a humiliating 4.5 per cent. The disillusionment of some left-wing voters with PASOK's policy of budget cuts allowed a modest revival in 1996 when the KKE polled 5.6 per cent. Both the KKE and the PCP will struggle to maintain even their current diminished status in the future. Although they may well survive, it is likely to be as vehicles for the protest vote of those disillusioned by the socialists rather than as the proud and militant 'vanguard' parties which they could once claim to be.

The PCE drew back from the brink of disaster in 1986 by joining with dissi-dent socialists, pacifists, feminists, and others to launch the United Left (IU) coalition. Conceived as a broad front of anti-NATO radicals, the IU has consoli-dated itself as the third force in Spanish politics. In June 1993 it polled just under 10 per cent and this rose to 11 per cent in 1996. Provided the IU can avoid splits, it has a good chance of occupying the space on the left vacated by PSOE. The IU is now a post-Marxist movement which articulates the concerns of the Green, feminist, and peace movements.

The moderate Greek communists launched the Greek Left (EAR) in 1987. Again this is very much a post-communist party committed to gender equality and radical reforms rather than classical Marxism. The retreat of the KKE into sectari-anism in 1990–92 left the EAR, together with KKE dissidents and others, fighting under the banner of the 'Coalition of Left and Progress' *(Sinaspismos)*. This forma-tion polled 2.9 per cent in the October 1993 elections, narrowly missing the 3 per cent required for representation in the Greek parliament. It did better in 1996 when its vote rose to 5.1 per cent and it won 10 seats in parliament. Both the Spanish IU and *Sinaspismos* – rooted as they are in significant social movements, and articulating concerns which many feel have been neglected or betrayed by the socialists – possess the potential to be dynamic, if minority, political forces in the future. However, they have yet to develop a strategy which does not condemn them merely to reacting to a pace of events set by the socialists.

The impact of the European Community/Union

Greece joined the EC in 1981, Spain and Portugal in 1986. There is no doubt that EC membership has had important economic, social, political, and cultural effects. Those who supported membership enthusiastically – the centre-right parties, and the Iberian socialists – argued that the EC would assist democratic consolidation, bring prosperity, and achieve cultural reintegration into the European mainstream. EC aid would facilitate infrastructural improvements and industrial modernisation; and the discipline of membership would force the southern European economies to bring inflation and budget deficits firmly under control. In other words, a powerful external guarantee of both democratic consolidation and balanced growth would result. Those who opposed EC membership totally – chiefly the KKE and PCP – argued that the EC would accentuate uneven development and suck their countries into increased dependency upon northern European (and American) capital. Membership would erode national sovereignty and imperil the recently won democratic freedom by shifting real power away from national governments and parliaments to Brussels. A third group – comprising the moderate Spanish and Greek communists – accepted EC membership as a guarantor of democracy and as a progressive development, but opposed the free market logic inherent in the EC and argued for a struggle to transform the Community from within. This would involve left-wing forces battling within a strengthened European Parliament to achieve a much stronger social Europe. PASOK, in Greece, has moved from outright hostility to warm support for EC/EU membership.

There can be little doubt that EC/EU membership has helped to stabilise democracy. On the other hand southern Europe has found itself battling for a greater share of EU resources and for increases in social spending. Greece has benefited from the Integrated Mediterranean Programmes (IMPs) which had their origins in PASOK's renegotiation of membership terms in 1982–83. Under the IMPs, southern Europe has picked up payments to assist with the readjustment of small businesses, agriculture, and tourism to the requirements of participation in the European single market. Portugal has gained significantly from EU structural funds. Greece and Spain have benefited from agricultural subsidies.

Nevertheless, there have been difficulties in adjustment, and it remains unclear how the region will fare when the last of the special transitional protective arrangements for fruit and vegetables expires. Familiar problems remain: high foreign debt, high inflation (except in Portugal), very high unemployment and the threat of growing regional imbalances. Mass tourism has damaged the Mediterranean coastline and overloaded waste disposal and sewage systems. The

Mediterranean is the dirtiest and most urbanised sea in the world with few underdeveloped coastal areas left. This could endanger the tourist trade.

Although southern Europe is relatively more prosperous now than it was prior to EU membership, its overall position as a poor and dependent region has not changed. Much now depends on the (unpredictable) nature of the EU's development. If a two-track or even three-track European Union develops, then it seems certain that southern Europe will find itself more dependent than ever on decisions taken in the developed core. Spain, Portugal, and especially Greece are hopelessly ill-equipped to meet the criteria for monetary and economic convergence; the enthusiasm of governments in the region to do so risks rising unemployment and mounting social tension. The ability to tackle inflation and debt is hampered by political factors. Squeezing living standards and reducing real wages, or reducing expenditure on health and education provision, imposes heavy sacrifices. Dashing people's expectations about living standards could lead to political instability. Measures to raise revenue by widening the tax base and tackling fraud, evasion, and corruption risk alienating farming and professional support for the ruling parties. Finally, such measures, and a more rational use of EU funds, require a change in political culture.

Conclusion

Spain, Portugal, and Greece face a number of difficult challenges. Their democratic political systems are all but secure. Nevertheless, as in northern Europe, signs of political malaise are evident. Irredentist nationalism which threatens to drift across the Balkans towards Greece, and the growing incidence of racially motivated attacks on immigrants in Spain and Portugal, present a challenge to democratic leadership. Political elites have yet to face up fully to the task of carrying forward the modernisation of politics and political systems. This is not merely, or primarily, a generational question. The relative weakness of civil society, the persistence of clientelism, and the tendency to resort to populist demagogy challenge the ability of political systems to express through democratic channels new socio-political cleavages as they arise.

Economically, southern Europe's fate is now firmly intertwined with that of the EU. Should the EU back away from the pursuit of a socially integrated political union, the region may suffer. Southern Europe now faces competition from eastern and central Europe, both in the export market and in the scramble for financial assistance from the EU. Finally, the Mediterranean region remains a potentially explosive area in the post-Cold War era and the maintenance of political stability on Europe's southern flank is scarcely less crucial now than before.

Further reading

Bruneau, T. (1997) *Political Parties and Democracy In Portugal: Organizations, Elections and Public Opinion,* Westview, Boulder, CO.

Danopoulos, C. (1991) 'Democratising the Military: Lessons from Mediterranean Europe', *West European Politics,* 14 (4) pp. 25–41.

Ethier, D. (1990) *Democratic Transition and Consolidation in Southern Europe, Latin America and South-East Asia,* Macmillan, Basingstoke.

Gillespie, R. (1996) *Mediterranean Politics,* Vol. 3, Pinter, London.

Gillespie, R., Story J., and Rodrigo, F. (1995) *Democratic Spain,* Routledge, London.

Gunther, R., Diamandouros, N. and Puhle, H.-J. (1995) *The Politics of Democratic Consolidation: Southern Europe in Comparative Perspective,* Johns Hopkins University Press, New York.

Heywood, P. (1998) *Spain: a European Democracy,* Frank Cass, London.

Lavdas, K. and Magone, J. (1997) *Politics and Governance in Southern Europe: the Political Systems of Italy, Greece, Spain and Portugal,* Westview, Boulder, CO.

Linz, J. and Stepan, A. (1996) *Problems of Democratic Transition and Consolidation: Southern Europe, South America and Post-Communist Europe,* Johns Hopkins University Press, New York.

Maxwell, K.. (1995) *The Making of Portuguese Democracy,* Cambridge University Press, Cambridge.

Pridham, G. and Lewis, P. (1995) *Stabilising Fragile Democracies,* Routledge, London.

Sapelli, G. (1995) *Southern Europe Since 1945,* Longman, London.

Veremis, T. (1997) *The Military in Greek Politics,* Hurst, New York.

9 The cockpit: central and eastern Europe

Introduction: central and eastern Europe in the 1950s

Chapter 1 indicated the traumatic common experience of eastern Europe in the years before Stalin's death. 1953 brought workers' strikes and demonstrations in several countries, especially East Germany, but the most dramatic protests against the Stalinist system followed Khrushchev's denunciation of Stalin at the Twentieth Congress of the Communist Party of the Soviet Union (CPSU) in 1956. The issues came to a head in Poland and Hungary. Yet while the Polish October and the Hungarian Uprising of 1956 arose from similar grievances, their outcomes and the countries' subsequent development were very different.

Khrushchev allowed the Polish Party, with workers' hero Wladyslaw Gomulka restored to its leadership, to pursue its own path, but the hopes of the October Rising faded as Gomulka disappointed the workers by sidelining the workers' councils and shelving reforms.

In Hungary the Soviets judged that premier Imre Nagy, pushed by popular pressures, had jeopardised Party rule by agreeing to reinstall a multi-party system and withdrawing from the Warsaw Treaty Organisation (WTO). Soviet troops and tanks 'restored order' and Party First Secretary Janos Kádár began the process of 'normalisation'. Yet five years later the initially detested Kádár launched the programme of 'goulash communism' which made Hungary the most tolerable Soviet bloc country to live in. Kádár seemed to be a model *apparatchik*. He moved cautiously, constantly reassuring the Soviets that the Party's leading role was not threatened, but his policies actually amounted to what would later (in the Prague Spring) be called 'socialism with a human face'.

Thus after the 1950s Hungary remained the only eastern European country outside the Balkans where the grinding authoritarianism and state-controlled centralism (itself controlled indirectly by the USSR) of the communist system was softened, and Hungary's modification of the system remained very slight and cautious. The revolts of the 1950s had all failed.

Figure 9.1 Central and eastern Europe 1994 (Yugoslavia = Serbia, including Kosovo, and Montenegro)

Developments from 1960 to 1989

Bulgaria

Until 1989, the Bulgarian Communist Party steadfastly and uncritically supported the CPSU and never let its people forget Russia's role in Bulgaria's liberation from the Turks in 1876–78. Todor Zhivkov controlled the Party and the state from 1962 to 1989. Bulgaria received the highest Soviet aid *per capita* in Europe and its trade was predominantly with the USSR. Growth was fairly good until 1985. Then problems mounted and the first signs of dissidence emerged.

Romania

Bulgaria's slavish conformity with Soviet wishes contrasted with Romania, whose deviant foreign policy attracted Western support well into the 1980s, despite the personality-cult of its leader ('Conductor') Ceausescu and his increasingly obnoxious domestic policies. Ceausescu made an art-form of opposing the Soviets, an ego-trip which reached its peak when he denounced the Soviet intervention in Czechoslovakia in 1968. He insisted on occupying personally all important positions in the state, and chairing a vast array of Party and state committees and commissions, but all errors were attributed to others. Hundreds of Bucharest's buildings were destroyed to accommodate a grandiose new city centre, in which an eight-lane Avenue of the Victory of Socialism led up to the Ceausescus' ostentatious new House of the Republic. His nepotism was derisively labelled 'Socialism in one family' (a reference to Stalin's programme of 'Socialism in one country'); his wife Elena became his acknowledged number two, his son was catapulted into senior positions, while some 50 relatives held significant posts.

Romanian society was transformed by his policy of 'systematisation'. Draconian rules were enforced in all spheres of life. A drastic programme of replacing crumbling villages by urban-style centres was supposed to raise living standards, but its real goal was to destroy the last remnants of private agriculture for the sake of vast and inefficient state farms by moving the peasants from their individual houses and plots of land to soulless blocks of jerry-built flats. This destruction of the rural community and family life particularly affected Transylvania, where ethnic Hungarians were already struggling to preserve their distinctive cultural identity. Many children ended up in orphanages, where large numbers became HIV-positive after injections with infected blood as a treatment for malnutrition.

The economy depended on guaranteed cheap energy, but the drop in domestic supplies from exhausted oil wells and the rising cost of imports from the Soviet Union meant that factories and the petro-chemical industry ran short. Drastic penalties for unfulfilled targets in militarised coal-mining lowered the quality of the output. By the 1980s living standards were dropping sharply and malnutrition was endemic. In 1989 a sixth winter of energy-saving brought reduced street lighting, a single 40-watt bulb in barely heated houses, and short-time working.

Ceausescu's excesses were belatedly recognised by Western governments and in 1987 the USA removed from Romania its most favoured nation status. Yet the Ceausescus felt to the end that they could defy the tide of change sweeping the bloc. However, a hidden hatred for the regime would burst out in December 1989.

Poland

After massive strikes in the Baltic seaports in 1970 following a 30 per cent rise in basic food prices, Gomulka fell from power. His successor, Edward Gierek, announced a two-year price freeze, and an import-led investment boom induced a false sense of prosperity. The freeze was unsustainable, the boom collapsed, and in 1976, once again, huge rises in prices of basic foods had to be imposed. Again there were strikes and demonstrations; again they were harshly suppressed. Intellectuals united with workers to form a Workers' Defence Committee. After further strikes in 1980, this movement developed into the bloc's first independent trade union, Solidarity, led by a shipyard electrician from Gdansk, Lech Walesa. This speedily attracted almost ten million members. But then the threat of Soviet intervention forced President Jaruzelski to declare martial law. The regime was detested; it survived only because people understood Poland's geopolitical situation.

In 1987 the economic situation forced Jaruzelski to announce a programme of radical reconstruction. A referendum asked Poles to approve a short sharp shock to get it off the ground and to reduce Poland's $35 billion foreign debt. In return he promised an elected upper house and expanded civic rights. Fewer than half the voters approved the programme, but Jaruzelski went ahead with it. Further strikes in 1988 forced Jaruzelski to seek political support from Walesa. Round table meetings between Party, Solidarity and Church leaders in early 1989 agreed that elections to the Sejm (parliament) would be held in June, with 65 per cent of the Lower House seats reserved for the Communist Party and its allies, but a free vote for the upper house. Solidarity swept the board in the new Upper House and won all the seats it was allowed to contest in the lower one. The Communist system was collapsing.

Hungary

In Hungary after 1956 Kádár, mindful of the limits of Soviet toleration, tried to reduce the direct role of the Party while safeguarding its political authority. From the late 1970s small-scale privatisation encouraged the economy. Garden plots worked by families in evenings and weekends produced a third of agricultural production. Groups of workers in state enterprises rented their machinery in the evenings and worked at higher rates negotiated with management. As an economic policy it was successful, but the more orthodox Party leaders became worried about society's ideological scepticism and indifference.

However, after 1985 economic problems mounted and Gorbachev's reforms in the USSR made Kádár seem increasingly conservative. Imre Pozsgay, his most radical Party critic, was demanding faster and more radical political and economic change. Opposition grew. The Hungarian Democratic Forum was formed in 1987, the Alliance of Young Democrats (FIDESz) and the Alliance of Free Democrats (AFD) in 1988. The Independent Smallholders, the Free Democrats and the Social Democrats, which had been disbanded or absorbed into the Communist Party in the late 1940s, were re-established. Kádár was shunted into an honorary Party Chairmanship, and eight of the 13 Politburo members were replaced. Political pluralism was seen as inevitable and in March 1989 the Party and the opposition groups agreed that there should be free multi-party elections. The Party's problem was how to preserve its leading role within that framework. The problem was soon to prove insoluble.

Czechoslovakia

Despite Czechoslovakia's democratic heritage and relatively advanced economy, de-Stalinisation – revived in the USSR in 1961 – began in Prague only after the Party Congress of 1962, during the presidency of Antonin Novotny, and it soon slowed down. By 1966 the economist Ota Sik was telling the Party leadership that genuine economic reform was impossible without political change. In response a New Economic Mechanism was established in 1967, but entrenched habits of bureaucratic interference greatly reduced its impact. However, dissent was mounting. Alexander Dubcek replaced Novotny as First Secretary in January 1968. Intra-Party democracy was promoted, censorship was abandoned, lesser parties and the trade unions began to establish a more separate identity from the Party, and a host of new, independent bodies emerged. The mood of change became infectious. In April the Party adopted an Action Programme. Its preamble admitted grave errors since the Communist takeover in 1948 and promised 'a new, profoundly democratic, Czechoslovak model of socialist society'. It saw Czechoslovakia as a bridge between East and West, bringing into Communism principles of separation of constitutional powers and civil rights, which echoed the ideas of Imre Nagy in Hungary in 1956. People felt that in this 'Prague Spring', a newly liberal Communist Party could rule benignly in 'socialism with a human face'.

The Soviets, however, saw in this (rightly) the beginning of the end of Party rule, and as in 1956 in Hungary they responded by invasion, supported by most other WTO members. Soviet tanks in the streets of Prague in October 1968 encountered popular execration but no military resistance. Dubcek, seized and taken to Moscow, was forced to agree to reverse the reform programme and 'normalise'. The Soviet government justified its action by declaring that bloc member countries had the right and duty to intervene if socialism was threatened in any other member state (the 'Brezhnev Doctrine'). After 1969, most Czechoslovaks retreated into political and social apathy. Small groups of intellectuals, like the 'Charter 77' movement, publicly protested at the suppression of democratic freedoms. There was widespread sympathy for them, but they aroused little active backing until Honecker's fall in East Germany in the autumn of 1989.

Figure 9.2 Memorial to a wall-builder (cartoon on the death of Erich Honecker, who supervised the construction of the Berlin Wall)
Source: *The Guardian*, 3 June 1994

East Germany

In August 1961 the government of the 'German Democratic Republic' (GDR) built the Berlin Wall round West Berlin to stem the flood of East Germans, many of whom previously had crossed the border to West Berlin and thus to West Germany in spite of all efforts to stop them. American President J.F. Kennedy came to Berlin in 1963 and declared America's commitment to the beleaguered West Berliners with the declaration '*Ich bin ein Berliner*' (which in local usage actually means 'I am a doughnut', but the Berliners knew what he meant). The Wall, however, remained as a nearly impenetrable barrier blocking escape from the East, and as a symbol of the failure of the communist regimes of the eastern bloc to fulfil the aspirations of their citizens. Some still tried to escape over it, and were machine-gunned in the attempt.

East Germans were forced back on their own resources, and succeeded in making the GDR a leading industrial country, while a wide-ranging social security system provided excellent benefits, especially for mothers and young families. This supported the fullest possible employment of women in a country from which many of the best young workers had emigrated before the wall was built.

From 1971 to the fall of the regime in 1989 the country was led by Erich Honecker. Under his rule the GDR claimed a distinctive identity produced by the building of socialism, and achieved a considerable reputation as a separate state, e.g. by the success of the sportsmen produced by a massively funded and ethically flawed training programme. Honecker adopted the policy of *Abgrenzung* (separation) which treated West Germans as foreigners, but by the mid-1980s the GDR had become so economically dependent on West Germany that it could no longer afford to antagonise it.

Honecker tried to ignore Gorbachev's policy of openness and democratisation; he even banned the German editions of some Soviet journals. But demands for political change grew increasingly, stimulated by meetings of new informal organisations (many sheltering under the umbrella of the churches). From these New Forum emerged in 1989 as the leading organiser of demonstrations.

The revolutions of 1989

Several sources of tension were growing within the bloc during the 1980s. One was the continuing influence of religion, despite all the years of state-supported atheism. In East Germany the Evangelical Church established discussion groups focusing on Christian goals, Green issues and an autonomous peace movement, and maintained close contacts with West German churches. Thus it constituted a centre for non-communist attitudes. In Poland the regime had always been aware that the institution to which the bulk of the population gave genuine deference was the Roman Catholic Church, and gradually the Church's influence undermined people's respect for the regime. The Polish Pope's visits to his homeland in 1979 and 1983, where television showed the people's devotion to him at vast rallies, greatly reduced the regime's prestige. As one writer said, the lasting impression was of a nation united with its Church; the Party seemed forgotten and almost irrelevant. But though most people identified the Church with rebellion against authoritarian constraints, the Church hierarchy saw its role more as that of a mediator in disputes between Party and people. Thus priests who got involved in politics, as many did, were something of an embarrassment. Nevertheless, many parish priests became active supporters of Solidarity, and under martial law their churches – the only places where more than three people could meet openly without breaking the law – often doubled as pro-Solidarity political forums. In 1984, however, a radical Warsaw parish priest, Jerzy Popieluszko, was murdered by state security agents, and the intense popular revulsion greatly increased hostility to the regime.

The bloc's economic system was also breaking down in the 1980s. Its Council for Mutual Economic Assistance (Comecon), which was supposed to coordinate economic activity in the bloc and promote integration through trade, achieved little. Integration, promoted by the Soviet Union, was resisted by the other states as tending to submerge them within the Soviet system. Neither of the two Comecon banks did much to foster intra-bloc trade, largely because the so-called 'transferable ruble' never lived up to its name, so member states relied instead on annual bilateral barter agreements. Generally low-quality production made member states loath to see a positive balance with one country offset by imports from another, and they tended to demand hard currency for deliveries outside the annual protocols, especially of the fuel and raw materials imported from the USSR (on which the other member countries' industries were very dependent). By the end of the 1980s, fuel beyond the established quotas could hardly be obtained at any price because Soviet production was falling and much of it was being exported to western Europe, and there were even difficulties in meeting the quotas. Thus industrial expansion was seriously hampered, and the problems were exacerbated by the absence of energy-saving measures in eastern Europe's industries. Pollution arising from energy-inefficiency was also extensive. The USSR, however, remained central to the economies of the whole bloc, and its increasing weakness relative to the West placed every eastern European economy in jeopardy. For instance, the Soviet Union had always been prepared to accept the bloc's manufactured products, even though these were often out-dated and qualitatively inferior to Western and latterly East Asian ones. But this guaranteed market shielded Comecon members from outside competition, and had the effect of blocking innovation and keeping efficiency low. In the 1980s, when increasing debts to Western banks and the increasing weakness of the Soviet economy necessitated exports to the West, the region's industries were unable to compete.

After Gorbachev came to power in 1985 he realised that the increasing decline of the Soviet economy made it impossible for the USSR to pursue the Cold War or impose its will on central and eastern Europe by military force. It gradually became apparent that the communist regimes of eastern Europe, under increasing pressure from their own growing difficulties, would not be propped up by Soviet power as had happened in 1956 and 1968. Thus revolu-tion was imminent all over the region. As Henry Kissinger said of the USSR, eastern Europe faced two crises – a political one if it changed the system, and an economic one if it did not.

Solidarity's electoral success in June 1989 was a portent for the region, but it was above all Hungary which precipitated the crisis. In March 1989 the Hungarian regime agreed to hold multi-party elections, and accepted the UN Convention on Refugees. In May Kádár was ousted. In July, Imre Nagy's remains were taken from an unmarked grave and reinterred, and he was honoured by a great ceremony on Heroes' Square. In the late summer Hungary's border with Austria was opened, and in September the Hungarian government announced that East German 'tourists' were free to cross Hungary's border with Austria and head for West Germany. Immediately there was a huge rush of people – espe-cially of East Germans – emigrating to the West through that border.

In the GDR enormous demonstrations in October 1989 became more and more openly threatening to the regime. The government is said to have consid-ered a 'Chinese solution' (sending in the tanks against the people as in Tiananmen Square, Beijing, in June 1989), but the idea was rejected after Gorbachev told the East German leadership that the USSR would no longer bail them out of any difficulties. Days later Honecker was removed from office, and the government announced that the Berlin Wall and all border-points would be opened. Berliners from both sides of the Wall were soon tearing it down and selling bits of it as souvenirs to tourists. The East German government opened discussions with New Forum and promised free elections.

In Bulgaria Zhivkov was overthrown by an inner Party coup in November, and arrested shortly afterwards. In Czechoslovakia the general public at last found the nerve to support openly the demands of the Charter 77 group. A political grouping of anti-communist forces called 'Civic Forum' was founded, led by one of the Charter 77 intellectuals, Vaclav Havel, who had been imprisoned for five years in the eighties. Street demonstrations in Prague by students and by Civic Forum bloodlessly overthrew the communist regime in the 'Velvet Revolution' of early December 1989. Havel himself became president. And finally, in Romania, only a month after the policies of the 'Conducator' had been as usual rapturously approved at the Communist Party Congress, demonstrations and violence in Transylvania and western Romania spread to the Romanian capital Bucharest. Here the revolution was far from bloodless, as Ceausescu's special police force, all through the week before Christmas, fought the demonstrators and soldiers who had joined the rebels in the streets. But the rebels eventually seized the presidential palace itself, and pursued the police through the city. Ceausescu was seized, and executed with his wife on Christmas Day.

At first the East German regime sought to survive by moderate reform. But it was now obvious that the GDR as a separate state made no sense, and people wanted to root out those whose orders had caused the shootings of attempted escapees on the Wall. In the elections of March 1990 the influence of the West German political parties was decisive, and pressure for union with the West became overwhelming. Negotiations for economic and monetary union between the two Germanies took place immediately, and full union was achieved on 3 October 1990.

Table 9.1 GDR: Elections to the National Assembly, March 1990

Party	Percentage of votes	Seats
CDU	40.82	163
DSU	6.31	25
Democratic Awakening	0.99	4
Free Democrats	5.28	21
SPD	21.88	88
PDS	16.40	66
Alliance 90	2.91	12
Others	5.41	21
Total	100.00	400

Developments since 1989

All the post-communist states of eastern Europe – including the states which once formed part of the USSR, which collapsed with communism in 1991, leaving Russia, the Ukraine, Belarus and the Caucasus states – have rejected an unsatisfactory past and sought connections with the West for both political and financial reasons. All of them claim to be creating a market economy, advanced financial institutions, and a Western-style democratic political system, but their levels of commitment vary, and both people and politicians have been sorely tested by the consequences of rapid market reform. The dislocation this involved resulted everywhere in reduced production for some years. Social services have had to be greatly pruned, many workers have been made redundant where full employment had been the norm, and the fear of unemployment has produced much cynicism and low morale. Significant proportions of the population are living on or below the poverty line, while a smaller group, including many of the old *nomenklatura* (party hacks in privileged positions), has become very rich. The economies of eastern Europe have gradually established stronger trading connections with the West, but the connections with Russia have remained important, and that has caused increasing difficulty since the partial collapse of the Russian economy in the later 1990s.

Political cultures change slowly, old habits linger, and the new democratic political institutions have not always functioned well. The strains of the rush to a market economy have shortened tempers and encouraged a narrowing of loyalties to one's own ethnic or national group, hindering progress towards a tolerant civil society. The greatest dangers come not from old-style communism (for the mainstream of the communist parties have turned to 'democratic socialism'), but from the extreme right and its ethnic hatreds. As political forces found more open expression after 1989 with the collapse of the communist system, ethnic hostilities often correspondingly became more open. But outside the Balkan area, these have not (so far) proved disastrous.

Poland

Poland made the most direct initial dash for capitalism, but the price rises engendered by the Solidarity-dominated government's policies strained the loyalties of Solidarity's rank and file. Solidarity's populist chairman, Lech Walesa, eschewed parliamentary politics and thereby stood above these conflicts by becoming president in 1990. For the next five years, he was regularly at odds with the Sejm (parliament) in seeking to increase presidential powers at its expense.

The low (43 per cent) turnout in the 1991 elections to the Sejm showed the public's disillusionment with politics. The Democratic Union (DU) and the Union of the Democratic Left (SLD – largely ex-communist) were almost equally supported. Jan Olszewski of the right-of-centre Liberal Democratic Congress was appointed as prime minister of a coalition government, though he had run against Walesa for the presidency. Walesa soon engineered a Sejm vote of no confidence and nominated the youthful Waldemar Pawlak in Olszewski's place, but the Sejm then overthrew Pawlak. The disparate ex-Solidarity parties then cobbled together a coalition government under Hanna Suchocka, who held on until she was overthrown by the pressure of health and education workers' pay demands on public spending limits in 1993, and new elections were called.

The 1993 elections returned to power parties committed to slowing down reform and emphasising social welfare – the ex-communists of the SLD and the Polish Peasant Party (PSL). It is noticeable that none of the six parties backed by the Catholic Church passed the 5 per cent threshold required for Sejm seats; the power of the Church in Poland had appeared great only because of its symbolic role in opposing communism, and women in particular resented the way Church pressure had imposed severe restrictions on abortion by a law passed in 1993. (The law was changed to permit abortion up to the twelfth week of pregnancy in 1996.) Pawlak was restored to the premiership, but was constantly harassed by Walesa, and accused of trying to slow economic reform. Walesa set up a range of presidential councils of prominent personalities and proposed a Charter of Rights and Freedoms. But he was losing popular support, and when Pawlak resigned in 1995 he was replaced by Jozef Oleksy rather than by Walesa's candidate, the SLD leader Aleksander Kwasniewski.

Kwasniewski, however, stood against Walesa in the presidential elections and defeated him. But instead of adopting the older-style socialist policies of the SLD, he promised as president to maintain the pace of economic reform and seek full membership of the EU and NATO.

In 1996 Oleksy resigned to avoid an investigation into charges (subsequently dropped) that he had been a KGB informer. An SLD–PSL government coalition was then formed, led by Wlodzimierz Cimoszewicz (SLD). But the coalition was increasingly strained by disagreements over privatisation, fiscal policy and power sharing, and after the 1997 elections, the right-wing parties returned to power with 261 Sejm seats out of 460. The new coalition, led by long-time Solidarity activist Jerzy Buzek, brought together Solidarity Electoral Action (AWS) and the Freedom Union (UW), with Leszek Balcerowicz of UW, the architect of Poland's 1989 drive towards capitalism, as deputy prime minister and minister of finance. In its first year in office the new government instituted major administrative decentralisation, introduced an employee-financed health system and initiated wide-ranging education and social security reforms.

Poland's economy has prospered since about 1993, especially in industrial production. The private sector's contribution has grown sharply, while the Gdansk shipyards have been allowed to go to the wall and agriculture now generates only 6 per cent of GDP, though it still involves over a quarter of the population. There has been a balanced growth of exports and imports, domestic and foreign investment have soared, and GDP has risen steadily – by 5 per cent in 1998.

Poland is a member of the Council of Europe and CEFTA, joined the OECD in 1996, and it is now seen as the most important of the countries in the first wave of prospective new members of the EU, following an association agreement in December 1991. It became a member of NATO in March 1999 – a particularly important step in view of Poland's long history of suffering invasion from its neighbours, since membership involves a guarantee of its frontiers. It favoured cessation of NATO's bombing of Yugoslavia in the Kosovo crisis of 1999, but rejected Russia's overtures towards a Pan-Slavic Front against NATO.

The Czech Republic and Slovakia

Free elections to establish the new non-communist Czechoslovakia were held in June 1990; Civic Forum and its Slovak sister-party, Public Against Violence, won handsomely. But the new government could not overcome the constitutional limits to its power. Czechoslovakia was a Federation of the Czech Republic and the Slovak Republic, and important issues required a 60 per cent majority with members from the Czech Lands and from Slovakia voting separately in each

Table 9.2 Poland: Elections to the National Assembly: 21 September 1997

Party	Sejm % votes	Sejm seats won	Sejm % seats won
Solidarity Electoral Action	33.8	201	51
Alliance of the Democratic Left	27.1	164	28
Freedom Union	13.4	60	8
Polish People's Party	7.3	27	3
Movement for the Reconstruction of Poland (Ruch)	5.6	6	5
Others, including non-partisans	12.8	2	5
Total	100	460	100

house. The two could rarely agree, and neither Civic Forum nor Public Against Violence would cooperate with the communists or the Slovak National Party. Demands for Slovak independence steadily mounted, and separation became inevitable when Vladimir Meciar's Movement for a Democratic Slovakia (HZDS) won 37 per cent of the votes for the Slovak National Council in the June 1992 elections and formed a coalition government with the Slovak National Party. Czech prime minister Vaclav Klaus thereafter aimed only to end the Slovak drain on Czech resources as quickly as possible, and two separate independent sovereign states emerged on 1 January 1993.

The split was relatively painless, but tensions arose thereafter over the division of property assets and liabilities and the distribution of privatisation shares. Border controls were tightened, making travelling between the two countries annoying and time-consuming, and relations were soured.

The Czech Republic's right-wing government, which was led by the Civc Democratic Party (ODS) under Klaus followed a determined policy of establishing capitalism, with considerable public support. 70 per cent of industry was privatised by 1994. Exports rose steadily and a substantial trade surplus of $350 million was achieved. Hard currency reserves reached $5.3 billion in 1994, and the Czech National Bank decided it was able to repay early an IMF loan of £471 million. Inflation was fairly low, although rises in wages exceeded those in productivity, while unemployment was among the lowest in Europe. But there was discontent at the replacement of the health service by an insurance system and other social problems and at a perceived neglect of the environment. The ex-communists were aggrieved by measures which lifted the statutory time limitations on prosecutions for ideologically motivated crimes committed in the communist period, though the Party had split. There was also controversy over whether all or only part of confiscated Church property should be returned. Klaus's rather abrasive personality often upset his coalition partners, and by 1996 the coalition was kept in power only by the fragmentation of the Left and the disillusioned apathy of the electorate.

In the elections of the summer of that year the coalition lost its majority, though it remained in power by negotiating for the support of the Czech Social Democratic Party (CzSSD) led by Milos Zeman, with its programme of free market economic reforms and concern for social and environmental issues. Klaus's government survived another year, but the economy performed badly in 1998, the ODS was accused of having traded privatisation benefits for donations, and Klaus resigned. The 1998 elections gave the CzSSD 11 seats more than the ODS.

One problem which increased the tensions of the 1990s was the fact that the Republic's constitution was generally thought to need reform. For several years it proved difficult to gather the necessary majorities for any particular changes, and the upper house (Senate) could not be set up at all until 1996. A Constitutional Court was established to enhance the separation of powers. But repeated difficulties in constructing majority support for coalitions led to opposition to the Republic's proportional representation electoral system. The long interregnum of 1998, when the largest party, the CzSSD, could not construct majority backing for a government, was particularly disturbing. The CzSSD was eventually able only to form a minority government which the ODS would not oppose in a vote of confidence, while the ODS would hold the chairmanship of both houses of parliament and a share of legislative committee chairmanships. But by now it was generally agreed that the electoral law would be changed to a first-past-the-post system in the hope of producing stable governments, so that these precarious arrangements might not be needed for too long.

Germany has invested heavily in the Czech Republic's finance and industry, often in joint-venture arrangements, and it has been important to resolve the painful historical inheritance of problems between the two countries (see Chapter 1). Prolonged negotiations concerning compensation for Czech victims of Nazism and for the three million Sudeten Germans expelled from Czechoslovakia in 1945 finally led to a treaty of reconciliation in 1996, in which Germany expressed regret for Nazi atrocities and the Czech Republic for Czechoslovakia's expulsion of the Sudeten Germans. The Czech Republic also agreed in 1994 to return property to Jewish families dispossessed by the Nazis. Improved relations between the two countries produced strong German support for Czech membership of the EU, and the Republic became a front-runner for full EU membership. In addition, it is a member of the Council of Europe, CEFTA, and the OSCE; it joined NATO in 1999.

Slovakia was the country whose nationalist resentments (allied to the abrasive policies of Klaus) brought about the break-up of Czechoslovakia, and there was a risk that this nationalism might connect with its earlier tendencies to clerico-fascism, and lead it into authoritarian rule. Further, Slovakia's enthusiasm for the new capitalism and its associated liberal and democratic politics was far less than that of the Czechs. And indeed, under Meciar's HZDS government the press was somewhat constrained and minority rights were not much respected – Slovakia's Hungarians were required to register their names in Slovak forms, for example. Privatisation proceeded slowly.

But Meciar's authoritarian style provoked opposition among the other members of his government and conflict with the president, Michael Kovac, and the

Table 9.3 Czech Republic: Elections to the Chamber of Representatives: 19–20 June 1998

Party	Percentage of votes	Seats won
Czech Social Democratic Party	32.3	74
Civic Democratic Party	27.7	63
Communist Party of Bohemia and Moravia	11.0	24
Christian and Democratic Union–Czechoslovak People's Party	9.0	20
Freedom Union	8.6	19
Others, including non-partisans	11.4	0
Total	100.0	200

Table 9.4 Czech Republic: Elections to the Senate: 15–16, 22–23 November 1996

Party	Percentage of votes	Seats won
Civic Democratic Party	49.1	32
Czech Social Democratic Party	31.8	25
Christian and Democratic Union–Czechoslovak People's Party	10.7	13
Civic Democratic Alliance	5.2	7
Communist Party of Bohemia and Moravia	2.1	2
Others, including non-partisans	1.1	2
Total	100.0	81

HZDS lost several defectors to other parties. In 1994 the party split when foreign minister Jozef Moravcik and deputy premier Roman Kovac left the government to set up a new party which, with the accession of the Alliance of Democrats, formed the Democratic Union of Slovakia. Meciar was overthrown and Moravcik became prime minister. Moravcik's more liberally orientated government began to revive the privatisation process and tried to attract greater foreign investment, though political uncertainty made this difficult. It also sought to improve relations with Slovakia's resident Hungarians, who had begun campaigning for educational and cultural autonomy, allowing names to be registered in Hungarian forms. But it lasted only a few months before elections in the autumn of 1994 brought Meciar back to power in combination with the Slovak National Party and the left-wing Association of Slovak Workers. The new government postponed privatisations and increased state control, including the renationalisation of radio and television. Relations with Hungary worsened and foreign investors took fright.

The conflict between Meciar and President Kovac was renewed, focusing especially now on Kovac's authority over the state intelligence agency, the Slovak Information Service (SIS). Meciar wrested control over the SIS and the armed forces from Kovac in 1995, though Kovac declared this move unconstitutional. Kovac's son, wanted by the German authorities on corruption charges, was abducted by the SIS, and taken to Austria for possible extradition to Germany. Slovak state television gave the case great publicity and proposed his father's removal. Investigation of the abduction came to nothing after a key witness died in a car bombing. The corruption charges were later dropped. In 1996 Kovac vetoed a Law on the Protection of the Republic, which criminalised demonstrations and the dissemination of what the courts would declare to be false information about the state. Western governments were alarmed by the authoritarian trend, but Meciar seemed still relatively popular in a country where politicians tended not to be highly regarded. The HZDS did quite well in the 1998 elections, with 43 of the 150 seats. However, a strong coalition was formed without Meciar and the HZDS from the Slovak Democratic Coalition (SDK), the ex-communist Party of the Democrat Left (SDL), the Hungarian Coalition Party and the Party of Civic Understanding. Led by Mikulas Dzurinda of the SDK, it has the necessary majority for reforming the constitution, so should be able to resolve the controversial issue of the status of the president.

The Dzurinda regime has been welcomed throughout the West. It is expected to democratise all aspects of the political and social systems, and to accelerate the privatisation process, as well as making it more open and equitable. However, the prospects for an economy too closely tied to Russian trade and energy supplies are poor in 1999, and this may hold back Slovakia's political connections with the West.

Slovakia is a member of the Council of Europe and CEFTA, though it was somewhat isolated in them till autumn 1998. It became an associate member of the EU in 1993, and entered NATO's Partnership for Peace in February 1994. It is tentatively scheduled to be in the second group of eastern European countries to be admitted to the EU.

Table 9.5 Slovakia: Elections to the National Council: 25–26 September 1998

Party	Percentage of votes	Seats won
Movement for a Democratic Slovakia	27.0	43
Democratic Coalition of Slovakia	26.3	42
Slovak National Party	9.1	14
Party of Democratic Left	14.7	23
Hungarian Coalition Party	9.1	15
Party of Civic Understanding	8.0	13
Others, including non-partisans	5.8	5
Total	100.0	155

Hungary

After the overthrow of the communist system, the 1990 general elections resulted in a right-wing victory and the Hungarian Democratic Forum (MDF) took power under Jozsef Antall. As in Slovakia, the politics of the following years was dominated by a conflict between the prime minister and the president, Arpad Göncz, mainly over Antall's attempts to appoint party loyalists to leading financial, media and military posts and to discriminate against minorities. The economy did badly, though in 1989 it had seemed to have good prospects. Unemployment more than doubled, living standards declined, and inequalities of income increased sharply. IMF credits were suspended in 1992. The MDF lost public support, and some of its ultra-nationalistic and anti-semitic elements left to form the Hungarian Justice Party. In the 1994 elections the MDF collapsed to less than 10 per cent of votes, while the Socialist Party (MSzP) gained 54 per cent. Its leader Gyula Horn formed a government with a programme of financial probity and the restoration of the economy. Austerity measures were introduced to reduce the level of debt and to make exports more competitive. Göncz was re-elected as president. Many dubious senior managers in financial and economic planning positions were sacked, and under their replacements positive economic trends began to emerge in production, productivity and exports. The new finance minister promised further prudence, cutting back the unprofitable state sector and reducing state funding for social programmes. Foreign investment rose.

There is considerable disquiet about the treatment of Hungarians in Serbia and Romania; it is unclear how this may affect future tensions in the region. Relations with Slovakia are also seriously impaired by disagreement about the Gabcikovo dam, initially part of a joint hydroelectric project to construct major dams in both countries and divert the Danube. In 1989 Hungary withdrew on environmental grounds, but Slovakia went ahead with its own dam. Hungary claimed that the consequent diversion of the Danube unilaterally altered the two countries' common border and endangered the environment. The two governments agreed to let the International Court of Justice arbitrate on whether Hungary had the right to renege on the 1977 agreement which initiated the entire project.

In the 1998 elections the centre right (the Alliance of Young Democrats (FIDESz) and the Smallholders) gained just enough to overthrow the Socialists and form a new government. It is as yet unclear how far policies will change. The economy is currently (1998 and 1999) growing well, but confidence is undercut by the collapse of the Russian economy and by the damage to Danube trade caused by the NATO airstrikes against Yugoslavia in 1999. Hungary joined NATO in 1999 and made bases available for NATO's airstrikes against Yugoslavia in the Kosovo crisis, but it insisted that no Hungarian troops participate in any ground war against Yugoslav troops (who might include ethnic Hungarians from the Vojvodina). Hungary expects to be admitted to the EU in the first group of eastern European adherents.

Table 9.6 Hungary: Elections to the National Assembly: 10 and 24 May 1998, First Round

Party	Percentage of votes	Seats won
Hungarian Socialist Party	32.3	134
Alliance of Young Democrats	28.2	148
Independent Party of Smallholders, Agrarian Workers and Citizens	13.8	48
Alliance of Free Democrats	7.9	24
Hungarian Justice and Life Party	5.5	14
Hungarian Democratic Forum	3.1	17
Others, including non-partisans	9.0	0
Total	99.8	385

Bulgaria

After Zhivkov fell in 1989, Bulgaria's communist party tried to find a middle path of democratic socialism, and to retain power within a multi-party system under a new name, the Bulgarian Socialist Party (BSP). In the 1990 National Assembly elections, its established apparatus enabled the BSP to win 211 seats, against 144 for the rightist Union of Democratic Forces (UDF), which had not yet established an adequate support network in the countryside. However, in an attempt to bring national unity, the UDF's leader, Zhelyu Zhelev, was elected president by the National Assembly, though the government was dominated by the BSP. Ignoring constitutional uncertainties, Zhelev initiated legislation to depoliticise the army, police and part of the civil service. But the BSP reform programme, with its very limited economic reforms, could not satisfy the new generation's demands for Western-style democracy, and the government fell within a year.

The resulting elections in 1991 gave the UDF a four-seat majority over the BSP, and the new UDF government, with the support of the (Turkish) Movement for Rights and Freedoms (MRF) embarked on a substantial but still rather slow programme of economic reform. In early 1992 some small shops, businesses and housing were privatised, and an amended land law provided for the abolition of collective farms. But privatisation proceeded slowly, due to disputes with former owners, arguments between the MRF and the UDF, and the continuing influence of the BSP. International organisations refused financial support until the country was on a better financial basis. Inflation, which had reached a staggering 334 per cent in 1991, continued high, and gross output dropped by 15 to 20 per cent, while unemployment reached 13 per cent. Not surprisingly, serious strikes occurred. Human rights legislation failed to mitigate the destitution of the Turks and gypsies in Bulgaria's south where redundancies were heaviest. Constitutional reform, which might have made a more determined economic reform programme possible, was blocked by the BSP, which also resisted moves to strip deputies of their immunity to prosecution. In 1993, amidst general discontent, the MRF voted with the BSP to bring down the government.

The MRF then backed a 'non-party government of experts' under Berov, with a programme of austerity and faster privatisation. But the government could not command the support it needed for this in the Assembly. New elections held in 1994, which produced a BSP government led by Zhan Videnov, failed to resolve the crisis. Privatisation was once more stalled, inflation rocketed and the lev collapsed. Videnov was forced to resign in December 1996, and in new elections in 1997 the UDF swept the board.

Ivan Kostov's UDF government then embarked on a programme of comprehensive political, administrative, economic and social reform. The lev was tied to the Deutschmark. Within six months interest rates and inflation were falling as monetary discipline was restored, though the economy remained depressed. Budget deficits have been overcome. Foreign investment was facilitated, and the IMF, World Bank and EU made substantial loans. Bulgaria joined the Central European Free Trade Agreement in 1998. It seeks to join the EU, and is assigned to the second group of prospective EU members.

Table 9.7 Bulgaria: Elections to the National Assembly: 19 April 1997

Party	Percentage of votes	Seats won
United Democratic Forces	52.2	137
Democratic Left	22.0	58
Union for National Salvation	7.6	19
Euro–Left Coalition	5.6	14
Bulgarian Business Block	4.9	12
Others, including non-partisans	7.7	0
Total	100.0	240

Romania

In Romania the task of dismantling communist economic and political structures proved equally difficult and prolonged. As in Bulgaria the Communist Party converted itself into a socialist reform party, renamed the National Salvation Front (NSF), led by Iliescu, an opponent of Ceausescu. Iliescu became interim president after the fall of Ceausescu, with the task of supervising multiparty elections in 1990. The opposition parties soon concluded that Iliescu was working to preserve the NSF's power, using the assets of the old Communist Party and its control of the radio, television, the secret police and the local authorities. But western observers validated election results: 66 per cent of the votes were for the NSF, and Iliescu was overwhelmingly endorsed as president.

However, there were further protests in Bucharest. The regime ordered a police crackdown, and Iliescu brought in 30,000 Jiu valley miners to end the demonstrations by force. The West lost confidence in the regime, and suspended all non-humanitarian aid. The government responded by introducing a drastic austerity programme in accordance with IMF demands. Price rises reduced real wages by about 40 per cent in a year and brought frequent strikes. The Jiu valley miners were soon back in Bucharest, but this time supporting demonstrations which brought down the government. A coalition led by Stoljan tried to stabilise the economy. It announced a six months' price freeze on staple items, and tried to improve Romania's international image. But the NSF split and pro-Iliescu elements set up the Democratic National Salvation Front (DNSF). This party won most votes in the 1992 elections, but could establish a majority in the Chamber of Deputies only in coalition with the chauvinistic Greater Romania Party, the communist-inclined Socialist Labour Party and the right-wing Party of Romanian National Unity. The new government, led by Nicolae Vacaroiu, failed to halt the collapse of the economy. The GDP dropped a further 16.5 per cent in 1992 and many families became destitute. Unemployment rose, and the lei and real wages dropped even further. Privatisation and real reform remained stalled. Major anti-government demonstrations rocked Bucharest in February 1993. The DNSF party restructured itself in 1993, merging with several smaller parties, and changed its name to the Party of Social Democracy of Romania (PDSR). Right-wing nationalist influence grew, led by Gheorghe Funar's Party of Romanian National Unity (PUNR).

However, reforms slowly began to have an effect through 1994 and 1995. A dynamic private sector emerged. Inflation dropped in 1994–95 and industrial output grew. In 1993 Romania signed an association agreement with the EU, joined the Council of Europe, and regained the status of most favoured nation with the USA. But Vacaroiu found it ever harder to hold the ruling coalition together, until in 1996 the PUNR left it. In the following elections (1996) the PDSR was defeated by the rightist Democratic Convention (CDR), and Emil Constantinescu replaced Iliescu as president. The CDR's Victor Ciorbea led a new coalition of the CDR, the Social Democratic Union and the Hungarian Democratic Alliance of Romania, with a programme of democratisation, privatisation and economic reform. But the coalition proved incapable of carrying through its programme. GDP dropped 6 per cent in 1997, and living standards shrank further. Ciorbea resigned in 1998 and was replaced by Radu Vasile, but little changed. A renewal of the IMF loan could not be negotiated, and in 1999 the economy's prospects were further damaged by the collapse of the Russian economy and by the obstruction to the Danubian trade caused by the NATO air-strikes against Yugoslavia. Romania's main hope must be that the West will provide substantial economic support in some Balkan Aid package which might be set up after the end of the Kosovo war. A lasting source of tension with Romania's neighbour Hungary is the presence of nearly two million Hungarians in Romania, especially in Transylvania and in its leading city Cluj. These tensions were exacerbated by the provocative treatment of Hungarians there in the early 1990s by Funar, the mayor of Cluj. Indeed, there has been a general rise in racial tensions since the fall of communism; anti-semitism has revived and there have been some nasty attacks on Transylvanian gypsies. But in September 1996 a treaty between Hungary and Romania guaranteed the rights of ethnic minorities

– a requirement for membership in the European Union and NATO – and since then relations between them have improved. However, racism remains a powerful force; the ultra-nationalist Greater Romania Party gained 17 per cent support in the 1998 elections.

Boundary disputes with neighbouring states continue to present possible sources of conflict, though the Hungarian frontier has been agreed. But Bulgaria and Ukraine both fear Romanian irredentist claims to parts of their territory, while Moldova, although ethnically Romanian, currently rejects any idea of union with Romania.

Table 9.8 Romania: Elections to the Chamber of Deputies: 3 November 1996

Party	Percentage of votes	Seats won
Democratic Convention of Romania	30.2	122
Democratic Social Party of Romania	21.5	91
Social Democratic Union	12.9	53
Hungarian Democratic Alliance of Romania	6.6	25
Greater Romania Party (Romania Mare)	4.5	19
Romanian National Unity Party	4.4	18
Others, including non-partisans	19.9	0
Total by proportional representation		328
Seats for Minority Organisations		15
Total	100.0	343

Table 9.9 Romania: Elections to the Senate: 3 November 1996

Party	Percentage of votes	Seats won
Democratic Convention of Romania	34.0	51
Democratic Social Party of Romania	25.6	41
Social Democratic Union	14.6	23
Hungarian Democratic Alliance of Romania	7.5	11
Greater Romania Party (Romania Mare)	5.0	8
Romanian National Unity Party	4.7	7
Others, including non-partisans	8.5	0
Vacant		2
Total	99.9	143

The Baltic States

The Baltic States, which had been forcibly incorporated into the Soviet Union after the Nazi–Soviet Pact of 1939, declared their independence shortly after the abortive Moscow coup of August 1991. But their small size in relation to their neighbour Russia, the presence of large Russian minorities within their borders, and the economic and political structures left to them by the Soviet system, presented particular difficulties. In particular, their attempts to confine full citizenship to non-Russians, or even to drive Russians out of their territories, clashed with the EU's requirements on respect for the rights of minorities, and thus tended to obstruct their attempts to become members of it. To counter any future threat from Russia they sought Western guarantees of their borders, and to this end hoped to be accepted as members of NATO. At first, moreover, they had to contend with the unpopular presence of Russian army units on their soil, and a major concern of their first administrations after 1992 was to negotiate their departure. Lithuania has a special problem in the existence within its borders of an isolated segment of Russian territory, the *oblast* of Kaliningrad, which contains a major naval base.

Estonia

In the 1992 elections, from which (as in Latvia) post-World War II Russian immigrants were excluded, the national-conservative Fatherland Front gained most seats with 29 out of 101. Its leader, Mart Laar, became prime minister of a broad-based coalition government, while Lennart Merl was elected president. The government fostered rapid privatisation and the depoliticisation of the administrative, police and judicial systems. But Laar had to deal with discord in his own party, and with an awkward relationship with President Merl, who refused to promulgate a number of laws passed by parliament. Nevertheless, the economy grew strongly in these years. The new currency, the kroon, was successfully tied to the value of the Deutschmark in 1992. It remained stable, and foreign investment grew. Foreign trade was redirected from Russia to the West. But the fast-growing economy brought with it relatively high inflation, by 1998 growth had slowed somewhat, and the trade deficit is expected to be substantial in 1999.

The 1995 elections brought to power a centre-left coalition government led by Tiit Vahi of the Coalition Party. He soon had to realign his coalition, however, when his first government collapsed after the interior minister, the leader of the Centre Party, was accused of illegal surveillance. Vahi's second coalition government had to survive sharp infighting over economic, social, and foreign policy, and it collapsed in 1996 when the Reform Party withdrew its support. Vahi then formed a minority government, replacing the six Reform Party ministers with members of the Coalition Party and Rural People's Union, but was soon replaced as prime minister by Mart Siiman. In 1999 it seems that the Rural Union parties may set up an electoral alliance with the Centre Party unless the coalition parties provide greater support for farmers, and all parties are engaged in trying to form electoral alliances.

Relations with Russia continue to be difficult – the borders are disputed near Narva – but the sea borders with Latvia (important for fishing rights) were agreed in 1996. Estonia was admitted to the Council of Europe in May 1992 and became a member of the new Council of Baltic Sea States. An associate membership agreement was signed with the EU in 1995, and an application for full EU membership was then made. Estonia is in the first group of eastern countries expected to be accepted for full membership.

Table 9.10 Estonia: Elections to the State Council: 5 March 1995

Party	Percentage of votes	Seats won
Coalition Party and Rural People's Union	32.2	41
Estonian Reform Party	16.2	19
Estonian Centre Party	14.2	16
Fatherland Union	7.8	8
Moderates	6.0	6
Our Home is Estonia	5.9	6
Conservative People's Party (right-wingers)	5.0	5
Others, including non-partisans	12.7	0
Total	100.0	101

Latvia

As in Estonia, Russians had no vote in the 1993 elections unless resident before 1940. The leading parties in the new parliament – the Saeima – were the Latvian Farmers' Union and the Latvia's Way Party; these two formed a coalition government led by Valdis Birkavs of Latvia's Way. The president was the economist Guntis Ulmanis of the Latvian Farmers' Union. A new currency – the lats – was established in 1993, and a tight fiscal policy kept inflation low. Foreign investment increased, but dependency on Russia for fuel supplies at world prices was (and remains) a constraint. Privatisation continued apace. The coalition lasted until 1994. A similar coalition led by Maris Gailis of Latvia's Way replaced it. This government was weakened by several serious bank failures, causing the finance minister to resign in 1995, and in the 1995 elections the Latvia's Way Party came only third. Nine parties won seats in the new Saeima, and no party had more than 18 out of the 100 seats. Two of the president's nominees were rejected before parliament accepted a charismatic non-party businessman, Andris Skele, as prime minister, with the support of seven of the parties. He concentrated above all on economic consolidation, and the economy grew strongly in 1996, while in 1997 GDP grew by 5.9 per cent and inflation dropped again. The Skele government lasted till 1997, when four ministers were forced to resign amid accusations of corruption. Skele was replaced by Guntars Krasts of the Fatherland and Freedom Party. Skele then founded a party of his own, the right-of-centre People's Party, which won 24 seats in the 1998 elections, becoming the largest party. But it was Vilis Kristopans who then formed a government. A referendum on the crucial issue of citizenship status and minority rights was held in 1998; 53 per cent approved the amendments which will liberalise the requirements for citizenship and naturalisation. However, the collapse of the Russian economy could be damaging for the Latvian economy in 1999.

The Russians remained concerned about the rights of Russians in Latvia, even after a new citizenship law in 1994 which satisfied the Council of Europe sufficiently for Latvia to be admitted in 1995. But a further liberalisation of citizenship rights was proposed, and approved in a referendum by 53 per cent in 1998. The Russian government welcomed this, and relations with Russia have improved with the departure of the last Russian base in 1998. But Latvia has joined NATO's Partnership for Peace programme in February 1994 and pursued its goal of full NATO membership by sending naval and army units to NATO exercises in 1995. Meanwhile, however, relations with Lithuania have deteriorated after Latvia agreed in 1996 to allow two Western companies to explore the seabed, though the sea borders were disputed by Lithuania.

Latvia signed an association agreement with the EU in 1998 and applied for full membership later that year. In the same year it became the first Baltic country to join the World Trade Organisation.

Table 9.11 Latvia: Elections to the Diet: 3–4 October 1998

Party	Percentage of votes	Seats won
People's Party	21.2	24
Latvia's Way	18.1	21
Fatherland and Freedom Party	14.7	17
National Harmony Party	14.1	16
Social Democratic Alliance	12.8	14
New Party	7.3	8
Others, including non-partisans	12.0	0
Total	100.2	100

Note: Turnout was 71.89 %.

Lithuania

Although the Lithuanian Communist Party had shifted a long way towards support for independence, it was the strongly anti-Soviet Sajudis coalition which won the relatively free election of 1990 and successfully established independence. But Lithuania's dependence on trade with Russia proved difficult to shift, the high price of Russian fuel contributed to a continuing decline in industrial production, and living standards declined. Lithuania lagged behind Estonia and Latvia in the race to the market and privatisation. Thus the attempt to reorganise the economy and trading connections, though it prepared the way for later development, at first caused a severe economic crisis. Moreover, even relations with neighbouring countries – like Latvia, because of the sea borders dispute – deteriorated. As a result, the former Communists (now the Democratic Labour Party (LDDP)), led by Algirdas Brazauskas, defeated Sajudis in the 1992 elections to the Seimas. Adolfas Slezevicius formed a left-inclined government. Brazauskas was elected president in 1993 with 60 per cent of the vote. The Slezevicius government lasted till 1996.

In the 1996 elections the LDDP was heavily defeated, damaged by financial scandals. The alliance of the Homeland Union and the Conservatives of Lithuania (TS-LK) (the grouping which succeeded Sajudis), formed the largest group and set up a coalition government, led by Gediminas Vagnorius, with the Christian Democrats. In February 1998, the former US citizen, Valdas Adamkus, who had spent decades working in the Environmental Protection Agency, narrowly won a run-off election and was inaugurated as president of Lithuania. He promised to establish an 'ethic of government service' as part of a reform process leading to EU and NATO membership, but how much power he will have in relation to the parliament is still uncertain. The Constitutional Court has ruled that Lithuania is a parliamentary rather than a presidential democracy. But the Russian economic crisis could seriously damage an economy in which, before the collapse of the ruble in 1998–99, 40 per cent of exports went to Russia and other ex-Soviet Union countries, and in which the trade deficit was already 13 per cent of GDP in 1998.

In 1993 Lithuania became the first Baltic state without Russian troops. But it affords access for Russia to the Kaliningrad *oblast*, and President Landsbergis offered aid when the Russian fleet there ran short of food. However, Polish and Russian speakers in Lithuania objected to the 1995 law which made Lithuanian

Table 9.12 Lithuania: Elections to the Seimas: 20 October, 4 November 1996

Party	Percentage of votes	Seats won
Coalition Party and Rural People's Union	29.8	70
Estonian Reform Party	9.9	16
Estonian Centre Party	9.5	12
Fatherland Union	8.2	13
Moderates	6.6	12
Others, including non-partisans	35.3	15
Undeclared	0.7	3
Total	100	141

Note: The Seimas has 141 members, elected for a four-year term, 71 members elected in single-seat constituencies and 70 by proportional representation. The five parties shown above won more than two seats in the 1996 elections:

the official language. Lithuania was accepted into the Council of Europe in 1993, joined NATO's Partnership for Peace, sending troops to the first NATO exercises held in a former Soviet republic (Poland), despite Russian opposition in 1994, and became an associate member of the EU in 1995.

The Balkans 1960–99

We consider here Yugoslavia and its successor-states, and Albania. The region is economically poor except for Slovenia and parts of Croatia, and suffers from serious ethnic and religious divisions. All areas except Slovenia were ethnically mixed until the appearance in the 1990s of policies of expulsion and massacre aimed at achieving ethnic purity within the separate countries and provinces, and politics is dominated by attempts to adjust to, or escape from, this situation. The state of Yugoslavia, created after World War I as a multi-ethnic state of the South Slavs, was always at best a precarious unity (see Chapter 1 for a closer historical view). In 1991 the total population was 23.5 million, of whom 35 per cent were Serbs, 19 per cent Croats, 8.5 per cent Muslims (mainly Bosnians who were non-Serb and non-Croat), 7.5 per cent Slovenes, 7.5 per cent Albanians, 5.5 per cent Macedonians, 2.5 per cent Montenegrins and 2 per cent Hungarians. Hardly any identified themselves as Yugoslavs. The state was divided into six republics and two partly separate provinces of Greater Serbia (Vojvodina and Kosovo). In Kosovo a large majority of the population was Albanian and Muslim, with a Serb minority which felt itself to be discriminated against in the 1970s and early 1980s. Albania itself was divided between two tribal groupings, and blood feuds remained endemic.

The disintegration of Yugoslavia

The Yugoslav leader Tito sought to smooth over divisions by a system requiring consensus on decision-making among the republics and autonomous provinces. However, Croatia and Slovenia, the two richest republics, increasingly felt they were being exploited to support the much poorer territories of Montenegro, Bosnia-Hercegovina, Macedonia and Kosovo. The system limped along for ten years after Tito's death in 1980 while tensions mounted and Croats in particular demanded greater autonomy. From 1987 onward the Serbs, under the nationalist leader of the Serbian Communist Party Slobodan Milosevic, responded by an aggressive reassertion of Serbian dominance, including in 1989 central Serbian control over Kosovo which was enforced by troops against strikes and demonstrations. The Milosevic-controlled Serbian media issued a constant diet of Serbian-nationalist propaganda including hatred of Croats (identified as Ustasha, the name of a group of murderous wartime fascist Croats), Muslims (identified as Mujahadeen, the Iranian terrorists) and Albanians. Fearing this new Serbian dominance, the Slovenian parliament in 1989 voted for a multi-party system and the right to secede from the Federation. Demands by the individual republics' Communist parties for independence from the central Yugoslav party (the League of Communists of Yugoslavia (LCY)) were rejected at a Congress in 1990; whereupon the Slovenes and Croats stormed out. Shortly afterwards Slovenia and Croatia installed non-communist governments and declared independence (1991). (The predominantly Serb province of Krajina immediately seceded from Croatia.) War began at once. The Serbian-dominated Yugoslav army, after failing to reconquer Slovenia, attacked Croatia, but was driven back, and Croatia's independence was effectively recognised in January 1992. Macedonia (known as FYROM – Former Yugoslav Republic of Macedonia to avoid upsetting Greece with its own Greek Macedonian province) also separated from Yugoslavia, and maintained a precarious balance between its populations of (majority) Slavs (who might be regarded as Serbs, Bulgarians, or as a separate nation of Macedonians) and (minority) Albanians.

Table 9.13 Yugoslavia: Elections to the Council of the Republic, 28 January 1993

Party	Seats won
Socialist Party of Serbia (SPS) (ex-LCS)	12
Serb Radical Party (SRP)	10
Democratic Party of Montenegran Socialists	18
Total	40

In Bosnia, however, with a mixed population of Muslims, Serbs and Croats, the attempt to separate from Yugoslavia, led by Bosnia's Muslim president, Aliya Izetbegovic, met the ferocious resistance of the Bosnian Serbs, backed by the Serbs of Serbia. They sought to resolve ethnic divisions by a savage policy of 'ethnic cleansing',[1] driving out or massacring whole populations of non-Serbs. The Bosnian capital Sarajevo was besieged from the Serb suburbs and the surrounding hills from 1992 to 1994, while its predominantly Muslim population faced sniper fire and shells in the streets, and 10,000 people were killed. UN peace-keeping forces could do little to restrain the violence, nor were the UN's economic sanctions against Serbia effective in this respect. In 1995 the town of Srebrenica, whose safety had been guaranteed by the UN, was taken by the Serbs and the entire male population massacred. Soon after, NATO (with UN backing) finally decided to intervene with a campaign of airstrikes against Serb forces in Bosnia (1995). The combined Muslim and Croat armies seized their chance to throw back the Serbs, while the Croats also reconquered Krajina, driving out into Serbia the 200,000 Serbs who had lived there. To avoid further losses the Serbs accepted a peace settlement in the 1995 Dayton accord.

Bosnia was divided almost equally between a Muslim–Croat Federation and a Serb Republic, under the shadowy authority of general Bosnian institutions. A NATO-led Implementation Force was installed to maintain the peace, a task in which it succeeded fairly well, but it proved unwilling to face the dangers involved in seizing war-criminals so the horrors of the war remained largely unpunished. From 1995 to 1999 Bosnia's federal institutions have been largely non-functional because the Serbs, fearing that a truly unified Bosnia would negate their aim of unification with Yugoslavia, have refused to participate in them. Few refugees have managed to return to their pre-war homes. Izetbegovic has remained president of this nominal federation. The Croatian areas of Hercegovina are *de facto* part of Croatia. But the 1998 elections did show that the voters continue to hope for improvement of the situation; the turnout was over 70 per cent. The moderate Zivko Radisic was elected to take Serbia's seat on the triumvirate Bosnian presidency, and the more moderate parties made gains in the parliamentary elections. And though the ultra-nationalist Nikola Poplasen won the presidency of the Serb Republic, the UN took advantage of the damage to the Yugoslav army during the Kosovo crisis in the summer of 1999 to depose him. At the same time the power of the Serb Republic of Bosnia was sharply cut back by the assignment of the key town of Brcko which connects its two parts, not to its own sole power but to a condominium.

Table 9.14 Bosnia and Hercegovina: Elections to the Republican House of Representatives: 12–13 September 1998

Party or Coalition	Percentage of votes	Seats won
Coalition for a Unified and Democratic Bosnia and Hercegovina	N/A	17
Croatian Democratic Community	N/A	6
Serbian Democratic Party-List	N/A	4
Social Democratic Party	N/A	4
Sloga	N/A	4
Others	N/A	7
Total		42

Table 9.15 Bosnia and Hercegovina: Elections to the House of Representatives of the Federation: 14 September 1996

Party	Percentage of votes	Seats won
Party of Democratic Action	54.3	78
Croatian Democratic Community	25.3	36
United List Bosnia and Hercegovina	7.9	11
Party for Bosnia and Hercegovina	7.4	10
Democratic People's Community	1.8	3
Croatian Rights Party	1.2	2
Others	2.3	0
Total	100.2	140

Table 9.16 Bosnia and Hercegovina: Elections to the National Assembly of the Serbian Republic: 23 November 1997

Party	Percentage of votes	Seats won
Serbian Democratic Party	26.5	24
Coalition for a Unified and Democratic Bosnia and Hercegovina	17.3	16
Serbian People's Alliance	16.0	15
Serb Radical Party of the Serbian Republic	15.7	15
Socialist Party of the Serbian Republic	9.9	9
Party of Independent Social Democrats	2.7	2
Social Democratic Party of Bosnia and Hercegovina	1.9	2
Others	10.0	0
Total	100.0	83

Slovenia, on the other hand, has had a relatively trouble-free existence since independence, due to its successful economy and its lack of a significant Serbian minority. It has joined the Central European Free Trade Agreement (CEFTA), was granted associate membership of the EU in 1996 and expects to be admitted to full membership soon. Its centrist government and its ex-Communist President Kucan remain solidly in power. Relations with Croatia are cool, but its comfortable relations with the West suggest that this may not matter much.

Table 9.17 Slovenia: Elections to the State Chamber, 10 November 1996

Party	Percentage of votes	Seats won
Liberal Democracy of Slovenia	27.0	25
Slovenian People's Party	19.4	19
Social Democratic Party of Slovenia	16.1	16
Slovenian Christian-Democrats	9.6	10
United List of Social-Democrats	9.0	9
Democratic Party of Retired People of Slovenia	4.3	5
Slovenian National Party	3.2	4
Others	11.1	0
Total	99.7	88

Croatia has hardly yet escaped from the traumas of the wars which attended its birth. Only in 1995 did it establish control over its territories with victory over the rebel Serbs of Krajina, and frictions continued over repatriations and property-claims of Croats expelled earlier from Krajina and Western Vojvodina and of Serbs who fled from Krajina in 1995. But economic growth has been good, the currency stable, and political stability was maintained up to 1999 through the continuing control of the Croatian Democratic Alliance Party (HDZ) and of President Tujdman until his death in December 1999. But its authoritarian style could lead to rising opposition. Croatia was admitted to the Council of Europe in 1996 and has applied to join the World Trade Organisation.

Table 9.18 Croatia: Elections to the House of Representatives, 29 October 1995

Party	Percentage of votes	Seats won
Croatian Democratic Community (HDZ)	45.2	75
Croatian Social Liberal Party	11.6	12
Croatian Peasant Party		10
Istrian Democratic Assembly		4
United List Croatian People's Party	18.3	2
Croatian Christian Democratic Union		1
Slavonian–Baranyan Croatian Party		1
Social Democratic Party of Croatia	8.9	10
Croatian Rights Party	5.0	4
Others	11.0	8
Total	100.0	127

Table 9.19 Croatia: Elections to the Chamber of Districts, 17 April 1997 (elected members)

Party	Seats won
Croatian Democratic Community	41
Croatian Social Liberal Party	7
Croatian Peasant Party	9
Istrian Democratic Assembly	2
Social Democratic Party of Croatia	4
Total	63

Macedonia (FYROM) was ruled from 1993 to 1996 by a coalition of Social Democrats and Liberals, but the economy stagnated and unemployment was high. Relations with Greece were normalised in 1995, thus easing trade through southern outlets, and FYROM was admitted to the Council of Europe and the OSCE. Albania was worried about Macedonia's treatment of its Albanian minority (e.g. its suppression of the Tetovo independent Albanian-language university). In the 1998 election the Macedonian nationalist party IMRO with its ally, the Democratic Alternative, won a dominant position, and seemed likely to form a coalition with parties representing Macedonian Albanians with a programme of honest government, economic reform, tax cuts and investment inducements for foreign capital. But in 1999 Macedonia's own ethnic difficulties were greatly exacerbated by the influx of hundreds of thousands of Albanian refugees from Kosovo, driven out by the Serbs' campaign of ethnic cleansing. The majority Slav population, already suspicious of their Muslim neighbours, became anxious about the possibility of a permanent swing of the ethnic balance of the state away from themselves, and about the huge cost of maintaining the refugees. They disapproved of the NATO bombing campaign and were nervous during 1999 in case they were to become involved in serious war if NATO used their territory as a base for a ground assault on Kosovo. Such fears proved unfounded, but they are likely to remain concerned about their future relations with their northern neighbour, Serbia.

Table 9.20 Macedonia: Elections to the People's Assembly: 18 October and 1 November 1998

Party	Seats won
Internal Macedonian Revolutionary Organisation (VMRO–DPMNE)	58
Democratic Alternative	
Social Democratic League of Macedonia	29
Party of Democratic Prosperity (Albanians)	
Democratic Party of the Albanians	24
Liberal Party	4
Socialist Party of Macedonia	2
Others	1
Undeclared due to voting irregularities	2
Total	120

Meanwhile, Albania had followed its own troubled path, constantly striving to maintain its territory against possible threats from Yugoslavia, looking for powerful supporters, and avoiding giving any excuse to its neighbours to attack it. It was protected by China from 1961 to 1977 and isolated in that period from the Soviet bloc. Until 1992 the ruling (Communist) party was the Albanian Party of Labour (APL) (led by Enver Hoxha from 1941 to 1985 and then by Ramiz Alia), but family feuds, plots and attempted assassinations, corruption and accusations of corruption, formed the stuff of politics.

As in the rest of eastern Europe, the economic situation deteriorated in the 1980s, and 1990 brought demands by the opposition (the Democratic Party (DP)) for open elections, backed by mass demonstrations which the army failed to suppress. The APL's organisation in rural areas enabled it to win the first elections in 1991, but further anarchy forced a new election in 1992 which broke the power of the APL. The DP's Salih Berisha became president, and the government was based on a coalition of the DP and the Social Democrats.

The economy, which was in crisis in 1992, made fair progress in 1993–95. The country's economic potential of off-shore oil and gas deposits and substantial mineral resources attracted the interest of major multinational companies, and Western influence became strong. Inflation was held to about 10 per cent, the currency was sound, and unemployment was down to about 15 per cent, though this success was partly due to the half million expatriate workers who sent money back to their families. But it was difficult to establish the framework of honest financial and commercial behaviour which could enable the country's economic potential to be realised. Though the legal system was reformed and it provided for private property, the judicial system was still open to pressure from powerful groups and corruption remained endemic. The government failed to respect the multi-party system it had fought for when in opposition, banned opposition public meetings, and settled scores by prosecuting leading members of the old regime, including Ramiz Alia and Hoxha's widow. In the 1996 elections, serious vote-rigging and other tricks – condemned by OSCE observers – secured a bogus DP victory, and again there were riots in the capital, Tirana. Pyramid investment schemes in which many Albanians had invested their savings collapsed in January 1997, and the resulting riots led to a near civil war. Arms depots were looted, and over 2,000 people died in the ensuing disorder, while tens of thousands fled by boat to Italy or by road to Greece. Berisha had to agree to a multi-national stabilisation force set up by the OSCE, and fresh elections in the summer. The Albanian Socialist Party (ASP) (the successor to the APL) won an overwhelming victory, Berisha was replaced as president by Rexhep Meidani and a Socialist-led coalition government took over, led initially by the ASP leader Fatos Nano and from 1998 by Pandeli Majko.

Table 9.21 Albania: Elections to People's Assembly: 29 June and 6 July 1997

Party	Percentage of votes	Seats won
Socialist Party of Albania (SPA)	52.8	99
Democratic Party of Albania (DP)	25.7	29
Social Democratic Party of Albania	2.5	8
Human Rights' Unity Party	2.8	4
National Front	2.3	3
Party of the Democratic Alliance of Albania	2.8	2
Republican Party of Albania	2.3	1
Others	8.8	9
Total	100.0	155

Though Western governments and international institutions such as the IMF supported the new government, it faced major problems of political violence and corruption. After further disorder in 1998 an OSCE-sponsored 'Friends of

Albania' was formed by 23 countries and eight international organisations to assist in improving the country's security situation, fight corruption, promote economic development, and help the Kosovan refugees who were increasingly escaping into Albania from the Serbs' intensifying persecution of them. Thus Albania came to be especially associated with the West, and was drawn by its situation into the West's actions against Yugoslavia. Already in 1995 the USA was using Albanian bases for reconnaissance flights over Bosnia.

Serbia and the Kosovo crisis

The new Federal Republic of Yugoslavia, as formed in 1992 and 1993, consists only of Serbia proper, its component provinces of Vojvodino and Kosovo, and an increasingly disaffected Montenegro. However, its Serbian nationalist regime under Milosevic remained in power even though the UN imposed economic sanctions for its support for the Bosnian Serbs, its economy was severely damaged and its people impoverished.

Table 9.22 Yugoslavia: Elections to the Council of Citizens, 3 November 1996

Party	Percentage of votes	Seats won
Socialist Party of Serbia (SPS) (ex-LCS) Yugoslav Left (JUL)	42.4	64
New Democracy–Movement for Serbia (ND) Together (Electoral Alliance)	22.2	22
Serb Radical Party (SRP)	17.9	16
Democratic Party of Montenegran Socialists	3.4	20
Hungarian Party of Vojvodina	1.9	3
People's Agreement (Electoral Alliance)	1.5	8
Others	10.7	5
Total	100.0	138

Only Russia and Belarus, and to some extent Greece, continued to support Yugoslavia against the pressure of the West, and it maintained its iron grip on Kosovo against increasingly violent opposition from the persecuted Albanian Kosovans. Through 1998 a serious conflict was clearly looming in Kosova. Many Kosovan Albanians, driven to desperation, joined the nascent Kosovo Liberation Army (KLA) and prepared to fight a guerilla war, while the Serbs burnt villages and shot villagers suspected of collaboration with the KLA, and there was a large build-up of the (Serbian) Yugoslav army. Many Kosovans fled to the woods in the late summer and autumn, enduring terrible sufferings, and Western governments feared an explosion of ethnic conflict which would destabilise the whole region, wreck the peace-keeping authority of NATO in Europe and the East, and open the door for aggressive nationalist forces. The prospect of the lifting of economic sanctions induced Yugoslavia to attend talks at Rambouillet in February and March 1999, but Milosevic would not agree to any arrangement in which an international force would be placed in Kosovo to guarantee a settlement protecting Albanian Kosovans, and the talks broke down. NATO (led by the USA and Britain) responded with a major campaign of airstrikes against the Yugoslav army and its infrastructure in Kosovo and Serbia, but Milosevic's response was to let loose his army and paramilitaries on a large-scale ethnic cleansing of Kosovo, driving out by massacres, rapes, and house-burnings whole populations of Albanians, and depositing in the neighbouring countries of Albania, Macedonia, and Yugoslavia's own republic of Montenegro huge numbers of refugees. In June 1999, after 78 days of bombing, the combination of serious damage due to the bombing, military pressure on the ground by the KLA, and the threat of invasion by NATO ground forces forced Milosevic to agree to terms similar to those which he rejected at Rambouillet. The Yugoslav forces withdrew and forces representing the UN (but essentially NATO and a Russian force) moved in to maintain a precarious peace within the theoretical sovereignty of Yugoslavia.

At the time of writing (June 1999) hundreds of thousands of destitute Kosovan refugees squatting in camps in the surrounding countries of Albania, Macedonia and Montenegro are returning home, while many Serbs are leaving Kosovo, fearing reprisals. Montenegro is threatened with conflict between the Republic's own police and these Serb emigrants, backed possibly by the Yugoslav army. The effects on the surrounding countries are as yet impossible to predict, but are certain to be major. Macedonia's internal ethnic tensions between Albanians and Serbs may increase; Albania is filled with armed men – KLA, NATO, or local Albanians waiting with the weapons they seized in 1997, and its economy and society remain fragile. Meanwhile, it is apparent that the destruction of Yugoslavia's bridges and oil refineries will produce major and long-lasting damage to the economy of Yugoslavia, and also to most of the surrounding countries, especially those dependent on Danube trade. Western aid will contribute substantially to the essential reconstruction, but the West has declared that Yugoslavia will not receive any while Milosevic remains in power, and possibly not until he is delivered to The Hague as a war criminal.

Conclusion

The West is seeking to draw eastern Europe into a Western-style polity of free market economics in a global financial system, democratic politics, technological development, and peace. Such a programme carries enormous costs in helping to transform and lift to another level the backward economies of these countries and in preventing conflicts, and it is not clear that the West's financial strength or its political will suffice for the sacrifices which the Western economies will have to incur to pay for it, especially if major war damage (of the

Table 9.23 Presidents of central and eastern european states

	Elected by	Term in years	Incumbent	Year elected
Albania	Parliament	5	Rexhep Mejdani	1997
Bulgaria	Popular vote	5	Petar Stojanov	1997
Bosnia & Hercegovina	Popular vote	2	Tripartite[1]	1998
Croatia	Popular vote	5	Franjo Tudjman	1997
Czech Republic	Parliament	5	Václav Havel	1998
Estonia	Parliament[2]	5	Lennart Merl	1996
Hungary	Parliament[3]	5	Guntis Ulmanis	1995
Latvia	Parliament	5	Arpad Göncz	1995
Lithuania	Popular vote	5	Valdas Adamkus	1998
Macedonia	Popular vote	5	Kiro Gligorov	1994
Poland	Popular vote	5	Aleksander Kwasniewski	1995
Romania	Popular vote	4	Emil Constantinescu	1996
Slovakia	Parliament	5	vacant	
Slovenia	Popular vote	5	Milan Kucan	1997
Yugoslavia	Parliament	4	Slobodan Milosevic	1997

1 Zivko Radisic (Serb), Ante Jelavic (Croat), Alija Izetbegovic (Muslim)

2 The president of Estonia is elected by parliament (3rd round) or an electoral college (4th round).

3 The president of Hungary is elected by parliament and becomes non-partisan after the election.

1999 air-strikes against Yugoslavia for example), major dislocation (as occurs with large movements of population or with natural or technological environmental disasters), or major economic collapses necessitate large and expensive recovery programmes analogous to the Marshall Plan of 1947. Furthermore, the programme carries the inherent disadvantage that it always has an eastern boundary; a boundary between countries advantageously included in the West's structures (like the EU or NATO), and those to the east which are not, and which may feel aggrieved or even threatened by the situation. Since 1989 this programme has been pursued with admirable resolve and a fair degree of subtlety, with the construction of various transitional institutions like associate membership of the EU to soften the boundary, and with no inescapable need for very large Western resources to be devoted to carrying it out. Most states of eastern Europe have embraced their part in the programme with more or less enthusiasm, and developed Western-style economic and political institutions accordingly. But the decision not to grant exceptional large-scale help to Russia in 1998 may have precipitated the Russian financial collapse (which then contributed to the world financial crisis involving also Japan and the Pacific Rim countries and Brazil) in 1998 and 1999, which clearly has very serious effects on eastern European economies. The involvement of NATO in the lethal ethnic wars of the Balkans will generate huge demands for financial support for reconstruction, even if its political outcome is satisfactory for the programme. It seems likely that the outcome of the Kosovo crisis will be some kind of NATO or UN protectorate over the Balkans (including Romania and Bulgaria) to prevent further destructive conflicts, to compensate for war damage, and to establish on a more prosperous basis the economies of the region. But it is obvious that such a protectorate carries immense dangers and difficulties, could easily generate resentment among the people of the region, and may well offend Russia, which would seek to maintain its influence in the region. Other countries likely to lie beyond the eastern boundary of reconstruction aid – Ukraine and Turkey – may also resent such developments. Thus the prospects for eastern Europe remain uncertain, even though there has been much progress and many possible disputes have been resolved peacefully, so far.

Further reading

Agh, A. (1998) *The Politics of Central Europe*, Sage, London.

Brown, J. (1991) *Surge to Freedom: The End of Communist Rule in Eastern Europe*, Adamantine, Twickenham.

Brown, J. (1994) *Hopes and Shadows: Eastern Europe after Communism*, Longman, Harlow.

Crawford, K. (1996) *East Central European Politics Today*, Manchester University Press, Manchester.

Crampton, R. (1997) *Eastern Europe in the Twentieth Century – and After*, 2nd edn, Routledge, London.

Dawisha, K. and Parrot, B. (1997) *The Consolidation of Democracy in East Central Europe*, Cambridge University Press, Cambridge.

Swain, G. and Swain, N. (1998) *Eastern Europe since 1945*, 2nd edn, Macmillan, Basingstoke

White, S. *et al.* (eds) (1998) *Developments in Central and East European Politics 2*, Macmillan, Basingstoke.

The most useful means of keeping up to date is the RFE/RL Newsline (http://www.rferl.org/)

Note

1. Radio Televizija Srbija used to say that the Yugoslav army was 'cleansing the terrain'; Western journalists partly unveiled this euphemism by calling the process of massacre of males, rape of women, and expulsion 'ethnic cleansing'.

10 Economic integration

Introduction

One of the most striking features of contemporary Europe is its organisation into groups of countries to achieve economic and political goals. Some of the present groupings are of very long standing – Benelux, the union of Belgium, the Netherlands and Luxembourg, dates back to 1948. One formerly important trading bloc, the Council for Mutual Economic Assistance (CMEA, popularly known as COMECON) dating from 1949 and active from the mid-1950s, was dissolved in 1991. The biggest bloc, the European Union (EU), has, as documented elsewhere in this book (particularly chapter 4), lurched in the 1990s through a series of fundamental debates about its future, but seems increasingly likely eventually to embrace all the countries of Europe. The purpose of this chapter is to examine why countries group together in this way, what tensions are generated by the process, and what are the main implications for non-members. We start with a brief discussion of the economic relationships between countries.

A world without trade

Let us start by thinking about a country, or region, which does not trade at all, but is dependent simply on what it can produce itself. Any society faces what economists regard as the basic economic problem – its citizens would like to have more goods and services than can be made with the available resources, so that choices have to be made about what is to be produced, including how this is to be done, and who is to receive the goods and services when they are available. Consider, for example, the family groupings in Europe in the late Stone Age. They grew crops, such as grain, and they made various tools, including polished stone axes. In order to quarry the stone and then shape it to make the axes, they needed to devote labour and other resources to the task. The axes were used to help to clear the ground for the cultivation of new areas; so more axes enabled more food to be grown in the long term. At any one time, however, the resources used to make axes had to be diverted from other activities, such as growing grain and making it into bread. The problems confronting any Stone Age family in any year can be considered in a stylised way as the choice between making axes and making bread, as represented in Figure 10.1.

The curve in Figure 10.1, known as a production possibility curve, represents the range of possibilities open to a family or community at any one time – for example, it could choose to make no axes, in which case it could have 10 loaves (point A). It could also make no axes and only 7 loaves (point B), but in that case it would not be using all its resources and would not be operating efficiently. A second economically efficient combination is point C, where there are four loaves and three axes.

The production possibility curve can also be used to identify how much of any one commodity the family has to give up to have more of the other. Look at Figure 10.2, which repeats points A, B and C from the first diagram. Starting at A, with 10 loaves and no axe, if the family wants one axe it has to give up one loaf of bread (because at point D there is one axe but only 9 loaves). A second axe (point E) requires a greater sacrifice of bread, because devoting enough resources to make two axes leaves the family able to make only 7 loaves, so in moving from D to E the extra axe requires resources that could have made 2 loaves. Except in very unusual circumstances, the efficient combinations will all lie along a curve, as in Figure 10.1 and 10.2. When axe production is very low (e.g. at point D), more axes can be made using labour that is not very useful for baking bread and by quarrying the stone from land that is not very good for growing wheat; but when more axes are made (e.g. at point C), the labour and other resources that need to be diverted into extra axe production are more and more efficient at making bread, so more bread is lost for each axe as axe production rises.

It should be noted that 'efficient' is here being used in the quite restricted sense that at any time with predetermined resources and technology as much is

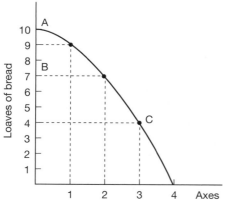

Figure 10.1 The production possibility curve

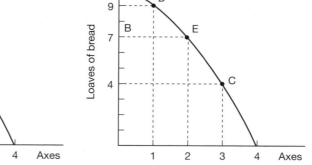

Figure 10.2 Trade-offs on the production possibility curve

produced as possible, or any achievable output is made with as few resources as possible. It usually excludes problems such as the depletion of natural resources or pollution (see Chapter 2), because it limits itself to relatively immediate matters. It also assumes that resources are available in the right mix and of the right quality to be fully used, and that what is produced will be demanded. Neither part of this assumption is necessarily valid, so there may be unemployment – see Chapter 3. Bearing these qualifications in mind, one can conceive a production possibility curve, drawn in multi-dimensional space to allow for a whole range of commodities, as representing the set of choices open to the family. If it is operating efficiently, it can select any combination on the curve, but it cannot go beyond it unless its options are increased. If the family remains isolated from other families, it can obtain goods and services in greater quantity if the technology available to it improves or if it increases the resources available to it – if more of its members can work, or it acquires more of the means of production, like more axes to clear land. The choice between bread and axes can be regarded as illustrating the choice between consuming as many goods as possible now – bread – or forgoing some present consumption to increase resources – axes – to enable more bread to be consumed in the future. Pushing the curve out, by increasing the resources available, or by improving technology so as to enable more to be made with given resources, or both, is the process of growth. There is, however, another way in which the family can increase the range of choices confronting it – by trading with others.

Why countries trade

We have just examined the production possibility curve representing the combinations of goods that a Stone Age family could produce, and found that its position depended on the technology available to the family and on the resources it could command. Even in Stone Age society, the mix of resources available would differ from one family to another – for example, one family might be living on flat land which is good for growing corn, whereas the other might be living fairly high up a mountain whose rock is ideal for making axes. In these circumstances, it would obviously make sense for the family on the flat land to bake more bread than it needs and exchange some of its surplus bread for axes, while the family on the higher ground makes more axes than it needs and exchanges its surplus axes for bread. This is the principle of the division of labour, where each family makes the products for which its resources are best suited, and surpluses are exchanged. When we consider not Stone Age families but modern countries, there will usually be quite big differences between countries in the kind of resources available, and these differences are the basic reason why trade is mutually advantageous. To see why, let us look at the example of Tayside, in Scotland, and Bordeaux, in France. The climate and the soil conditions in Tayside are such that the only way to grow grapes is to do so in a greenhouse, but raspberries grow very well in the fields. In Bordeaux, raspberries grow quite well, but grapes flourish in the vineyards and hence wine can readily be produced. We can illustrate the options for each region in a stylised way in Figure 10.3, where on diagram (a) TT represents the production possibility curve for Tayside and on diagram (b) BB that for Bordeaux.

If there were no trade between Tayside and Bordeaux, each region would at most be able to choose some combination of raspberries and wine on its curve, like for Tayside point T1 (with R1 raspberries and W1 wine) and for Bordeaux point B1. However, both regions can probably do better for themselves if they trade. Look at diagram (c) in Figure 10.3, in which curves TT and BB are repeated from diagrams (a) and (b). Suppose, to simplify the analysis, consumers in both regions would like the combination of wine and raspberries represented by point A, where each region would have RA raspberries and WA wine. This point is not available to either region without trade, because it lies outside the range of possible combinations on both TT and BB, but point A can be reached by trade. We can reach A, if Tayside grows R2 and Bordeaux R3 rasp-

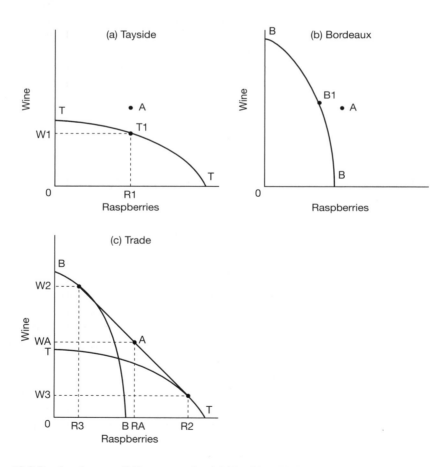

Figure 10.3 Production possibility curves for (a) Tayside, (b) Bordeaux and (c) both regions

berries, Bordeaux makes W2 and Tayside W3 wine, and Tayside sells to Bordeaux RA-R2 raspberries in exchange for WA-W2 wine. As common sense would suggest, Tayside grows more raspberries, the product in which it has an advantage over Bordeaux, than it wants to consume, and exports the surplus to Bordeaux. At the same time, Bordeaux makes more wine that it wants to consume, and exports the surplus to Tayside for raspberries.

Although Figure 10.3 portrays a much simplified analysis, its results generalise into the real world of many products and many countries. Provided countries differ from each other at all in the mixes in their basic factor endowments, trade can always make available combinations of goods that are otherwise unattainable. If these new combinations are what the citizens of participating countries want, trade will be mutually beneficial, by making more goods available to everybody. This can happen because trade lets each country specialise in making the products in which its resources give it a relative advantage: countries, like our Stone Age households, adopt the principle of division of labour.

Once the division of labour has occurred, its advantages may be compounded by economies of scale, which occur if the average cost of production declines as output grows. Economies of scale do not exist for all products (indeed in some cases average costs may actually rise as output grows) but they are a common phenomenon and hence frequently add to the benefits available from trade. In advanced modern economies, trade can take sophisticated forms, including that of intra-industry trade, in which what is in some sense the same product is both imported and exported. All western European countries both import and export cars, exporting those they produce themselves (perhaps under licence arrangements from another European country or Japan) and importing different models. Intra-industry trade seems paradoxical; if France is relatively good at producing Renault cars, why is it not also relatively good at producing Audi cars? It is, however, readily explicable by a mixture of accidents of history (which determine where goods were made in the first instance), economies of scale (which perpetuate the accident of initial location), and the extent to which the citizens of prosperous countries demand a wide range of goods (so that some Germans want Audis and some want Renaults).

Markets

Whether in prehistoric society or in a modern one, families play two economic roles. They are consumers of the goods and services that are available, and they make (or help to make) them. As soon as families move away from the self-sufficiency we described above, they will wish to exchange their surpluses of unwanted goods for goods of which they would like more. Those with surpluses wish to supply goods, those who want more demand them. The exchange can happen in two ways.

In theory, the more straightforward method of exchange is barter – the swapping of goods at some agreed rate – for example, one axe for 10 loaves of bread.

However, simple bilateral swaps may not be possible. The practical complications of barter can be illustrated by an example from the early career of Robert Maxwell. In the early 1950s most international trade had to be conducted by barter because of currency restrictions. In one deal brokered by Maxwell, chemicals were exported from Britain to East Germany in exchange for an assortment of china, glass and textiles, which were sent to Argentina. In return, Argentina sent pork to Britain. Unfortunately for Maxwell, the pork was condemned by the British authorities as unfit for human consumption, but nothing daunted he arranged for it to be re-exported, some to the Netherlands (where it was canned and sent to East Germany in exchange for cement which was eventually sold to Canada) and the rest to Austria in exchange for prefabricated houses. Because of the difficulties of barter, economies have evolved the use of a specialised good – money – to act as a medium of exchange. Whether with a barter system or with a monetised one, the principles are similar – those who demand goods and those who wish to supply them meet to try to arrive at a deal. This process of meeting, whether it takes place physically in a market place or without buyer and seller ever coming into direct contact with each other, is called a market. Figures 10.4 and 10.5 illustrate the principles.

Figure 10.4 shows the operation of barter in the Stone Age community. The family that wants to supply axes and receive bread will be willing to supply more axes the more bread it gets for each axe, so the supply curve for axes slopes up from left to right. The family that wants to obtain axes and to barter its surplus bread for them will demand more axes the fewer the loaves it has to pay for each axe, so the demand curve for axes slopes down from left to right. If, as in the diagram, the two curves intersect, it is possible to find an equilibrium price for axes in terms of bread – here 10 loaves, so at the equilibrium point 3 axes will be exchanged for 10 loaves each, 30 loaves in total. At any other price, one or both of the families will not be satisfied – for example, if the price of each axe was 5 loaves, only one axe would be supplied but 6 axes would be demanded, so there

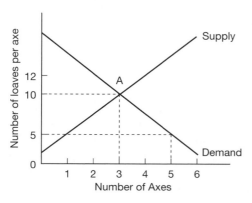

Figure 10.4 Supply and demand in the barter economy

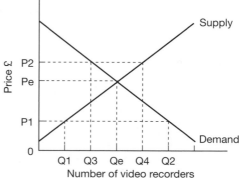

Figure 10.5 Supply and demand in a modern economy

would be an excess demand of 5 axes. Similarly, if the price were above equilibrium, for example at 12 loaves per axe, there would be an excess supply of axes. Only at the equilibrium price can the families strike a bargain by agreeing on the number of axes to be exchanged.

Figure 10.5 illustrates exactly the same principle for a modern economy – the price in the UK of video recorders. The equilibrium price is Pe and quantity Qe; at prices below equilibrium, such as P1, there will be excess demand (Q2–Q1) and at prices above equilibrium there will be excess supply (Q4–Q3).

International exchange markets

We glanced earlier at the complexities of conducting trade on a barter basis; in practice international trade usually entails financial transactions, rather than direct swaps of goods. The financial arrangements for international trade are one step more complicated than those for the purchase of goods and services in any one country. Consider, for example, a group of Tayside farmers selling raspberries. They will want payment in sterling. Households in Bordeaux buying the raspberries will want to pay in francs. So the farmers (or an agent acting for them) must convert the francs into sterling. Each time any item is sold from one country to another, if the two countries have different currencies, there is a foreign exchange transaction as well as the transaction of selling the good or service. If the foreign exchange rate is determined by the operation of market forces, the price of any currency in terms of any other depends on the interaction of supply and demand like any other price.

We can now look at the effect on the exchange rate between sterling and francs of the sale by our raspberry farmers to Bordeaux. The vertical axis in Figure 10.6(a) shows the price of francs in terms of sterling, and the horizontal axis the quantity of francs, with supply and demand intersecting at the exchange rate £0.1 (1 franc = £0.1 or 10p, 10 francs = £1). A rise in the exchange rate from, say, £0.1 to £0.2 represents an appreciation, or rise in the value, of the franc (1 franc = £0.2 or 20p, 5 francs = £1). The supply curve represents the transactions of people who currently want to sell francs and buy sterling – UK exporters to France, like the Tayside farmers. The more francs are worth, and therefore the less sterling is worth, the more attractive it is to convert francs into sterling now rather than wait, so the supply curve slopes up from left to right. It is, however, quite steep – most UK exporters will want to convert their francs into sterling more or less regardless of the exchange rate. The demand curve represents the transactions of people who currently want to sell sterling and buy francs – French exporters to the UK, like the Bordeaux wine makers (and slopes down steeply from left to right because if sterling is worth relatively few francs some of the people holding sterling are likely to postpone converting it into francs, in the hope of being able to do so at a more favourable rate later). Now, the raspberry farmers make their sale to France, and want to convert francs into sterling. Figure 10.6(b) illustrates the result. The raspberry farmers' sale of produce means an increase in the number of people supplying francs, so the supply curve shifts from S to S1. As a result, the price of francs falls, to, say, £0.09 (11 francs = £1) – the franc has depreciated (or fallen in value) against sterling because of the import to France of British goods. We can see the converse effect if France exports more to the UK, by looking at Figure 10.6(c), which illustrates what will happen if the Bordeaux wine merchants sell more wine to Tayside. They will have received payment in sterling, and wish to convert it to francs, so they represent an addition to the people who are supplying sterling and demanding francs, and so the demand curve shifts from D to D1, with the price of francs accordingly rising to, say, £0.11 (9 francs = £1), where the franc has appreciated against sterling.

In reality, because many exchange transactions are taking place in any one day, the value of transactions from francs into sterling is normally nearly equal

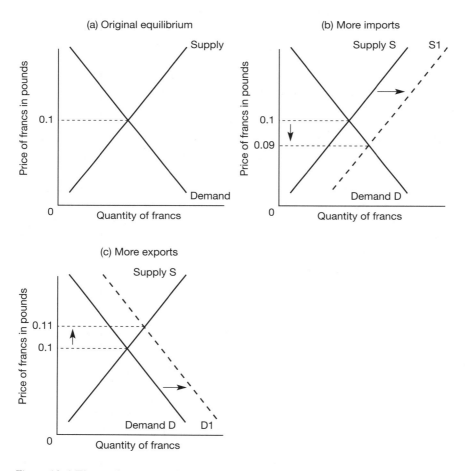

Figure 10.6 The exchange rate between francs and pounds (a) in equilibrium, (b) after an increase in imports to France, and (c) after an increase in exports from France

in any day to the value of transactions from sterling into francs. The difference between the two flows is what causes the exchange rate to change, and so normally there is very little movement from day to day in the exchange rate. Where dramatic changes do take place, as with the Russian ruble in August and September 1998, they are caused by speculative transactions which swamp the small changes resulting from trading flows. To understand speculation in currency markets, we have to consider what activities, other than trade, produce foreign exchange transactions.

Besides importing and exporting goods, firms and households can also import and export factor services. For example, Irishmen might work in Belgium on reconstruction of the EU Commission headquarters in Brussels. If they do, this is an export from Ireland to Belgium – instead of providing goods to Belgium, Ireland is providing labour. The Irishmen will be paid in Belgian francs, and will want to convert some of their wages to Irish punts, perhaps to send money home when they are working in Belgium and to take their savings home at the end of the contract. Imports and exports of labour are, however, small in volume in comparison with the international flow of financial capital. When a British company issues shares, some of the shares may well be bought by people in other countries – e.g. Spain. The initial transaction – the purchase of the share – is an 'export' from Britain to Spain, and money has to be converted from pesetas to sterling to pay for the share. When dividends are paid on the share, the flow is the other way (an 'export' from Spain to Britain because the dividend is payment for a factor service provided by Spanish finance) with sterling being converted to pesetas.

Some of the financial flows are very volatile, because they represent surplus cash which is being lent out for short periods (often a matter of days) to whoever gives the highest return. The return on money is the rate of interest, so if it wants to attract more of these volatile financial flows a country should offer a rate of interest a little higher than that prevailing elsewhere. However, this may not be enough, because with international currency lending there is also the question of what is happening to the exchange rate.

Suppose a Spanish household has some spare cash. Suppose the best interest rate available to it in Spain is 10 per cent per annum and that it therefore decides to lend it to the British government for a year by buying some savings certificates, which offer interest of 15 per cent per annum – for each £100 the household lends, it will get £115 in a year's time. Provided the rate of exchange between the peseta and sterling is constant, the family will obtain a return of 15 per cent in terms of pesetas. If, however, the exchange rate alters, it will do better or worse than this. Suppose that when it made the loan £100 = 20,000 pta. If, when the loan matures, sterling has depreciated against the peseta, so that £100 = 15,000 pta, the £115 will give the family only 17,250 pta, a loss of 14 per cent on the investment. If, however, sterling has appreciated against the peseta, to, say, £100 = 25,000 pta, the £115 gives the family 28,750 pta, a return of 44 per cent.

To simplify the arithmetic of the illustration, we have assumed 25 per cent appreciation or devaluation, which is a quite high figure even for a year, but it is not unrealistic for currency movements to swamp interest differentials. To see why, we must remember that the really volatile financial flows are lent for periods of days, not years, so the interest they expect to attract is normally measured in fractions of a per cent, and can easily be outweighed by quite small exchange rate changes. That is why in currency crises, when a country is trying to stave off a devaluation, it is not uncommon for interest to have to be offered for one-day loans at 100 per cent or more, because 100 per cent per annum is under a third of a per cent per day, not much return if the currency is expected to depreciate tomorrow.

Exchange markets exist, then, to facilitate trade both of products and of factors. Because of the extra risks (of unfavourable exchange rate movements) implied by foreign trade, various arrangements have been developed to insure traders against the risk. If the raspberry farmers are worried that, by the time they are paid, the pound will have appreciated against the French franc (so that the French francs they expect to be paid will give them less sterling than they expected to receive), they can obtain protection against that risk by operating in a futures market, today buying sterling for francs which they promise to deliver in, say, three months' time. Then, when the farmers are paid in francs for the raspberries, they use the francs to pay for the sterling they have agreed to buy. Thus the farmers know now how much sterling they will get for the francs they have not yet received, whatever the exchange rate becomes. The farmers have, of course, to pay for avoiding the risk of devaluation, because the extra transaction will involve extra brokerage fees and the future price they are quoted may not be attractive, but if the currencies are volatile the protection may be thought to be worth the payment.

Futures markets were thus created to facilitate trade, but once they exist their nature changes, with agents buying and selling foreign currency as a commodity in its own right and not because of trade flows. Such agents are speculators, who make their living by anticipating movements of the exchange rate. If, for example, a speculator thinks that sterling will depreciate against the franc, he or she will buy francs for sterling now and then sell the francs for what he or she expects will be more sterling in the future. Thanks to the existence of futures markets, the speculator does not have to pay for the francs now, and so can operate in terms of a set of contracts to buy and sell large amounts of currency which he or she does not in fact have, because all that will have to be paid for is any net loss on the contracts. Speculators can have a powerfully destabilising effect in the short run on currency markets whenever they share opinions which therefore become self-fulfilling. Suppose most speculators expect sterling to depreciate against the franc. They therefore sell sterling and buy francs. As they do this, the price of sterling in terms of francs falls – i.e. the 'market sentiment' has produced exactly the outcome the speculators expected. Such speculative activities have, as we shall see, been important in the recent history of monetary union in Europe. However, market sentiment is unlikely to hold strongly to some opinion without some definite underlying basis for it in the economic or political realities, so most of the time speculation simply hastens the inevitable.

Volatility in exchange markets is not welcome to those who are trying to trade products or factor services, because of the uncertainty it causes for them. Nor is it welcome to governments, who are sensitive both about the country's trade and about its international capital markets, and who also attach prestige to the strength of the currency. For these reasons, it is not uncommon for countries to intervene in the operation of currency markets. This intervention can take many forms. It can consist simply of *ad hoc* action in particular circumstances to nudge the exchange rate in the desired direction (operated usually by the government or the central bank using foreign exchange reserves to buy the country's own currency to push the exchange rate up). It can, as we shall see later in this chapter, involve bilateral or multilateral international agreement to fix exchange rates at some particular level and to use appropriate instruments to ensure that the level does not change. It can be the outright prevention of any official free market in a currency, by the use of various exchange controls such as preventing citizens and visitors from taking more than a minimal amount of currency out of the country and by conducting foreign trade in barter terms. Until the end of the 1980s nearly all the internal trade, and a high proportion of the external trade, of the former Soviet bloc was based on swapping commodities because the USSR ruble, Polish zloty, etc., were either not convertible at all to other currencies or were convertible only at official rates that bore very little relation to reality.

Inconvertibility of currency leads to all the complications of barter trade. If currency is convertible, but only at rates which do not reflect market forces, there is the potential problem of excess supply or excess demand which we discussed earlier in this chapter. For currencies, as well as for goods, unofficial or black markets may emerge as a result. For example, in the latter days of the USSR, when a policy of exchange control was still being operated, there were wide divergences between official, tourist and unofficial market exchange rates (on 31 December 1990, officially 0.55 rubles exchanged for one US$, the tourist rate of exchange was 5.1 rubles for one US$, and on the unofficial markets around 20 rubles exchanged for one US$).

Forms of trading groupings

In Chapter 11 we shall examine some of the circumstances in which countries might seek to prevent trade occurring between each other, by erecting various barriers to trade. The theme for the rest of this chapter, however, is the forms of closer partnership which countries might wish to consider, assuming that trading relationships are successful.

We can regard the possible forms of trading groupings as lying along a spectrum. From the loosest to the tightest relationship we meet: free trade areas, customs unions, common markets, monetary unions, and economic unions. Although the boundaries between the different types are sometimes somewhat unclear in practice (and also in popular discussion), they can be distinguished sharply in principle. In a free trade area, member countries abandon barriers to trade between each other. A customs union is a free trade area with common external barriers. A common market is a customs union with freedom of movement for factors of production. A monetary union is a common market with what is *de facto* a common currency. An economic union is a rather more nebulous concept, but is probably a monetary union with common fiscal and other macroeconomic policy. The further countries proceed along the spectrum, the more they are ceding, to whatever organisation controls the grouping, powers which in principle are part of their national sovereignty. Whether in practice they would otherwise have really been free to exercise those powers is, however, another matter.

In entering into any of these arrangements, countries agree to act in some spirit of commonality of interest which must have political as well as economic content. It is difficult, for example, to imagine the members of a free trade area seriously trying to restrict the sale of arms to each other. Unless the arrangement is a free trade area, the commonality also applies to attitudes to non-members. This can give problems for new members of a customs union, who have a set of pre-existing special arrangements which are inconsistent with those of the union. Such difficulties were, for example, evident for France, the UK and, to a lesser extent, Italy and the Netherlands, for all of whom membership of the European Economic Community (EEC) cut across previous trading relationships with countries formerly in their empires. We shall consider these issues in the next chapter.

Europe contains an interesting range of trading groupings. The Nordic Council, founded in 1952, contains some element of cooperation on economic matters between its members (Denmark, with the Faroes and Greenland, Finland, with the Åland Islands, Iceland, Norway and Sweden) but on a fairly *ad hoc* basis. A similar function has been performed since 1947 for all the European countries together with Canada and the USA, by the Economic Commission for Europe. By contrast, the European Free Trade Association (EFTA) performs for manufactures and some agricultural products exactly the functions its title implies. It was established in 1960, to some extent deliberately as a counterweight to the EEC. Many of its members have joined the EU, the remaining members are in the process of being considered for membership of the EU, and EFTA and the EU have agreed to form an European Economic Area (EEA) as an interim measure. The CMEA, which embraced the USSR and the other communist countries of eastern and central Europe (except Albania and Yugoslavia) together with Mongolia, Cuba and Vietnam, functioned to some extent as a customs union and to some extent (reflecting Soviet dominance) as a kind of economic union. In the CMEA as economic union, planning aimed at enabling each member to enjoy economic growth by specialising in the products in which, relative to the other members of CMEA but not necessarily in world terms, it had most advantage. Now that the CMEA has been dismantled, this has left some of its former members specialised in products in which, in world terms, they are not efficient. The EU is a common market, in the process of incomplete conversion into a monetary union and with ambitions to become an economic union. Unified Germany is a very interesting case of a full economic and monetary union created almost literally overnight from very limited prior cooperation.

The contrast between the EU on the one hand and CMEA and EFTA on the other is striking. The economic difficulties of the planned economies and the disintegration of the USSR, which we discussed in Chapter 9, perhaps sufficiently explain the collapse of CMEA. Why, however, is EFTA in the process of being absorbed by the EU? This seems particularly puzzling in the light of the travails of the EU over monetary union. The answer must lie in the extent to which the EU dominates European trade.

As the exporters of non-member countries become more and more reliant on EU markets, membership of the EU becomes more and more attractive to them. If their countries were in the EU, they would be free from any barriers the EU applies to imports from their country; they would enjoy the benefits, if any, that EU industrial or agricultural policy confers on their competitors in member countries, and, if their country joins EMU, they would not have to worry about exchange rate movements on trade with other EMU members because there would be none. The disadvantages to them of EU membership might be higher barriers to trade in some of their traditional markets (but as they trade more with the EU the traditional markets are becoming less important to them); any problems they might experience from the changes in their country's macroeconomic policy required by membership of the monetary union, and any further costs in net contributions to the EU budget.

Monetary unions

A monetary union need not imply that its member countries have a single currency, but if there are different currencies the exchange rates between them must be fixed. This can be achieved only if monetary policies are harmonised, so that the different countries follow agreed plans about the rate of expansion of their money supply, and operate and maintain agreed interest rate differentials. The history of the EC's Exchange Rate Mechanism (ERM) in late 1992 and early 1993 gives ample illustration of the difficulties that occur if these conditions are not met. One of these was that the exchange rates were not quite fixed. Each currency could move up and down within a prescribed range (usually 2.25 per cent) against the ecu (a weighted average of all EU member currencies). The fact that movement was permitted at all enabled the market to read signals into the extent to which currencies persisted at the top or bottom of the permitted range, because if there is a big underlying problem it may be predictable what the monetary authorities will do. Speculators might continue to push the currency to the limit until either they see the action they expect or they are forced to make losses by powerful countervailing action by the monetary authorities.

For example, in early September 1992, when sterling was in the ERM, it was at the bottom of the range for some time partly because of market belief that the UK economy was weak, and partly because UK interest rates were low relative to those in Germany. Germany had a stronger currency, with no danger of devaluation, but high interest rates because of its domestic macroeconomic situation arising from German unification. In the UK interest rates had been cut, for macroeconomic reasons, to try to stimulate economic growth. Market sentiment was that sterling was overvalued, and so speculators sold it. By the rules of the ERM, when sterling reached the critical level, the governments of the UK and the other member countries had to act. They tried to support sterling by buying it in exchange for other currencies, but the reserves available were small relative to the strength of speculative selling. The UK government raised interest rates in one day from 10 to 12 and then to 15 per cent, to try to strengthen sterling by encouraging financial inflows. But by then it was too late for the move to be credible to the markets, and later that day ('Black Monday') sterling had to be devalued (in fact by leaving the ERM rather than changing its parity within it). Depreciation of the French franc in 1992 was, however, averted because in that case the monetary authorities' support for the currency was stronger than speculators' determination to sell it, but when the French franc came under renewed pressure in August 1993 the only economically and politically possible solution was a radical review of the ERM, widening the bands of permissible movement of currencies to +/– 15 per cent – bands so broad as to be almost useless in achieving the exchange rate stability which was the whole objective of the ERM. A successful monetary union requires a degree of policy harmonisation which was evidently lacking overall in the ERM in its successive crises in 1992 and 1993.

Even when countries are not in a monetary union they may wish to behave as if they were, to try to maintain stability of the exchange rate to help their exporters. This is much more difficult than if they are in a union, because, as we have just seen, monetary unions include provisions whereby all the members act together to maintain the fixed exchange rates, by concerted action in the foreign exchange markets using their pooled reserves. Thus whilst non-members trading with a monetary union frequently find that it is in their best interests for their exchange rate to 'shadow' that of the union, they have to bear the burden of administering this on their own and thus at greater cost than if they were members. So full membership might in fact actually give more, not less, scope for independence of macroeconomic policy.

The last form of economic grouping we shall consider is the most complete of all – full monetary and economic union, of which the most dramatic recent European example is Germany. Because East Germany was much the smaller party in the union, the effects there were greater than in West Germany, but even in what used to be West Germany unemployment has risen at least partly as a consequence of the economic dislocation caused by the unification. The German case illustrates well the problems of monetary and economic unions, and is worth detailed consideration. (What follows is a summary account; for more detail the reader is referred to H. Giersch, K. Paque and H. Schmieding (1992) *The Fading Miracle: Four Decades of the Market Economy in Germany*, Cambridge University Press and to G. and H. Sinn (1992) *Jumpstart*, MIT Press.)

One of the first questions which arise when countries decide to enter a monetary union is the exchange rate at which they are going to merge their money supplies. In the case of German monetary union on 1 July 1990, political considerations led to a decision to use what, by all economic criteria, was at best a compromise rate. Considering exchange rates in terms of what currencies can buy, in principle exchange rates in the long term should reflect what is known as purchasing power parity – a representative collection on goods is identified, and the exchange rates should be such that the amount of one currency needed to buy it is equal to the amount of the other currency needed to buy it. Various German economic institutes tried in early 1990 to estimate what purchasing power parity would imply, and concluded that a rate of about 1 East German Mark (M) to 1 West German Mark (DM) was about right. This assumed existing relative prices for different goods, but taking likely price changes induced by reunification into account led to much the same answer. Another way of looking at it, however, was to consider supply considerations, by comparing the productivity of factors of production in export industries in the two Germanies, and to set a rate at which East German exporters could compete with those in West Germany. On this basis, the right rate was about 4.4 M to 1 DM. More generally, factor productivity was thought at the time to suggest a rate of about 2 M = 1 DM. To add to the confusion, whilst the (pegged) official exchange rate was 1 M = 1 DM, the unofficial market rate in early 1990 was between 7 and 11 M = 1 DM (the unofficial market was, of course, heavily influenced by political uncertainties, and a rather more normal value might have been about 6 M = 1 DM).

The choice confronting the two German governments was, then, whether to try to protect East German exporters (by going for a rate of 4 or 5 M = 1 DM), to protect East German production generally (by a rate of about 2 M = 1 DM) or to protect the savings of East German consumers (by a rate of about 1 M = 1 DM). In fact they opted for a rate between these solutions. For current transactions (prices, wages etc.) the conversion rate used was 1 M = 1 DM. Most financial assets and liabilities were converted at the rate 2 M = 1 DM, but up to a certain limit household savings by East German families were converted at 1 M = 1 DM. The overall average for all financial assets and liabilities was 1.8 M = 1 DM.

As perhaps should have been expected, the compromise created difficulties for producers and both gains and losses for consumers in the former East Germany. The problems for producers are predictable from our earlier analysis – industrial production in the former East Germany fell in the last six months of 1990 by about 50 per cent. Part of this fall was presumably due to the switch from a planned to a market economy and the consequent drastic changes in relative prices; a reasonable estimate based on the experience of other countries such as Poland is that these effects account for about half the fall in industrial output. The rest of the fall is attributable to two factors. One is East German loss of trade with its former CMEA partners (on which it relied for 65 per cent of its foreign trade) because of their economic difficulties. The other is the combination of initial overvaluation of East German production due to the failure of the exchange rate to reflect productivity, with rapid rises in the costs of producers in former East Germany due to wage inflation.

In deciding the rate to use for converting East German Marks into DM for general current payments purposes such as calculating prices and wages, the two German governments tried to balance issues of labour productivity against the need to make sure that wages in the East were high enough to prevent any further outflow of labour from the East into West Germany. Wages were initially converted at 1 M = 1 DM, which, since East German money wages were about a third of the West German levels would have been consistent with East German labour productivity being a third of that of West Germany. What determines wage inflation, however, is not so much the initial figure but the expectations of both workers and employers. The two German governments had promised to reduce the gap in living standards between West and East Germany, so it was reasonable for the workers and employers in the former East Germany to expect subsidies from the new German government (i.e. from West German taxpayers) to cover the period until their capital equipment and their labour training levels were brought up to previous West German levels. When these subsidies were not forthcoming on the scale expected, labour unrest resulted. Money wages in East Germany (as measured in DM) rose by about a third in 1990.

The consequence of the rise in East German wages, however, was that the existing capital equipment became uneconomic very quickly (because using obsolescent equipment causes labour productivity to be low, and unless wages are correspondingly low, producers cannot cover their costs). Thus capital equipment required immediate replacement across nearly all of the former East German economy. The impossibility of achieving this meant that the former East Germany simply could not make its output competitive, even with generous subsidies. The fall in total East German output in 1990 was about 30 per cent (less severe than the decline in industrial production because of transfers from the West) and before long employment fell by a comparable amount. Unemployment, obviously, is a blow to consumers – if members of the household lose their jobs, household income falls. Those in work, however, benefited from the wage rises. Average income rose by some 5 per cent in 1990. Living standards also improved because west European and especially West German goods were much more readily available and could be substituted for inferior East German or Soviet bloc products – e.g. people bought second-hand Volkswagen cars instead of new Trabants. But the real income of many households fell because of the loss of free or heavily subsidised services, especially assistance for newly-wed couples to set up house and for families with young children to use crèches and kindergartens.

The other major impact on East German households was on their wealth. In terms of purchasing power parity, the average rate of 1.8 M = 1 DM reduced the wealth of East German households by about a third (the effect varied from family to family, with the wealthier families losing more). The effects of this wealth loss are more widespread than might at first sight be expected, because in East Germany, as in the other planned economies, the economic strains of the late 1980s had led people to accumulate savings. There had been shortages of goods to buy and, in a controlled economy, they could not spend their savings to buy other financial assets (like company shares) or real assets (such as houses). After unification, they wished to convert some of their savings from money into assets such as shares. In the process, they pushed up the prices of the shares, thereby losing a bit more of the real value of their wealth. The economic and monetary unification of Germany therefore in two ways reduced household wealth in East Germany and thereby the willingness of East German households to buy goods and services. The effect of all these considerations is that the experience of East German households was very diverse, some clearly gaining and others losing from the monetary union.

German economic and monetary union is obviously a very special case, because of its abruptness and because it combined a planned and a market economy. Some of the lessons apply, however, to any monetary union, such as the conversion of the EC/EU into a full monetary union. In particular, the choice of the exchange rates at which to fix conversions in the monetary union is important. The obvious technique seems to be to try a gradual reduction of the volatility of rates over time, to head towards stability at some exchange rate sanctioned by the market. This was the method adopted by the EU in its progress towards full EMU, but, as we have seen, gradualist approaches do not always work, and in the case of the ERM failed spectacularly in late 1992. Nevertheless, the insistence by the Treaty of Maastricht on the importance of convergence of key macroeconomic variables as a precondition of monetary union was wise, because the absence of such convergence between the two Germanies has led to acute problems for East German producers.

The Maastricht convergence criteria were carefully chosen to test how far potential EMU members have converged in economic policy and performance, and thus how far a common monetary policy is viable for them. A common monetary policy implies commonality in interest rates and fixed exchange rates, so two of the five criteria assess the extent of practical convergence in these measures. A common monetary policy can work, however, only if the participants broadly agree on how to react to internal pressures – for example, the aspirations of their trade unions for increased real pay levels, and of their citizens for more jobs and for improved public services – and to external shocks, such as the abrupt downturn in many formerly rapidly growing Asian economies. From the perspective of monetary policy, good measures of the extent of such agreement are the inflation rate and the size of public sector borrowing and total national debt, the remaining three criteria. Economies running with similar inflation rates and with similar amounts of public sector borrowing and debt are likely to have similar responses to pressure to risk more inflation by expanding the economy or to pressure to let the public sector grow at the expense of the private sector. The Maastricht Treaty insisted, in specifying the convergence criteria for EMU membership, not just on similarity but on convergence to the performance of the economies with the lowest inflation and on adherence to tight public sector borrowing targets. This reflected the monetary orthodoxy of the 1990s, and also the extent to which the other EC members sought to make their economies more like West

Germany's, because in practice West Germany, with low inflation and relatively fast growth, had dominated the EC in the 1970s and 1980s.

The Maastricht criteria are appropriate for monetary union. They are not – and do not profess to be – all that is needed for full economic union. Even if their governments were in complete agreement on matters such as the relative importance of inflation and unemployment, different countries do tend to react to common external shocks in a different way because they affect their economies differently – for example, an abrupt change in the world price of petroleum and derivatives would affect the UK, the Netherlands and Norway (as oil- and gas-producing countries) in a way different from its impact on Spain, Portugal and Italy. If all six of these countries were EMU members, they could not use exchange rate or interest rate changes to cushion the shock. So such an external shock would almost certainly have a greater effect on output and employment in their economies than if they were not in EMU. The provisions in the Treaty of Amsterdam for harmonisation of employment and labour market policies are partly a reaction to international pressures – to be discussed in the next chapter – but also part of what is needed as background for full economic union. Economic union cannot make economic volatility go away, and a careful set of policies, including appropriate transitional assistance through regional policy, is needed to ensure that harmonisation elsewhere does not produce unbearably severe pressures in the face of unexpected shocks.

Let us return, then, to the question of why countries might want to join monetary or economic unions rather than stopping at some earlier stage in the process of economic integration. The answer lies in the extent to which a successful economic integration leads to a desire for closer and closer links. If the countries of the EU become increasingly interdependent in trade, it is more and more in the interests of their producers and consumers to cut out avoidable costs in transactions between member countries. This means first dismantling the internal barriers to trade – completed, for the EU, by the Single European Act. Once this has been done, exchange costs are the obvious next barrier to remove, together with impediments such as different systems of taxing goods and different tax rates on goods – hence the centrality of these matters in the Treaty of Maastricht. Governments may worry about the loss of sovereignty over economic matters, but they are in practice gradually ceding genuine sovereignty to the EU by the extent to which achieving exchange rate stability requires them to make their monetary and fiscal policy coherent with those of their EU partners (or, more strictly, those of the strongest currency countries in the EU, like Germany). If a customs union is working well, it takes major national political events, like the need to ratify the Treaty of Maastricht, or major externally induced difficulties, like the partial collapse of the ERM in late 1992, to occasion serious questioning of this gradual apparent inevitability of monetary union.

There is, however, an obvious tension between the desire to deepen the links between existing EU members, by proceeding to monetary and economic union, and the desire to broaden the EU by bringing in more countries. The applications by some of the former CMEA countries to join the EU raise the

Table 10.1 Performance in relation to convergence of EU member states – late 1990s

	Inflation		Government budgetary position						Exchange rates		Long-term interest rates (4)
	HICP (1)	Existence of an excessive deficit (2)	Deficit (% of GDP) (3)	Debt (% of GDP)		Change from previous year			ERM participation		
	January 1998		1997	1997		1997	1996	1995	March 1998		January 1998
Reference value	2.7 (5)		3	60							7.8 (6)
Belgium	1.4	yes (7)	2.1	122.2		−4.7	−4.3	−2.2	yes		5.7
Denmark	1.9	no	−0.7	65.1		−5.5	−2.7	−4.9	yes		6.2
Germany	1.4	yes (7)	2.7	61.3		0.8	2.4	7.8	yes		5.6
Greece	5.2	yes	4.0	108.7		−2.9	1.5	0.7	yes (8)		9.8 (9)
Spain	1.8	yes (7)	2.6	68.8		−1.3	4.6	2.9	yes		6.3
France	1.2	yes (7)	3.0	58.0		2.4	2.9	4.2	yes		5.5
Ireland	1.2	no	−0.9	66.3		−6.4	−9.6	−6.8	yes		6.2
Italy	1.8	yes (7)	2.7	121.6		−2.4	−0.2	−0.7	yes (10)		6.7
Luxembourg	1.4	no	−1.7	6.7		0.1	0.7	0.2	yes		5.6
Netherlands	1.8	no	1.4	72.1		−5.0	−1.9	1.2	yes		5.5
Austria	1.1	yes (7)	2.5	66.1		−3.4	0.3	3.8	yes		5.6
Portugal	1.8	yes (7)	2.5	62.0		−3.0	−0.9	2.1	yes		6.2
Finland	1.3	no	0.9	55.8		−1.8	−0.4	−1.5	yes (11)		5.9
Sweden	1.9	yes (7)	0.8	76.6		−0.1	−0.9	−1.4	no		6.5
UK	1.8	yes (7)	1.9	53.4		−1.3	0.8	3.5	no		7.0
EU	**1.6**		**2.4**	**72.1**		**−0.9**	**2.0**	**3.0**			**6.1**

(1) Percentage change in arithmetic average of the latest 12 monthly harmonised indices of consumer prices (HICPs) relative to the arithmetic average of the 12 HICPs of the previous period.

(2) Council decisions of 26 September 1994, 10 July 1995, 27 June 1996 and 30 June 1997.

(3) A negative sign for the government deficit indicates a surplus.

(4) Average maturity 10 years; average of the last 12 months.

(5) Definition adopted in this report: simple arithmetic average of the inflation rates of the three best-performing member states in terms of price stability plus 1.5 percentage points.

(6) Definition adopted in this report: simple arithmetic average of the 12-month average of interest rates of the three best-performing member states in terms of price stability plus 2 percentage points.

(7) Commission is recommending abrogation.

(8) Since March 1998.

(9) Average of available data during the past 12 months.

(10) Since November 1996.

(11) Since October 1996.

Source: European Commission Report 'Euro 1999', 25 March 1998. Reproduced by permission of the Publishers, The Office for Official Publications of the European Community.

same kind of issues as those confronted by the two Germanies in seeking unification – what is the best way quickly to assimilate a new member country whose economy is in many ways very backward in comparison with those of existing members? Now that it is clear that not all the existing EU members will join the first round of EMU, either because they are not sure whether EMU is good for their own economies or because they cannot meet the convergence criteria, we are going to witness some manifestations of a multi-speed Europe.

11 Europe in the global economy

The global economy

As we enter the millennium, it is increasingly obvious that to understand the major forces influencing the economies of the individual European countries, and even the economy of a major block like the EU, we must look at the global context. The objective of this chapter is to see how influences outside Europe have shaped the operation of European economies in the 1990s.

A hundred years ago, the question of a global context to economic performance barely arose, other than in the relationship of imperial powers to the dominions over which they had control. World trading relationships were dominated by trade in goods rather than services. Transport costs were a significant proportion of the costs of producing goods and delivering them to their purchaser, and the time taken to ship goods from Australasia or the American or Asian continents to Europe was an important constraint on trade. The economies of scale from increased volumes of international trade and the development of commercial aircraft and, more recently, electronic communications have transformed the global economy, as has the increasing importance of trade in services and in intellectual property. To take a very small example of globalisation which would have been inconceivable even twenty years ago, the first edition of this book was written and edited in Scotland, sent on floppy discs to our publisher in England, who in turn sent the text to its subsidiary company in Singapore where the book was typeset and printed and shipped to the UK for distribution by the publisher. All this was made possible not just by new technology but also by the growth of transnational corporations (TNCs) and by the changing patterns of world production (see Chapter 2).

Our publisher is far from unique in running a worldwide operation, with production and distribution capacity in many countries of the world. The big TNCs are major players in the economic scene – the biggest of them, like some of the oil giants, have an annual turnover greater than the annual output of many countries, and thus can have a huge impact on the economies of the countries in which they establish production. Governments thus usually welcome the decisions of TNCs to set up new plants in their countries, because foreign direct investment can be a source of badly needed jobs, often in industries whose technology is in advance of that in the firms already operating in the country. The TNCs themselves usually locate new production on the basis of hard-headed calculation of costs in one location compared with another; any tax breaks offered by the potential host country are important, but for industries not dependent on some primary resource the major economic consideration is the quantity, quality and cost of labour available in the host country. The TNC may also be concerned with political risks such as civil unrest which might damage its property or the risk of its nationalisation by the state, so that TNCs favour stable political regimes.

Until the late 1990s the Pacific Rim countries, such as Singapore, were highly favoured by TNCs as locations for inward investment, and thus achieved startlingly rapid economic growth. Western European labour costs by contrast were regarded by many TNCs as too high, and the political stability of eastern Europe was regarded as doubtful both before and in the aftermath of the collapse of communism. In the newly emerging Pacific Rim countries, wages were low and the additional costs of employing labour (such as social security contributions by employers) very low by western European standards, expansion and contraction of the workforce to meet variations in demand was easy and (by west European and US standards) cheap, and the quality of labour was highly satisfactory for the kind of assembly work most TNCs wanted. Which east Asian country was the most favoured location changed from time to time; extensive foreign direct investment in Taiwan, for example, pushed wages up there to such an extent that other Pacific Rim countries became more attractive to the multinationals.

It is easy to overdraw the picture of Pacific Rim expansion at the expense of Europe. Some of the TNCs locating production outside Europe were themselves European companies, whose success fed back to their European shareholders. Foreign direct investment into western Europe, by US and even by Japanese and other Asian companies, continued. We will explore one important reason for this later in the chapter. In general, however, in the early and mid-1990s the prognosis for the long-term health of manufacturing in western Europe seemed poor. By 1997 many were concerned that EU labour was becoming uncompetitive with that in the rest of the world, including the USA, and the Treaty of Amsterdam sought to reduce the rigidity of EU labour markets and to improve the quality of labour by better education and training.

In the late 1990s these perspectives have changed a little since the Pacific Rim economies have experienced recession, partly because of a sustained downturn in Japan, one of their major markets, partly because, like that of Japan, their financial systems became overextended, and partly because of political and environmental problems. But the fundamental problems of the European economies have not changed. Can western European labour markets compete with those in other countries such as the USA? How can the weaker eastern European economies find a new role after the collapse of communism? What, if anything, can the EU do to help its present and future members? Let us look first at one possible solution – protection.

Free trade and restrictions on trade

The advantages of specialisation, as we have seen, are considerable, but cannot be realised unless trade occurs. There is thus a strong case for permitting trade to take place without hindrance. Yet the history of any European country gives numerous examples of devices adopted to prevent free trade. To understand why, we must consider why countries can perceive trade as threatening to their national interest.

There are three main kinds of reason for a state to intervene in trade flows: strategic and social, industrial, and macroeconomic. Certain materials or ideas may be regarded as either important to national defence (as in the embargoes during the Cold War on the export from western Europe to the USSR of products incorporating advanced computer technology) or socially undesirable (such as restraints on the import of pornographic films), and for such strategic or social reasons trade in them may be restricted. Countries may also seek to protect their home producers in important industries from competition as part of their industrial policy, e.g. from 'dumping', where surplus stocks of a product are sold abroad at less than the cost of production. Or an infant industry not yet sufficiently developed to achieve the economies of scale which would enable it to compete may be protected in its home market for the sake of future industrial development. But in modern Europe most of the restraints on trade have been for reasons of macroeconomic policy. There are two different ways in which a country's trading balance affects its macroeconomic position.

The more direct impact is the immediate effect on total output. When a country exports goods and services (including factor services), the total demand for its products is greater than that represented by the home market, so exports cause the country's output to rise. Conversely, when households or firms buy imported goods and services, not only is there no stimulus to the country's output but some of the country's demand for goods and services has leaked abroad, so its output is less than if the imports had not occurred. Therefore, the difference between the total of exports and the total of imports (the balance of payments if we include service flows) is one of the determinants of total output in the country. If the balance of payments is in surplus, exports are greater than imports, and output is boosted. If the balance of payments is in deficit, the country is losing more sales to other countries than it is gaining in export orders, and so output is reduced. So if a government wishes to boost output, perhaps because the economy is in recession, one attractive route is to reduce imports and try to stimulate exports. The more roundabout influence of trading on the macroeconomic position is from the exchange rate. As we have seen in Chapter 10 the balance of payments affects the exchange rate, causing the rate to depreciate if imports are greater than exports (balance of payments deficit) and to appreciate if there is a balance of payments surplus. Exchange rate movements help to solve the original problem. (Depreciation, for example, makes exports more competitive and imports dearer, and so helps to reduce the original balance of payments deficit.) Exchange rate fluctuations do, however, bring with them their own macroeconomic problems because the volatility of international financial flows tends to magnify their effects. Hence governments have an added reason to try to reduce any imbalance, either way, between imports and exports.

Practical action in restraint of trade can take many forms. It can be an outright ban on the export or import of certain goods or services, administered through the legal system. There are, for example, legal penalties imposed on people found guilty of importing certain addictive drugs to the UK, and UK firms violating trade embargoes to Iraq or to Serbia have been liable to prosecution. Alternatively, bureaucratic devices can reduce trade to a trickle even without any legal restrictions – as when France decided to try to curb the import of Japanese video recorders (to protect its own infant industry) by processing the documentation and inspection of all such imports through a small customs post in Poitiers. Producers who feel threatened by imports may also take the law into their own hands and physically prevent imports – for example, both British and French fishermen have blockaded fishing ports, and farmers in various parts of the EU have destroyed imported food. The more common forms of restraint on trade are, however, operated through governments and are 'voluntary' agreements, quotas, tariffs and non-tariff barriers.

'Voluntary' export restraint agreements are bilateral arrangements between exporting and importing countries. Recently there have been such agreements between Japan or South Korea, as exporter, and the USA or European countries as importer – for instance, agreements that the number of Japanese cars imported in any year to a particular country shall not exceed some prescribed level. There are major problems in agreeing and unambiguously defining such arrangements. For example, when Japanese cars are manufactured in Britain does France regard these as British or Japanese? In fact, by EU law they must be regarded as British – with interesting consequences, as we shall see. Quotas identify a maximum number of items of any particular product that may be imported to a certain country in a particular year, but they apply on the same basis to all potential exporting countries. Tariffs are special taxes levied on imports. Their main intended effect is to make imports more expensive and hence to make home-produced goods relatively cheaper in the domestic market. Moreover, they increase the government's tax revenue, which lends them added political attractiveness. The so-called 'non-tariff barriers to trade' are much more subtle, and take the form of requirements imposed at least apparently for reasons quite different from trade protection – e.g. the 1992 German requirements that all packaging must be recyclable – but which discriminate in favour of home producers because of the extra expense to exporting countries of meeting these standards. The demolition of many non-tariff barriers within the EU was one main object of the Single European Act.

Thus there are in principle many measures countries can take to protect their home markets from foreign competition, but in practice their freedom of manoeuvre is fairly limited. In the short term the most powerful limitation is usually the fear of retaliation. If a country feels it is being treated unfairly in one of its export markets it may itself threaten to discriminate against what it regards as the offending country – for example in 1992 the USA announced it would impose tariffs on EC agricultural exports such as French wine in retaliation against what it regarded as unfair levels of subsidy to farmers in the EC. Spirals of such retaliations are called 'trade wars', the eventual outcome of which could be to reduce each country back to its own production possibilities and make points like A in Figure 10.1 (p. 222) unattainable.

Recognising the advantages of free trade, countries have agreed in several arrangements mutually to reduce barriers to trade, thus voluntarily foregoing the power to restrain trade flows. The most wide-ranging of these international compacts is the World Trade Organisation (WTO). The WTO has subsumed the General Agreement on Tariffs and Trade (GATT) which, since 1947, has bound its signatories not to increase existing barriers to trade and periodically to negotiate agreement to reduction of barriers. In addition to this process, the WTO also involves agreements to reduce barriers to trade in services and in intellectual property. The WTO exists to prevent spirals of retaliatory trade barriers of the sort which added to the severity of worldwide economic depression in the 1930s. Trade barrier reductions under WTO take place after complex and protracted discussions generally known as 'rounds' and named after the initiator or the place in which discussion started. The most recent major negotiations, the 'Uruguay round', started in 1986 and took a decade to complete; they were particularly difficult because they tried to address problems of agricultural subsidies and involved head-on clashes between the USA and the EC/EU, both of which subsidise farmers but in a different way. Because agriculture is an interesting case, we shall devote the next section of this chapter to an in-depth examination of the issues.

The main theme of Chapter 10 was an examination of trading groupings from the point of view of their members. One of the major aims of the WTO is to ensure some equity of treatment of non-members (and ultimately to bring about the demolition of all barriers to trade from non-members). Membership of the EU and its predecessor organisations cut across pre-existing special trading relationships, especially those of France and the UK with countries in their former empires, and, whilst these organisations achieved reductions in and eventually the abolition of barriers to trade between EU countries, they also led to the erection of new or higher barriers to trade between non-members and EU countries. The EU has tried to counter this and to preserve special relationships with some of the less developed former colonies by the Lomé Conventions, but with limited results.

It is possible in principle to analyse any special trading grouping by examining whether it is trade-creating – i.e. stimulates imports from cheaper sources than those used previously – or trade-diverting – i.e. switches imports to higher-cost sources than previously. Consider for example the effect on the UK of its membership of the EU. One effect was trade diversion in butter as the UK erected barriers to imports from New Zealand and lowered those to imports from the Netherlands, since New Zealand was a lower-cost butter producer than the Netherlands. Thus in the short term UK membership of the EU damaged third party interests and was in this case economically inefficient. But the much more important question in the long run is the effects of growth rates; if, for example, UK membership of the EU increases the UK growth rate, then the New Zealand economy may benefit by being able to sell more apples to the UK than would otherwise have been the case.

In such respects trading groups are in principle second best to free trade and distort trading patterns to the ultimate disadvantage of some producers and most consumers. In particular, they systematically disadvantage producers in low-cost non-member countries. However, to assess their effects in reality, we have to compare their outcome not with a hypothetical free trade position but with what is likely otherwise to have occurred – for example, the actual position from which their members started. Any conclusions from such studies must be tentative; as Balassa remarked in 1975,

> there exists no wholly satisfactory way of measuring the effect of a customs union or free trade area on trade flows. International transactions are governed by many factors, and it is difficult to isolate the influences exercised by regional integration.

But all studies of the effects of the EU have concluded that on balance all countries (and not only EU members) have gained from its creation (although they differ in their estimates of the extent to which they have benefited). However, the benefits are not spread evenly even within the EU; the member states on its periphery show little capacity to catch up, even in growth rates, with the countries at its heart. Nor are non-members all affected in the same way and to the same extent. It is clear that some of the developing countries not protected by the Lomé Convention as well as some of the developed British Commonwealth countries have lost export markets to EU countries.

Agriculture – a special case?

The problems of agriculture constitute a good illustration of the tensions between the conflicting objectives of trade blocs. Most countries regard agriculture as a strategic industry because of the importance of being self-sufficient in times of national emergency. The founders of the EU, sensitive to the lessons of the Second World War, were alert to the danger of being dependent on imports of basic foodstuffs. Add to that the political strength of the small farmers' lobby, especially in France, and it is easy to understand why a complicated set of policies directed towards agriculture was one of the key elements in the EEC. Essentially, what these policies sought to do was to increase EC food output and particularly to ensure food supplies in times of shortage, and to protect farmers' income whilst giving incentives for improved efficiency in agriculture, whilst at the same time ensuring that prices faced by customers were reasonable. This set of objectives is not entirely internally consistent, as we shall see.

Agricultural output is subject to fluctuations because of year-to-year variation in factors such as weather and the incidence of diseases affecting crops and livestock. Applying the market analysis developed in Chapter 10 we can see in Figure 11.1

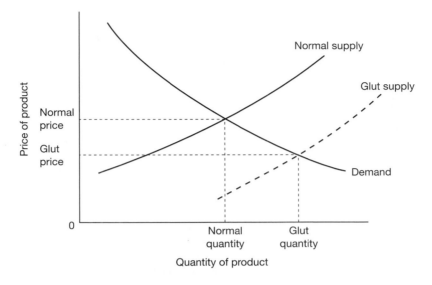

Figure 11.1 Abnormally high supply

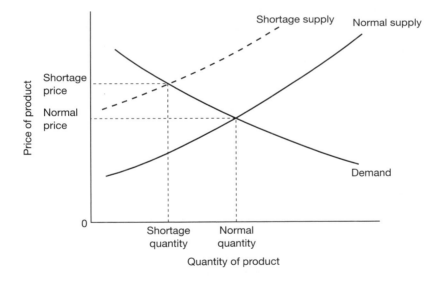

Figure 11.2 Abnormally low supply

that if supply rises because of favourable conditions, the equilibrium price falls and output rises; while if (Figure 11.2) supply falls because of adverse conditions, the equilibrium price rises and output falls. In the situation of Figure 11.1, consumers clearly gain because the product is abundant and cheap, whereas in Figure 11.2 consumers find that food is dear and relatively scarce. The effect on farmers

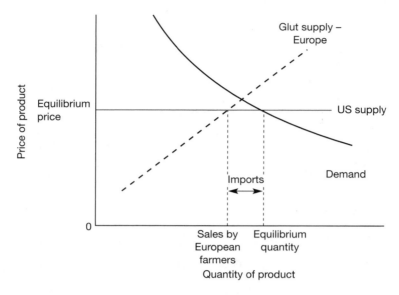

Figure 11.3 Imports, with abnormally high European supply

is more complicated, because in Figure 11.1 they are selling a lot of their product but at low prices, and in Figure 11.2 they are selling less but getting a high price. Nevertheless, their income is likely to vary between seasons of glut and shortage.

Now let us consider what happens when the product variations affect only Europe, with another major producer – say, the USA – unaffected. We can now

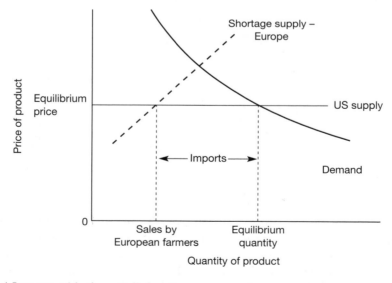

Figure 11.4 Imports, with abnormally low European supply

add to the diagrams a horizontal line to represent supply from the USA, available in Europe at a more or less constant price regardless of the quantity imported into Europe. If there are no barriers to imports from the USA to Europe, then when there is glut in Europe relatively little will be imported (Figure 11.3), but when there is shortage in Europe (Figure 11.4) much more is imported. For customers, the availability of American imports has the effect of stabilising prices, which are not as high in Figure 11.4 as in Figure 11.2, and reducing the variation in quantity available, but the effect on European producers in years of shortage of their supply is catastrophic because they can sell very little and do not enjoy prices as high as in Figure 11.4. The solution adopted in the EU's Common Agricultural Policy (CAP) was to prevent prices in Europe from falling below a predetermined level. Farmers would be able to sell their product at a guaranteed price. If in a year of glut the price turned out to be higher than that which customers were willing to pay, the surplus produce would be bought by public funds and stored, for release in times of shortage. A tariff would be levied on imports, so that goods from elsewhere, e.g. the USA, could not be sold at a price which undercut the guaranteed price. Figure 11.5 illustrates the way the system was meant to work in a year of glut.

The CAP solution was designed to protect European farmers at the expense of farmers in other countries. An effect which was not intended, but gradually became more marked, was to support European farmers at the expense of European consumers. This happened because the guaranteed price gradually drifted further and further above the market clearing price, because the increasing efficiency of European farmers, especially from the early 1970s onwards, was not reflected in falls in the guaranteed price. A further unintended effect, also

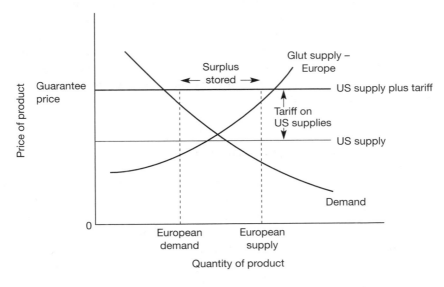

Figure 11.5 The operation of price guarantees with abnormally high supply

arising from increased efficiency in European farming, was that stocks of produce bought to honour the guarantee price steadily accumulated, into the grain mountains and wine lakes which eventually brought the CAP into public disrepute. If surplus stocks were destroyed, public reaction was to object to the waste. If surplus stocks were given to the needy in the EU, that simply increased the size of next year's surplus. The best solution seemed to be to give the surplus in overseas aid, to prevent famine in the USSR or in Third World countries, but more recently it has been recognised that this too is unsatisfactory because it reduces profitability for farmers in the recipient countries and may drive them away from the land.

Thus there has been strong public pressure against the CAP, criticising high food prices, the large surpluses and the unhappy measures to dispose of them, and the high proportion of the total EU budget absorbed by the guaranteed price system. In response, the EU initially adopted rather *ad hoc* measures to address particular surpluses, by imposing ceilings on the output for which EU farmers could receive the guarantee prices, or by compensating farmers for leaving land fallow (the 'set-aside' scheme). More fundamental reform of the CAP was, however, required for three reasons. First, enlargement of the EU to incorporate the eastern European countries would increase the proportion of EU output coming from agriculture (some of it very inefficiently) and add to the cost of running the CAP. Second, the USA had lost patience with the EU's tariffs on imports (a crucial element of the guarantee price mechanism), so a major structural change in agricultural support was needed if the WTO Uruguay round was to be successfully completed. Third, a growing environmental lobby in western Europe raised public concern about the impact of intensive farming methods on the countryside, and, indeed, on human health (the BSE cattle disease raised acute concerns). The Agenda 2000 reforms under discussion in 1999 are designed to take a much more radical approach, by a steady reduction in the guaranteed prices of cereals, beef and milk towards world price levels. The fact that this can be done without completely crippling European agriculture is in some respects a tribute to the success of the CAP in delivering improved efficiency in European agriculture, but many EU farmers are finding the process of adjustment extremely painful.

Competition policy and competitiveness

The CAP is interesting both as a topic in itself and as an illustration of the tensions between the aspirations of a powerful trading grouping like the EU and the rest of the world. A basic objective of the EU is to ensure fair competition between its members – and so to abolish barriers to such competition – whilst protecting them if necessary from competition from the rest of the world. Where EU producers are genuinely competitive in world terms, there is no conflict between the aims of the EU and of the WTO. But where EU producers are not competitive, it may not be in the interests of the EU to support trade liberalisation.

The existence of barriers to trade, however, has this further advantage for the EU. They constitute a motive for TNCs to locate production within the EU for sale within it, thus evading the barriers, and this both increases output and employment in the host country and brings new technology and new production methods to the EU. Most of the investment in the EU by overseas companies has been at the leading edge of technology; typical products of such activity are modern consumer-orientated goods such as cars and personal computers and cash dispensers, usually made by the latest automated techniques. Thus foreign direct investment by multinationals, at least some of which would not have occurred in the absence of the EU's barriers to trade, has been directly and indirectly beneficial to the EU. The disadvantage of such investment is that if the TNC hits adverse circumstances it is more likely to withdraw production from its EU operations than from its home base, but overall the effects of TNC investment are beneficial.

Competition policy within the EU is therefore rather ambivalent. The initial focus of EU competition policy was firmly on intra-EU international trade; each country had its own legislation on restrictive practices by companies within its boundaries, and the idea of the EU policy was to prevent cartels and restrictive agreements from distorting international trade within the EU. These powers were extended from 1989 by giving the EU Commission the authority to examine and, if necessary, to prevent proposed company mergers and takeovers which crossed national boundaries. The Treaty of European Union includes provisions to prevent aid from EU national governments to companies, including state-owned concerns, unless this aid is consistent with EU objectives. All of these measures are designed to ensure fair competition within the EU and to prevent dominant producers from exploiting consumers. But what if some proposed restrictive practice damages the interests of EU consumers in the short run but is designed in the long run to enable EU producers to meet foreign competition or to exploit global market opportunities – an updated version of the infant industry argument is on p. 243.

A good example of these tensions can be seen in EU competition policy on telecommunications, a big, profitable and still rapidly growing industry, of literally global scale. Writing in the Spring 1996 edition of the European Commission's *Competition Policy Newsletter*, Alexander Schaub, the Director General responsible for the policy, explained:

> We are in favour of commercial initiative and partnerships when they are in the interests of the Information Society. But alliances must have a competitive not an anti-competitive logic behind them. With this in mind we have two general conditions: The first is that such a powerful and radical revolution in telecoms as we are experiencing must be overseen by competition safeguards: basic principles which need to be as flexible and global as the moves and players themselves. The second is that the markets must be liberalised before we can allow their dominant players to join forces. We cannot risk that such markets as digital interactive TV, or global mobile satellite systems, are sewn up by defensive commercial moves before they are even opened up to competition. New gateways must be opened to avoid gatekeepers strengthening their positions.

The key issue in this policy is what to do with the 'gatekeepers' or currently dominant operators in the market. Commenting on the problems to be expected here, Schaub remarks:

> Timing is critical. We must ensure that markets are not foreclosed by the defensive strategies of the dominant incumbent players before effective competition has had a chance to 'bite'. The next five to ten years will demand particular attention as the ex-monopolists reposition themselves and adjust their behaviour to the new commercial environment. Competition policy dictates that we allow normal 'performance based' competitive behaviour on the part of dominant companies, whilst preventing defensive and anti-competitive behaviour. The distinction between the two is both complex and dynamic, depending upon, *inter alia,* the state of deregulation, the structure of the market, intent of the dominant player and the effect on actual and potential competitors...
>
>   Although dominant positions pose risks to consumers and competitors, this clearly does not mean that alliances 'caught' by the EU competition rules will always be disallowed. Often the benefits of agreements will be seen to counterbalance the potential risks, and/or such benefits will be judged to be the legitimate advantages of normal competitive strategy... I hope that an understanding of the logic... will encourage investment in competitive and innovative alliances and restructuring, as well as discouraging defensive agreements aiming at market distortion and foreclosure. Real synergies between telecoms and broadcasting, and really global service offerings are benefits which should be promoted. But this will always be weighed against the risks of extending dominance and harming competition.

In short, each case has to be judged on its merits, including trying to understand what is the real motivation behind apparently anti-competitive practices.

Underlying many of the recent deliberations of the EU, including some of the provisions of the Treaty of Amsterdam, is concern not about competition within the EU but about the competitiveness of EU producers vis-à-vis those in other countries. As we have just seen, there is a complicated relationship between these two considerations, and the Agenda 2000 proposals include under the general rubric of policies for growth and employment specific priorities to promote research and development and to make 'social protection systems more employment-friendly'. Research and development matters are important in the case we have just examined – telecommunications – as suggesting some possible 'innovative alliances' which are to be welcomed.

The issues regarding the relation of social protection systems to employment are primarily these. The amounts of unemployment benefit and other payments to those who might otherwise be at work, and the eligibility rules, affect the costs of employers through taxation. More generally, the extent to which employers have to foot the bill generally for social security and specifically for matters such as redundancy payments and maternity and paternity leave for their employees will also affect their costs. What can be done to reduce these costs, or indeed whether anything should be done, is currently controversial. Some commentators point to the USA as a successful economy whose social protection schemes give very strong incentives to those who can work to do so, and urge the adoption within the EU of approaches modelled on US policies. In particular, as in the UK, this line of argument leads to strong pressure on young people to undertake serious training and then obtain employment, thereby breaking the 'cycle of dependency' where successive generations of families depend principally on state support. Others argue that the best strategy for growth is to try to generate genuine security so that people can feel long-term commitment to their work, and that generous social security provisions are important to the atmosphere of stability. The existence of a relationship between competitiveness of economies and labour market flexibility is rather doubtful and indeed some would doubt whether the concept of national competitiveness is measurable or indeed meaningful. (A good summary of the literature can be found in D. Rapkin and P. Avery: *National Competitiveness in a Global Economy* (1995).) At present, EU policy is simply to encourage member governments to exchange ideas about best practice, in the hope that some consensus can emerge.

Eastern and central Europe

We have alluded at various stages in this chapter and in Chapter 10 to the economic problems of the eastern and central European countries. In this section we will briefly discuss the economic implications of the momentous events discussed in Chapter 9 and offer some tentative comments on the potential contribution the eastern and central European countries can make to the future prosperity of Europe.

In Chapter 10 we analysed the basic economic problem, but said little about its solution. The solution adopted in western countries was to let the market determine what is made and who gets the goods and services produced – 'the consumer is king'. Of course, this was never the complete answer even in the most market-orientated economy, because all governments regard themselves as having a role in providing activities such as defence and a police and judicial system and in protecting the most vulnerable members of society from penury, but a market-driven approach coupled with extensive private property is the basis on which the western economies operate. In the communist economies of eastern and central Europe a radically different solution was adopted: economic policy started from a concept of public ownership of most of the means of production (except people's labour) and from an idea of how goods should be distributed – 'to each according to his needs'. In operating such a system markets are of little use, and instead what is needed is an apparatus of state planning, to ensure that what is made matches what people need. So the Soviet economy was centrally planned from 1917 (apart from a brief flirtation with markets in the 1920s), as were the economies of most of the eastern and central European countries from 1945, until the collapse of communism. (Yugoslavia adopted its own solution, market socialism, which combined elements of market and of planned economies.)

Central planning is enormously complicated. As operated in its most complete form – in Stalin's USSR – it requires that each producer is given targets, in physical terms, of what to produce, allocations of equipment, material and labour to make the goods, and instructions about where the goods should be delivered – to shops for purchase by final consumers, to other producers for further processing, etc. The system further requires that each producer's performance be monitored to ensure that the targets have been achieved and the products correctly allocated. In situations of emergency – such as wartime – when there are clear objectives which command public assent, central planning is relatively easy to operate (and used in many countries) and planning is efficient in mobilising resources to address the emergency. When, however, central planning is being used year after year in circumstances where consumer aspirations are rising, it is much more difficult to ensure efficiency. The planners lose touch with what are realistically demanding targets to give the producers (who, of course, have every motive to make the targets as undemanding as possible). When the range of goods and services which the economy is providing grows, as a result of increased prosperity, the planning process becomes much more complicated because there are many more interrelationships between producers which have to be identified and incorporated into the plan. It is particularly difficult for planning to be flexible in responding to changing consumer tastes, because the planning mechanism involves making binding decisions for at least one year ahead, so if consumers want the latest fashions in clothes or music they will have to get their hands on imported products.

Across eastern and central Europe various attempts were made, intermittently from the mid-1960s but in a more sustained way from the early 1980s, to make the planning system less unwieldy and more responsive to consumer tastes and to reduce the inefficiency which was becoming endemic in production. The mechanisms of incentives for producers were modified many times to try to make them operate more efficiently. Markets were increasingly being given at least semi-official recognition, particularly for small-scale producers and farmers. However, the economic reforms did not really address fundamental problems, but instead tinkered with details, and by the later 1980s were overtaken by political events, as we have seen in Chapter 9.

For eastern Europe the CMEA, discussed briefly in Chapter 10, was of decisive significance. In 1988 about half of the USSR's trade was with other European CMEA members, and nearly 70 per cent of the other CMEA members' trade was with the USSR. Thus, because the USSR was in both political and economic terms the dominant member of the CMEA, the non-Soviet members became more dependent on trade with the USSR than the USSR did on trade with them. When the Soviet economy began to seize up in the 1980s, this had profound effects on all these east European countries, because the main export market of all of them shrank. They could not quickly develop new markets, because many of their products were too old-fashioned to be attractive, at any price, to western markets. At the same time, the new liberalisation of trade enabled consumers who could afford to do so to buy imports from the West.

Their difficulties were compounded by rapid inflation. To understand why, we will need to consider the role of prices in a planned economy. In a market system, prices are the key variable which relates supply to demand so that, unless prices are controlled, as in the CAP guarantee system, quantity demanded is matched to quantity supplied. In a centrally planned economy, supply is determined by the decisions of the planners, which may not reflect what consumers want. Prices are more or less artificial, because all the prices do is determine who is to obtain the goods made available as a result of the planners' decisions. If the price is set too high, goods will be left unsold, but lowering the price solves that problem. If the price is set too low, more of the product is demanded than is supplied. To maintain or increase their popularity, the governments in the centrally planned economies typically kept down the prices of foodstuffs and other basic household commodities, and in the process created excess demand. Figure 11.6 illustrates the problem.

Suppose the government decides that the price of the product cannot exceed Pmax, which is below the market-clearing price Pe. It is obvious that there is excess demand of Q1–Q2 and so there are queues of people who want the good but are unable to obtain it, and shopkeepers can choose to whom to sell (perhaps their favoured customers). In some circumstances, such as the USSR in 1990, the central or local government tries to override shopkeepers' preferences by introducing its own allocation system. One such system is rationing, whereby people wishing to buy a good need both the money and a government-issued coupon. The number of coupons would be set to equal total supply, Q1, and the coupons distributed to households in what the government regards as a fair way – for example, local authorities might use rationing to limit purchases to local residents. Exactly that device was adopted by the city of Leningrad to cope with shortages in late 1990

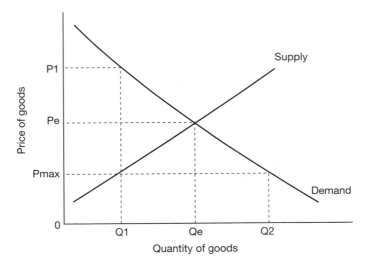

Figure 11.6 Price controls

and 1991 by restricting sales of consumer goods to local citizens. Figure 11.7 shows coupons for wine, strong alcoholic drinks, tea and soap. The coupons for strong alcoholic drink issued for the same period by different district offices in our illustration were obtained from one family; this neatly demonstrates that once coupons are issued they are traded between households.

Any government which tries to control a market, whether or not it operates a rationing policy, must expect that the price ceiling may be violated. Usually, it is relatively simple for a planning authority to control fairly completely what is produced, so output is unlikely to be much more than Q1, but it is much more difficult for the government to control the distribution network, and so to stop the goods being sold at a price greater than Pmax on the black market. If all the supply available, Q1, were sold on the black market it would command a price P1, even further above Pmax than the market-clearing price Pe. If only some of the supply is diverted to the black market, the price can be even greater than P1. How far the government chooses to tolerate black markets depends on the circumstances. In the USSR by 1990–91 a vast variety of meat and produce was being sold openly by individuals in city centres, and the government did nothing to prevent this because the availability of extra produce to cities helped to reduce social unrest.

The decision of a government to operate official price ceilings but to acquiesce in the existence of a black market can serve both to make most of the goods available at low prices to those who are prepared to queue and to make small quantities (sometimes of superior quality) available at a much higher price to those who are prepared to pay for it. It does not, however, address the basic problem that the overall quantity of goods is being kept artificially low (Q1 rather than Qe). A further problem of shortages is that, when durable goods are available, buyers hoard them. This is true both for producers, hoarding supplies of raw materials, and for households. The average Soviet family in 1990, fearing even worse shortages or sharp price rises, was storing about 6kg of soap and washing powder and vast holdings of toilet rolls and sugar. The confusion in the retail market turned Soviet flats effectively into small warehouses. Hoarding serves, of course, only to make the shortages worse for those not holding stocks. The shortages of consumer goods were one cause of the dissatisfactions underlying the developments discussed in Chapter 9.

Why were these developments associated with rapid inflation? When planning was abandoned and the market mechanism introduced in its place, demand adjusted much more quickly than domestic supply. The black markets meant that at least the more affluent households in cities had some experience of the price mechanism, but producers (especially those in what had been the USSR, who had known nothing but central planning for up to 70 years) were used to being told what to make (and, sometimes, how to make it) and found it difficult to learn how to adapt output to demand. That meant that for commodities whose price had been set artificially low, as in Figure 11.6, output remained very low (at or only just above Q1) and so the free market price was P1. Once output adjusted, prices would fall, but the initial price rises were very steep. Faced with steep price rises,

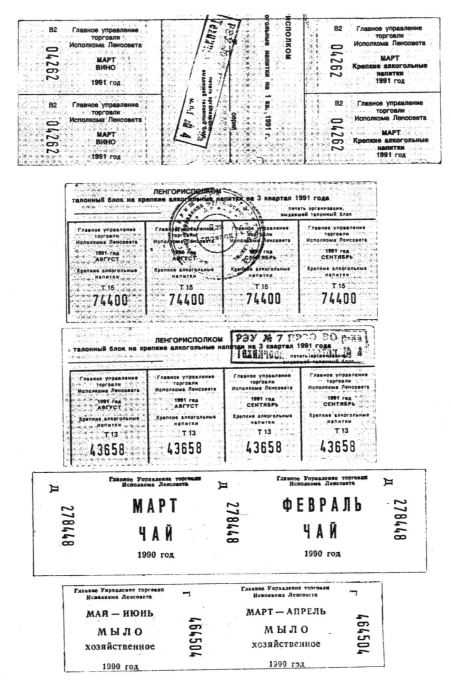

Figure 11.7 St Petersburg ration coupons of 1990–91. From top, coupons for one person for wine and strong alcoholic drinks (March 1991), two sets for strong alcoholic drinks (August/September 1991), tea (February/March 1990) and soap (March–June 1990)

workers demanded substantial pay rises, thus fuelling the whole process of inflation. Families with two or more members in employment fared reasonably well,
with rises in pay roughly matching those in prices, but those with no or limited
earning capacity suffered badly, so overall demand fell for many products.

Falling demand makes it less attractive for producers to expand output and
prolongs the problem. Furthermore, the government, knowing that prices
should fall when output grows, will be reluctant to see incomes rise very far
because of the inflationary consequences. This will result in particular in a
squeeze on public sector pay, adding to the depression in the economy. All this
is compounded by a further problem. To meet the excess of demand over
supply, more goods are imported – for example, in Russia in early 1993 much of
the supply of vodka and spirits, and nearly all paper handkerchiefs, were
imported, as were vast quantities of consumer durables. The growth in imports,
together with inflation, led to rapid devaluation of currencies such as the ruble.

The economies of eastern and central Europe suffered drastically in the
immediate aftermath of the collapse of communism. Few escaped the deadly
combination of a sharp decline in real output and inflation of 100% or more
(i.e. prices doubling in a year). Unemployment, which in theory and to some
extent in practice was unknown under the planning system, rose to high or very
high levels. For many of these countries the resulting social and political problems were very serious. Since social security arrangements had been sharply cut
back or even abolished, many individuals went hungry or even starved to death,
though others did well for themselves.

How fast and how sustained can we expect economic recovery to be? At the
time of writing it is difficult to be optimistic. In all the eastern and central
European countries the ending of communism was marked by extensive privatisation of hitherto state-owned means of production and by the creation of financial
markets, to deal, for example, in the shares of the newly privatised companies. But
these financial markets are thin – in many cases, there are still few quoted companies and few people interested in buying and selling shares – and so the markets
are very vulnerable to destabilising forces. The newly reconstituted banking system
lacks experience; in particular, the central banks are ill-equipped to perform their
main functions of acting as banker to the state, overseeing and controlling the
money supply and acting as effective regulators to prevent doubtful practice by
privatised financial institutions. The events in the Pacific Rim countries, to which
we alluded at the beginning of this chapter, are exactly the kind of shock which an
inexperienced central bank working with thin and underregulated markets
cannot easily withstand, and the effects on Russia in particular have been very
marked, with the ruble crashing in value yet again because of (well-founded) fears
about the capacity of Russia to honour her debts.

The West is seeking to ensure that Russia adheres to the market system, by
linking assistance to promises that there will be no turning back from reform.
Countries which believe that there is a realistic prospect for them of early membership of the EU similarly face strong pressure not to deviate from the path of
capitalism. The European Council met in Copenhagen in 1993 and laid down

three criteria for EU membership to be applied to the countries of eastern and central Europe; one of these criteria requires that the applicant has a functioning market economy and can cope with competitive pressure and market forces within the EU. For many of the east and central European economies, the worst of the pain of reform may now be over – see, for example, the declines in inflation rates and moves towards positive output growth for many countries towards the end of the period. There must, however, be a strong temptation for the people of Russia and some other ex-USSR countries (such as Ukraine) to conclude that the miseries of their experiment with capitalism are never-ending, and that they would be better off resurrecting some sort of socialist system even if it does mean cutting themselves off from the West and sinking into further long-term decline.

In general, however, and if they keep their nerve, the eastern and central European economies have the potential for rapid growth once the world economy, and particularly that of western Europe, starts to recover. They start with the flexibility that springs from a major refocusing of their economic activity. Their pay levels are low by west European standards, and their workforce generally well educated. Their main current problem is that they are hampered by poor capital equipment. We alluded in the last chapter to the involvement of what had been West Germany in rebuilding the economy of former East Germany. In the same kind of way, investment from outside in the other eastern and central European economies will lead to high returns for the investors and will modernise the host economies.

12 And nation shall speak unto nation: the communications network

Introduction

When people try to do something together, everything depends on how they communicate with each other. We can send messages into deep space in the hope that some extra-terrestrial beings might find them and interpret them; but the project of setting up a Joint Galactic Research Programme in High-Energy Physics or Forms of Social Organisation is blocked by the fact that it will take about 22,000 years or more for one message to travel from sender to receiver. Similar – though less drastic – difficulties for centuries reduced effective European contact with China to very limited exchanges of trading information. But even where the technical possibility exists of passing information quite quickly from A to B, that technology may be so expensive or cumbrous to install that it does not in practice operate as a network. Royal messages might be carried on selected routes by relays of fast horses kept in readiness along the route, but for ordinary traders in the grain-market towns of eighteenth-century Poland or the coastal wool ports of northern Spain, messages depended on the pace of barges on the River Vistula or schooners on the Bay of Biscay, or at best on the efforts of a single messenger managing one horse on a difficult journey over bad roads. The peasants in their villages hardly heard anything of the events of the world outside a radius of about 30 kilometres.

Gradually, communications improved in Europe, but for a while only along limited routes of communication, from city to city by state postal systems, for example. What has happened to Europe in the twentieth century is a transformation of its communications into an ever speedier and more widely spread fast network, in which very many messages pass very quickly in many different directions. The tendency of any such network is to produce a loose and fluid exchange of understanding spreading through the whole network. One effect of this – wherever it becomes established – is to change drastically the underlying structure of political and social life, of power structures, of economic activity, and of culture.

But for Europe – as opposed to the USA and Canada – any such tendency meets a counter-tendency: the effects of Europe's division into separate units –

separate countries, separate strategic and economic regions, etc. These divisions have produced another major barrier to communication – language difference. The tendency of the technology is towards a uniform, swift and transparent network of communication, producing a correspondingly swift and uniform framework for the European economy and commerce and tending towards a unified structure of political power. But the cultural differences of Europeans – reinforced by political power – divide this network into partially separated smaller ones because of the problems of understanding one another across these divisions. Of these cultural barriers the most substantial – but not the only one – is language difference.

Language difference and the sense of identity

People tend to feel a strong emotional bond with those they understand, and with whom they share ideas, attitudes, social activities and jokes. All these depend on language, so it is not surprising that people often have a sense of their own identity as members of groups (e.g. nations) which are defined by speaking a common language. Also, for any job except unskilled labouring, carrying out your work tends to require a knowledge of the language of those with whom you have to cooperate, both those working in the same organisation and in other organisations. In this way, people's career paths also tend to be determined by language; you can hope to get a job or be promoted, generally, only in organisations which use a language which you can write and speak fluently. So all these factors – emotions, sense of identity, interest – tend to steer people into groups of those who share a language; and all these factors also interact with each other. Thus we get a strong tendency for nation-states to be formed with a common language, a tendency first identified (and proclaimed as a political programme) by Johann Georg Herder in the eighteenth century.

Nevertheless, strong though these tendencies are, reality is much less tidy. Once a population has an established language, it becomes very deep-rooted, and cannot easily be eradicated even by the determined efforts of the state to make people speak some other language (even a closely related one). For example, Spanish governments from the eighteenth century to the 1960s tried to eradicate the Basque language from its north-eastern provinces and the Catalan language from its eastern province of Catalonia. But they failed completely, and only aroused in the oppressed Basques and Catalans greater resentment and greater determination to preserve their own identity. Soviet governments from about 1930 right into the 1980s downgraded and disadvantaged languages other than Russian in the USSR with a very similar result; when the Soviet regime began to disintegrate in the late 1980s (partly because of these national resentments) many non-Russian peoples demanded some degree of independence and recognition for their own languages. Ukraine and Belarus established their own sovereign states and made their languages official within them; while in

Russia itself, even after the break-up of the Soviet Union in 1991, separate component republics have been trying to make their own languages official.

However, it should be remembered that languages may die or fade away to an insignificant status; Manx (in the Isle of Man, UK), Dalmatian (in Croatia), and Jutish (in northern Germany) are examples, while the position of Scottish Gaelic, Friulian (in northern Italy), and Sorb (in east Germany) – to mention only a few examples – looks somewhat insecure.

So the idea that every nation-state has its own language unique to that nation is a myth (one which some nation-states themselves sedulously promote). In fact, virtually all states contain minority populations whose native language is different from the official one, or else have two or more quite different official languages spoken by substantial elements of the population of the state, as in Switzerland (official languages: French, German, Italian, Romansh) or Belgium (French and Flemish). Moreover, many of the languages are spoken (in various forms or dialects) by substantial populations of two or more different states of Europe. That applies to English (UK, Ireland, Malta); French (France, Belgium, Switzerland, Luxembourg); German (Germany, Austria, France (Alsace), Luxembourg, Belgium (an area in the east), the Netherlands, Poland (Germans in Silesia), Romania, and Italy (in Südtirol, the Alto Adige)); Albanian (Albania, FYROM Macedonia, and the Kosovo province of Serbia); Hungarian (Hungary, Slovakia, Romania, Serbia); Turkish (Turkey, Bulgaria, and Greece); Swedish (Sweden and Finland); Finnish (Finland, Sweden and Russia); and Russian (spoken in the Baltic states and in every state of the CIS). Then there are states where an older language once dominant and a more recently established one are both official languages (like Ireland: Irish Gaelic and English). There are also states where a variant of the older official language now enjoys official status for some purposes, for instance Spain: Spanish and Catalan; and France: French and Occitan (Provençal).

We can see from these examples how far reality is removed from the myth that one language goes with one nation-state. If we add that there are about 30 million people in Europe who are immigrants from countries not adjacent to the state in which they have settled – immigrants from other European countries and from all over the world, speaking more than 100 different languages, then we can see that what is normal (i.e. nearly always the case) for a 'nation-state' is, in fact, to be multi-lingual. In Britain, for example, about 100 minority languages are in regular use by residents.

Nevertheless, most states do exert pressure in the direction of one official language. The reasons are obvious enough. Economic efficiency within a state is promoted by easy exchange of information; the legal system works better if everyone in the courts understands what is being said; the armed forces and the civil service work better if they use the official language and can recruit the personnel they want from the entire population; and in times of crisis the state is more likely to be able to call on a loyal population (ready, for example, to sacrifice its blood on the battlefield) if its people have a sense of loyalty to 'their country' which is greatly promoted by a shared language and culture. Modern states can promote the official language in many ways: via the education system; via the influence of the legal system, and of the civil service, on the language needed for commerce; via the prestige and influence of the armed forces; via the broadcasting system (both radio and television), especially if it is a public (government-controlled) broadcasting system, but also by influence and legal control exerted on commercial broadcasting. We shall consider later how these forms of pressure are in some circumstances becoming less powerful. States may also take steps to *define* the official language, as with the activities of the French Academy, though many states are content to leave this to organisations like universities and publishing houses which are anyway usually closely involved with state policy, power and organisation.

It is important to see that the very definition of one 'language' is nearly always (in the developed world) the outcome of this official determination of what the official language of some state is. In the beginning of any such process there are just a lot of overlapping dialects, usually mutually intelligible in neighbouring villages and regions, but becoming more different from each other as distance between them increases. One of these dialects is reduced to writing, extended and developed by dictionaries, terms for specialised uses, refinements of grammatical rules, etc.; and it then receives the enormous boost which comes from the backing of a state. (In the earlier history of Europe the backing was very often more from the Church, and associated especially with the language used for translations of the Bible.) But it remains the case that the official language is different (to varying degrees) from the various dialects of most people who 'speak that language'.

For these reasons the definition of a dialect as a 'language' rather than merely a dialect of some other language is a *political* matter, fraught with political consequences and fought over by adherents on each side. Slovak was distinguished as a separate language by native nationalists in the second half of the nineteenth century, but was not recognised by their Hungarian masters. In the same period the similar speech-form of Czech (readily comprehensible to Slovaks) was defined as a separate language by Czech nationalists, trying to establish recognition for Czech identity within the Austrian Empire. In both cases the establishment of defining written forms of the language by new national literature was of central importance. When the power of both Austrians and Hungarians was overthrown by the First World War, the victorious powers at Versailles (trying to apply the 'national principle' of 'one language one state') were persuaded by the Czech leader, Masaryk, to treat the two speech forms as one language and so to constitute Czechoslovakia as a unitary state with Czechoslovak (undefined) as its official language. Since power was centred in Prague there might have been a tendency for a predominantly Czech unitary language to become established and accepted (as happened in England through the Middle Ages with the gradual fading to dialect status of northern English forms).

However, in 1939 the Nazis forced the Slovaks to set up a clerico-fascist independent Slovak state, promoting Slovak as a separate language, and after the war

Slovak – now more thoroughly established – was treated as a speech form and written form parallel with Czech. (On television two newscasters – one Czech and one Slovak speaker – would sit together and take it in turns to read news items, both of them understood well enough by both Czech and Slovak viewers.) So a sense of both political and linguistic separateness developed together. When democracy arrived in 1989 the Slovaks soon separated themselves from the Czechs as the independent state of Slovakia and established international recognition of Slovak as a separate language, even though by the criterion of linguistic science only (i.e. languages are the same if mutually comprehensible to a reasonably high degree) the two *are* one language.

In a rather similar way the state of Yugoslavia was founded in 1919 on the idea that the Serbs and the Croats spoke essentially the same language ('Serbo-Croat'), which – because of the accidents of history – was written in two different scripts, the Roman for Croat, and the Cyrillic (like Russian) for Serbian. But from the late 1980s it became clear that the Serbs and the Croats did not regard themselves as one people, and consequently some – including Croats and Serbs themselves – have come to regard Croatian and Serbian as two separate languages, partly just because of that difference in scripts.

The status of Catalan as a separate language from Spanish (though closely related) became established in a similar way through political pressure associated with semi-independent status for the province of Catalonia within Spain. On the other hand the dialect of Ruthenian has no official status within Ukraine; the Provençal (Occitan) dialect of French has a literature and some limited official recognition, but is regarded as a dialect; and the dialect of Scots English has no recognition at all within the UK.

The many dialects of German (grouped into the 'High German' of south Germany, Switzerland and Austria, and the 'Low German' of north Germany) are not treated as separate languages, and official German (a version of High German) prevails everywhere as the written form. But in Switzerland, for example, the spoken Swiss dialect is so different from the official written German that Swiss children have to be taught both – as separate linguistic skills – in schools; while in Luxembourg the local German dialect – Letzebürgisch – enjoys official recognition as one of the three languages of the state along with French and standard official German, which all Luxembourgers are taught.

In Norway (which had been part of Denmark until 1814 and then of Sweden until 1905) an official language related to the linguistically similar Danish had been set up in the eighteenth and nineteenth centuries, called the Riksmål ('the King's tongue') or the Bokmål ('the book tongue'). In the later nineteenth century some Norwegians trying to establish their separate national and linguistic identity came to think that the Riksmål was too Danish-influenced and too different from the speech of the people (especially in the country districts); so they defined and promoted the Landsmål ('the country tongue'), also known as Nynorsk ('New Norwegian'). Today both forms of Norwegian are officially recognised and taught.

Among the south Slav dialects the speech of the Macedonian region might be regarded as a dialect of the official language Serbian, or of the official language Bulgarian, or as a separate language official in the state of Macedonia (FYROM); and which decision is taken has major political implications in a region tense with the potential for ethnic conflict. (The Greeks, for example, are determined that Macedonia proper is part of Greece, and that its proper language is Greek. They are therefore opposed to recognition of the Slav dialect as a Macedonian language.)

The official languages of Europe are often quite recent creations (as with Norwegian), and associated with the establishing of political rights or separate statehood. Finnish was defined and recognised as part of the nationalist movement against the Russians in the nineteenth century and up to 1914, as were Estonian, Latvian and Lithuanian. Modern Greek, Romanian, Bulgarian, Hungarian, Serbian, Slovenian, Czech, Albanian, Maltese, and Icelandic were all defined and established as official, separate languages in the nineteenth and twentieth centuries, in association with separatist movements and (later) the backing of state power. By contrast, Romany (the language of gypsies), Sardinian (in Italy), Corsican (in France), Kashubian (in north-west Poland), Sami (Lapp) (in Norway) and many others, receive little official recognition and are consequently not flourishing.

Disputes about linguistic recognition and official support for languages can arouse very serious political tensions. In 1968 the government of Belgium fell because of protests by the Flemings (Flemish-speaking Belgians) about state backing for a French-speaking university (the university of Louvain). Post-Franco Spanish governments have staved off political trouble from their separatist provinces (frequently seeking recognition and official status for their language/dialect) by granting substantial provincial power (including power over language policy) to certain provinces. In Russia, where more than 100 different languages are spoken, 89 separate territories are accorded powers as 'subjects' within the Russian federal state. But there are considerable pressures in many of these territories for greater powers; and one factor encouraging this is their fear that their own language may be swamped by the influence of Russian as the official language. Of course claims for languages are not the only forces working for separate political power for provinces of modern states. Indeed in Germany where a federal system is well entrenched as a way of representing local interests, the separate *Länder* (states) do not particularly promote local dialect forms.

Organisations like the European Union which seek to promote cooperation and inter-communication across several European countries also have an interest in ensuring that all workers in Europe – more generally all people living in Europe – are treated in a way which enables them to realise their full potential and to play their full part in the life of Europe. This interest is partly economic, to maximise the efficiency of work and partly political, to reduce the chances of political conflict arising from discontent. The powerful transnational corporations (TNCs) may share these concerns, favouring not only the recognition of minority languages but also a general mastery of the languages most used for international commerce, English, French and German. (Russian is spoken by about 150 million people in Europe, as compared with roughly 60 million each for English, French and German, but the role of Russian in commerce outside the CIS is so far small. Spanish is a major world language, but mainly because of its widespread use in South and Central America; in Europe its role is smaller than that of English, French or German.)

In addition, one motive for the founding of the EC/EU was to reduce the potential for destructive wars in Europe by promoting human rights. Thus we should expect the EU, the TNCs and other similar organisations to favour rights for minority languages and to promote the teaching of languages so as to produce a sizeable population speaking at least one or two of the major languages. In fact the Treaty of Rome did not mention languages or education. The EC only gradually recognised the importance of language issues, despite the enormous translation and interpretation costs of conducting its own business in all the official languages of the EC. (In the late 1990s 40 per cent of the administrative costs of the EU were absorbed by translation of documents; the EU employed more than 2,000 people in translation and interpretation.)

Language issues have been neglected until recently because national governments are particularly touchy about their own languages, and the politicians drafting the Treaty of Rome and subsequent EC directives and treaties were trying to avoid stirring up a hornet's nest. So the EC itself absorbed the ever-rising costs of recognising all the official languages of member states as official EC ones. It relied on commercial pressures to determine the dominating language in the European economy.

But in 1977, migration pressures provoked an EC directive pledging member states to 'take appropriate measures', as far as consistent with domestic requirements, to provide free and adequate tuition to the children of migrants to teach them the official language of the country, and also to provide teaching in their mother tongue. An EC directive is binding, but member states differ in the extent to which thus far they have implemented this directive. In 1990 the EC established the LINGUA programme of encouraging bilingualism (or multilingualism) in EC countries. Article 126 of the Maastricht Treaty stresses the Community aim of developing 'the European dimension in education, especially through the learning and the development of the languages of the member-states'. But the Treaty also expects (and endorses) continuation of linguistic diversity, specifically mentioning its value and its connection with national cultures. Of course, it leaves the content and organisation of education to member states. But it is significant that education and language are seen as sufficiently important to appear in this Treaty. We may expect growing pressures to develop these policies, so the EU is unlikely to retreat from this position. However, every additional member with a language distinct from those previously recognised increases greatly the cost and delay of translation and interpretation, so that in practice the EU's business is increasingly conducted in English and French.

Thus as the structure of European commerce, quasi-governmental activity and society becomes more international, so the influence of the major European languages will surely grow. The power of governments of nations with minor languages to influence the language of their citizens may be expected to diminish. Three-quarters of the world's letters and 80 per cent of electronic databases are in English, while simplified and technical forms of English have been developed for universal use in air and sea traffic control and for much of scientific and technical interchange. (These figures are, of course, heavily weighted by North America; for Europe alone the balance between English, French and German is not so unequal, with German especially significant in eastern Europe. Nevertheless, it is clear even in Europe that English is fast becoming the essential international language.) Thus for those with jobs involving international commerce, the language crucial for personal advancement is likely to be one of the major languages, perhaps together with the language of one's own country. For this reason, the Dutch, the Danes, and the Finns have a very large proportion of speakers of two, three or more languages, and devote large proportions of their education time to learning them. Other small and medium-sized countries in Europe are likely to develop similar policies. The inhabitants of countries such as Norway, Poland, Portugal and Hungary are increasingly becoming used to material in one of the major languages. Television and magazines – as well as scholarly and scientific publications which the advanced student must study at university and even at school – have much wider coverage in the major languages. In such ways the power of the state to influence its citizens to adopt its own official language exclusively is diminishing. In countries using the major languages English and French, this trend to multi-lingualism is much less marked, but even so it is considerable, since no one language is really adequate for anyone whose work has an international dimension.

Modern communications technologies

Languages determine what people can understand, but it is the communications available that determine what messages can reach them. In the mid-nineteenth century people communicated by letters, and by newspapers, pamphlets and books. By 1960 Europeans generally had supplemented these with radio, television, telephones and telex, films, posters, etc., and newspapers were adapted for mass circulation and carried hot news (i.e. the previous day's). Notice how far these developments worked by enabling *one* sender of messages to send the same messages to *very many people* – that is what 'broadcasting' means for radio and television, but the same effect worked for films and for mass circulation newspapers. The effect of such a dominating one–many system of communication is to centralise the sources of information and ideas (and thus cultural power) in a smallish elite, usually located in capital cities. Because of these technologies, information and ideas spread much more widely, and quite a lot faster. The culture of Europe changed accordingly.

Effects of development of communications technology to 1960

The principal effect of new communications technology before 1960 was that commerce became much easier: orders could be sent more quickly, invoices sent out and payment received, problems with delivery of orders chased by telephone messages, and so on. Markets could be built up and secured by advertising campaigns. As a result, trade increased sharply and on a more international scale, the market reacted faster to conditions, and the major firms became larger and more powerful.

Another effect was that cultures became more evenly spread and more pervasive within their areas of effective influence. For many countries – though not for some smaller ones – the effective range of the mass communication of information and ideas was the nation-state. Radio and television transmitters were controlled by each nation-state, and each set up its own state broadcasting corporation to communicate its culture to its own people, such as BBC (UK), TF1 and Antenne 2 (France), ARD and ZDF (Germany), BRT (Belgium, Flemish language), RTBF (Belgium, French language), RTVE (Spain). This arose partly because setting up broadcasting facilities was hugely expensive, and partly because the technology then available permitted only a few non-interfering radio frequency channels and television transmitting channels, which had to be shared out between the European states. Differences of language between the populations of some European states and their neighbours stopped them from listening to the broadcasts of other states. In this way, state broadcasting corporations provided an opportunity to promote the sense of national identity and solidarity among their citizens. Newspapers in many states also assumed a national range, although the regional press remained influential.

Thus cultures became more national and more sharply separated from those of other nations, while within each state they became more uniform. These effects were always less marked in smaller states, especially if their populations shared a language with other states. Viewing figures for foreign-language broadcasts reached about 13 per cent in some smaller states by the mid-1980s. But for the larger states there was a great concentration of effective cultural communication within the country.

Because broadcasting systems were controlled by the state, they were thought of as agents of education and of the promotion of national consciousness. Thus they tried to encourage and develop (a) 'high' culture – programmes about the history of painting, serious drama, classical music etc.; (b) especially the *national* achievements of high culture – Shakespeare and Galsworthy for the British, Molière and Anouilh for the French, Dante and Betti for the Italians, etc.; (c) a folk culture specific to that nation – e.g. comedy programmes like *The Goon Show* full of British humour and in-jokes about British characters and history; (d) sport, especially international contests seen from the point of view of whether one of 'ours' is playing; (e) political information, focused on the politics of the state concerned – so that in Germany a listener or viewer would become familiar with the views of German politicians such as Adenauer, in Hungary with those of Hungarian politicians such as Kádár; (f) political and social history of the nation concerned; and sometimes, sad to say (g) outright propaganda, either by cutting out any information about embarrassing events, like the attacks by police on Algerians in Paris in 1960, or by promoting distortions and lies, as in the Portuguese broadcasting corporation's optimistic version of Portugal's efforts to put down revolts in its African colonies, or in Czechoslovak radio's happy tales about the contented and progressive Czech and Slovak people under communism. But even where the state broadcasting corporation did not go in for crude propaganda, such national educational broadcasting policies strongly promoted a sense of national identity and loyalty (and to some extent support for the government) by reinforcing the distinctive elements of the national culture such as the language, the style of humour and the pool of shared knowledge of literature and of broadcast shows.

Developments in communications technology 1960–99

During these years there has been an extraordinary (and continuing) revolution in communications technology. To understand these developments we need to look more closely at the technology itself.

Technological advances have come mainly in five areas; (i) the physical medium of transmission of messages; (ii) the coding of the message; (iii) switching – the systems for controlling the passage of different messages in different directions; (iv) the interfaces – instruments for transposing voice, video image, keystrokes etc. into radio waves or electric impulses along a wire, and vice versa; (v) data and communication systems.

The physical medium
Fibre-optic cable is a (sheaf of) glass-fibre thread, along which the signal is transmitted as laser-controlled pulses of light. It transmits at 565 megabits per second (565,000,000 electric blips per second), i.e. 4,000 times as much information per second as copper cable carries. In 1956 the transatlantic telephone cable (copper) carried 36 telephone channels; the 1988 fibre-optic one carried the equivalent of 40,000. A new multiple-fibre transatlantic cable link, due to be completed in the year 2000, will be able to carry 7.7 million calls simultaneously.

Geostationary satellites (i.e. satellites which travel at the same speed as the earth beneath them, thus remaining always above the same point of the earth's surface) receive radio signals (including television signals) from a transmitter (an uplink) and retransmit them from their own transmitters (transponders) over a wide area of the earth's surface (the satellite's footprint). They can be received either by a special large receiver and retransmitted by cable, or directly by private consumers using a small satellite dish receiver; the latter method (DBS – Direct Broadcast by Satellite) requires a larger and more powerful satellite.

The coding of the message
The old method was analogue representation; the new method is *digital representation,* in which every represented feature of the message is coded (ultimately in

a binary code of blip-or-no-blip-in-a-position). Digitisation makes possible better interfaces and more efficient transmission of the messages, which can be inter-leaved with each other along transmission lines within microsecond 'packets', so utilising the greatly increased speed of transmission for carrying many more messages along the same line (cable or radio). This makes possible the use of the same transmission line for different kinds of message; thus teletext, interactive videotex, network services and so on can be carried on the same line as the ordinary telephone. This is the idea of integrated services; so the information technology made possible by digitisation is called ISDN, Integrated Services Digital Network. A crucial stage in the development of ISDN is the conversion of television reception to digital form, since this both makes possible higher quality reception but also enables the television to be utilised for the display of material derived from other sources than the standard television transmissions; possibly interactive connections with commercial, educational and even private sources hooked up to a home computer. These developments are just beginning serious penetration of the market at the end of the twentieth century, with the help of massive investments by large TNCs like Rupert Murdoch's News Corporation. It seems likely that they will transform society within ten years.

Switching

The old electro-mechanical systems of rotating cogs are now superseded by electronic switching by large computers switching digitised messages in 'packets' in accordance with codes on the front end of each message. These make possible a great increase in the volume of information passed through the system.

Interfaces

Among many developments, some of the most important are cellular mobile telephones, fax transmission of documents, fax transmission of graphics, videophones (cheaply available now for the deaf as outline representation), videoconference, consultation of computerised databases, direct transmission of data from one computer to another, teletext, and interactive videotex.

Data and communication systems

In the 1990s there has been a huge development of the internet and the world-wide web. These are essentially worldwide structures which tend to be centred in the USA, but their importance for Europe (and everywhere else) is very considerable, and wherever cable connections of sufficient capacity have been installed the internet is tending to take over from communication by surface mail and telephony.

Character of the new communications technology

Telecommunications have become more plural; they do not have the same tendency to be dominated by a few people or by the state. Partly this is because telecommunications are not a one–many kind of communication, but a many–

many network, with messages going in many different directions between many different senders and many different receivers. The more efficient and widespread the telecommunications network becomes, the less will the technology allow a few powerful controllers of communications to exercise an effective monopoly over the messages in the culture. This is partly because the technology now permits a much larger number of radio or television channels to be utilised without interfering with each other; so there can be many different message senders available for any individual to receive. It is also partly because some of the technology is relatively cheaper; desk-top publishing allows anyone who owns a small computer to design and print high-quality pamphlets, flyers or magazines, and it is not too hard to make one's own video.

The number of communications has become so large that nobody could control it. The demand for television programmes has grown by a factor of 10 to 20. Local radio stations are spreading fast. Newspaper sales have increased, and the size of newspapers – and thus the information they carry – has also grown enormously. Similarly, telecommunications traffic has grown so greatly that state organisations cannot monitor it effectively, even if they should wish to do so (except in the case of specially targeted telephones used by people already identified as suspicious). The speed of communication in 1999 is no greater than it was in the best cases in 1960 (e.g. in ship-to-shore radio). But so much more of it gets through, to so many more destinations, at great distances, and so much more reliably, that there has been a transformation in everybody's way of life and of working and in the character of their relations with other people. In effect, we now have a fast and dense network.

Effects of the application of this technology in Europe

Telecommunications
A modern economy hinges on its communications. According to the World Bank, investment in telecommunications produces for the economy as a whole a better rate of return than any other type of investment. In 1986 the average number of telephone lines per person in the world was about 9; in the EC it was 36, in Japan 37, in the USA 50. Telecommunications used to be the kind of business that provided a basic service for as many customers as possible, for which they paid only the basic subscription and a call charge. That pattern was suited to public provision, which became the structure of the service throughout Europe, usually linked to the postal service. Each state set up corporations for posts, telegraphs and telephones: PTTs.

By the late 1970s, however, information technology could provide many 'value-added services' – i.e. optional facilities. The new need for large-scale risk investment and the opportunity for sales of value-added services favoured a private competitive structure. In addition, the increasing role of international telecommunications, especially automatic transfers of data to computers or searches of databases for commercial investment purposes, favoured commercial investment by very large international TNCs. For these reasons, and because of the application of EU competition policy, the telecommunications sections of the western European PTTs were rapidly privatised in the 1980s and 1990s to permit the formation through mergers of European telecommunications companies large enough to compete in the world market. However, through mergers (especially with American companies) in an effort to compete in the global market, these companies are coming to be international TNCs and their specifically European character is melting away.

The crucial issue for all of them is the increasingly fierce competition for global markets. The world telecommunications market is worth 52.8 million ecu in 1999, and is expected to grow to 2.7 billion ecu by 2004. It is businesses, not private individuals, which make the most extensive use of the new communications technology; increasingly, modern business operates through intensive use of databases, tele-negotiated deals with faxed back-up, transfer of computer data, video-conference to save the travel time of executives, etc. Much of this traffic is transatlantic, which is why a new transatlantic cable is being laid at a cost of 1.6 billion ecus by a consortium of American and European telecommunications companies. Some 60 per cent of jobs in the EU are in information-related activities.

Within the EU telecommunications are unevenly distributed, as you would expect in the light of the division between core and periphery and the after-effects in eastern Europe of the years of isolation from western technological and commercial developments; hence the EU has a policy (STAR – Special Telecommunications Action for Regional Development) of targeting regional aid on to the establishment of a modern telecommunications infrastructure in the peripheral parts of the EU – currently Ireland, Portugal, most of Spain, Corsica and Sardinia, southern Italy, and Greece. The policy is having some success, but development in the core regions and countries of the EU is proceeding even faster, so it is doubtful whether the peripheral regions are really catching up. At present strenuous and successful efforts are being made to establish modern telecommunications for eastern Europe, especially in Poland, the Czech Republic and Hungary. Further east and south of these countries development is as yet very partial.

The effects of better communications on the European economy have been accentuated by the further developments of these tendencies to greater speed and effective circulation. A recent tendency worth noting is towards less centralised organisation of companies. The many-to-many pattern of the recent trends has had an effect on the character of the economy. The network of communications is so large and various that it cannot be so tightly controlled by centrally organised structures like states or firms. This has not meant that these organisations have ceased to matter; rather, they now exercise their power more loosely, by a more devolved system of management and by interlocking relationships with each other. Thus the dominant pattern of economic organisation is one of different firms with connections between them. The links may be by partial shareholdings held in common, by finance companies or banks, or by agreements to operate under licence to share markets. Thus the firms form loose networks rather similar to the communications network itself (see Chapter 2).

Television

In the 1980s and 1990s the key technical development was satellites, whose telecasts could reach consumers either by direct reception by a small satellite receiver dish, or through cables. Since the footprint of each satellite extended over several countries there was never any question of the individual state broadcasting corporations using them. Nor have they in general operated as adjuncts to the terrestrial commercial television companies. Instead they have been used by major TNCs transmitting on the many channels they make available, as rivals to terrestrial television, though technical improvements have also allowed for increases in the number of terrestrial channels transmitted.

But the big development of the end of the century has been digital television, which can be transmitted either by satellite or by terrestrial transmission. Getting the market to invest in the more expensive digital televisions and the black box set-top decoders required involves huge financial resources, and the competitors for this market are all large TNCs. The main field for competition in 1999 appears to be between reception by satellite receiver and reception by cable. Murdoch's News Corporation is committed to the former, Bill Gates's Microsoft Corporation seems to be opting for the latter. The significance of Gates's move into this market is that if the reception is by cable then there is scope for the same technical equipment to be used for the wider purposes sketched above for ISDN – use of the television screen for internet connections covering home shopping by computer and other commercial and educational uses. The fact that such companies with their huge financial resources are committing themselves to this competition suggests that the market will be transformed fairly fast, and the social and commercial character of Europe will correspondingly be changed.

The role of the state public broadcasting corporations

Broadcasting as domination of cultural space

Nation-states have used their control of the space of their territory to promote within it a national culture which will strengthen the sense of national identity for the population; thus a state will promote the national language(s), national history, national styles of literature and film, etc. In effect, nation-states have for about 200 years operated as culture-dominators within their own territories. Broadcasting which crosses national boundaries (especially satellite broadcasting with a broad footprint) or which broadcasts programmes predominantly of some other culture, threatens this cultural domination.

Many people think that the space determined by the range of a widely watched television channel *is* a cultural space, just as a nation used to be; and that it is important for their own (or their nation's) cultural identity that this space be dominated by the right culture. Larger countries (with some prospect of controlling their own 'audiovisual space') may make strenuous efforts to combat foreign culture within it. The French are particularly committed to this, promoting the idea of a *pays audiovisuel français* (or thinking globally, in resistance to American and other English-language cultural domination, a *pays audiovisuel latin*). This policy tends to cost France heavily. But note that the French are promoting French culture against *any* other.

The EU tends rather to promote *European* culture against American or Australian culture. This partly derives from the EU's keenness to promote European cultural integration and partly because of the drive to protect European markets for European programmes, broadcasting control, and equipment provision. This partly overlapping campaign *also* had strong French support in the 1980s, and nearly led to the breakdown of the GATT Talks in 1993, when the Americans tried to insist on open access for their programmes to European markets. Jack Lang (French minister of culture in the early 1980s) especially publicised the idea of a *'guerre des images'* (a war of the television images). He was thinking especially of French versus American television programmes, seeking at that time to preserve French public broadcasting control of television channels. In this he failed; it proved commercially impossible to maintain the range of state television channels he wanted. Control of audiovisual space by nation-states within the EU, then, is very difficult, and it seems can succeed only to a limited extent.

Increasingly, many programmes are made with dubbing or voice-over provided in various languages for versions aimed at different language groups. Thus there is a tendency for the major languages to dominate a cultural space, even without any state controls intended to produce this result.

These issues are traversed and complicated by the issue of high culture versus low (or popular) culture. In the past, the idea of high culture has always been determined as part of national cultures and associated with national elites. Thus the defence of high culture tends to be also the defence (now often a losing battle) of national cultures in their elite forms. Hence the partial rejection of high culture (as expressed in viewing figures) partly reflects the rejection by the people of their middle-class national elites, the classes which have dominated them in the past.

Low or popular culture is commonly associated with the USA. What is the reason for the almost universal appeal of American culture as reflected in Westerns, pop music, police thrillers and soaps? Some alternative (but not necessarily exclusive) answers: (a) taste not guided by an aspiration towards excellence tends to sink towards the crude, kitschy, and superficial; (b) for Europeans American culture seems free from the traditional culture of established – and oppressive, i.e. snobbish – national power; (c) American culture actually *is* European culture (because of the large-scale immigration from Europe into America), but more go-ahead, less tied to tradition; (d) American tastes actually are world tastes; (e) American culture has a crucial edge in the production market for programmes because of its large financial backing and large home market.

But all these considerations are cut across by the suspicion that television broadcasting does *not* in fact determine a 'cultural space' in any important sense. For viewers attend to television in a much less focused and absorptive way than to books they study (especially if these are reinforced within an educational system) or even to newsprint; they chat to family and friends, go in and out of the room, and tend to retain only a vague general impression of the material of the telecast. And they don't just swallow the attitudes of the programmes they see; very often they watch with a detached and ironic stance based on more deeply embedded aspects of their minds and their cultures. So it is not clear that cultural space should be fought over in the way it has been (at least in connection with television). Perhaps the crucial factors are, rather, the education systems and career paths.

A public service broadcaster may buy in foreign programmes and so not really be the standard-bearer of national high culture. The largest proportion of American programmes on a British TV channel is on BBC 1. Czech state TV broadcasts on two channels; on one channel many programmes are controlled by IP Praha, which is half owned by Information Publicité (French independent), broadcasting, for example, *Walt Disney Presents, Dallas, Derrick* (German crime series), children's programmes sponsored by Mattei toys, etc; and on its other channel, programmes in French, English and German (not Czech) from La Sept (French), CNN (American), Screensport (British), RTL Plus (German), MTV Europa (French). Such a public service broadcasting corporation is driven to become just another player in the commercial market by the difficulty and expense of finding sufficiently interesting programmes, and it is totally wrong to take it as a force for Czech culture or national feeling. Alternatively, a corporation which tries to preserve its tradition of trying to inform and educate people risks becoming so boring to the majority of the population that few watch it. They tend instead to watch broadcasts from neighbouring foreign countries (this happened to Norway).

Programme production

In the effort to preserve national culture in the television its people watches, a country may require by law that a specified proportion of the programmes shown are made in the country, or have been originally made in the country's native language. France requires, for any channel broadcasting in France: 50 per cent of audiovisual broadcast material must be originally made in French; 60 per cent must originate in an EU country; 120 hours of French-produced programmes must be broadcast between 18.00 hrs and 23.00 hrs each year; 15 per cent of turnover must be spent on original French production. But the effects of this policy on French television have been alarming; channels have lost money and had to close down, and the most successful commercial channel is run by a pay-per-view channel, Canal-Plus.

But now a large proportion of programmes is co-produced, by privately backed or public corporation-backed groups. For instance, a consortium of mostly public broadcasters comprising Channel 4, RAI (Italian), ORF (Austrian), ZDF (German), Antenne 2 (French), SRG (Swiss), and RTVE (Spanish) was set up in 1985 to back European productions. But many smaller independent producers make use of whatever resources, of whatever nationality, seem to serve their purposes, though their marketing is frequently aimed at the television of several different countries. Thus it seems to make more sense (within the EU) to require that a given proportion of programmes originates in *some* European country. The EU does indeed require this, hoping not only to preserve something of Europe's 'audiovisual space' against the Americans and Australians but to foster the European production industry. In addition some EU aid (Eurimage) assists European co-productions.

But of course this directive does not adequately protect individual national cultures and production industries. Moreover, any such rules are very hard to enforce; very many productions use contributions and editing from different studios in different countries. At present there is not much American–European co-production. But it might easily develop – there is quite a lot of American–European co-ownership of broadcasting companies, especially for satellite broadcasting in eastern Europe. Thus the trend is quite strongly towards a broadcasting regime of private channels financed by advertising, in competition with each other.

In spite of the tendency to pluralism inherent in modern communications technology, at present the control of major communications (especially television broadcasting, telecommunications networks, and newspapers) is becoming concentrated in the hands of a small number of private companies, and a smaller number of powerful individuals ('media moguls') each of whom controls or exerts influence over a considerable number of these companies. Well-known figures are:

- Rupert Murdoch – Australian by birth, now an American citizen; controls especially (but not exclusively) English-language satellite broadcasting and newspapers, in Europe and North America; uses these to oppose trade unions and public service expenditure and European integration, and to promote close connections with the USA;
- Silvio Berlusconi – Italian; controls most of Italian television and a lot of its publishing and newspapers, a big slice of Spanish television, some French and German television, and has major interests in Poland, Hungary, etc.; was elected as Italy's prime minister in 1994 on the basis of a campaign which utilised his control of the media, but could not maintain his position; now (1999) leads a major political party;
- Robert Hersant – French; controls much of Hachette;
- Karl-Heinz Bertelsmann – German; interests in RTL Plus (German-language independent based in Luxembourg) and in CLT, Luxembourg-based company;
- Leo Kirch – German; extensive interests in German television and newspapers.

However, these men and their organisations usually focus mainly on profit rather than the promotion of their own political viewpoint, though Berlusconi and Murdoch are notable exceptions. This commercialism may, of course, have indirect effects on the political messages conveyed; for instance, advertisers must not be offended, and the audience attracted should feel relaxed and inclined to think in terms of spending money on a high standard of living.

European integration

These and other tendencies have led some people to promote the idea of a European identity – a 'European village' (Delors), or a 'European space' (Felipe González). The public justification for the idea of an overarching European sense of identity is usually the need to overcome the old, bitter national conflicts of European nations. But a powerful consideration is the attempt to gather together European resistance – especially economic resistance, most notably in the communications industries – to the economic power of America and Japan. How far this attempt to organise a sense of identity for an entity which was previously just a (vaguely defined) geographers' conception will succeed is doubtful. But, more than the discovery of European traditions, the decisive consideration is likely to be the extent to which Europe as a power bloc – especially an economic trading bloc – operates as a unity which needs to strengthen the loyalty of its population in a similar manner to the way the nation-states operated in the past.

Further reading

Council of Europe (1998) *A Virtual New World?*, Council of Europe Publishing, Strasbourg.

Council of Europe (1998) *Radio and Television Systems in the EU Member States and Switzerland*, Council of Europe Publishing, Strasbourg.

Council of Europe (1998) *Radio and Television Systems in Central and Eastern Europe*, Council of Europe Publishing, Strasbourg.

Council of Europe (1998) *Radio and Television Systems in Northern Europe and the Baltic*, Council of Europe Publishing, Strasbourg.

Council of Europe (1998) *Radio and Television Systems in Southern Europe*, Council of Europe Publishing, Strasbourg.

Crystal, D. (ed.) (1997) *Cambridge Encyclopaedia of Language*, 2nd edn, Cambridge University Press, Cambridge.

Crystal, D. (ed.) (1994) *An Encyclopedic Dictionary of Language and Languages*, Penguin, Harmondsworth.

Kellerman, A. (1993) *Telecommunications and Geography*, Belhaven Press, London and New York.

Negrine, R. and Papathanassopoulos, S. (1990) *The Internationalization of Television*, Pinter Press, London and New York.

Noam, E. (1992) *Telecommunications in Western Europe,* Oxford University Press, Oxford.

Noam, E. (1992) *Television in Western Europe,* Oxford University Press, Oxford.

Packer, J. and Myttin, K., for the Abo Akademi Institute for Human Rights (1993) *The Protection of Ethnic and Linguistic Minorities in Western Europe,* Abo Akademi University Press, Turku, Finland.

Tunstall, J. and Palmer, M. (1991) *The Media Moguls,* Routledge, London.

13 How Europeans see themselves: culture, belief and writing

Introduction

The idea of Europe has always been not so much that of a stretch of land but rather the idea of a centre of a certain kind of culture producing a stable political and social structure – a centre thought of as located in a particular group of countries. These countries are pictured in an idealised but not wholly unrealistic way, as embodying these cultural ideals.

This chapter considers that cultural tradition with which people seek to identify. Not surprisingly, different people hold different views about this essential character of Europeanness. So it is important to examine competing conceptions of the idea of being European and to consider both what is genuine in them and what is myth or propaganda. It is also necessary to examine how these cultural traditions have developed since 1945 in Europe – how Europeans have tried to understand their own situation and who they are. It will be no surprise that the cultural development described in this chapter will be mainly focused on the 'heart' of Europe; though for the period from 1945 to the 1980s there was a different cultural area operating separately, that of the eastern bloc, and some of its thinkers will be considered as well.

The European cultural tradition

From 600 BC to 200 BC the ancient Greeks built up an extraordinarily fertile intellectual tradition; one of rational inquiry into the causes and explanations of everything, and of development of the individual spirit as free, self-understanding, and valuable in itself. The Romans took over this intellectual tradition as their own culture, and spread it throughout their empire, adding Roman Law and a political tradition of disciplined participation in the state. From the Near East came the Hebrew tradition, which in a fruitful junction with Greek thought produced Christianity and Judaism, religions in which the individual spirit is seen as having its own individual responsibility and destiny within the Creation. So at the roots of the culture of Europe are the curiosity, open-mindedness and ratio-nality of the Greeks, the civic responsibility and political individualism of the Greeks and Romans, and the sense of the significance of the free individual spirit to be found in the main tradition of Christianity.

In the sixteenth and seventeenth centuries Europeans discovered and con-quered North and South America, and their trading posts and privileged trading towns were established in remote parts of the coasts of Asia and Africa, in India, Arabia, China, the islands of the East Indies and Japan. Old certainties cracked open; the authority of tradition was rejected in favour of new attempts to under-stand the world from out of the newly strengthened conception of the power of individual reason; and the Europeans tried to make sense of their own domi-nance and advanced civilisation as against the less dynamic cultures of the East, of Africa, of Islam, and of the native Americans. For many of them the crucial European cultural possession was Christianity. For others, who saw the churches as conservative opponents of the typically European reliance on individual reason, it was reason itself, as developed from the Greeks and preserved in classi-cal culture. For others it was the Roman virtue of self-reliant and socially responsible republicanism.

In modern times the Europeans have understood themselves precisely as the centre of modernity. Modernity began in the eighteenth century in the movement also known as the Enlightenment, at the time when confidence in reason as the power which could enable European civilisation to master the world reached its peak. Thinkers of France, Britain, Germany, Sweden, and Switzerland built up the idea that all of nature, and also man himself and his societies, could be understood as a rational system. The one who would do the understanding was the individual man, the free thinking mind which devel-oped its own fulfilment in understanding, the subject for whom the whole world was object.

In the Enlightenment view, tradition is of little interest and certainly need not guide people, since they can start at the beginning and by rational effort reach a complete understanding of everything. Not only can the enlightened mind understand everything and communicate everything in clear and coherent lan-guage; it can also construct society so as to make it produce the best outcome, which is, of course, the happiness of each individual member of it. And if the existing social and political arrangements include features now seen as non-rational, like kings, aristocracies, traditional religions and classical forms in the arts, then that only shows that we need to get rid of these cobwebs from the dusty past – if necessary, in a revolution. Meanwhile, we shall continue to develop our scientific knowledge, in an advance in which everything will always get better, because all progress is ultimately an expression of ever-developing knowledge. All structures of the world around us, therefore, are merely provisional; change will move endlessly onward, and is not to be feared or resisted because history itself moves us onward and upward. Politically, the confidence of the Enlightenment in human reason tended to line it up with liberal causes – with defence of human rights and with democratic forms of government and society.

This Enlightenment creed is far from dead. It was originally a specifically European creed (even though it was soon exported to America), expressing Europe's sense of its own pre-eminent destiny in history as the bearer of 'progress'. But since the French Revolution of 1789 ended in the Terror and then in the military imperialism of Napoleon, and since the Romantics came to see the meaning of the individual's life, not in an attainable happiness but in an agonising yearning towards an unattainable infinite dream, modernity has been shadowed by a sense of loss and failure. Maybe, people thought, the constant shifting of the structures of the world is not guaranteed to lead always onward and upward; maybe our efforts to build our lives for ourselves in the modern world only lead us into destruction and the release of dark forces of the human mind. The controversial findings of Freud concerning the mysterious workings of the unconscious (the role of instinct, repression, neurosis), further discredited the view that individuals were capable of exercising reasoned control to achieve a progressively more harmonious society. Europe's self-confidence then came to seem to some Europeans like a dangerous over-confidence, a belief in rational mastery which betrays the modern consciousness and casts it back into the unsolvable puzzles of life. But this mood of doubt did not appear as a rejection of modernism, but rather as an assertion of the true nature of modernity. So modernism came to mean both the individual mind's drive to understanding (the Enlightenment), and its shadowing by a sense of incompleteness and doubt.

Even in this aspect of negativity and uncertainty, however, a crucial element of the confident Enlightenment was retained: the idea that the centre within which we must wrestle with the problems of doubt is the individual soul or spirit. Whether in its confident, 'Enlightenment' mode, or in its mode of doubt, modernism saw the issues as lying *within*, in the human mind, free even when it was struggling with its own incapacities. It is not surprising, then, that the mood of incompleteness and doubt is politically ambivalent. Some expressions of it have led to a rejection of reason and thence to the conclusion that political authority needs to be asserted above the carping of critics in democratic argument; while other expressions of it have led to a reassertion of true democracy as against the mere appearance of it (discerned by this spirit of suspicion) where it cloaks a subtle form of dominance or imperialism. The irrationalist fascism of the 1920s and 1930s is an example of the former, reactionary kind of critique of the Enlightenment. The 'Critical Theory of Society' originating in the same period (Adorno and Marcuse) and some aspects of the feminist movement are examples of the latter, left-wing kind.

Around the beginning of the twentieth century this loss of confidence in the power of reason was coupled with a tendency to question the adequacy of language to express any objective reality. Thinkers and poets – especially those involved in the Symbolist, Expressionist and Surrealist movements – began to regard the use of language in a plain and obvious way as a trap; the kind of trap which had led a whole generation into thinking that such an insanity as the slaughter of millions of men in the First World War was based on rational and sensible decisions. To use language in the traditional straightforward ways was to go along with the crude propaganda of wartime patriotism and the complacent authority structures of traditional society. To use it was to give way to the illusory objectivity of language which only blocked any possible access to reality as it is actually to be reached: fragmentary, subjective, filtered through dreams and images. Such writers sought new ways to use language, and their writing has shifted the sensibility and understanding of Europeans in ways that have affected the rest of the twentieth century.

The tradition of Christianity generally stood apart from the brasher expressions of the Enlightenment, but has by no means always taken up the mood of doubt and incompleteness. Sometimes it has fostered rather a rejection of the Enlightenment in favour of the assertion of authority and the rejection of democracy (especially in southern Europe, as in the clerical fascism of Franco in Spain or the Colonels' regime in Greece). But in northern Europe some Christian thinkers have stood out as critics of the materialist capitalist society. And perhaps we should attribute to the Christian background of European culture the fact that even wholly secular thinkers tend to regard the question of the meaning of life as a meaningful question which each individual man or woman must face, even where they think the question cannot be answered. For that failure seems to them a ground for agonised meditation, not for a shrug of the shoulders.

It is in the second half of the twentieth century especially that the sense that the pride of Europeans has led them into the worst disasters has been most acute. After two terrible world wars, after the overthrow of democratic values and democratic politics in many of the most advanced states of Europe, in Germany, Italy, Spain; after the building of extermination camps equipped with official gas chambers for the scientific liquidation of whole peoples; after the burning of tens of thousands of people in bombed cities; after purges, grotesque show trials, and hysterical panics about spies and foreign contamination; in the midst of a 'Cold War' in which Europe seemed to be irretrievably divided between oversimplified ideologies accusing each other of crimes, and all the peoples of Europe – and maybe of the whole earth – were threatened with extermination if their nuclear weapons were unleashed; how could anyone in Europe feel that the modern European spirit could be relied on to lead mankind towards happiness? So it is not surprising that much of the culture of Europe since 1945 has been a culture of doubt, of criticism, of a search for radical rethinking.

Critics and activists

This strain within contemporary European culture has shown itself most clearly in the work of artists, writers and thinkers. In some cultures artists and thinkers have generally been the ideological props and cheerleaders of society and of its political power structures. But in modern Europe the most significant artists and thinkers have usually been critical or oppositional in temper; they have registered in their own emotions the strains of the culture, and tried to find a way for society to be less oppressive, less fragmented into lonely individuals struggling against each other, less inclined to promote aggression and the drive for mastery. These concerns have often been embodied in the political left, in which they find expression in a political programme of some kind based on support for the poorer and (individually) less powerful in society, the workers and peasants, often linked to the hope of a politically driven transformation in society, a 'revolution'. Horror at the results of fascism and Nazism during the Second World War gave a strong impetus to the left in the period from 1945 to 1968. European civilisation was in crisis; its power structures and culture seemed to have proved deeply and irremediably flawed. For many artists and thinkers the need for some kind of hope in the face of this sense of crisis was overwhelming.

The left

For the left this aspiration had to be centred on the hope of a revolution to enable Europeans to start building a good society from a different base than the old corrupt power structures. The most influential left-wing ideas about the possibility of forming a good society were those of Marxist-inspired cultural critics of capitalist society who had little connection with the Soviet model, the eastern bloc or the Leninist movement. For instance, an Institute of Marxist research had been founded in Frankfurt in 1923, producing notable work before 1934, when all its members had to flee. Most spent the war years in the USA, especially in the free-wheeling atmosphere of California. It was there that Theodor Adorno and Max Horkheimer wrote their penetrating critique of the Enlightenment as an essentially imperialist, domination-justifying system of thought, *The Dialectic of Enlightenment* (1947).

It was particularly the Frankfurt School (as it came to be called after Adorno and Horkheimer had returned to Germany after 1949 and refounded the Institute) that established that kind of critique of the Enlightenment confidence in reason, which has been so influential ever since. Indeed, a great deal of European thought since then can be seen as successive attempts to identify a way of thought which is not trapped in the totalitarian dominance-strategies which, according to Adorno and Horkheimer, hide behind the apparent liberal openness of Enlightenment thought. In their view, the whole structure of a modern, late-capitalist society is a kind of anonymous system, which oppresses, restricts and distorts the lives of everyone living in it, but which is not consciously operated by anyone or any class as a system of control and exploitation of others. Thus the oppression and alienation is as much cultural as economic, and it operates as destructively for managers and professionals with quite a high standard of living as it does for unskilled labourers earning very little. The task of a writer, then, is to be a critic of culture, awakening the consciousness of people living in the midst of this system to its destructive, all-pervasive grip, provoking them to what the Italian writer Italo Calvino called a 'Challenge to the Labyrinth'. For example, the linguistically experimental texts of the German poet Hans Magnus Enzensberger, who was familiar with Adorno's ideas, sought to expose the insidiously mendacious nature of so-called normal language, particularly that of bureaucracy and advertising,

But whether such a challenge could result in a social or political revolution seemed dubious to the writers of the Frankfurt School; they were too deeply aware of the way the system absorbs all challenges against it, turning them into what critics called 'radical chic' (i.e. expressions of radical style and opinion which are really no more than gestures to make a smart impression on others). However, the ideas of this 'Critical Theory of Society' (as it was called) spread widely. In the 1960s the most influential Frankfurt School writer was Herbert Marcuse, who had stayed in California; his influential *One-Dimensional Man* of 1961 presented the critique of late-capitalist society as one which made its members atrophy into just one dimension when their real human potential should have enabled them to develop many dimensions of life.

It was from about this time (and partly because of Marcuse's vivid book) that the mood of these critics of 'the System' or 'the Establishment' changed from mere analysis to the thought that revolt might overthrow it. And a few years later factors such as acute student discontent in practical matters, for instance hopelessly overcrowded lecture theatres and soulless campuses, came together with this steadily developing intellectual attitude of anti-Establishment revolt to generate the mass rallies, demonstrations, and riots of 1968 in Paris, Berlin, London and other university cities of western Europe as well as the USA whose overtly imperialist Vietnam policy further kindled the anti-authoritarian fire. The hope among students for socialist revolution continued into the early seventies in many western European countries, fuelled by the protest songs of dedicated left-wingers such as the Spanish singer, Paco Ibañez, who set to music politically committed poems by Gabriel Celaya and others.

But throughout the post-war years, right up to 1991, the left was bedevilled by the question of the Soviet Union: was Soviet communism the model for the left and the cause to which it should be loyal, or was it some kind of perversion of the socialist ideas of a good society? Already in the late 1940s the British socialist writer George Orwell pinpointed in ferocious satires the dangers of socialist revolutions. Gradually, it became more and more difficult to believe in the Soviet Union as a progressive force. News of the purges and mass imprisonments of the 1930s became harder to deny or minimise; eastern Europe under the domination of the Soviet Union looked less and less like a model of happy socialism and a beacon of hope. New purges and show trials and revolts suppressed by tanks in Berlin and Budapest were followed by Khrushchev's account at the twentieth CPSU Congress in 1956 of some of the crimes of Stalin. This contributed to the causes of the Hungarian uprising later that year and further Soviet army intervention. Those who still believed in Soviet socialism were further disillusioned in 1968 by the suppression by WTO (mainly Soviet) tanks of the Prague Spring, which was feeling its way toward a humane form of socialism.

The political left increasingly turned to the attempt to bring about a socialist revolution in western Europe in a direction wholly different from that of the Soviet Union. This movement, however, always suffered from a tendency to be merely a movement of the intellectuals and students; the political weight of the workers as a mass force never settled into a clear focus on bringing about a socialist revolution, but directed itself more to short-term aims. When the student revolt of 1968 failed to take with it any substantial support from the workers, this kind of socialism ceased to be a basis for practical hope; and even the reformist socialist programmes of the big parties of western European countries (in any case less satisfying to those who are looking for a major change on which to pin their hopes), ran into all kinds of difficulties in the 1970s and 1980s.

To those within central and eastern Europe itself the situation seemed very different. Before 1968 some thinkers, especially in East Germany, Czechoslovakia and Hungary, tried to think constructively within the framework of Marxist socialism, to help their own societies to a better, freer society, 'socialism with a human face' as the programme of the Prague Spring was called. But one after another, after more or less of a struggle, they felt forced to abandon this hope, either by leaving eastern Europe altogether, or by writing in a more and more critical or individualist way. Bertolt Brecht, the playwright, and Ernst Bloch, the philosopher and author of *The Principle of Hope*, returned from wartime exile in the USA to live in and identify with communist East Germany. Brecht was assigned a prestigious position in Berlin theatre, Bloch one in the University of Leipzig. But when they criticised the government for its suppression of the East Berlin uprising of 1953, Brecht's work was severely restricted and Bloch was forbidden to publish or teach and was put under house arrest. In 1961 he finally gave up hope for the East German regime, and escaped to the West, where his work became one of the inspirations of the 1968 student revolt. Wolf Biermann, the folk-singer and political poet, followed a parallel course a few years later; his voice was also silenced while he lived in the East, so he returned to the West. Rudolf Bahro in 1977 published in the FRG (not in the GDR where he lived) a book describing a humane socialism, *The Alternative*; he was given an eight-year gaol sentence. Christa Wolf, the novelist, remained in East Germany, but her writing became more and more individualist, more distant from any clear kind of political hope.

Karel Kosik, the Czech philosopher, published analyses of Marxism in the early 1960s which helped to inspire the programme of the Prague Spring; after the suppression of that programme he stopped all publication. Agnes Heller and Ferenc Feher of Hungary, followers of the Marxist philosopher Georg Lukacs, continued to pursue their left-wing political thinking, but in a way more and more remote from the reality of communist power in their home country, and increasingly they worked in the West.

Worthwhile writers in the Soviet Union tended more frequently to be dissidents or outright opponents of the communist regime, writing in defence of the freedom of the individual and against the oppression and terror of the Gulags (the prison camps). Consequently, they were more likely to be subjected to serious harassment or imprisonment by the government. Such were Andrei Sakharov, the physicist, and Alexander Solzhenitsyn, the novelist. But the outcome for such dissidents was often that they left the Soviet Union (voluntarily or involuntarily), their home country where people understood their feelings and their language, and lived in a kind of exile. Andrei Tarkovsky, the film-director, Rudolf Nureyev, the dancer, and Mstislav Rostropovich, the cellist-conductor, were other Soviet artists who followed this road to exile. Sometimes (as for Milan Kundera, the Czech novelist) exile in the West seemed to be a solution for these artists. But for some – like Solzhenitsyn and Tarkovsky – their creative power dried up away from their home country. In the 1980s, however, some thinkers made their protest and stayed in the East, often in prison or in preventive detention, as symbols of defiance for their people. Sakharov did this, as did Vaclav Havel, the Czech playwright, who called on men to resist the lies they were expected to subscribe to, in *The Power of the Powerless* of 1985. He described the regime in a way highly reminiscent of Adorno's critique of capitalism, as 'post-totalitarianism', dependent not primarily on force but on the indifference of a people whose initiative was smothered by bureaucracy. Havel subsequently became president of Czechoslovakia and then of the Czech Republic, and Sakharov a key figure in the 1989 Soviet parliament.

But for thinkers and artists of the West the fading of hopes of a revolutionary transformation of society left them more uncertain about where they stood. A common reaction was to stand aside from large-scale, positive political programmes, but to engage critically with the system of European society and its established power structures, and with its terrible history. Much of this work took the form of a focus on individuals trying to live their lives and give them meaning in the deadening framework of ideologies and power structures in which the weight of Europe's history imposed its force against any divergence from the norm. Gunther Grass, the German novelist, in *The Tin Drum* of 1959, embodies his 'individual', with bitter humour, in the person of a dwarf who even when he grows up has the mental age of a young child (thus retaining his 'innocence' and avoiding adult entanglement in the corruptions of society), but whose tin drum disrupts the music of the military-political brass band and whose magically piercing scream breaks the shop-windows of capitalist cities.

Although Germany's neighbour, Switzerland, had maintained an official position of neutrality throughout the Second World War, the Swiss writer Max Frisch appeared fully involved in the contemporary socio-cultural crisis, exposing in his satirical plays the insidious phenomenon of self-delusion and complacent complicity with evil totalitarian regimes. His compatriot Friedrich Dürrenmatt in his play *The Physicists* (1962) used paradox and parody to identify courageous personal endeavour to fulfil one's obligations to humankind as the only possible line of conduct, however futile, in a materialistic world embarked on a crazy course to self-annihilation. Primo Levi, the Italian chemist-turned-novelist (who survived the Auschwitz extermination camp), wrote of the decency of following the rational and useful structure of chemistry within a world in which decency was constantly lost.

One field of this struggle was precisely the issue of how recent European history should be understood, and in particular the horror of Hitler's Germany and the Nazi Holocaust. That such atrocities were possible at all overwhelmed many thinkers. Ever since 1945 successive writers have revealed the crimes of the Nazis, the extent of collaboration with them, and other awful crimes of the period. More recently, historians have explored both the psychology of mass anti-semitism and complicity in mass-murder on the part of many ordinary Germans. (See, for example, Daniel Goldhagen's *Hitler's Willing Executioners: Ordinary Germans and the Holocaust*, Abacus, London, 1996.)

Especially cases of hitherto-concealed collaboration aroused the greatest shock: Rolf Hochhuth's play *The Representative* of 1963 portrayed the wartime Pope as agreeing to the extermination of the Italian Jews; John Cornwell's biography of Pius XII (*Hitler's Pope: the Secret History of Pius XII*, Viking, 1999), based on hitherto unavailable Vatican archives, paints a damning picture of the Pope's Nazi sympathies. The admired philosopher Martin Heidegger was shown by Victor Farias and Hugo to have been deeply committed to the Nazi cause. Further investigation has shown the extent of French collaboration with the occupying Germans during the war, and with their extermination programmes, and so on. Trials of some of those responsible took place, sometimes 50 years after the crimes, as in the trial of the French collaborator Klaus Barbie in 1992. In Austria the chancellor Kurt Waldheim was disgraced when his wartime military record in the German Army was revealed. In Germany the attempt to gain any kind of sympathetic understanding of the actions of Germans who had gone along with the government during the Nazi period caused outraged controversies, as in the row over Chancellor Kohl's tribute to the dead soldiers of the war at the Bitburg Cemetery, while the philosopher Jürgen Habermas led the protest at sympathetic (or, fellow-travelling) history of the time in the 'Historiker streit' (Historians' controversy) of 1986–89. The wounds left in European consciousness by that terrible time still hurt 50 years after the end of the war.

Existentialism

This sense of the life of the individual as the place of freedom apart from society, but also of suffering and of struggle to achieve meaning, could also be the focus of concern for writers in itself. This was the character of the extraordinary success of existentialism in the years after the Second World War, from 1945 to about 1955 or 1960. Existentialism arose especially in France, where it was the label given to the ideas of Jean-Paul Sartre, who tried to give a direction to European culture by which it could avoid the feebleness of liberalism (as he saw its pre-war character) and the brutality of fascism. Sartre argued that the self has no fixed being and no preordained destiny, but has always to be created by each individual person, following no rules, no prescription about how to live or how to understand oneself, but has his or her own freedom to live up to even while being perpetually threatened by the absurd. The self has its most fundamental meaning just in preserving its own integrity, in not going along with the norms of society or the requirements of others, even when these requirements are perhaps morally right. In existentialist plays and novels the characters who do this are often defeated, and their cause often fails, sometimes even in a way which shows it was perhaps the wrong cause; but if, in failing, they stick to their own sense of what their path in life is while not trying to impose it on other people, then they have kept true to their own humanity. So there came to be a great fashion for the *film noir*, in which the hero is killed and utterly defeated after everything he hoped for has turned out to be betrayed, or to have been a mistake; often these films were literally *noir* (black) or at least dark, as their scenes were often night scenes in the streets and alleys of cities, with figures appearing out of the shadows.

Perhaps it could be said that the fashion for existentialism reflected a deep sense in Europe that all grand talk, all messianic ideologies and great programmes for society, all claims to have seen the meaning of history, are illusions and frauds, which are used as covers for aggressive power structures like those of the Nazis. This is a rejection of the Enlightenment confidence about reason, a way of going over to the other side of modernism, the side of criticism and doubt. And what survives this scepticism about great causes and all-embracing interpretations of history and moral uplift, is the sense of individual freedom and commitment preserved in the very heart of each individual person.

Existentialism seems at first like the extreme negative side of modernism, the side of doubt and negativity, with all the positive, Enlightenment side eliminated. But it is not really like that. If it had been, then nothing at all would have been left, no hope, no meaning, no point in living in one way rather than another way. But the existentialists were really deeply, passionately committed to something. What they were committed to was the belief in the value of human freedom, of the integrity and responsibility of the individual man or woman, lying behind all the religious creeds and political programmes and moral values, at the pure centre of the human consciousness. If everything else fails, if you go wrong in the pattern of all your actions and all your attempts to make sense of the world, still there will be, if you hold on to it bravely, this one thing, the freedom at the heart of your consciousness. It was a philosophy which struck an answering chord in post-war Europe, in which many people remembered how difficult it had been for those living in occupied Europe under the Nazis to keep faith with a belief in the victory of the Allies, and in some cases to die fighting for the Resistance without any certainty that the sacrifice would be of any use. Sartre wrote several plays and novels about just that situation, as did Albert Camus. For Camus the notion of solidarity with others became increasingly significant, while Sartre remained suspicious of the potential that solidarity has for fascist notions of blood and soil.

But that was in the years immediately after the war, when that sense of heroism and of the possibility of a socialist society was still fresh in people's minds. The hopes of social renewal faded, as people felt more the falseness of the ideologies of communism and of the anti-communist, capitalist West, both of them wielding the threat of horrible destruction which might be unleashed on the peoples of Europe, and responsible meanwhile for injustice and suffering. The ordinary entanglement of people's lives in selfish aims and corruption took hold, and the heroic style of existentialism came to seem less real. As a philosophy, it has died. Its overblown faith in the being of transcendental consciousness, the self behind all particular contents of the mind, in control of its instrument – language – no longer convinces anyone. But its long afterglow is still with us in the form of pop culture.

Pop culture

Pop culture, the youth culture of our time, came originally from the USA. But it spread fast all over Europe. By the 1960s it was as thoroughly based in Europe as in North America. The Iron Curtain could not stop it; the young people of Moscow and Leningrad, Warsaw and Prague, took to the concerts, the songs, the records, the pop-star cult, the discos, the jeans, in a way that the staid Party officials and the members of the *nomenklatura* could do nothing about. Pop culture has done more to dissolve the pompous prestige of official ideologies in Europe than any intellectual argument or great book. But how did it happen? Why did this culture of individual self-expression sweep Europe in the second half of the twentieth century when it had not done so before? People had always sung songs and listened to music when they could. But pop culture is different; it has a special individualist, anarchic style which the folk songs of the eighteenth century or the music-hall songs of the 1920s lacked. How did it come to have such an appeal to the generations of the 1960s, 1970s, 1980s and 1990s?

Pop culture has a style of approach to life which is like existentialism without the heroism and strong sense of commitment to action. Typically, pop culture is anarchic, avoiding all involvement with causes, creeds, or moral rules imposed on others. Like existentialism, it takes each individual back to his or her own naked self, without rules or pretences or frameworks to guide life. But what is left at this centre of individual life, for pop culture, is not usually the drive towards commitment and responsibility, social or political action, which marked out Sartre's thought. Sartre's own political position was strongly left-wing, and he wrote a long and deep analysis of freedom and alienation in society (*The Critique of Dialectical Reason*) which pointed to the need for a Marxist revolution. One would not, of course, expect pop culture, since it is expressed mainly as song lyrics, to include analyses of anything. But its style and tenor tend in any case to be far less earnest than existentialism, more focused on the emotions and less on the possibility of action, on individuals and their immediate relations rather than the social or political.

This retreat from any sense of possible action to ameliorate the social conditions in which we all live is expressed also in a pervasive cynicism and materialism. The cynicism especially concerns political programmes or social causes involving politics. People feel that there are no great social or religious causes to identify with or believe in, that any political movements which exist are liable to be only fronts behind which self-seeking politicians can feather their own nests, and those who proclaim great causes are probably only in it for what they can get. More and more young people who in a previous generation might have been expected to be idealists passionately committed to a cause which might offer hope of some kind of New Jerusalem, were impressed by the thought that the consequences of attempts to establish a New Jerusalem were usually appalling. Instead, they increasingly focused their efforts simply on getting a good job with a large salary. This combination of cynicism and materialism began to be noticeable in the 1960s, but after the failure of the 1968 students' revolt it was much more marked. Only time will tell whether it will continue to be so noticeable a feature of the Europe of the future. But it is worth noting that the collapse of the Italian political system in 1992–93 was essentially a product of this cynicism and materialism. Politicians, seeing that people expected little else from them, only nominally subscribed to political beliefs and used their power to feather the nests of themselves and their friends; but when the public became fully aware of this fraudulent power structure they overturned it in a general rage with all politicians.

Of course, this cynicism and withdrawal from social commitment were never universal. Increasingly, from the time of the 1968 debâcle, people took up causes which might be called radical life-programmes: ideas for the reordering of attitudes and social action which were not total ideologies, not programmes for changing the whole social and economic structure, but which impinged on only one aspect or dimension of social life. It was in the 1970s that feminism took off in Europe. It built on the ideas of Simone de Beauvoir, whose *The Second Sex* of 1949 inspired a whole generation of thinkers who argued for a deep-rooted change in consciousness and in ways of living to combat what they saw as a consistent suppression of women. A series of issues focused the more theoretical discussions on practical action: rights to abortion, rights to equal employment opportunities, rights to equal political representation. Such claims brought controversy to many countries in Europe, which in turn further stimulated feminist thinkers and writers. It was in the 1970s also that active concern for the environment and for its degradation by the impact of modern human life and technology became widespread. These issues – altogether outside the structures of traditional politics – seemed to offer the possibility of really making a difference to life.

Literature and the language problem

As we have seen, since the end of the nineteenth century rejection of the Enlightenment's overweening confidence in reason had been accompanied by a challenge to conventional assumptions about language – a challenge which was articulated above all in avant-garde poetry and theatre. This preoccupation with and exploration of the nature and status of language became more marked in the years after the Second World War, manifesting itself in novels as well as in poetry and plays. After the shattering experience of hypocrisy, propaganda, and violence, after the trauma of exile which often brought about separation from one's native language and confrontation with a strange new one, the notion of a logically consistent, pre-existing reality, in relation to which coherent individuals could have coherent thoughts which they could communicate in coherent language to other individuals capable of relating them to their own coherent world-view, seemed totally bankrupt. In many texts of the late 1940s, 1950s and 1960s conventional linguistic and conceptual categories were dislocated to the point of virtual breakdown, articulating grotesque and disturbing hallucinatory visions of human isolation and degradation in a hopelessly fragmented, alien environment.

Such traits are present, for example, in the works of writers as diverse as Fernando Arrabal, a Spanish playwright who wrote in French during self-imposed exile from Franco's dictatorship, Eugène Ionesco, a dramatist of mixed Romanian and French origin, and Paul Celan, a German-speaking Romanian Jew who settled in Paris after living through the deportation of his parents to a death-camp. Major questions and dilemmas haunt the works of poets like Celan – the possibility that there may be no way of escaping sufficiently from the corrupting effect of established language systems to articulate anything original or, alternatively, the possibility that the attempt to operate on the fringe of these systems may render texts so opaque and private that they are inaccessible to others. However, there are also hints of hope that the complex layers and networks of meaning generated by the experimental language will somehow open up new perspectives to humanity.

In the novels and plays of Samuel Beckett, an Irishman who spent much of his life in France and who wrote in both English and French mainly in the 1940s and 1950s, experimentation with language became a major feature and indeed a central theme. So also did exploration of its communicative power, and its relationship not only with thought and reality, but also with personal identity. In Beckett's trilogy of novels, parody of logically ordered language presented a vision of absurdity which not only pointed towards the meaninglessness of the world, but also called into question the integrity of the individual who confronts it. Beckett's characters are caught between the basic need to encapsulate their unique identity and the impossibility of doing so. Identity can be expressed only within the framework of language, since to pass beyond language is to pass into silence and non-being, and yet language is hackneyed and impure. Thus the contours of 'characters' who are no more than fragile linguistic constructs become blurred, and identities become at least partially interchangeable. Now, not only is our world devoid of meaning and our actions ridiculously futile, our language is suspect and yet we are trapped within it, so that our very identity as individuals is a dubious fiction. This is far from the existentialist belief in the freedom to shape the self or to construct an original and coherent book. Apparently nothing is left but a tissue of language compulsively filling the void and questioning itself – and perhaps laughter at the crazy incongruity of it all.

Modernism and post-modernism

Let us now consider, not so much the general movements of feeling and opinion which were widespread in Europe in these years, but how the leading writers and artists and the deepest thinkers were responding to the spiritual crisis of the age.

Structuralism

The end of existentialism came, as we have seen, with the realisation that its secure fortress to which consciousness retreated, the freedom of the transcendental self at the heart of consciousness, is really a kind of dream, a piece of philosophical wishful thinking. For if there were such a centre of the self, it would have to be possible to discern it as it expressed itself in some pure expression of free consciousness, with all the illusory and uncertain structures of tradition and old philosophies and rational constructions wiped away to reveal pure consciousness itself alone. And this just cannot be done.

The impossibility of such a pure expression comes out in the impossibility of 'innocent' writing; that is, of writing which could be completely free of traditions and inherited value-systems and pre-specified ways of understanding. All writing is already involved with some such structures; and since our traditions are always involved with failure and the crimes and disasters of history, all writing is 'complicit' with these failures and crimes, however it may try to approach all issues with the best of good intentions, in a spirit of pure starting-from-scratch. That was what Roland Barthes meant when he denied the possibility of innocent writing. Equally, the idea that any writing can be the expression of just the fresh response to the world of this one consciousness, the author's, is also an illusion. An author does not have a fresh consciousness which could start from nothing but its own freedom, any more than any human being on earth has such a fresh consciousness. What an author writes should be understood, rather, as an expression of a development of already given structures of thought and value in response to the changing reality of the world. So a reader should not interpret a text by using it as a key to the state of mind and understanding of the author who expressed his or her consciousness in it. Rather, a text should be read as an expression of cultural structures.

This line of thought began as a theory of literary criticism, first argued by Barthes in *Writing Degree Zero* in 1953. But it was never merely a theory about literature (if such theories are ever 'mere'). The reason why a text cannot be interpreted as the expression of a pure individual consciousness is that *nothing* can be interpreted as the expression of a pure individual consciousness; no music, no painting, no face-to-face speech, no looking into the eyes of another person, no love-making – nothing. And since there is no way in which expression of any kind can be innocent, the very idea of a pure transcendental self can only be an illusion – a figment of metaphysical dreaming. It is not just the text which has to be interpreted as a net of structures of cultural tradition; the consciousness which lies behind it is itself nothing but such a net of shifting structures. The tissue and substance of the conscious mind (and of the unconscious mind too) is made up of structures of thought and value and patterns of desire; and behind them there is no transcendental self freely accepting or rejecting these structures as if they were goods on offer in a supermarket. There is no transcendental self at all.

This view, that texts and thought and the life of individuals should be understood in terms of the structures of the cultures in which they are embedded, is what is meant by 'structuralism'. It is essentially connected with the rejection of the idea of a transcendental self.

The structuralist overthrow of existentialism, then, went much further than just to propose a different method of interpreting texts in literature courses in universities. Its implication was that the author, as he or she had previously been conceived, does not exist at all. The author as the constructing, inventing consciousness behind the text, who expresses his or her own individual and original response to the world, owing nothing to anyone, does not exist. Barthes expressed this view, melodramatically perhaps, as 'the death of the author'. 'Death' in this sense: that the *idea* of the author, which for centuries has governed Europe's idea of the source from which ultimately all culture comes, has been destroyed by Europe's development to the point where it has given birth to structuralism. The shock, nostalgia and almost grief which this event produces is like the effect on a family of the death of a loved one on whom the family had relied. A few years later, in the 1960s, Michel Foucault expressed the full implications of the death of the author by speaking of the end of humanism. Individual man as the transcendental source of all culture, free in himself, is now revealed as an illusion. And the effects on our understanding of ourselves, of our hopes, fears and values, are sure to be profound.

The general character of this change was a retreat from the subjective basis to which European culture had ultimately referred all issues. The positive side of modernism, the Enlightenment, the confident assertion of mastery by the advance of knowledge, is detached from the base on which it had previously rested – the faith in the capacity of the pure self to proceed by reason alone towards rational truth. But equally, the negative pole of modernism, the scepticism and doubt, had been understood as resting on the power of the free mind to detach itself from rational schemas and discern for itself that they could not be proved and that their grounds were unsound. The emotion and sense of personal meaning to which the doubting mind then retreated took its value from the idea that it was a genuine, totally individual response. With the advent of structuralism, none of this could still be maintained.

At first sight it might seem that structuralism would lead to a depressing kind of determinism: to the belief that every thought and any feeling that anyone could have has already been determined by the causal forces of society and history. Human beings would really be marionettes, pirouetting around the stage of life imagining that they were important and really doing something, while all the time the forces of the structures of society and history were pulling the strings which moved them. And that may indeed have been the implication of the ideas of the anthropologist Claude Lévi-Strauss, who showed how the cultural life of any society is built on structures of meaning and metaphor; for instance, the pattern of food taboos of the Australian aborigines relate to the structures of their family relationships, of their myths and their picture of the world, to their idea of history, and to the inter-relationship of the different tribes. Indeed, in a way all these structures are just one structure, translated into a different dimension each time. This seems to describe the aborigines' way of understanding the world and themselves, and their ways of acting, as not really the result of any conscious planned decisions by the aborigines themselves but rather as the outcome of these structures underlying their lives, which they themselves did not grasp in a theoretical way at all. But if all societies are like that – including our own – then indeed it seems that it is the structures of culture which really determine everything.

Lévi-Strauss's ideas had great influence on the first generation of structuralist thinkers. But the structuralists who followed him and who made such a strong impact in the 1960s – Barthes, Foucault, Althusser, Todorov – were not at all inclined to see cultural life in this determinist way. Still less were the novelists who wrote under the structuralist influence – Alain Robbe-Grillet, Nathalie Sarraute, Italo Calvino – inclined towards determinism. Rather, they set up texts which are devoid of traditionally recognisable characters and sequential plots and where obsessive language patterns invite the reader to interact with them, sensing the close and intricate influence of the cultural structures. Precisely in this way the reader may be able to discern how the new, fragile and barely attained expression of freedom within and among these structures might be found.

In political terms we could say that these writers wanted to face without any wishful thinking the complexity of the structures of power in society and their capacity to 'recuperate' (i.e. turn to their own purposes) all attempts to overcome or mitigate them by a progressive social or political movement. Calvino called this pervasive power 'the Labyrinth'. But still he wanted, as arguably they all wanted, to reveal the possibility of a 'Challenge to the Labyrinth', not by escaping from it completely – that was impossible – but by a continued and constantly renewed effort of fighting for what could be seen to make some freedom possible, some renewal of humanity.

Post-structuralism

In 1967 three remarkable books were published by the French thinker Jacques Derrida. In them Derrida made clear that, like the structuralists, he rejected the idea of a transcendental self and a pure consciousness, and that he accepted the view of thought as a deep entanglement of traditions of cultural understandings. But the main focus of his thought was on the indeterminacy of the way these traditions exerted their continuing influence within texts; and indeed on the precarious, shifting nature of these traditions – the structures – themselves. He wanted, he later said, to make these structures *tremble*; or rather, to show that they already trembled and shook and were not fixed, and that there is a perpetual tendency to go wrong in interpreting tradition by thinking of it as if its meaning had finally been determined. The way to show this is to examine the texts themselves in which these structures appear, which carry the cultural traditions in which we live, and *deconstruct* them; that is, interpret them so as to show their shifting, fragile character, in which their own internal tensions break down all attempts to find fixed meanings for them.

The idea of deconstruction proved enormously influential. Derrida himself was not very attached to the label 'deconstructionist', which journalists applied to his work, because he viewed all such labels as misleading in suggesting that there is a clear doctrine and defined method for people to adopt, whereas (he thought) all thinking must be acutely aware of its own tendency to pretend to a fixity which it cannot have. People also labelled his thought 'post-structuralist', thinking that it was a new movement in philosophy and came after structuralism, and that its attack on fixity of interpretation must be an attack on structuralism with its belief in structures.

This is clearly too crude a view; the structuralists never wanted to see the structures they studied as determinate. But what is true is that Derrida brought into much clearer view a way in which thinkers could do what structuralists had always wanted to do: to reveal within texts the complexity of interplay of cultural structures and the element of possible freedom in the way new texts and new thinking can use their own traditions. So in that sense it is true that there is a movement which can be called 'post-structuralism'. At any rate, after 1967 philosophy, literary criticism and avant-garde writing could never be the same again. There is a new focus on difference as such; on the possibility of writing and thinking in a way which looks outside its own framework to the different, the Other.

Who, besides Derrida himself, could be said to be part of this movement? We should notice the appearance of an important group of feminist thinkers, who brought together Derrida's thought of difference with the idea that women as such think in a way which is more open to difference than the thought of most men. In the 1970s and 1980s a new generation of women thinkers and writers – Julia Kristeva, Luce Irigaray, Hélène Cixous – took up this idea and developed the idea that women's thought-styles can carry further the post-structuralist focus on difference and plurality.

Post-modernism

Let us now draw these threads together. The governing conception of Europe, as a cultural focus for the late twentieth century, is that of modernism. We have seen how the overthrow of existentialism really undercuts both the positive side of modernism, and its sceptical and doubting negative side. The crucial question for late-twentieth-century Western culture then becomes, how is modernism to be rethought; or, if we abandon modernism, what do we need to put in its place? This question remains open. But one answer has come into view. This is the thought that modernism has been succeeded by a culture of post-modernism. According to this view (put forward by the American Martin Berman and the French thinker Jean-François Lyotard), modernism, in bringing everything back to the basis of thought in a single self-determining consciousness, imposes a simple, one-centred system on all understanding, at least as the direction in which thought should go.

The overthrow of the idea of the transcendental self should be understood as the overthrow of this ideal of one-centred, single-picture understanding. Instead we have to get used to thinking of a world in which there are always many perspectives, many viewpoints, which are never resolved into one right one. Difference, multiplicity, relation to others whom we do not fully understand, is what a post-modern society is like for everyone in it, and not just for those who have not acquired the established, final, approved view of the elite who know. On this view, post-structuralism is really the philosophy of a post-modern condition of life.

Whether this view is right or fruitful, it is as yet (1999) too early to say. What is clear is that these movements will have a very marked effect on how the Europeans can conceive of their own imperfect unity-in-difference, in their renewed attempts to understand what it is to be European. To some extent there is already in a number of domains a shift in focus from the exploration of difference to the notion of the extension of consensus, but consensus which can never be other than provisional, multi-faceted, and problematic.

Further reading

(a) You should read a few of the notable post-war European novels and plays published since 1945, choosing some from different countries. Possible authors you might read include George Orwell, Heinrich Böll, Gunther Grass, Christa Wolf, Friedrich Dürrenmatt, Simone de Beauvoir, Samuel Beckett, Albert Camus, Alain Robbe-Grillet, Italo Calvino, Milan Kundera, and Alexander Solzhenitsyn.

(b) You could usefully study the following books on movements of thought and culture:

Baumann, Z. (1992) *Postmodernity and its Discontents*, Routledge, London.

Hoffmann, S. and Kitromilides, P. (1981): *Culture and Society in Contemporary Europe*, George Allen & Unwin, London.

Hughes, H.S. and Wilkinson, J. (1991) *Contemporary Europe: a History*, 7th edn, Prentice-Hall, Englewood Cliffs.

Jervis, J. (1998) *Exploring the Modern: Patterns of Western Culture and Civilisation*, Blackwell, Oxford.

Kearney, R. (1986) *Modern Movements in European Philosophy*, Manchester University Press, Manchester.

Maier, C. S. (1988) *The Unmasterable Past: History, Holocaust and German National Identity*, Harvard University Press, Harvard, MA.

Ramet, S.P. (ed.) (1994): *Rocking the State: Rock Music and Politics in Eastern Europe and Russia*, Westview Press, Boulder, CO.

14 Living with diversity? Nation-states and national identities in contemporary Europe

A notable fact about human beings in modern political systems is their tendency to define themselves as part of an identified group, such as a nation, which goes far beyond the immediate communities, rooted in family, locality, or workplace, to which they tangibly belong. Both nationalism, and a universalised sense of national identity, are essentially modern phenomena. Of course, it is neither the case that a sense of national identity automatically makes one a nationalist; nor that even a 'shared' national identity will necessarily evoke the same response in different individuals. Two people may both 'feel' German or British; but whereas one may take pride in a perception of past or present national 'greatness', the other may feel shame and even pain in a perception of past or present injustices perpetrated in the country's name. National identity, after all, is a complex phenomenon – the product of complex interactions between social, economic, political, and cultural histories. Moreover, one's sense of national identity is rarely one's only politically significant identity, even when it is of prime importance to the individual; national identity coexists with identities rooted in region, class, religion, gender, sexuality, etc.

Identification with a nation need not be an identification with only one such group. For example, one might be proud to be Welsh as well as British. One might identify oneself as a supporter of the football club Juventus, a citizen of Turin, a Roman Catholic, and an Italian, all together; as well as a European perhaps. So these group identifications about which people feel so strongly can and do overlap, in multiple identities. Sometimes they reinforce each other: a citizen of the Irish Republic may feel Irish partly as a Catholic, so that Catholicism and Irishness reinforce each other. Sometimes they challenge each other: an Irish Protestant, Jew, or atheist, living in what has been until recently a devoutly Catholic society, may reject attempts to conflate Irish national identity with membership of one religious denomination and argue for a more inclusive and pluralist definition of 'Irishness'. Above all group identifications change, as societies change. Nowhere does a sense of national identity remain static. As with all identities, national identity is constantly reinterpreted and reconstructed, even if some nationalist political movements, appealing to myths of racial or cultural 'purity', seek to obscure this fact.

Many of the more powerful group identifications are associated with institutions such as the Church or the state. These institutions build up their strength by doing all they can to promote in their supporters a sense of identification and loyalty. The state in modern times takes measures on an extensive scale to build up a sense of nationhood in its citizens, to make people think of themselves as loyal Greeks or loyal Swedes and so on, and moreover to disseminate the belief that it is the state which embodies the sense of nationhood shared by at least a majority of those living within its boundaries. The success, or otherwise, of the state in disseminating this belief will critically affect the extent to which ruling elites enjoy political legitimacy (that is, a widespread acceptance, active or passive, of their right to exercise state power in the name of the collective group).

This relates to another characteristic of the modern era: the fact that most modern states tend to be nation-states, the territorial limits of which are justified by reference to the perceived common national characteristics of a majority of those inhabiting the state's territory. In so far as features of physical geography – such as oceans, seas, or mountain ranges – may contribute to cultural differentiation between peoples, the myth of 'natural state frontiers' may be deployed by those engaged in the process of nation-state building. Of course the reality is that – geography notwithstanding – few, if any, states in modern Europe are ethnically or nationally homogeneous. There are few universally or even commonly perceived 'natural' frontiers. Furthermore, European history has been marked – and looks set to be marked for some time to come – by disputes between the rival aspirations of peoples and ambitions of their rulers, on the one hand, and by the increasingly necessary search for a means of defusing potentially violent conflicts and accommodating clashing identities within a 'common European home', on the other.

National feeling can arise in people even if they are not already united in a state. Often (but not always) demands may be made for some degree of national self-government, or even outright independence from an existing state. A group of people who have come to regard themselves as distinctive may seek the institutional structure of a state to uphold and to maintain their own special features – language and culture, for instance, or a commonly shared religion, or sufficient respect for people who share their (perceived) national characteristics. Frequently, the belief that economic prosperity and advancement will be facilitated by a degree of self-government or independence adds powerful stimulus to the emergence of a movement seeking to articulate a sense of national identity in terms of 'self-determination', that is, a nationalist movement.

Though many states have come into existence as a result of such nationalist movements, they are almost never ethnically uniform; there are nearly always different ethnic groups within the state, and often some of these groups identify themselves as being of different 'nations'. So a modern nation-state is a paradox. It is supposed to be a state which is the institutional organisation of one nation on a definite territory whose borders it protects, but frequently it is also a state which holds together as citizens people of different ethnic groups, some of which may well think of themselves as separate nations. Thus Spain holds together the

Castilians of the centre, the Basques of the north-east, the Catalans of the east, the Galicians of the west, and the Andalusians of the south; Switzerland holds together the people of the different cantons, speaking four different languages and belonging to two different major religious groupings; the United Kingdom holds together England, Wales, Scotland and Northern Ireland; Russia holds together many different semi-autonomous nations and ethnic groups; Belgium holds together French speakers (Walloons) and Flemish speakers (Flemings), and so on. It is therefore normal for a state to have to operate with some potential for political danger arising from these separate national groupings within it.

How dangerous such tensions can be was shown in a terrible fashion when Yugoslavia broke up from 1991. Many people identified themselves as Slovenes, Croats, Serbs, Montenegrins, Muslims, Hungarians, Macedonians, Albanians, Romanies (Gypsies), and amongst several of these peoples aspirations and demands for separate states – or, in the case of the Serbs, for dominance within the Yugoslav state – were manipulated and exacerbated by ambitious and sometimes ruthless political leaders. In practice many people were of mixed ethnicity, and at the start of the 1980s more than one million people (5.4 per cent of the total population of Yugoslavia) refused all 'divisive' national categories and simply defined themselves as 'Yugoslav' (Kellas, 1998: 21). Moreover, even where people defined themselves as Serbs, Croats and so on, they were frequently intermingled in adjoining villages and in the same villages and towns throughout the southern Balkans. Thus it was never completely obvious where the boundaries of new states should be. Extreme nationalist forces fought each other to try to secure territory which could be regarded as Croatia, or Serbia, etc. In such tragic situations, even individuals who have no desire to participate in wars, and whose sense of belonging to a common humanity transcends the narrow confines of nationalism, are often forced to identify with one group or another. Only in that way can they obtain protection, by being regarded as potential citizens of one or another incipient or possible nation-state.

The basis of these identifications is quite various. It can be language, though most states have substantial minorities speaking different languages from the majority. It can be just a matter of decision when two people are regarded as speaking a different language rather than just variant forms or dialects of one language. Or the criterion can be religious; for example, when by the Treaty of Lausanne of 1923 it was agreed to end the Greek–Turkish war by resettling a million 'Greeks' in the territories designated as part of Greece and a million 'Turks' in the territories designated as part of Turkey, the criterion which determined whether a person was Greek or Turkish was whether they were Christian or Muslim. As a result, many Turkish-speaking Christians found themselves labelled Greek and removed to Greece. In the eastern parts of Poland the criterion determining whether someone was Polish or Ukrainian was partly linguistic and partly whether the person was Roman Catholic or Orthodox (at least by family tradition). And in Bosnia the group whose ancestors had once favoured a Christian heresy and had largely adopted Islam subsequently, became identified as the 'nation' of Muslim Bosnians who later suffered such losses in the Bosnian war of the 1990s.

It has also often been supposed that another criterion for classifying peoples as belonging to one national group or another might be 'racial'. The use of this idea is nearly always dangerous. Europe in the twentieth century has been scarred indelibly by the murder of millions of men, women, and children on the grounds of alleged 'racial impurity'. And in fact this notion of determinate characteristics of a race is an illusion or a myth. People do, of course, differ in their physical appearance, and this is to a large extent determined by their genetic inheritance. But every human being inherits a very mixed set of genes, and people's appearance (colour of skin etc.), intelligence, and moral character vary very greatly, so that there are no coherent groups in which people can all be said to be of the same 'race' in the sense of physical, intellectual, or moral characteristics. Indeed, the latest scientific research shows that gene differences between individual members of the same ethnic group or race are much more significant than differences between actual ethnic groups or races, thus undermining any scientific basis to racism. Racism is therefore a myth, though a powerful one. It differentiates human beings from one another by constructing an entirely spurious hierarchy of 'superior' and 'inferior' peoples on the basis of what are supposed to be inherited genetic features, both physical and (in association with these physical features) behavioural qualities of 'character'. This view – allied to nationalism – has been symptomatic of the far right of the European political spectrum, especially its Nazi and fascist variants.

Over and above these criteria of nationhood everything depends on what people *feel* themselves to be. It is important to pay attention to the *idea of a nation* which people care about and in which they believe, and to bear in mind that such ideas are obviously subject to historical change. Benedict Anderson (1983) calls a nation an 'imagined community'; imagined, that is, by people who go along with the idea of the nation. Its basis is a sort of vision of collective identity, history, and so on, but on this basis the community can become very real indeed. To establish such an idea which can grip people's imagination it is necessary to have a history, a tradition – or at least to believe in such a history or tradition. (Many national traditions are in fact invented, exaggerated, or distorted ones, like the Spanish history of El Cid, the medieval warrior who fought the Moors, or the Hungarian tradition of the horsemen of the Milky Way who will return to aid the Hungarians in their hour of need; and there are much more recent – and widely accepted – examples also.) So attempts to build up the idea of a particular nation often involve the invention or bolstering up of a tradition, as well as the accentuation of the special distinguishing features of a nation, like its language or its folk songs. The Finnish independence movement of the nineteenth century involved the collection of fragmentary ancient stories and myths and putting them together as a coherent set of stories, the *Kalevala*, to play the role of the national tradition of the Finns, while the folk-musical traditions of Finns were raised by the great composer Sibelius to the status of the national music.

Nationalist movements

It is clear that movements which make loyalty to a nation central to their purpose will have a very different character depending on whether they direct their appeal to the dominant national group in an existing nation-state, or to a minority which seeks separation to form its own state. The former might be called a *status quo movement*; its purpose will tend to be the assertion of the unity of the existing nation-state and therefore it will tend to play down other loyalties and other divisions within the state (notably class divisions and the status of ethnic minorities). The latter is a *disruptive movement*, which seeks to limit or break the power of the existing state in order to detach part of its territory. It is also possible that an ethnic nationalist movement might seek the advancement or protection of its own ethnic group within a (reformed or decentralised) nation-state without seeking actual separation, or that such a movement might be only pushed to a separatist or 'disruptive' stance by the intransigence of the existing state. Status quo nationalist movements do not necessarily want to leave everything as it is. They may be opposed to forces in the state which emphasise divisions within it, like movements for social change or parties which represent the workers against the middle class. The Franco regime in Spain (1939–75), the Salazar regime in Portugal (1926–74), and the regime of the Greek colonels (1967–74) are examples of authoritarian regimes which invoked defence of the status quo and preservation of the existing nation-state in attempted justification of their repression.

The most dangerous status quo nationalist movements (from the point of view of democracy and stability) are those which add to their promotion of national unity in their state (a) hostility to particular minority groups within the state, and (b) aggressive hostility towards other nations in other states. European history can show many examples of nationalism of this kind, and there is ground for serious concern that manifestations of reaction and resentment against immigrants, now widespread in Europe, might develop into such more extreme forms of anti-democratic, aggressive, and minority-persecuting nationalism. The risks of such movements in contemporary Europe will be considered shortly. But it is important to remember that not all status quo nationalist movements, either on the right or the left, reach these extreme forms.

Disruptive nationalism – since it is based on the discontent of its supporters with their place within existing states – is sometimes apt to be more populist, invoking the loyalty of ordinary people whilst attacking the existing social, political, economic, or cultural hierarchy. Like status quo nationalism, such movements have milder and more extreme forms. In their mild form they shade off into cultural movements promoting minority culture in the form of language and literature, folk music, and so on. They assume a disruptive form (in the sense of demanding political change) when they seek some kinds of special rights for the minority (such as teaching in the minority language in schools) which can easily develop into demands for a degree of local self-government. Sometimes, perhaps in response to state repression or due to frustration with their inability to command sufficient support through democratic channels, such movements can produce a wing which is prepared to use violence to secure total independence. The IRA (Irish Republican Army) in Northern Ireland and ETA in the Basque lands of Spain are examples of such groups. By the end of the 1990s both these movements were seeking ways of advancing their causes through less violent methods, having apparently learned that states which enjoy a high degree of democratic legitimacy cannot easily be brought to their knees through terrorism. In the 1990s the Corsican nationalist movement, though it has an extreme wing seeking separation from France through armed force, mostly operates as a movement seeking only a degree of local autonomy and recognition of the Corsican language.

On the other hand, the nationalist movements in Latvia, Lithuania, and Estonia applied peaceful mass pressure to obtain total independence in 1991 from the state which had previously exercised sovereignty over them (the Soviet Union). Such movements (in so far as they use peaceful methods) may be tolerated by the existing state structure, and their demands to some degree conceded, as they have been by Spain and Belgium, which have tried in this way to defuse the potential danger from the separatist movements of the Basques, the Catalans, and the Flemings.

Alternatively, the state may resist the demands of ethnic groups and find itself in this way confronted with demands for total secession backed by the threat of force. Such a situation may develop into one of endemic terrorism and state repression, as in Turkey in its relations with its Kurdish minority, or in Britain during the 1916–21 period in its relation with Irish nationalists.

Disruptive or revolutionary nationalist movements are often led and inspired by middle-class people who feel that their social, political, or economic ambitions are being thwarted within the existing state, and that they are being excluded, because of their nationality, from the important positions in society to which they feel entitled. To understand why this is so we need to realise that the modern nation-state is (among other things) a way of organising the job opportunities and career paths of people in a complex modern economy, in which many jobs require expertise so that candidates for them have to be found through some open competitive system. The state's institutional framework for this system of competition always favours the official culture and the official language, and in this way talented people with energy and organisational capacity may feel themselves to be held back by this power structure, and so come to support movements which give some kind of recognition to their own different culture; they may even reach the point of supporting revolutionary nationalism.

The question arises, then, how such movements will relate to social issues and class conflict. This is an issue which has perplexed and confounded the European left throughout its history. Many socialists have argued that nationalist movements are regressive, opposed to socialist internationalism and to workers' interests. This may be because they have the effect of dividing workers along national or ethnic lines; or because, in the name of what they claim is the 'national interest', they submerge or suppress issues pertaining to social injustice and class inequality. But other socialists have argued that they may represent the interests of workers because of their perceived anti-imperialist and democratic character, and that the class structure of modern states rather often operates by suppressing both minority cultures and the workers who share them.

State strategies for dealing with national or ethnic minorities

The paradox of the nation-state, described above, implies that virtually every state will have a more or less serious problem with minorities. How can they try to deal with it in contemporary Europe? Various strategies can be distinguished.

Melting pot assimilation

This strategy involves submerging by every possible means any separate national feeling within the state, so as to strengthen as much as possible the new nation which is to be formed on the basis of the sense of identification with a new state. The classic example of this strategy in the nineteenth and twentieth centuries is the USA, which had such a large and various influx of immigrants that this seemed the only tactic which could build any sense of 'Americanness'. In Europe there is no real example of this since new states have always been based on one existing ethnic group. Lenin and the early Bolsheviks certainly envisaged in the immediate post-1917 period that the new Soviet Union would solve the problem of national and ethnic tensions through a process of 'melting pot assimilation', the end product being a new Soviet national identity. But under Stalin especially, such ideals were all but reduced to empty rhetoric as Russian nationalism and Russian domination of other national groups took centre-stage again under the guise of Soviet patriotism.

One-nation dominance

The end goal of this strategy is apparently very similar; but the sense of national identity which the state seeks to promote is that of an existing nation or ethnic group, already present as the most powerful (and usually the majority) element in the state. In fact the two strategies operate very differently, since the dominance strategy places citizens on an unequal footing depending on whether they are, to start with, already members of the dominant ethnic group or are members of a minority group which it is the state's policy to extinguish as a separate group. It is thus more likely to arouse resentment.

Such a strategy has been applied by, for example, Poland, which after the end of the Second World War transferred great numbers of its citizens of Ukrainian background and language to a part of Poland (the north-west) remote from their former homes and from other Ukrainians, and dispersed them in isolated pockets while giving them a purely Polish education. The idea was that in a generation or two they would feel themselves to be simply Polish, and so become loyal members of the Polish nation. Several of the states which emerged from the break-up of Yugoslavia in the early 1990s – notably Serbia and Croatia – applied similar strategies under the slogan of 'ethnic cleansing'. Indeed, the brutal imposition of one-nation dominance by the Serbs upon the overwhelmingly Albanian population of the region of Kosovo in the late 1990s provoked a new civil conflict as Serb forces attacked Albanian civilians and the newly formed Albanian Kosova Liberation Army (KLA) retaliated with attacks on Serbs. 1999 saw a massive escalation of this conflict as the Serb-dominated Yugoslav army, assisted by paramilitary terrorists, drove almost one million Albanian civilians from their homes into refugee camps in neighbouring countries, thousands of Albanian men were kidnapped and feared murdered, and NATO responded with massive airstrikes upon targets in Yugoslavia. NATO's goal was implementation of an agreement which would end one-nation dominance in Kosovo whilst leaving Kosovo as a semi-autonomous region of Serbia. The total lack of trust on both sides, and the ascendancy of a virulently chauvinist leadership in Serbia, boded ill for future stability.

A less bloody variant of the strategy of one-nation dominance was attempted in some of the Baltic states, to discourage their large Russian minorities from exerting an unwelcome influence in states which were founded precisely to get away from the power of Russia. Whilst Lithuania offered automatic citizenship to its Russian speakers, Estonia and, especially, Latvia imposed a second-class status upon their Russian-speaking populations after independence. Latvia's denial of citizenship to Russian speakers and their descendants unless they officially 'naturalised' after passing stringent language tests meant that around one-third of the country's population of 2.6 million people had no right to vote, had their housing and social benefits removed or reduced, and were branded as 'aliens'. A combination of pressure and threats of economic sanctions from Russia, and dire warnings from the European Union that such discriminatory policies would jeopardise Latvia's chances of greater integration with the EU, forced a retreat in October 1998. In a referendum, 53 per cent of Latvians voted to give passports to all children of Russian speakers born in Latvia since independence and to make it easier for older Russian speakers to gain passports also.

In the case of most European states the nation has been established for a long time as based on its dominant ethnic group, with usually one official language and an education system and broadcasting system which favours that group and its traditions. For such long-established states a one-nation dominance strategy is unnecessary. For any state such a strategy is a high-risk option because it involves an active suppression of the special characteristics of the minority groups it seeks to merge into the dominant nation; for example, a suppression of their language, their religion, even sometimes their national dress (as with Highland dress in Scotland in the late eighteenth century). If, in their resentment at this, they resist by founding nationalist movements, a one-nation dominance strategy involves active suppression of these movements, which, as we have seen, can lead to a vicious spiral of violence. Quite apart from the undemocratic nature of such policies, the implications for both long-term political stability and human rights are usually pretty grim.

An extreme form of one-nation dominance strategy is the attempt to eliminate a minority (or all minorities) altogether from the territory of a state, by forced mass emigration or by genocide. The most recent large-scale European examples of mass expulsions at the time of writing are the expulsions of Germans from east of the Oder–Neisse Line (the new Polish border) and from Czechoslovakia in 1945–46, and the refugee exodus from former Yugoslavia which had reached more than 800,000 by the end of 1998, with a further 4.5 million persons left displaced or homeless within the former state. It seems very likely that any lasting settlement in Bosnia, Kosovo or other parts of the Balkans will involve further large transfers of population so as to produce less ethnically mixed mini-states. Genocide as a policy of one-nation dominance has cast its infamous shadow over European history in the Nazi Holocaust of World War II, in which six million Jews, about a million Poles, and 400,000 Romanies (not to mention trade unionists and socialists, homosexuals, and others who failed to fit the Nazi image of being a true German) were exterminated. But though the Holocaust is unique in its scale (so far), the strategy has been applied by other racially motivated nationalists, as by the Turks in 1915–16 against the Armenians and by the Serbs in the 1990s ('ethnic cleansing') against the Muslim Bosnians and Kosova Albanians. There is a continuing risk that any extreme nationalism could use the tactic; from the extremist's point of view, it has the great attraction of seeming to be a 'Final Solution' of the problem of minorities (though it is never really a final solution).

One-nation hegemony with tolerance

This strategy is different from the dominance strategy because it does not seek the legal or violent suppression of minority cultures. Instead, it seeks to use state power to 'discourage' them in the hope that they will fade away, being gradually displaced by the officially backed culture of the dominant nation. For instance, the language of the law courts, of government, and of the education system is the language of the dominant ethnic group; the best job opportunities in practice go to those with the right language (or dialect) and culture; the history and traditions taught in schools and favoured in the official broadcasting system are those of the dominant group. Such a policy relies on the minority group's language, traditions, and so on, fading away as the style of an older generation, without arousing too active a resentment. This is the sort of policy allegedly followed by France and the United Kingdom, and with some success. But one should remember that Britain's attempt to apply such a policy in Ireland in the period 1800–1916 ultimately failed. Although the Irish language suffered irreparable damage as the spoken language of most Irish people, great resentments were aroused, and discontent took a nationalist form, so that active nationalism arose and – after bloody conflict – led to the secession of most of Ireland from the United Kingdom in 1921. Italy has had a long-standing problem of a similar kind in the Austrian national feeling of many people in the Italian Tyrol (Südtirol). Attempts to assimilate these people led to bomb outrages in protest at

Italianisation, but the situation was defused by the retreat of the Italian government from an assimilation policy to the strategy of regional pluralism.

Regional pluralism

Not all minorities occupy definite regions within a state. Indeed many of central Europe's Romanies (Gypsies) follow a wandering life all over the countryside, and most Jews in pre-war Europe were scattered over central and eastern Europe, living usually in towns. Nor is the problem of immigrant groups one for which there could be a regional solution. But where a minority *does* occupy a particular region, one possible strategy for the state is to grant the region a substantial degree of self-government. Under such a system the regional government will support the culture and language of the ethnic group dominant within the region, but within the framework of the state which holds sovereignty over it. This solution has been applied quite widely in post-war Europe, and especially since 1980. Switzerland has long had a federal structure giving local power to its separate cantons, and it is in this way that a state containing four language groups and two main religions has been able to hold together. Similarly in 1948–49 the representatives of the *Länder* who set up the constitution of the FRG reserved a great deal of power to the separate *Länder*.

Belgium has responded to growing tensions between its two language groups by devolving power in the state to three regions, a Walloon region, a Flemish region, and a Brussels central region. Spain, after the death of Franco, decided on a strongly devolved structure, in which the strong sense of regional loyalties, especially in Catalonia, in the Basque region, and in Galicia could be satisfied. But such policies are also risky. They can easily develop in either direction. They can encourage the sense of separateness of regional ethnic groups as distinct nationalities, and so lead to the break-up of the state or to substantial clashes between separatists and the state (arguably, something like this happened in Slovakia's separation from Czechoslovakia). Alternatively, the sovereignty of the state can exert itself to make sure that the concessions to minority identity are just tokens and that the real power still rests with the dominant group. To succeed, the strategy of regional pluralism would seem to require a fairly well-developed civil society with wide acceptance by both the state and the political movements representing various national groupings of the values of democratic tolerance and constitutional rule.

The Soviet Union – in which these conditions were absent – landed itself with the worst of both worlds. In the 1920s it encouraged the sense of separateness of its component nations, so that they came to feel more of a sense of separate nationhood as a result; while from the 1930s the separate nations were in fact suppressed, thus arousing resentments which ultimately contributed to the break-up of the state.

Cultural pluralism

This strategy tries to accommodate the policy of the state to the reality of the pluralist, multi-ethnic character of all states, and especially (perhaps) of modern European states. The aim is to acknowledge this reality and use the state as a legal framework holding together many different kinds of people with different cultures which should all – so far as possible – be recognised and encouraged. This leads to the idea that national identity is not ethnic – that it does not depend on particular cultural characteristics or possessions like language – but is simply that of a citizen of the state.

This inclusive nationalism fits well with the ideology of liberalism, which conceives of the state as a neutral legal framework within which people can each pursue their own lifestyles. But, in practice, application of the strategy meets with severe difficulties. For one thing, the role of the state in a modern economy, as explained above, favours a single official language and a reasonably uniform education system to ensure reliable qualifications acceptable throughout the state. For another, the sense of identity on which modern states build the loyalty of their citizens tends to need more content than just the idea of a state with a particular name and flag. People associate the state with the dominant culture within it, and this tends to be thought of as the identity of the nation. So the old Soviet Union, though its constitution recognised many component nationalities within it, tended to be thought of as 'Russia' and its citizens as Russians even when they were Ukrainians, Lithuanians, or Uzbeks. This corresponded to the reality that the Russian language and Russian culture were the ones which were promoted and encouraged by the state and by the CPSU, and the fact that ethnic Russians tended to occupy the best jobs and the most powerful positions.

Even apart from the direct influence of the state, minority languages have difficulty in maintaining more than a peripheral status in a modern economy, since most parents want their children to learn and use the language which will enable them to succeed in the job market, and time spent on minority languages is time not spent on chemistry, or geography, or some other 'useful' subject.

Sometimes a policy of cultural pluralism is legally entrenched as a system of minority rights; sometimes, indeed, such a system of legal minority rights is demanded by international pressure or treaty obligations. The League of Nations in the 1920s tried to protect Europe's minorities by requiring member states to grant specific rights to minorities. The policy failed, but it may be that it did so mainly because of the more general failure of the League of Nations. The most disastrous problems were those of German minorities in Czechoslovakia and Poland, and Nazi Germany was not interested in protection of Germans by the League, of which, in any case, it had ceased to be a member in 1934. Perhaps the prospects for protection of minority rights are better since 1945, but the policy is still fraught with dangers and difficulties. Since 1975 the human rights clauses of the Helsinki Final Act have contained some provision for protection for minority groups, but these have not so far been very effective. The reason for this is not only lack of will; to implement any *general* form of protection for minorities is very difficult, since entrenched positions for special groups cannot be made available to every group, and it seems nearly impossible to formulate criteria for how big or how different or how vulnerable a group needs to be to deserve protection. Nevertheless, the prospect of possible future admission to, or association with, the European Union (with all its economic advantages) is sufficiently attractive to many states of eastern Europe for the EU to be able to exert a considerable influence in favour of tolerance and liberal democratic standards.

The main problems of ethnic feeling in contemporary Europe

Regional self-government and inter-regional disputes

These problems are substantially different in the old communist bloc and in western Europe.

Central and eastern Europe
The removal of the old structures of authority with the fall of the communist governments led to a situation in which people were uncertain what political authority might ultimately be established. In some cases the fragility of state structures and political institutions in the post-communist period, combined with uncertainty about the future, made many people afraid that their own national group or region might lose out, unless as much local control as possible was established. This was especially true, perhaps, of many of the semi-autonomous regions and republics of Russia – rich in natural resources and anxious to by-pass central control from Moscow. In addition, economic instability, poverty and high unemployment fuelled fear and discontent. The situation was ripe for ambitious and often unscrupulous political leaders – many of them recycled from the old communist ruling *nomenklatura* – to whip up prejudice and ultimately aggression against vulnerable minorities who could be made the scapegoats for society's problems by being portrayed as undermining the cohesion of the national group, or seeking to attack it or gain advantages over it.

Both Russia and eastern Europe are ethnically very mixed; every state contains substantial minorities and the concept of ethnically 'natural' boundaries between one state and another is potentially a very dangerous myth. To add to the instability, the area has a confused and destructive history of national and ethnic conflicts, so that many families retain sad and bitter memories of past injustices which can easily give rise to present-day hatreds. It is precisely these 'historical experiences of national humiliation' which can be whipped up into 'ethnic paranoia' (Caplan and Feffer, 1996: 219) by political elites seeking to advance their own careers on the back of national chauvinism. Against this the main force preventing the descent of the whole area into conflict is the people's own awareness of how futile, destructive, and terrible such conflicts are. Moreover, common economic interests are beginning to pull countries of eastern Europe together into an array of regional organisations in the 1990s. There are a surprising number of possible conflicts in the area which have not (so far) got out of hand; the peaceful separation of the Czech Republic and Slovakia in 1992, the avoidance of *serious* conflicts arising from the presence of sizeable ethnic minorities in Romania, Bulgaria, Slovakia, and the Baltic republics, and so on. That said, the prevalence of 'narratives of victimization and of threat, linking the present with the past and projecting onto the future' (Brubaker, 1996: 74) remains a frightening danger.

Just how dangerous such narratives can be is, of course, illustrated by the terrible examples of the war between Serbia and Croatia, the awful Bosnian war which began in 1992, and the war between Serbia and the Kosovo Albanians which began in earnest in 1998 (following almost a decade of Serb attempts to impose their dominance in Kosovo). It is possible that eventually a counter-movement of unification may set in, because of the substantial economic ties connecting the different regions and states, making them mutually dependent on each other. But it seems very likely that the pattern for any such overarching structure will not be a reunification of separate states into one larger state, but looser arrangements of economic connection.

Western Europe

In western Europe the people of richer regions may feel that poorer regions of the same state are living off their backs and holding them back; whilst the people of poorer regions may feel trapped in a relationship of underdevelopment, exploitation and worsening dependency. For the richer regions, there are two possible tactics in this situation: to get control of the central government and make it reduce its subventions to the poorer regions by free market policies, or to split off the richer region from the state. The Northern Leagues in Italy are a movement which veers between these two approaches, combining a neo-liberal assault on central government's public spending with occasional calls for the rich north to secede from the rest of Italy so as to stop having to 'subsidise' the south.

One possible development is that Europe may ultimately operate with the EU as its overarching structure (corresponding to the effective economic unit, the European market as a whole). Within it the units representing territorial interests could be of the size of (present-day) regions like Lombardy or Alsace or Jutland, while existing large states cease to exist or to be significant. Such a structure might be utilised either in the interests of the richer regions, entrenching their position, or as a structure to enable redistribution of wealth and resources from the richer to the poorer regions. But in practice it is mostly those who favour redistribution who tend to favour it. Such a 'Europe of the regions', embodying the 'principle of subsidiarity', would require very drastic changes in the present structure of the EU itself as well as to the entrenched political structures which depend on the existing states.

Of course, most of the larger European states, and some of the smaller ones, have already progressed some way on the road of regionalisation, following the model of Federal Germany. Spain has devolved a great deal of power to its regions, while Italy has devolved quite a lot of power; and Switzerland, Belgium and the Netherlands have long-established entrenched rights for their regions. Under Conservative governments the UK continued to centralise power in London, and in fact was the only large-scale centralised state in the EU. However, following the election of a Labour government in May 1997, constitutional reform – including directly elected regional assemblies for Scotland, Wales and Northern Ireland – sought to change this anomaly. If a devolved structure in the EU as a whole is to serve as a basis for a redistributive polity, the control over its operation exercised by EU institutions themselves – especially the Social and Regional Funds – would have to be much stronger than it is at present. Of course, these considerations provide part of the reason for the strong opposition of sections of the political right to enlargement of the powers of the EU.

Racism and contemporary anti-semitism

Since the latter half of the 1980s there has been a perceptible growth in manifestations of racism and of anti-semitism in many European countries. Regrettably, this is nothing new; they have a long history in European culture, and 'the dark side of Europe' is as much part of Europe's political legacy as the Enlightenment ethos. How far Europe will outgrow them, and how far it is likely to become caught in a vicious spiral of racism and ethnic conflict, is one of the most important issues facing us today.

It is not so difficult, though, to discern some causes of the current wave of racism and anti-semitism. Continuing economic recession seems to have condemned many millions to long-term unemployment and has compounded social problems. The policies pursued by governments show little sign of being able greatly to improve the situation, and many people give up hope in democratic politics, identify closely with a narrow group of their own people, and take out their frustrations in hatred of outsiders.

Racism may appeal to those who feel their material security, or their sense of identity, or both, threatened by processes of change which are too complex to grasp or to control easily.

Racist ideology focuses on *difference* as constituting a threat. Those who are defined as different – the Outsider, the Stranger – are constructed as scapegoats for the resentments and frustrations of ordinary people. In fact, even the physical presence of minority groups is not always necessary for such 'scapegoat' hatreds to become established. It has been noted, for example, that strong anti-semitism has persisted in Poland, despite the fact that the Nazi Holocaust, followed by decades of discrimination at the hands of the Polish Stalinist regime, effectively reduced that country's Jewish community to a tiny handful (currently less than 5,000). Throughout the continent the Jewish community has once again been exposed to insult (manifested in the daubing of Nazi slogans on Jewish graves and synagogues and in attacks on Jews). However, the main targets of racist attacks in recent years have been immigrants, and these attacks have often been associated with prejudices about those with different skin colour, those who are simply desperately poor, and those from predominantly Moslem cultures – not just north African societies, but also Bosnia and Albania, for example.

Immigration and immigrants

Since 1945 Europe has seen very substantial immigration into all the richer countries of western Europe. The immigrants came especially from southern Europe (Italians, Portuguese, Yugoslavs, Spaniards) and from North Africa particularly to France, from the West Indies, India and Pakistan to Britain, from Indonesia to Holland, and from Turkey to Germany. It proved impossible either to send them back again or to keep their families out (though Germany tried to operate both these policies for quite a while), so the outcome in each of these states was a substantial population of people of a different ethnic group from the dominant nation of the state.

In recent years the patterns of immigration have altered. It is estimated that between 1980 and 1992 some 18 million people entered western Europe as migrants. But many of these came as refugees from war and persecution, or in flight from economic collapse, from eastern Europe. It has been estimated that the war in Yugoslavia had left some four million displaced people by the end of 1993, with the international community struggling to prevent a mass exodus westwards.

The recent upsurge in racism is manifest in rising support for far-right political parties and in a sharp increase in physical (often murderous) attacks upon refugees and immigrants, in many western European countries (a 74 per cent increase from 1991 to 1992 in Germany, for instance). Far-right parties which openly advocated policies against immigrant peoples made substantial gains in elections in France, Germany, Italy, Austria, Belgium and Denmark in the 1990s, leading to the presence of neo-fascists in a European government in 1993 for the first time since 1945, in the government of Italy formed by Berlusconi. And the policies of many European parties on the 'respectable' right moved sharply in a racist direction in anti-immigrant policies adopted by, for example, the French interior minister Charles Pasqua in 1993.

In January 1994 the European Commission tried to promote a constructive European policy on immigration by issuing a 'Green Paper'. As a result the member states of the EU agreed to allow easier movement of immigrants between member states without the need for visas, to guarantee security of residence for immigrants and their families, and to outlaw racial discrimination at work. This is to go with moves to reduce migratory pressure on the EU by improving economic and social conditions in the immigrant-exporting countries, and tough moves against illegal immigrants. Whether these agreements will eventually become the law in the member states remains to be seen. A much more controversial development was the decision by the EU in 1995 to fund a barrier on the north African coast to keep illegal immigrants out of Europe. Classified as a military project, this high-tech 8.5 kilometre wall was to be constructed on the border between the Spanish enclave Ceuta and Morocco at a cost of $29 million. Comparisons with the former Berlin Wall and accusations of institutionalised racism in a new 'Fortress Europe' were inevitable.

A big step forward, as far as immigrant rights and status are concerned, was undoubtedly the election of a new Social Democrat–Green coalition government in Germany in October 1998. Germany had long operated one of the most restrictive nationality and citizenship laws, denying even the right to vote to millions of German-born children of immigrants. The new government of Chancellor Gerhard Schröder promised a radical overhaul of the antiquated 'blood and soil' citizenship law, dating from 1913, to make a person's place of birth rather than who their mother was the key criterion in deciding citizenship. The proposed new law – vigorously opposed by the centre-right Christian Democrats as well as the far-right neo-Nazis, of course – was aimed at conferring full citizenship rights on 3 million immigrant children born in Germany, making it easier for several million others to acquire German citizenship (by reducing the length of the residence requirement), and challenging racism head-on by countering an exclusive, blood-based view of what constitutes the national community with an inclusive and democratic view.

The meaning of Europe: an overarching identity?

It has been emphasised in Chapter 12 and at the beginning of this chapter that people's sense of identity is typically multi-faceted, with overlapping loyalties to different groups. Throughout the modern period the nation-state has been the largest, most inclusive, of the *political* groupings with which people have identified. But in Europe since the time of the Ancient Greeks people have also had some sense of being 'European' as a significant kind of identity. The European leaders who set out to build up a European Community (as opposed to merely a pattern of arrangements for limited economic cooperation) sought to build on this sense of 'Europeanness' by making the European Community a *political* unit, with which people could identify politically. Partly they did so to bind together the quarrelsome European nations and so reduce the risk of a recurrence of the European wars which had been so disastrous in 1914–18 and 1939–45. But the project also arose from a deeper sense that the age of the nation-state of moderate size was over; that the political and economic troubles of Europe of the 1930s had resulted from the attempt to organise life in separate units when in fact the activities of these nations intersected so much that they could not construct coherent policies as separate units, and instead fell blindly into destructive policies of injuring each others' interests. The technical, economic, and military conditions of the twentieth century made organised cooperation essential.

In this way the idea of Europe as an overarching political unit, encouraging a plurality of identities in its peoples, came to seem the best solution to Europe's problems. So from the start the European Community was conceived as an overarching entity, a unit of cooperation; not as a replacement for the European nations. It was envisaged that people would feel more vividly the plural character of their identities; that they would feel themselves to be both French and

European (as well as, say, Breton, and a citizen of Dinard, and so on). Such a programme can work only if people feel happy to accept the overarching unit, 'Europe', and if they feel involved in it as participants.

By the end of the 1990s it was clear that there had been a tendency for the EU to be built from above, and that the decision-making processes of the EU were seen as technocratic and elitist, and often heedless of the needs and feelings of the different nations. Indeed, as the constitutional structure of the EU changes from unanimity to majority decisions the prospect of substantial clashes of policy between some member states or parts of the EU's population and the EU as a whole increases; and the larger the EU becomes, and the more extensive the range of competence of its policies, the more such clashes are likely to happen. Thus the sense of an overarching European identity is damaged or overthrown by a fairly widespread feeling that it is associated with structures which are not sufficiently accountable to the peoples of the EU. The scene is thus set for an accumulation of grievances which nationalistic forces, and those nostalgic for the past, may seek to exploit.

So what policy might now be adopted for Europe? On the one hand, *federalists* argue that incremental progress in the direction of economic integration has reached the point where a relaunch of the EU along democratic federalist lines is necessary in order to safeguard and protect European democracy. They envisage a federal European Union, in which a European government elected by and accountable to the European Parliament would share power with regional and national governments and parliaments. Such a Union would have the power to operate a positive policy to ameliorate the ills of European society, to combat regional and sectoral imbalances and tackle the problems of mass unemployment and migration. On the other hand, *anti-federalists* argue that we should construct an EU-wide free market based on free movement of labour, capital, goods and services. Following the Gaullist slogan of *'l'Europe des patries'*, they seek to retain control over political and social matters at the level of the nation-state.

Both the Maastricht and Amsterdam Treaties leave the institutional framework of the EU intergovernmental, rather than supranational, in character. The European Parliament, for example, is still a long way from becoming transformed into a legislature; people refer to the 'democratic deficit': the fact that control of European institutions is a long way from the democratic control of the people, because the European Parliament has so little power. David Marquand (1994) has argued that the European project found itself confronted by four paradoxes as it entered the late 1990s. The first is a paradox of *identity*. Born in the shadow of the Cold War, the identity of the EU was implicitly accepted, originally, as essentially western European, developed, and mainly Roman Catholic. Expansion towards the Protestant north and the non-western and underdeveloped east obviously forces reconsideration of a European identity. Clearly what it is to be European as a citizen of the EU has now become more complex and problematic, culturally, socially and historically.

Second, there is a paradox of *territory*: the more the EU expands and grows, both economically and geographically, the greater the potential imbalance between its prosperous 'core' and its dependent 'periphery', with all the potential for political tension that brings. To overcome this paradox would require mechanisms of redistribution. As has been explained, redistribution requires some significant transfer of power from national governments to EU institutions.

Third, there is the paradox of *supranationalism*. So long as the political control of the EU remains substantially devolved to its member states, it can operate effective policies only if the more powerful of its member states (i.e. especially France and Germany) exert firm and dynamic pressure to get such policies accepted. But the result of the development of the EU is that these states 'have become stronger because they have created a chain of interdependencies which has made it impossible, or at the very least extremely expensive, for them to act unilaterally in certain key areas' (Marquand, 1994: 24). Although they remain the focus for citizens' political loyalties, these interdependencies limit the capacity of nation-states to put in place policies which could effectively resolve the other paradoxes.

Finally, Marquand refers to the paradox of *functionalism*. The very success of the European project to date has brought us to the point where it is no longer clear that the hidden hand of economic integration can of itself deliver an answer to the question, 'What is Europe?' But it is not clear how the political basis for a more extensive function for European institutions could be constructed.

Clearly we cannot really speak of European culture, democracy, or civil society, unless we accept that there is more to 'Europe' than just a marketplace, and more to being a 'European' than just being a consumer – albeit a consumer of a greatly increased range of goods and services. As Jacques Delors, the former President of the European Commission, warned: 'You can't fall in love with a Single Market!'

The construction of the EU has, until recently, been guided largely by technocratic logic. Political elites in the EU have begun to show recognition of the fact that new ways will have to be found of listening to the ordinary peoples of Europe – particularly the tens of millions of unemployed, low-paid and marginalised who feel most threatened and betrayed by socio-economic change – and engaging them seriously with the project of the construction of Europe. This is likely to be the greatest political challenge in the years ahead. As European history shows, the price of failure could be high.

Further reading

Anderson, B. (1983) *Imagined Communities: Reflections on the Origin and Spread of Nationalism*, Verso, London.

Brubaker, R. (1996) *Nationalism Reframed: Nationhood and the National Question in the New Europe*, Cambridge University Press, Cambridge.

Caplan, R. and Feffer, J. (eds) (1996) *Europe's New Nationalism: States and Minorities in Conflict*, Oxford University Press, Oxford.

Cohen, R. (1994) *Frontiers of Identity: the British and the Others*, Longman, London.

Cohn-Bendit, D. (1993) 'Europe and its Borders: the Case for a Common Immigration Policy', in Ogata, S., *et al.*, *Towards a European Immigration Policy*, Philip Morris Institute for Public Policy Research, Brussels.

Harvie, C. (1994) *The Rise of Regional Europe*, Routledge, London.

Hobsbawm, E. (1990) *Nations and Nationalism Since 1780: Programme, Myth, Reality*, Cambridge University Press, Cambridge.

Kellas, J. (1998) *The Politics of Nationalism and Ethnicity*, 2nd edn, Macmillan, Basingstoke.

Marquand, D. (1994) 'Prospects for a Federal Europe. Reinventing Federalism: Europe and the Left', *New Left Review*, No. 203, Jan–Feb., pp.17–26.

Milward, A.S. (1992) *The European Rescue of the Nation State*, Routledge, London.

Ogata, S., *et al.* (1993) *Towards a European Immigration Policy*, Philip Morris Institute for Public Policy Research, Brussels.

Appendix: European regional organisations

1	2	3	4	5	6	7	8	9	10	11	12	13	14	
x	x											x		Albania
x	x											x	x	Armenia
x		x	x	x						x				Austria
x	x											x	x	Azerbaijan
x	x												x	Belarus
x	x	x	x	x	x		x							Belgium
x										x				Bosnia & Hercegovina
x	x		x									x		Bulgaria
x	x	x												Canada
x										x				Croatia
x			x											Cyprus
x	x	x	x							x	x			Czech Republic
x	x	x	x	x	x			x	x					Denmark
x	x		x						x					Estonia
x		x	x	x				x	x					Finland
x	x	x	x	x	x		x							France
x	x											x		Georgia
x	x	x	x	x	x		x		x					Germany
x	x	x	x	x	x		x					x		Greece
x	x	x	x							x	x			Hungary
x	x	x	x	x		x		x						Iceland
x	x	x	x	x	x					x				Ireland
x	x	x	x	x	x		x			x				Italy
x	x												x	Kazakhstan
x	x												x	Kyrgyzstan
x	x								x					Latvia
x			x	x		x								Liechtenstein
x	x		x						x					Lithuania
x	x	x	x	x	x		x							Luxembourg
										x				Macedonia
x			x											Malta
x	x											x	x	Moldova
x														Monaco
x	x	x	x	x	x		x							The Netherlands
x	x	x	x	x		x		x	x					Norway
x	x	x	x						x	x	x			Poland
x	x	x	x	x	x		x							Portugal
x	x		x									x		Romania
x	x								x			x	x	Russia
x			x											San Marino
x	x		x							x	x			Slovakia
x			x							x				Slovenia
x	x	x	x	x	x		x							Spain
x			x	x	x			x	x					Sweden
x			x			x								Switzerland
x	x												x	Tajikistan
x	x	x	x									x		Turkey
x	x		x										x	Turkmenistan
x	x											x	x	Ukraine
x	x	x	x	x	x		x							United Kingdom
x	x	x												USA
x	x												x	Uzbekistan
x														Vatican

1	Conference on Security and Cooperation in Europe	8	Western European Union
2	North Atlantic Cooperation Council	9	Nordic Council
3	North Atlantic Treaty Organisation	10	Council of Baltic States
4	Council of Europe	11	Central European Initiative
5	European Economic Area	12	Visegrad Group
6	European Union	13	Black Sea Economic Cooperation Council
7	European Free Trade Area	14	Commonwealth of Independant States

Source: Adapted from Clarke, D.L., *Europe's Changing Constellations* RFE/RL Research Report, Vol. 2, no. 37, 17/9/93, p. 14

Chronological table

1917   Lenin and the Bolsheviks seized power in Petrograd (November). Finland declared independence from Russia on the outbreak of the Bolshevik Revolution and was recognised by the Bolshevik government (November–December).

1918   Finnish civil war between the Whites and Reds won by Whites under General Mannerheim (January–May). Civil war began in Russia and continued until the Bolshevik victory in March 1921 (May). Armistice ended the First World War (November).

1919   Completion of Treaty of Versailles under which Germany surrendered Alsace and Lorraine to France and made other concessions over territory, reparations and armaments (June).

1920   Treaties of St Germain (with Austria) and Trianon (with Hungary) completed break-up of the Austro–Hungarian Empire (June and September).

1921   Treaty of Riga confirmed new Russo–Polish borders (March). 'Vivovdan Constitution' adopted in Yugoslavia, ensuring Serb dominance in inter-war period (June).

1922   Mussolini and Fascists came to power in Italy (October).

1923   Coup d'état in Bulgaria toppled Alexander Stamboliski and ended democratic government (June).

1924   Death of Lenin (January). Stalin finally prevailed in ensuing five-year power struggle, and from 1929 embarked upon a drastic transformation of Russian economy at huge cost in lives.

1926   Pilsudski seized power in Poland, ending Polish democracy.
Beginning of Sanacja regime in Poland (May). In Portugal, right-wing dictatorship came to power. From 1928, its leader and strong man was Antonio de Oliveira Salazar.

1929   Start of the Great Depression. King Alexander of Yugoslavia began dictatorship, trying to suppress local nationalism and create a 'Yugoslav nationalism' (January).

1930   King Carol II of Romania began more personal regime ending with his dictatorship by 1938 (June).

1932   Gyula Gömbös became prime minister in Hungary and pushed Hungary to the right over next four years (October).

1933   Hitler became chancellor of Germany (January).

1935   Germany repudiated military clauses of Versailles Treaty (March).
King Boris's coup d'état in Bulgaria began period of 'benevolent dictatorship' until 1943 (April). Elections in Czechoslovakia resulted in Sudeten German Party becoming largest party in Czech parliament (May). Italy invaded Abyssinia (October).

1936   Germany remilitarised the Rhineland (March). Spanish Civil War began and continued until April 1939 (July).

1938   *'Anschluss'*: Austria incorporated into Germany (March). The question of the future of the Germans in the Sudetenland (in Czechoslovakia) came to a head, reaching its climax at the Munich conference at which Hitler's demands were largely satisfied by Britain and France (August–September).

1939   German troops occupied Prague, followed by German annexation of Czech areas, with Slovakia becoming a German satellite state (March).
At end of March Britain and France guaranteed Polish independence, already under threat from Germany.
Spanish Civil War ended with defeat of the democratically elected Spanish government; Franco's dictatorship began (April).
In Yugoslavia central government made a special agreement (*'Sporazum'*) with Croatia, granting the Croats wide autonomy (August).
Germany and USSR signed Nazi–Soviet pact settling division of Poland and their future spheres of influence in eastern Europe.
Germany attacked Poland on 1st, Britain and France declared war on Germany on 3rd (September).
USSR attacked Finland without declaration of war (November).

1940   The 'Winter War' between Finland and USSR ended. Finland lost some eastern territories (March).

In series of whirlwind campaigns, Germany defeated Denmark, Norway, the Low Countries and France. Britain struggled to survive in the following 12 months, though with some moral and economic support from USA (April–June).

Britain and US occupied Iceland. US established airbase at Keflavik (May).

Fall of King Carol of Romania; period of brutal rule by 'Iron Guard' (1940–41) and regime of Marshal Antonescu (1941–44) (September).

1940–41 Hungary, Romania and Bulgaria drawn into alliance with Germany, Italy and Japan (Tripartite Pact).

1941   Germany invaded Yugoslavia and Greece. Independent Croatian state set up under Ustasha regime which began genocide of Serbs (April).

Germany invaded USSR (June).

Finland joined Germany in attacking USSR though on a restricted front and with limited objectives.

Reinhard Heydrich began 'regime of terror' in the Czech lands. Heydrich assassinated May 1942 (September).

German declaration of war on USA (December).

1943   German surrender at Stalingrad, followed by defeat during summer in battle of Kursk. Soviet forces advanced steadily westward thereafter (January).

Outbreak of civil war between factions of Greek anti-Nazi resistance movement (September).

Tehran conference between Churchill, Roosevelt and Stalin which did much to shape future (November–December).

1944   American and British forces landed in France and began their drive to victory from the west (June).

Bretton Woods conference – 44 countries led by UK and USA devised plans for the post-war international financial system, including the establishment of the International Monetary Fund (IMF) and International Bank for Reconstruction and Development (World Bank) (July).

Warsaw uprising put down brutally by Nazis (August–September).

Germany's ally, Finland, concluded an armistice with the USSR (September).

Germans began to withdraw from Greece. Stalin agreed to assign country to British sphere of influence (October).

Fall of Admiral Horthy in Hungary; brutal rule of fascist 'Arrow Cross movement' until April 1945.

British forces began to take action against the communists in Greece (December).

1945   Moscow recognised Lublin Committee as the provisional government of Poland (January).

Yalta conference on future of Europe attended by Churchill, Roosevelt and Stalin (February).

Italy finally liberated from Fascism. Benito Mussolini executed by partisans (April).

Suicide of Adolf Hitler (30 April).

Allied forces met in heart of Germany and war in Europe ended (8 May).

Labour Party, led by Clement Attlee, won British general election (July).

Allied leaders met at Potsdam, and USA tested and then used atomic bombs against Japan (July–August).

Potsdam: agreement on conditions for signing peace treaties with Bulgaria, Hungary and Romania (August).

Alcide de Gasperi became Christian Democrat prime minister of Italy (December).

1946   Forced merger of Social Democrats (SPD) with Communists (KPD) in Soviet Occupation Zone in Germany to form Socialist Unity Party (SED) (April).

Peace treaties negotiated with all former enemy states except Germany and Austria (April–December).

Italians rejected monarchy and voted in a referendum for establishment of a republic (June).

Constitution of French Fourth Republic promulgated (October).

Greek civil war began when communist resistance fighters, organised as the Democratic Army of Greece, refused to accept a right-wing royalist government under British tutelage.

1947   Economic merger of British and American occupation zones in Germany to form Bizonia (January).

Peace treaties signed with Bulgaria, Finland, Hungary, Italy and Romania (former allies of Germany) (February).

France and UK signed a 50-year friendship treaty (March).

Benelux states agreed to establish a customs union, commencing in January 1948.

Truman Doctrine formulated in general terms to assist 'free peoples in the struggle against communism'. It was prompted by British warning that it could not continue to back Greek government, and by fear of communist gains in Greece and Turkey (March).

Communists expelled from French and Italian governments with American encouragement (May).

First steps taken in the creation of the Marshall Plan, which, after departure of Soviet delegation, was directed to economic recovery of western Europe (June–July).

Cominform set up by USSR in response to Truman Doctrine and Marshall Plan (September).

Establishment of General Agreement on Tariffs and Trade (GATT) (October).

1948   Political crisis in Czechoslovakia left communists as dominant political force (February).

Brussels Treaty signed by Benelux states, France and UK providing for military cooperation (March).

USA granted massive economic and military assistance to right-wing forces in Greece.

Organisation for European Economic Cooperation (OEEC) set up in Paris (April).

Finland signed Treaty of Friendship, Cooperation and Mutual Assistance (FCMA) with USSR.

Congress of Europe called for political and economic union of European nations (May).

American Senate approved Vandenberg Resolution which opened way to American defence cooperation with western European states (June).

East–West differences over German questions led to interruption of western supply lines to West Berlin (the Berlin blockade). West responded with airlift.

Cominform expelled Yugoslav Communist Party and approved Soviet model of industrialisation and agricultural collectivisation for the 'people's democracies' (July).

UK Labour government implemented major health and social security reforms, establishing National Health Service.

1949   Comecon set up by USSR and its partners (January).

North Atlantic Treaty (NATO) signed by Belgium, Britain, Canada, Denmark, France, Iceland, Italy, Luxembourg, Netherlands, Norway, Portugal and USA (April).

Southern Ireland became completely independent of British Commonwealth when Irish parliament promulgated Republic of Ireland Act.

Federal Republic of Germany (FRG – West Germany) adopted its post-war constitution (May).

Berlin blockade ended.

'Show trials' began in eastern Europe.

Statute of Council of Europe signed in Strasbourg by ten states.

First Soviet nuclear test (August).

Konrad Adenauer became first chancellor of FRG (September).

Greek civil war ended with defeat of communist forces (October).

German Democratic Republic (East Germany – GDR) established.

Cominform denounced Yugoslav regime. Soviet bloc countries broke off diplomatic relations with Yugoslavia (November).

1950   France proposed European Coal and Steel Community (Schuman Plan) (May).
Outbreak of Korean War (June).
Start of Western talks on West German rearmament (September).
France proposed Pleven Plan resulting in attempt to establish the European Defence Community (EDC) (October).
Growing East–West tension led to major increases in defence spending by NATO and a larger and firmer commitment by USA to defence of Europe (December).

1951   Benelux states, FRG, France and Italy signed treaty establishing European Coal and Steel Community (ECSC) which operated from July 1952 (April).
Conservatives returned to power under Winston Churchill in UK (October).

1952   New constitution promulgated in Greece (January).
Greece and Turkey entered NATO (February).
USSR proposed German peace treaty based on withdrawal of foreign troops and neutralisation of Germany (March).
Benelux states, FRG, France and Italy signed treaty to create EDC (May).
Yugoslav Communist Party renamed League of Communists of Yugoslavia (LCY) (November).
Right-wing forces won elections in Greece.

1953   First American thermo-nuclear test (first deliverable bomb tested in March 1954) (February).
First session of Nordic Council comprising Denmark, Iceland, Norway and Sweden. (Finland joined in October 1955).
Death of Stalin (March).
Soviet intervention put down demonstrations in East Berlin and other cities in East Germany (June).
Korean armistice signed.
Soviet–Yugoslav diplomatic relations resumed.
Recently appointed prime minister Imre Nagy introduced 'new course' in Hungary (July).
First Soviet thermo-nuclear test (August).

1954   French National Assembly refused to ratify EDC treaty (August).
London and Paris conferences opened way to creation of Western European Union (WEU), rearmament of West Germany, its membership of NATO and achievement of full sovereign status (September–October).

1955   Leadership struggle in USSR: Malenkov replaced by Bulganin (February) with Khrushchev (CPSU General Secretary) increasingly influential, taking over premiership in 1958.

Nagy replaced as prime minister in Hungary (March).

Churchill succeeded as UK prime minister by Anthony Eden (Conservative) (April).

Austrian Peace Treaty provided for withdrawal of occupation forces and establishment of a neutral Austria. The Warsaw Pact between USSR and its eastern European allies concluded in same month (May).

Khrushchev's rapprochement with Tito.

FRG became a sovereign state.

Messina conference of foreign ministers of the six ECSC states discussed further integration (June).

A Four-Power summit in Geneva failed to reach any substantive agreements, but reflected a temporary easing of Cold War in Europe (July).

Introduction of so-called 'Hallstein Doctrine' in FRG (December).

1956   Khrushchev denounced Stalin at 20th Party Congress (February).

Cominform dissolved (April)

Strains developed in Poland. Poznan riots. Gomulka restored to leadership in October (June).

Rakosi removed from Hungarian Party general secretaryship after visit of high-level Soviet delegation (July).

Nagy restored as prime minister in Hungary. Uprising ended with heavy bloodshed after Soviet military intervention occasioned by USSR's refusal to accept end of one-party rule and Hungary's departure from WTO (October–November).

Anglo-French action at Suez led to temporary crisis in Anglo-American relations, and deeper rift between Paris and Washington (November).

1957   Harold Macmillan (Conservative) succeeded Eden as UK prime minister (January).

Treaties of Rome signed, establishing the European Economic Community (EEC) and the European Atomic Energy Community (EAEC) (March).

1958   Treaties of Rome came into force (January).

USSR agreed to withdraw troops from Romania (May).

Long-running crisis in French Fourth Republic came to a head with army coup in Algeria; Charles de Gaulle returned to power in France, promising end to colonial war in Algeria and return of political stability at home (May–June).

French referendum approved Constitution of Fifth Republic (September).

A Soviet note on future status of Berlin led to period of intermittent and at times serious tension between East and West over Berlin (and Germany) until end of 1961 (November).

De Gaulle elected president of France (December).

1960   European Free Trade Association (EFTA) Convention signed in Stockholm by Austria, Denmark, Norway, Portugal, Sweden, Switzerland and UK (January).
Four-Power summit in Paris a dismal failure (May).
Growing evidence of a rift between communist China and USSR (June).
Cyprus became independent republic within British Commonwealth (August).
OEEC reorganised into Organisation for Economic Cooperation and Development (OECD) (December).

1961   USSR cancelled aid to Albania (April).
Denmark, Ireland and UK applied for EC membership.
Berlin Wall erected to stop growing numbers of East Germans going to the West (August).
22nd Congress of CPSU – Khrushchev renewed de-Stalinisation (October).
Move to 'goulash communism' in Hungary (December).

1962   French colonial war in Algeria ended. Algeria became an independent republic in July (March).
Norway applied for EC membership (April).
A Soviet attempt to deploy nuclear missiles in Cuba followed by most serious crisis in the Cold War (October–November).
De-Stalinisation began in Czechoslovakia (December).

1963   De Gaulle vetoed UK bid to enter EC. Franco-West German Treaty of Friendship and Cooperation signed (January).
Sino-Soviet rift made public (June).
Yaoundé Convention between the EEC and 18 African states and Madagascar (July).
FRG opened a trade mission in Poland (September).
GDR adopted New Economic System.
Alec Douglas-Home became Conservative prime minister of UK (October).
Ludwig Erhard succeeded his fellow Christian Democrat Konrad Adenauer as chancellor of FRG.
In Greece, Centre Union, led by George Papandreou and his son, Andreas, won office (November).
New crisis in Cyprus: clashes between Greeks and Turks (December).

1964   Constantine II succeeded to throne of Greece (March).
Central Committee in Romania issued declaration asserting independence of all communist parties (April).
FRG opened trade mission in Hungary (July).
Hungarian Socialist Workers' Party Central Committee accepted principles of New Economic Mechanism.

UK elections returned Labour government under Harold Wilson (October).

Khrushchev relieved of all his posts in USSR. Brezhnev shared power with Kosygin, but steadily became the more influential figure.

1965   Signing of Treaty (Merger Treaty) establishing a single Council and a single Commission of the EC. Treaty took effect in July 1967 (April).

France began a boycott of EC institutions to register its oppositon to various proposed supranational developments (July).

Constitutional crisis in Greece ended in defeat for elected government of George Papandreou when King Constantine forced its resignation to appease army.

1966   Luxembourg Compromise ended French boycott of EC institutions (January).

De Gaulle announced French withdrawal from military participation in NATO (March).

Grand Coalition government formed in FRG with Social Democrat Willy Brandt as foreign minister (December).

Kurt Georg Kiesinger became third post-war Christian Democrat chancellor of FRG.

1967   FRG established diplomatic relations with Romania (January).

Military coup in Greece led to establishment of 'Dictatorship of the Colonels'. In December, King Constantine left for exile in Rome having failed to remove colonels (April).

EC Merger Treaty came into force (July).

De Gaulle vetoed UK entry to EC again (November).

1968   Dubcek elected first secretary of Czech Communist Party. A wide variety of reforms followed, but 'Prague Spring' ended by Warsaw Pact invasion in August, the USSR once again fearing that matters were drifting out of control. In November so-called 'Brezhnev Doctrine' laid down that a socialist state was bound to intervene if socialism was threatened in another socialist state (January–November).

Paris rocked by strikes and demonstrations as students and workers revolted against the perceived authoritarian and paternalistic nature of de Gaulle's regime. Benefiting from fears of revolution, French right wing won a parliamentary majority in general elections in June. Similar student protests elsewhere in Europe (May).

Completion of EEC Customs Union (July).

Marcello Caetano succeeded ailing Salazar as dictator of Portugal (September).

1969   De Gaulle resigned French presidency following defeat in referendum on constitutional reforms (April).
Georges Pompidou became president of France (June).
British troops arrived in Northern Ireland, ostensibly to keep peace between the province's Protestants and Catholics. A split in para-military Irish Republican Army (IRA) produced hard-line 'Provisional' IRA in August–December, which began serious campaign of violence against British presence in Northern Ireland (August).
Massive labour unrest in Italy led to trade union reforms and to forms of collective bargaining which increased strength of labour movement. An extreme right-wing backlash saw neo-fascist terrorist groups carry out some bombings.
Brandt became FRG chancellor heading an SPD–FDP coalition. In October he made overtures to USSR and Poland, and showed his desire to open a dialogue with GDR (September).
The Hague summit of EC leaders (December).

1970   First FRG–USSR agreement on supply of Soviet natural gas to FRG by pipeline (February).
Brandt's 'Ostpolitik' led to first conference of FRG and GDR leaders (March).
Conservatives returned to power in UK, led by Edward Heath (June).
EC membership negotiations reopened with Denmark, Ireland, Norway and UK.
FRG–USSR treaty of non-aggression (August).
FRG–Poland treaty of non-aggression (November).
Riots occurred in Gdansk in Poland. Edward Gierek replaced Wladyslaw Gomulka as first secretary (December).

1971   Erich Honecker replaced Walter Ulbricht as general secretary of GDR Communist Party (SED) (May).
Quadripartite Agreement on Berlin (September).
UK parliament approved EC membership (October).

1972   Enrico Berlinguer became leader of Italian Communist Party. Over the next four years, he articulated the ideology of Eurocommunism and sharply criticised the USSR (January).
President Nixon visited Moscow and signed first Strategic Arms Limitation Treaty (SALT I) and Declaration on Basic Principles of Soviet–American relations (May).
FRG and GDR signed 'Basic Treaty' on mutual relations (December).

1973   Ireland, Denmark and UK joined EC (January).
Conference on Security and Cooperation in Europe (CSCE) opened in Helsinki, including representatives of all European states (except Albania), Canada, USA and USSR (July).

FRG concluded a treaty with Czechoslovakia and established diplomatic relations with Bulgaria and Hungary (December).

1974   British Labour Party regained office; Wilson prime minister again (March).
Portuguese radical army officers overthrew right-wing dictatorship of Salazar–Caetano, initiating a period of revolutionary upheaval and ultimately consolidation of multi-party democracy. First free elections for 50 years held in 1976 (April).
UK government demanded renegotiation of terms of accession to EC.
French president Georges Pompidou died; succeeded by Valéry Giscard d'Estaing (April–May).
Helmut Schmidt (Social Democrat) succeeded Willy Brandt as chancellor of FRG (May).
Greek military intervened in Cyprus; driven back by the Turks.
Cyprus divided into Greek and Turkish zones. Greek military regime collapsed (July).
In Greece, democratic elections returned centre-right New Democracy Party led by Constantine Karamanlis to power (November).
Greeks voted by huge majority to abolish monarchy and declare a republic (December).
EC Heads of State and Government decided to meet regularly as European Council.

1975   First Lomé Convention between EC and 46 African, Caribbean and Pacific states (ACP states) (February).
Elections to a new constituent assembly in Portugal established Socialists as biggest party (April).
UK referendum; two-to-one majority in favour of remaining in EC (June).
Greece promulgated a new constitution and applied for EC membership.
Final Act signed at Helsinki Conference on Security and Cooperation in Europe (August).
General Franco died and transition to democracy began in Spain under King Juan Carlos. Free elections held in June 1977 (November).

1976   James Callaghan succeeded Harold Wilson as Labour prime minister in UK (April).
Portuguese general elections won by socialists.
Italian elections. So-called government of 'national solidarity', 1976–79, sought communist support in parliament in return for consultation. Communists, however, denied cabinet seats (June).
Socialist leader, Mario Soares, became prime minister of Portugal (July).
The Committee for the Defence of Workers (KOR) set up in Poland (September).

1977   Charter 77 formed in Czechoslovakia (January)
Legalisation of political parties began in Spain (February).
Portugal applied for EC membership.
A NATO summit agreed to increase defence spending by 3 per cent a
year in real terms as confidence in détente weakened (May).
Spain's first free elections for more than 40 years (June).
Spain applied for EC membership (July).

1978   China cut off aid to Albania (July).
Polish Archbishop Karol Woytila elected as Pope John Paul II (October).

1979   European Monetary System (EMS) came into operation (March).
Margaret Thatcher led British Conservatives to election victory and
became first female prime minister of UK (May).
SALT 2 was signed but not subsequently ratified by USA (June).
First direct elections to European Parliament.
Second Lomé Convention between EEC and 58 ACP states (October).
NATO took twin-track decision to negotiate with USSR on intermediate-
range nuclear systems and, if Soviet SS-20s not removed by 1983, to
deploy Pershing and cruise missiles in Europe (December).
Soviet invasion of Afghanistan.

1980   Karamanlis became president of Greece (May).
Death of President Tito of Yugoslavia.
Price increases in Poland led to establishment of the Solidarity free
trade union under leadership of Lech Walesa (August).
Turkish government toppled by military coup (September).

1981   Start of Ronald Reagan's presidency of USA (January).
Greece joined EC.
Attempted military coup in Spain failed (February).
Nationalist disturbances in Kosovo (March–April).
François Mitterrand became first socialist president of French Fifth
Republic, defeating Giscard d'Estaing. In June, Mitterrand's Socialist
Party also won general elections. A left-wing government formed which
included four cabinet ministers from French Communist Party (May).
Giovanni Spadolini, a Republican, became Italy's first non-Christian
Democrat prime minister since 1945 (July).
Elections in Greece returned socialist party, PASOK, to power. Andreas
Papandreou became prime minister October.
Further FRG–USSR gas pipeline agreement (November).
Martial law declared in Poland by Jaruzelski. Solidarity leadership
arrested. American sanctions against Poland and USSR followed. In
1982 this led to serious controversy between USA and its European
allies over handling of issue (December).

1982   Greenland referendum voted in favour of withdrawal from EC (February).

Argentina invaded Falkland Islands. Hostilities continued until UK victory in July (April).

Spain joined NATO (May).

FRG Chancellor Schmidt lost vote of confidence and was succeeded by Helmut Kohl, who led a CDU/CSU–FDP coalition government (September).

Brezhnev died. He was briefly succeeded by Yuri Andropov (1982–84) and Konstantin Chernenko (1984–85) (November).

1983   Reagan announced intention to proceed with Strategic Defence Initiative (SDI). The anti-nuclear movement became increasingly active in western Europe (March).

Conservatives under Thatcher returned to power in UK elections (June).

Martial law lifted in Poland (July).

Anti-communist Bettino Craxi, leader of Italian Socialist Party, headed CD-dominated government (August).

NATO began to deploy Pershing and cruise missiles. USSR broke off East–West arms talks (November).

1984   Free trade area established between EC and EFTA (January).

Mitterrand shifted France to more pro-federalist position, implicitly recognising failure of 1982–83 'socialist experiment' largely due to pressure of world economic trends; in July, French communists left government in protest (June).

FRG granted DM950 million loan to GDR in return for further relaxation of travel restrictions. By August there was a growing USSR–GDR rift over détente and relations with FRG (July).

Third Lomé Convention between EC and 65 ACP states (December).

1985   USA and USSR took the first steps towards renewal of arms talks (January).

Mikhail Gorbachev became general secretary of Central Committee of Communist Party of Soviet Union. USA–USSR arms talks renewed in Geneva (March).

Karamanlis resigned as Greek president (May).

Greek Socialists, led by Papandreou, returned to power in elections (June).

Geneva Summit between Reagan and Gorbachev marked beginning of end of 'Second Cold War' (usually dated as starting with Soviet intervention in Afghanistan in December 1979) (November).

Anglo-Irish Agreement gave Irish government a consultative role in Northern Ireland.

European Council agreed principles of Single European Act (SEA) (December).

1986   Spain and Portugal joined EC (January)
        SEA signed in Luxembourg, fixing end of 1992 as completion date of Internal Market.
        Assassination of Swedish prime minister Olaf Palme (February).
        Mario Soares replaced General Eanes as president of Portugal.
        Right-wing parties won parliamentary majority in France, forcing a period of 'cohabitation' between Jacques Chirac as prime minister and Mitterrand as socialist president. This continued until May 1988 (March).
        Major accident at nuclear power plant in Chernobyl, Ukraine (April).
        Gorbachev proposed 30 per cent cut in strategic nuclear arms (June).
        Stockholm Security Conference: agreements on observers and on notice of military movements (September).
        Reagan and Gorbachev met in Reykjavik. Western Europeans alarmed by USA's unilateral (though unsuccessful) proposals on strategic nuclear arms cuts (October).

1987   FRG coalition government (CDU/CSU–FDP) returned to power in elections (January).
        USSR proposed Intermediate-range Nuclear Forces (INF) agreement (March).
        Gorbachev, in a Prague speech on a 'common European home', emphasised the shared history and culture of Europeans (April).
        Italian prime ministership passed from Bettino Craxi to the Christian Democrat Amintore Fanfani.
        Slobodan Milosevic, who became Communist Party leader in Serbia in 1986, exploited unrest in Kosovo.
        Conservatives won third term of office in UK (June).
        Single European Act came into effect (July).
        Slobodan Milosevic became general secretary of the League of Communists of Serbia (October).
        Proposed economic reforms in Poland failed to win support of 50 per cent of the people. Strikes followed in spring and summer of 1988 (November).
        INF treaty provided for elimination of all INF weapon systems in Europe within three years (December).
        Slobodan Milosevic removed Ivan Stambolic as president of Serbia.

1988   Janos Kádár, Hungarian leader, replaced; radical reforms promised (May).
        Mitterrand won second presidential mandate in France. Socialist Party also won general elections. Michel Rocard became prime minister.
        Rallies in former Baltic states calling for autonomy (August).
        Lech Walesa invited to help end strikes in Poland.

1989   Independent opposition political parties legalised in Hungary (January).

Talks began between Polish communists and Solidarity; agreement reached in April on trade union, economic and political reforms.

Solidarity won all but one of the seats it was allowed to contest in June elections (February).

Serbia removed autonomy of Kosovo (March).

The Delors report proposed three-stage progression to economic and monetary union (EMU) (April).

Hungary opened its borders to allow East German 'tourists' to cross to the West (May).

European Council of the EC agreed to begin Stage 1 of programme for EMU on 1 July 1990 (June).

Greek elections resulted in stalemate. A short-lived and unprecedented communist–conservative coalition took office to 'clean up' alleged corruption of outgoing socialist administration.

Slobodan Milosevic celebrated 600th anniversary of Battle of Kosovo.

Franjo Tudjman founded new political party: Croatian Democratic Union (HDZ).

Human chain across Lithuania, Latvia and Estonia marked 50th anniversary of Molotov–Ribbentrop pact (August).

Solidarity-led government formed in Poland.

Hungarian government agreed to hold multi-party elections

Hungarian Socialist Workers' Party became simply Socialist Party.

Party's leading role dropped from Constitution (October).

Serbia removed autonomy of Vojvodina.

Pro-Milosevic regime installed in Montenegro.

Soviet statement effectively ended the 'Brezhnev Doctrine'.

Massive demonstrations in East German cities (November).

GDR government promised free elections and free exit on 8 November. Within hours, Berlin Wall breached.

Zhivkov replaced in Bulgaria.

All-party government formed in Greece.

Coalition government formed in Czechoslovakia (December).

European Council of the EC agreed to convene an Intergovernmental Conference (IGC) on economic and monetary union and subsequently (June 1990) to establish an IGC on political union.

Union of Democratic Forces formed in Bulgaria.

Romanian communist leader, Nicolae Ceausescu and his wife Elena executed.

Communist Party of Lithuania left CPSU.

1990   GDR government proposed unification of Germany (January).

Extraordinary Communist Party conference in Belgrade: Slovene and Croatian Communists left the organisation.

Balcerowicz plan for economic shock therapy adopted in Poland.

First free general election in GDR. Christian Democrats won almost 50 per cent of vote, paving way for unification (March).

Lithuania declared its independence from USSR.

Free elections in Hungary produced right of centre coalition government led by Josef Antall's Hungarian Democratic Forum.

Centre-right New Democracy won one-seat majority in Greek elections. In May, Karamanlis returned as president (April).

Milosevic changed Serbian constitution to ensure his positon.

Franco-German proposal for IGC on political union.

Free elections in Croatia won by Democratic Union (April–May).

Free elections in Romania won by Iliescu's National Salvation Front (May).

Communists defeated in free elections in Slovenia and Croatia. Parties of Milan Kucan and Tudjman took power.

FRG–GDR treaty on monetary, economic and social union.

Boris Yeltsin elected president of Russian Republic.

Free elections in Czechoslovakia won by Civic Forum and its Slovak counterpart Public Against Violence (June).

Free elections in Bulgaria won by Socialist (ex-Communist) Party.

Germany adopted single currency (July).

NATO summit in London began to consider implications of post-Cold War era.

Group of seven states (G7) discussed integration of eastern Europe into world economy.

First stage of EC plan for EMU came into effect.

28th CPSU Congress. Yeltsin and others left Party.

State treaty on German unification signed by FRG and GDR (August).

Treaty on Final Settlement on Germany signed by two German states and France, UK, USA and USSR ('2+4' Treaty) (September).

Albanians of Kosovo organised referendum for independence.

Formal declaration of suspension of Four-Power rights in Germany (October).

Croatia and Slovenia proposed 'confederal' model for Yugoslavia which was rejected by Serbia.

Germany became a single state once again. Helmut Kohl (FRG chancellor) elected chancellor of reconstituted state in December and led a CDU/CSU–FDP coalition.

Margaret Thatcher forced from office in UK due to internal Conservative Party coup. John Major became party leader and prime minister (November).

CSCE summit – Charter of Paris declared that the Cold War was over.

Lech Walesa elected president of Poland (December).

Bulgarian government resigned following widespread strikes.

Elections in Serbia and Montenegro won by ex-Communists.

Elections produced a weak coalition government in Bosnia-Hercegovina and a nationalist one in Macedonia.

Central Committee plenum removed hardliners from Albanian Party of Labour as anti-government demonstrations mounted.

Opening sessions of the two Intergovernmental Conferences on economic and monetary union and political union.

1991   Harder line by Gorbachev reflected in OMON (para-military force) attacks in Vilnius and Riga. Yeltsin recognised sovereignty of Baltic states (January).

Italian Communist Party (PCI), under leadership of Achille Occhetto, voted to dissolve itself and to give birth to the Democratic Party of the Left (PDS). A minority seceded to form rival Party of Communist Refoundation (PRC) (February).

Growing crisis in Yugoslavia. Kucan and Tudjman agreed that Yugoslavia could only survive as a voluntary league of sovereign republics.

Milosevic and Tudjman discussed partition of Bosnia between Serbia and Croatia (March).

Albanian Party of Labour (APL) won Albania's first free elections (April).

In France, President Mitterrand appointed a new socialist prime minister – Edith Cresson (May).

Albanian government replaced by coalition following widespread strikes. APL became Socialist Party of Albania (June).

Declarations of independence by Croatia and Slovenia.

Yugoslav army invaded Slovenia, but was forced to retreat. Serbia accepted Slovenian independence.

Comecon dissolved.

Bundestag voted Berlin capital of united Germany.

Warsaw Treaty Organisation dissolved (July).

Serbo-Croat war began in Croatia.

Attempted putsch failed in USSR. Gorbachev lost all credibility on return to Moscow. Communist parties banned and much of their property taken over by republican governments following Yeltsin's lead in Russia. Estonia, Latvia and Lithuania declared independence and Yeltsin urged world to recognise them (August).

Romanian government forced to resign. Coalition government formed (September).

Social Democrats defeated in Swedish elections; right-wing government came to power.

Indecisive Polish elections resulted in formation of weak coalition government under Olszewski in December (October).

Union of Democratic Forces narrowly defeated Socialists in Bulgarian elections.

Bosnian parliament debated motion to declare Bosnia a sovereign republic; Serbs walked out of session.

Start of EC sanctions against Serbia (November).

NATO Rome summit announced the new strategic concept. Alliance to have a wider security role.

Fall of Vukovar to the Serbs.

Caretaker government formed in Albania (December).

EC association agreements with Czechoslovakia, Hungary and Poland provided for free trade within 10 years and possibility of eventual EC membership.

EC heads of state and government meeting in Maastricht agreed on a treaty framework for European Union incorporating agreements on economic and monetary union and political union, and introducing a new security/defence dimension to EC cooperation.

USSR replaced by Commonwealth of Independent States (CIS).

1992   EC recognised independence of Croatia and Slovenia (January).

Cease-fire in Serbian–Croatian war signed in Sarajevo.

Zhelyu Zhelev re-elected president of Bulgaria.

Broadly effective cease-fire in Croatia.

Treaty on European Union signed in Maastricht (February).

Democratic Party decisively won Albanian elections. Its chairman, Salih Berisha, was elected executive president in April (March).

Proclamation of independence by Bosnia-Hercegovina. War started in Bosnia; siege of Sarajevo until 1994.

Italian general elections confirmed crisis within corruption-tainted Christian Democrats and their Socialist allies. But the former Communists also polled poorly. New parties did well, especially right-wing secessionist Northern Leagues (April).

Serbia and Montenegro created 'Federal Republic of Yugoslavia'.

Conservatives returned to power in the UK, but with a much-reduced majority (May).

EC and EFTA signed treaty establishing the European Economic Area (EEA).

Yeltsin won Russian presidential election.

UN imposed sanctions on Serbia and Montenegro.

Leningraders voted to restore name of St Petersburg (June).

Olszewski government fell in Poland. In July, Hanna Suchocka formed a seven-party coalition government, which survived until May 1993.

General elections in Czechoslovakia. Strong performance of Meciar's Movement for a Democratic Slovakia made early dissolution of Federation inevitable.

Danish voters rejected Maastricht Treaty.

Tudjman's Croatian Democratic Union consolidated its grip on power after lower house and presidential elections (August).

UK hosted London conference on Bosnia.

Horrors of Serb concentration camp at Omarska made public to world media.

Iliescu re-elected president of Romania, but general election results forced his Democratic NSF into a government coalition with 3 hard-line nationalist parties (September).

French referendum narrowly approved Maastricht Treaty.

Brazauskas' Democratic Labour Party (former Communist Party of Lithuania) won general election (October/November).

Czechoslovakia, Hungary and Poland (Visegrad group) signed free trade agreement (December).

'Non-party government of experts' led by Lyuben Berov installed in Bulgaria.

Dissolution of Czechoslovakia into Czech Republic and Slovakia at midnight on 31 December.

1993   EC formally became a single market (January).

EC opened negotiations with Austria, Finland and Sweden (and Norway – April 1993) on their applications for membership (February).

Attempt to impeach Yeltsin failed (March).

French general elections returned a parliamentary landslide for right-wing parties. Edouard Balladur became the new Gaullist prime minister, heralding new period of cohabitation with Mitterrand.

Russian referendum: 59 per cent backed Yeltsin (April).

Danish referendum voted in favour of Maastricht Treaty (May).

Athens summit: Bosnian Serbs forced to sign Vance–Owen plan. War crimes tribunal began to be set up.

Spanish general elections returned a minority Socialist government, dependent on Catalan nationalist support (June).

EC finance ministers agreed to alterations in EMS following turmoil in financial markets (August).

Polish elections. Ex-Communists of Democratic Left Alliance returned to power in coalition government with old allies in Polish Peasant Party. Solidarity and church-backed parties did poorly. Pawlak became prime minister (September).

Yeltsin dissolved Russian Republic Supreme Soviet, intending to rule by presidential and governmental decree until elections to new State Duma on 12 December. Vice-president Rutskoi announced he had taken over presidency and was supported by Supreme Soviet, which also attempted to replace defence minister Grachëv by hardliner Achalov. Deputies, led by Rutskoi and speaker Khasbulatov, occupied Parliament Building.

Army units stormed White House. Rutskoi, Khasbulatov and other leaders arrested (October).

Socialists, led by Andreas Papandreou, returned to power in Greece, inflicting a heavy electoral defeat on New Democracy. The latter elected a new leader, Miltiades Evert.

Maastricht Treaty on European Union formally came into effect (November).

Elections to Russia's State Duma and Federation Council. Disarray among pro-Yeltsin parties and public apathy and disillusionment boosted Zhirinovsky's inappropriately named Liberal Democratic Party and also Communist Party of Russia. New Constitution approved in referendum (December).

Elections increased majority of Milosevic's Serbian Socialist Party.

114 countries agreed on treaty for liberalisation of world trade following seven years of GATT negotiations (Uruguay round) (December).

1994   Second stage of EMU came into effect with establishment in Frankfurt of European Monetary Institute (EMI) as a precursor to European central bank (January).

NATO Brussels summit announced intention of the alliance to enlarge its membership.

European Economic Area (EEA) came into existence creating a free trade zone comprising all EU member countries and six of the seven EFTA countries – Switzerland having voted against participation in December 1992.

Russia's State Duma granted amnesty to leaders of parliamentary resistance to President Yeltsin in October 1993 (February).

Shelling of Sarajevo marketplace resulted in death of 69 people and led to Serb forces pulling back heavy artillery from siege of the city.

Croatia agreed cease-fire with self-declared Republic of Serbian Krajina (March).

Austria, Finland, Norway and Sweden agreed terms for joining European Union in January 1995.

Italian general elections confirmed collapse of old discredited Christian Democrat and Socialist parties. The main beneficiaries of the crisis of the old party system were the neo-fascists, the right-wing Northern Leagues, and a new right-wing, pro-free market movement, *Forza Italia*, led by media mogul and billionaire, Silvio Berlusconi.

Slovak prime minister Meciar lost no-confidence vote and was replaced by Jozef Moravcik, leading a five-party coalition governnment.

Hungary and Poland became first former communist states to apply for membership of EU (April).

Silvio Berlusconi became Italian prime minister. His government included five neo-fascist cabinet ministers, raising concern in many European capitals (May).

Hungarian Socialist Party (ex-Communists) won overall parliamentary majority in elections.

Austrian referendum voted in favour of EU membership (June).

Russia joined NATO's Partnership for Peace and signed a 'partnership and cooperation' agreement with the EU, which stopped short of setting full EU membership as the final goal. After being accepted as a full political partner at G7 summit, Russia also seemed about to apply for admission to the Paris club (of government creditors).

The Supreme NATO Commander in Europe and the Russian defence minister agreed to set up working groups to draft a programme of joint activities. NATO missions to be established in Russia and Russian military missions at NATO's European headquarters.

Jacques Santer appointed to succeed Jacques Delors as president of European Commission (July).

Tony Blair elected leader of British Labour Party.

Withdrawal of all American military forces from West Berlin after five decades of presence in the city.

Italian anti-corruption judges resigned in protest at bail for prisoners on remand accused of corruption. Berlusconi's brother accused of corruption.

1995   Austria, Finland and Sweden joined the EU (January).

Kostas Stephanopoulos, a veteran centre right (ND) politician, became president of Greece (March).

Bosnian Serb forces took Srebrenica and massacred male Muslim inhabitants.

Chirac succeeded Mitterrand as president of France (May).

Croatia drove Serb forces out of western Slavonia.

Cannes European Council meeting agreed that the introduction of a single currency by 1997 was unrealistic (June).

Croatian 'Operation Storm' retook Krajina area of Croatia (August).

Latvia and Slovakia applied to join the EU.

Socialists won Portuguese general elections; António Guterres became prime minister (October).

Estonia applied to join the EU (November).

Dayton Accord, supported by NATO forces under UN mandate, brought end of hostilities in Bosnia.

Andreas Papandreou found it increasingly difficult to discharge his duties as Greek prime minister due to recurrent ill health; power struggle developed within PASOK.

Lech Walesa defeated by SLD leader Aleksander Kwasniewski in Poland's presidential elections.

Bulgaria and Lithuania applied to join the EU (December).

Dayton Accord provided for a bipartite state of Bosnia and Hercegovina and for a NATO-led Implementation Force to supervise the implementation of the accords.

1996   Jorge Sampaio of the Socialist Party was elected president of Portugal (January).

Deployment of NATO forces in Bosnia to implement Dayton Accord.

The Czech Republic and Slovenia applied to join the EU.

Andreas Papandreou was forced by ill health to relinquish the post of prime minister of Greece to Kostas Simitis.

Basque terrorists attempted to destabilise Spain's general election campaign by murdering several political leaders from the ruling Socialist Party. One million people protested against ETA's violence in Madrid (February).

Jorge Sampaio formally succeeded Mario Soares as president of Portugal (March).

IGC convened to review the Treaty on European Union (Maastricht Treaty).

Portuguese conservatives (PSD) elected Marcelo Rebelo de Sousa as their leader, in a bid to restore party unity and morale after recent defeats and divisions.

Spanish socialists (PSOE) lost power to a minority conservative (PP) government which was led by José Maria Aznar and relied on Catalan nationalist support.

Death of Andreas Papandreou. He was succeeded as leader of PASOK by Kostas Simitis (June).

Spanish conservative government, despite its hard-line anti-ETA stance, hinted at negotiations with ETA in return for a permanent cease-fire.

Greek general elections returned PASOK under Kostas Simitis to power (September).

Czech Republic and Germany signed a treaty of reconciliation in which Germany expressed regrets for Nazi atrocities and the Czech Republic for Czechoslovakia's expulsion of the Sudeten Germans (November).

Tough austerity budget introduced by Greek government saw huge farmers' protests which threatened to paralyse the country (November–December).

Dublin European Council meeting agreed a single currency Stability Pact (December).

1997   Renewal of trade union protests in Greece against government cuts in order to qualify for entry into the European single currency (January).

Kostas Karamanlis replaced Miltiades Evert as leader of ND party in Greece (March).

Spanish government secured PSOE support for an economic stabilisation plan which aimed to secure Spain's entry into the European single currency through 'drastic' government spending curbs (April).

Election of Labour government in UK (May).

French general elections – called a year early saw the rout of Chirac's right-wing allies and the return of a left-wing coalition government under Lionel Jospin (June).

Felipe González resigned as leader of PSOE, to be succeeded by Joaquín Almunia who was regarded as a González supporter.

Amsterdam European Council meeting agreed the Treaty of Amsterdam following the IGC review of the Treaty on European Union (Maastrich Treaty).

NATO Madrid summit agreed to admit the Czech Republic, Hungary and Poland as new alliance members in 1999 (July).

After parliamentary elections in Albania (June/July), a Socialist-led coalition government took office under Fatos Nano. Rexhep Meidani succeeded Sali Berisha as president (August).

Scottish and Welsh voters approved proposals for national assemblies in Scotland and Wales in referenda (September).

Parliamentary elections in Poland brought to power a coalition government comprising Solidarity Electoral Action (AWS) and the Freedom Union (UW).

Gordon Brown, British Chancellor of the Exchequer, specified five economic tests for UK entry into the Euro zone and indicated that the UK would not be ready for entry before the end of the current parliament (October).

Greek government unveiled tough budget which imposed effective freeze on wages in public sector and abolished some tax perks for the better-off; measures were declared necessary if Greece was to qualify for entry into the Euro in 2001 (November).

Serbian operations intensified in Drenica region of Kosovo, following clashes with the ethnic Albanian Kosova Liberation Army (KLA).

Luxembourg European Council meeting invited Cyprus, the Czech Republic, Estonia, Hungary, Poland and Slovenia to start membership talks in March 1998 with a view to entry to the EU early in the next century (December).

Entire leadership of Herri Batasuna was imprisoned in Spain for collaborating with Euskadi Ta Askatasuna (ETA).

1998   Serbian operations against Kosovar Albanians killed hundreds of civilians, many the result of deliberate or indiscriminate attacks. 60,000 Kosovars fled their homes (February–June).

Greek PASOK government adopted austerity package which reduced rights of workers in the public sector by giving managers new powers to curb overtime, reduce collective bargaining rights and reduce benefits (February).

UN Security Council Resolution 1160 urged Yugoslavia and Kosovar Albanians to reach a political solution, with wide autonomy for Kosovo (March).

Greek government devalued the drachma by 14 per cent and rejoined the exchange rate mechanism.

European Commission ruled out Greek entry into the Euro in 1999 saying that Greece had yet to meet any of the criteria contained in the Maastricht Treaty.

Good Friday peace settlement between Irish and British governments, parties in Northern Ireland, and parliamentary representatives was signed and approved in simultaneous referenda in both parts of Ireland (April–May).

11 of the 15 EU states agreed to proceed to the third and final stage of EMU (scheduled for 1 January 1999) with provision for the establishment of the European Central Bank, the fixing of exchange rates and the introduction of a single currency – the Euro. Denmark, Sweden and the UK had previously obtained opt-outs from this timetable, while Greece was deemed to have failed to qualify (May).

After parliamentary elections in Hungary, the Alliance of Young Democrats (FIDESz) formed a centre-right coalition government with the Smallholders Party.

Unemployment in Spain stood at 19.63 per cent – first time it had fallen below 20 per cent since 1982.

Referendum in Portugal on easing the country's abortion law; narrow majority voted against but the result was not binding because of a turn-out of only 32 per cent (June).

NATO threatened military intervention if Milosevic did not withdraw troops from Kosovo. Milosevic and Yeltsin agreed that Serbia would resolve the Kosovo situation by political and peaceful means.

Elections to new Northern Ireland assembly saw pro-agreement forces triumph, but by a very narrow majority on the Ulster Unionist side.

In the Czech Republic, the Czech Social Democratic Party formed a minority government.

ETA announced an 'indefinite and total' unilateral truce in Spain; moderate Basque parties welcomed this as a breakthrough; Spanish prime minister Aznar who had followed a policy of harsh repression of ETA since 1996 gave first indication of willingness to make concessions to secure peace (September).

UN Security Council Resolution 1199 expressed concern at the 'excessive and indiscriminate use of force by the Serbian security forces' in Kosovo.

Serbia agreed to peace agreement negotiated by US Balkan envoy Richard Holbrooke; OSCE to put 2,000 unarmed monitors into Kosovo (October). 700 monitors were sent in, but by the end of 1998 Yugoslav military action against the KLA was escalating.

After parliamentary elections in Slovakia, Mikulas Dzurinda, leader of the Slovak Democratic Coalition (SDK), formed a coalition government.

Renegade IRA terrorists tried to sabotage Northern Ireland peace process by exploding huge bomb in Omagh, Co. Tyrone, which killed 29 people and injured over 300.

Election of SPD–Green government in Germany.

Gerhard Schröder became federal chancellor in Germany, with Oskar Lafontaine as finance minister and Joschka Fischer as foreign minister (October–November).

EU agreed in principle to lift the ban on the export of British beef (November).

British and French governments agreed principles of a defence policy for the EU (December).

1999 The Euro, the new EU single currency, was formally launched, with 11 of the 15 EU states participating (January). In the following six months its international value declined considerably.

Massacre of Kosovar Albanians at Recak lent greater publicity to Serbian oppression in Kosovo. Officials of War Crimes Tribunal were refused access to massacre sites.

Blair announced a 'national changeover plan' for the possible replacement of the pound sterling by the Euro (February).

Talks organised by the EU and USA were held at Rambouillet chateau (Paris) between Yugoslav and Kosovar Albanian (including KLA) delegations, under threat of NATO airstrikes if a peace agreement, involving the continuance of theoretical Serbian sovereignty over Kosovo but the stationing of 30,000 NATO troops there to maintain peace, was not agreed (February–March). Kosovar Albanians finally agreed but Yugoslavia refused (March).

Oskar Lafontaine (finance minister of Germany) resigned.

OSCE monitors were withdrawn from Kosovo. NATO began airstrikes against Yugoslav army and Serbian infrastructure.

European Commission resigned in response to a critical report on fraud, nepotism and mismanagement by a Commission of Independent Experts established by the European Parliament.

European Council meeting in Berlin agreed a package of budgetary, agricultural and regional policy reforms to improve the financial stability of the EU and prepare for its expansion into eastern Europe.

NATO's Washington summit agreed as part of *Agenda 2000* that the EU could use NATO equipment, personnel and infrastructure in operations which did not directly involve the USA (April).

Romano Prodi appointed new President of European Commission (May).

International War Crimes Tribunal indicted Milosevic for organising murders in Kosovo.

EU announced economic/political 'Stability Pact' to stabilise the Balkan region.

The WEU member states agreed in principle to incorporate the WEU into the EU.

Treaty of Amsterdam took effect.

Yugoslavia agreed to NATO demands after 72 days of bombing, after almost one million Kosovar Albanians had fled Kosovo as refugees (June).

78 days of NATO bombing ceased after Yugoslav army fully agreed to NATO terms on withdrawal from Kosovo (10 June). Yugoslav forces withdrew, while NATO–Russian force (KFOR) of 51,000 troops under

the auspices of the UN entered Kosovo, quickly followed by mass return of refugees, while many Kosovar Serb civilians fled to Serbia. Numerous mass graves of Kosovar Albanians discovered.

Elections to European Parliament showed a swing to the right in very low turnout (June).

Index